Haunted Laughter

Haunted Laughter

Representations of Adolf Hitler, the Third Reich, and the Holocaust in Comedic Film and Television

Jonathan C. Friedman

LEXINGTON BOOKS
Lanham • Boulder • New York • London

Published by Lexington Books
An imprint of The Rowman & Littlefield Publishing Group, Inc.
4501 Forbes Boulevard, Suite 200, Lanham, Maryland 20706
www.rowman.com

86-90 Paul Street, London EC2A 4NE

Copyright © 2022 by The Rowman & Littlefield Publishing Group, Inc.

All rights reserved. No part of this book may be reproduced in any form or by any electronic or mechanical means, including information storage and retrieval systems, without written permission from the publisher, except by a reviewer who may quote passages in a review.

British Library Cataloguing in Publication Information Available

Library of Congress Cataloging-in-Publication Data

Names: Friedman, Jonathan C., 1966- author.
Title: Haunted laughter : representations of Adolf Hitler, the Third Reich, and the Holocaust in comedic film and television / Jonathan C. Friedman.
Description: Lanham : Lexington Books, [2022] | Includes bibliographical references and index.
Identifiers: LCCN 2022001946 (print) | LCCN 2022001947 (ebook) | ISBN 9781793640154 (cloth) | ISBN 9781793640178 (paperback) | ISBN 9781793640161 (ebook)
Subjects: LCSH: Holocaust, Jewish (1939-1945), in motion pictures. | Holocaust, Jewish (1939-1945), on television. | Hitler, Adolf, 1889-1945--In motion pictures. | Hitler, Adolf, 1889-1945--On television. | Nazis in motion pictures. | Nazis on television. | Germany--In motion pictures. | Germany--On television. | Comedy films--History and criticism. | Television comedies--History and criticism.
Classification: LCC PN1995.9.H53 F75 2022 (print) | LCC PN1995.9.H53 (ebook) | DDC 791.43/6584053--dc23/eng/20220222
LC record available at https://lccn.loc.gov/2022001946
LC ebook record available at https://lccn.loc.gov/2022001947

Contents

Introduction	1
Chapter 1: Famous Comedies from *The Great Dictator* to *Jojo Rabbit*	19
Chapter 2: Comedy Films and TV Shows about Hitler	61
Chapter 3: Contesting the Nazis and Their System of Terror through Humor	101
Chapter 4: Memory, Trauma, and Comedy	145
Chapter 5: Humor as Social Criticism	193
Conclusion	215
Bibliography	219
Index	227
About the Author	233

Introduction

The purpose of this book is to address the question: Is it ever appropriate to engage the Holocaust through the medium of comedy? I felt the need to ask this question after seeing a flood of Holocaust-themed humor in films and television that appeared in the latter half of 2019. In July of that year, Jeff Ross' Netflix series, *Historical Roasts,* featured a fictional Anne Frank on the hot seat, taking barbs from Hitler and FDR. In the fifth and final season of the groundbreaking series, *Transparent,* showrunner Jill Soloway ended with Judith Light's character Shelly, joined by the entire cast (without Jeffrey Tambor), singing an "anti-Holocaust" song complete with the following lyrics: "We need a 'Joy-A Caust' for all the lives we lost. . . . Need a celebration of the soul. . . . For this extermination super bowl."[1] In November 2019, Taika Waititi premiered his comedy *Jojo Rabbit*, which focuses on a German boy who, despite having Hitler as an imaginary friend, ends up helping a Jewish girl in hiding. Then in December, comedian Louis CK joked before an audience in Tel Aviv: "I'd rather be in Auschwitz than New York City. . . . I mean now, not when it was open."[2] This came two years after comic actor Larry David appeared on *Saturday Night Live* and said:

> I've always been obsessed with women, and I've often wondered: If I'd grown up in Poland when Hitler came to power and was sent to a concentration camp, would I still be checking out women in the camp? I think I would. . . . The problem is, there are no good opening lines in a concentration camp. . . . "How's it going? They treating you OK? You know, if we ever get out of here, I'd love to take you out for some latkes."[3]

A joke about the Holocaust even impacted the 2021 Olympics in Tokyo when the director of the opening ceremony, Kentaro Kobayashi, was fired after video clips surfaced of him making fun of "massacring Jews" in a comedy act from the late 1990s.

At a conference sponsored by the Vienna Holocaust Institute in 2014, I addressed Larry David's utilization of Holocaust humor in an essay about his infamous "Survivor" episode from his series *Curb Your Enthusiasm,* which features a subplot about a Holocaust survivor who engages with a star from the television show, *Survivor*.[4] Fictional depictions of the Holocaust in drama have a contested history, encountering opposition from the likes of Elie Wiesel and Theodor Adorno, but the issues over comedy and the Holocaust that I grappled with in 2014 seem to be even more relevant now. I am unnerved by the trend in cinema away from the core narrative of the Holocaust in favor of national narratives of resistance or narratives of trauma and memory, but the appearance of, and then praise for, *Jojo Rabbit* seemed to legitimize the pattern in filmmaking from the past decade that would I label comedic-fantastic. One could argue that Quentin Tarantino opened the floodgates with his 2009 revenge fantasy, *Inglourious Basterds*, whose eponymous Jewish American soldiers scalp Nazis and blow-up Hitler and his henchmen in a theater in occupied France. The German satire from 2015, *Look Who's Back* (*Er ist wieder da*), pushed moments of incongruity further by envisioning Hitler being transported through time and space from his bunker in 1945 to Berlin 2015 and becoming a reality-tv star. Both films fit squarely within the trend of alternative universe narratives that have emerged in the past twenty years, a trend that includes Philip Roth's book from 2004, *The Plot Against America*, about Charles Lindbergh and antisemites defeating FDR, and the 2015–2019 serial, *The Man in the High Castle,* based on Philip K. Dick's 1962 science fiction novel set in a world in which the Nazis and Japanese defeat and occupy the United States.

By analyzing how comedy films, television productions, and other forms of performance art have depicted Hitler, the Third Reich, the Holocaust over time, I hope to shed light on the "third rail" relationship between the Holocaust as a subject of immense human devastation and the literary medium of comedy. The book's specific focus is on film and television comedies, areas of the performing arts that have a foundational impact on global popular culture. With such power comes great responsibility; films and television shows are often the first encounters with a subject from history like the Holocaust, and they can, and should, open doorways to further exploration and inquiry. Film and television productions can illuminate and inspire, but they can also diminish and commodify. Through my analysis, I advance both an overarching framework for understanding the purpose of comedic productions on the Holocaust and a set of criteria for distinguishing the inspirational from the trivializing.

In describing a scene from his movie *Borat 2,* Sacha Baron Cohen said there is "nothing less funny than explaining why a joke is funny,"[5] advice that may be resonant for comedians, but not for academics who want to know how comedy operates and what lurks behind the scaffolding of a comedic premise, and so to begin, we need an exploration of terminology. Although such an exercise may confirm Baron Cohen's adage, because nothing silences a room quite like a discussion of semantics, it is a logical place at which to begin a study where there are as many descriptors of comedy as there are comedians. The *Oxford English Dictionary* defines comedy as "entertainment with jokes, short acts, etc., that is intended to be funny."[6] The *OED* includes words like humor and wit as synonyms for comedy, but they are not necessarily interchangeable. Comedy is a performance designed to evoke laughter, while humor is a disposition that enables one to find what is funny about our existence as humans. The two words are related and complementary but distinct as well. Wit is also a cognate, but it refers to intellectual acuity or sharpness with words. An effective comic probably needs all three ingredients—a sense of humor, wit, and performance ability.

Philosophers such as Plato and Thomas Hobbes contended that comedy makes us laugh because it makes us feel superior. This can take the form of *Schadenfreude* or taking pleasure in the misery of others, but it can also be a scenario of disempowerment, in which elites become the subject of ridicule. Thus, comedy can also facilitate group solidarity and "emotional management," as Linda Francis has demonstrated in her work. She has found that humor generates "positive sentiments among members of an interacting group by bonding them and/or reducing an external threat, often at the expense of some excluded person(s), event(s), or object(s)."[7] In the 19th century, Henri Bergson suggested a corollary that it was one's inflexibility that made one laughable. According to philosophy professor David H. Munro, laughter was for Bergson "society's defense against the eccentric who refuses to adjust himself to its requirements."[8] Sigmund Freud offered his impression of laughter as the release of pent-up energy—a psychological relief from the suppression of the id.[9] Other thinkers saw comedy as stemming from incongruities or situations involving mutually opposing contexts, in which laughter arises out of surprise.[10] A more recent take on the notion of incongruity is the benign violation thesis, advanced by scholars Peter McGraw and Caleb Warren, who argue that humor occurs in a scenario in which one's view of the world as it should be is challenged in a nonthreatening way and that the person can see this simultaneously.[11]

Comedy also comes in myriad forms, from parody and satire to farce and slapstick. To these, one could add burlesque, romantic comedy, tragicomedy, and many others. Wikipedia's article on comedy forms is illuminating, offering over twenty different subgenres, and Asa Berger, in *The Genius of the Jewish Joke*, lists over forty.[12] Some forms are easier than others to define; romantic comedies are about romance, while dark comedies deal with serious or difficult subjects, like death. Farces are stories with "zany goings-on" that often incorporate slapstick. Distinguishing parody from satire is more of a challenge, and I consider several films that fall into these categories, which makes critical a basic definition of the two genres. Parody is a humorous or ironic imitation in which "an author exaggerates distinctive aspects of an original text,"[13] while a satire ridicules something to subvert it and to provoke outrage on the part of an audience. As linguist Kerry L. Pfaff suggests, in satire, "the author assumes that readers will recover the absurdity of the created text which hopefully will prompt readers to consider issues beyond the text."[14] In addition to forms of comedy, Conrad Hyers has delineated archetypes of the comic in his book, *Spirituality of Comedy,* including the tragic and comic heroes, the clown, trickster, rogue, humorist, underdog, and simpleton, and many of these archetypes come through in the productions I include in this book.[15] Ultimately, as Hyers admits, it is difficult, if not impossible, to try to divine an overarching "essence of comedy." At best, there may be "family resemblances between comedies, but no single feature [that] delineates all members of the family."[16] The point of this scan is to show that the language and theory of comedy are complex and that precision of language may help us distinguish effective from ineffective representation, but one of my first admissions here is that the following analysis is done by someone trained in history and not linguistics. The above descriptors re-appear throughout the manuscript, and while I do not spend time deconstructing them, I demonstrate that they are not static terms. In the pages that follow, we will encounter many different types of comedic films, and I take a broad, inclusive approach to comedy, analyzing films that many would see as pure comedies, that is to say, they have entirely comedic storylines and characters, while others are dramas that may have comedic moments or characters within tragic or otherwise dramatic frameworks. Perhaps there are subgenres of comedy and comedic archetypes that occur more frequently in, or are better suited to, narratives about Hitler, the Third Reich, and the Holocaust, but perhaps not.

Applying the above concepts to this discussion, one can see how making fun of Hitler and the Nazis could result in something beyond the physical response of laughter. Mockery can generate a sense of superiority, provide relief, or reinforce group solidarity; indeed, Mel Brooks has said that his intention through his films and stand-up has been to exact "revenge through ridicule."[17] However, Brooks has said that humorous incongruities specifically about the Holocaust, like the one in Larry David's *SNL* monologue, are a different matter, and while they might elicit laughter—the kind of laughter that might lead one to utter the words "that's bad" as they laugh, they provoke almost an involuntary negative response from listeners who see the transgression as malicious rather than benign. Some might say that timing is the issue. For instance, it is easier to joke about something that has receded in historical memory, like the plague (in Monty Python's *Holy Grail*), while the Holocaust is still so immediate, but content also matters. Joking about the Third Reich is different from the Holocaust, and they both possess a similar temporal distance. Some scholars, such as Sander Gilman, argue that the messenger matters. In an article in *Critical Inquiry* from 2000, Gilman pointed to video testimonies of survivors who noted the "pragmatic function of humor as a means of coping."[18] Survivors might laugh and discuss humor as a survival mechanism, but there is no intention on their part or their interviewers, for that matter, to elicit laughter either among themselves or the viewer. One can accept survivors talking about how they used humor to get them through the day, but a 21st-century comedian removed in time and place from the genocide? Much more problematic.

It also does not seem to matter if the comedian is Jewish or not. Jews have been a major, if not defining, presence in American comedy, and even Freud asserted that he did not know "whether there are many other instances of a people making fun to such a degree of its own character."[19] According to scholars who have written on Jewish comedy, such as Elliott Oring, Ruth Wisse, and Jeremy Dauber, Jewish comedy has long roots from the Torah, Talmud, and other medieval writings, but the modern variant, which is self-deprecating, is borne out of insecurity and despair, the result of an unfulfilled premise of modern life for Jews in western and central Europe that they could be embraced as citizens.[20] As a tactic to make Jews "accessible" to non-Jews, self-deprecating humor was a way for Jews to advocate for their inclusion into society. That the central victims of the Holocaust were Jews makes it a part of Jewish experience, and since Jewish joking is, in the words of Ruth Wisse, "the product of an intricate culture, conceived in a Jewish language or idiom, drawing on Jewish memory, and responsive to shared experiences, especially of the deleterious kind,"[21] it follows almost logically that Jewish comedians would be the primary conduits of Holocaust humor. However, this does not mean that it is appropriate only when Jews joke about the Holocaust. If the examples of Larry David and Sarah Silverman are any indication, Jews do not get a free pass on this terrain either.

Some comic writers like Larry Charles, of *Seinfeld* and *Borat* fame, view comedy about the past that is more transgressive as more effective because it reveals deeper, hidden truths about the present, and maybe he is on to something. Israeli psychologist Avner Ziv has posited five functions of humor: 1.) An aggressive function, stemming from a sense of either frustration or superiority; 2.) A sexual function; 3.) A social function; 4.) A defense mechanism (specifically, gallows humor and self-humor); 5.) An intellectual function.[22] In the case of Larry David, in both his "Survivor" episode and his *SNL* monologue, the humor does not come at the expense of Holocaust victims but rather people who are alive now who think their problems are all that matter. David employs multiple functions with his humor—aggression, self-critique, and social criticism—all aimed at people who lack perspective. People like

Larry David. He directs his humor inward to amplify the schmuckiness of his television persona.

Elaborating on the notion of purpose is one of the major contributions of this book to research on Holocaust comedy. Monographs on the subject are relatively new, although over thirty years ago, literary scholar Terrence Des Pres, who authored the harrowing account of life in the concentration camps, entitled *The Survivor*, wrote against what he saw as the limits set on Holocaust representation, i.e., that it should be approached as a sacred, unique event and that depictions of it should be as "accurate and faithful as possible to the facts and conditions of the event, without change or manipulation for any reason." [23] He argued in defense of humor and satire, declaring that the "value of the comic approach is that by setting things at a distance it permits us a tougher, more active response."[24]

Recent research is as supportive of humor as a mode of criticism and analysis, whether that focus is on the Holocaust period itself, as in the books by Steve Lipman, *Laughter in Hell* and Chaya Ostrower, *It Kept Us Alive: Humor in the Holocaust,* or different contexts in the postwar era—Liat Steir-Livny's *Is it OK to Laugh About it?: Holocaust Humour, Satire and Parody in Israeli Culture*) and David Slucki's edited volume, *Laughter After: Humor and the Holocaust*.[25] The consensus among these scholars is that Holocaust comedy by survivors is a legitimate form of defiance. Their joy and laughter constitute a way of denying Hitler a posthumous victory over their lives. In the words of survivor Viktor Frankl: "Humor [is] another of the soul's weapons in the fight for self-preservation. It is well known that humor, more than anything else in the human make-up, can afford an aloofness and an ability to rise above any situation, even if only for a few seconds."[26] For those who are not survivors, humor can serve the same purposes, but it can also be a conduit for channeling commentary about the here and now.

From the first days of the Hitler regime, when it criminalized "malicious gossip," to the war years, when ghetto inhabitants and camp prisoners performed, sang, or told jokes, humor was an element of life and death during and after the Third Reich. Scholars like Lipman, Wisse, Ostrower, Dauber, and others[27] have richly demonstrated this in numerous contexts. John Efron has studied the Yiddish cabaret performer Shimon Dzigan, who fled to Russia after the German invasion of Poland, and, having survived both Hitler and Stalin, went on to have a successful career as a comic in Israel. In 1935, Dzigan performed in a sketch entitled "The Last Jew in Poland," which imagines a scenario in which all but one Jew has been driven out of the country, causing economic collapse and leading the government to try to convince the last remaining Jew to stay by showering him with praise and medals, which he pins to his backside.[28] Another joke, taken from *Laughter in Hell,* and reprinted in Dauber's book on Jewish comedy, serves as an example of the kind of humor that Jews would engage in to make it to the next day:

> Two Jews are sitting on a park bench, reading newspapers. One looks over and notices, with some surprise, that the second Jew is reading *Der Stürmer*. . . . "Why are you reading that?" The second Jew sighs and looks at his paper. 'What does your paper say about the Jews?" "Well it says that the Jews are being harassed; that they're being beaten, and that their property is being taken away from them; that they're being gathered up and taken away in trains to who knows where." "Exactly," nodded the second Jew . . . "Now, look at this paper. In this paper, we control the world's economy; we have our men inside all the world's governments; we're an unstoppable force. Now, tell me the truth; which Jews would you rather be?"[29]

In the postwar era, a handful of novelists and memoir writers have constructed Holocaust narratives that explore tragedy through a comedic framework. There are Tadeusz Borowski's short stories, *This Way for the Gas Ladies and Gentlemen* (1976), Ruth Klüger's memoir, *Weiter Leben* (1992—published in English in 2001 as *Still Living*), and Art Spiegelman's graphic novel, *Maus* (1986). There are also the well-known novels that preceded their film versions, such as Jurek Becker's *Jakob der Lügner* (*Jakob the Liar*), from 1969, about a ghetto inmate who makes up the story of an impending Russian invasion to lift morale; *The Dance of Genghis Cohn* (1968), by the Lithuanian and Jewish-born novelist, Romain Gary, about the ghost of a Jewish clown who perished during the Holocaust possessing his murderer; and Jonathan Safran Foer's *Everything Is Illuminated* (2002) about a boy who goes to Ukraine to find out the story of how his grandfather survived the Holocaust. To these can be added numerous stand-alone comedic novels. In *Mendelssohn Is on the Roof* (1959), Czech-Jewish novelist Jiří Weil wrote a story about Nazis who are ordered by Reinhard Heydrich to take down a statue of Jewish-born composer Felix Mendelssohn on the Prague Opera house amidst several other statues, but who do not know which one is Mendelssohn, so they accidentally dismantle a statute of the antisemite, Richard Wagner, instead. When they get around to toppling the correct statue, it comes to life and seeks revenge. Another Czech novelist, Ladislav Fuks, in his dark comedy from 1963, *Mr. Theodore Mundstock,* set up the premise of the eponymous character preparing for his inevitable deportation to a concentration camp by creating such an atmosphere in his apartment. In 1971, German-Jewish survivor Edgard Hilsenrath published the book, *The Nazi and the Barber,* about an SS guard who goes to Israel after the war, takes on the identity of his Jewish childhood friend, and becomes a hairdresser. Anne Frank has made appearances as well, brought back from the dead by Philip Roth in *The Ghost Writer* (1979) and by

Shalom Auslander, as an embittered, foul-mouth old woman who says "blow me" at one point in *Hope: A Tragedy* (2012). Finally, Tova Reich satirized Holocaust commodification in her novel, *My Holocaust* (2007), which features numerous out-of-control characters looking for a way to make a profit from genocide.[30]

Comedic films about the Third Reich have a similarly long history, such as Charlie Chaplin's *The Great Dictator* (1940), Ernst Lubitsch's *To Be or Not to Be* (1942), and Mel Brooks' *Producers* (1967). However, comedies about the Holocaust specifically have been few and far between, increasing in number only in the past twenty to thirty years. Film historian Lawrence Baron views the 1975 film *Seven Beauties* by Lina Wertmüller as the first production to "extract laughter from the plight of an inmate at Auschwitz," although he notes that Jerry Lewis' never released film from 1972, *The Day the Clown Cried,* about a clown in a concentration camp, was operating on the same level at least in the abstract. Baron argues that more comedic or comic-tragic films about the Holocaust began to emerge in the 1990s because the generation of filmmakers who lived through World War II as adults had passed and filmmakers who experienced it as minors wanted new formats and assumed that the general public was already familiar with "the basic facts of the Holocaust."[31] Apart from Baron's analysis, which is itself a part of a more extensive study of the evolution of Holocaust cinema, there are only a couple of specific books, articles, and theses about comedy films on the Third Reich and the Holocaust, and it is curious that an analysis in monograph form that attempts a comprehensive approach has yet to take shape. The dearth of commentary changed in 2017 when filmmaker Ferne Pearlstein premiered the documentary, *The Last Laugh,* a groundbreaking scan of Holocaust humor in film and stand-up. The voices she incorporates offer a primer in the history of American comedy, including Mel Brooks, Carl Reiner, Sarah Silverman, and Larry Charles. To punctuate the seriousness of the topic, however, Pearlstein anchors the film around Holocaust survivor Renee Firestone, who offers her thoughts about humor as defense and survival through joy. In 2019, Valerie Weinstein published a volume on antisemitism in comedies produced in Nazi Germany, a study that is part of a broader trend in examining how minorities have been used as comedic foils to reinforce bigotry and solidify the position of those in power.[32] Here, I think of Donald Bogle's work on racism in American films, *Toms, Coons, Mulattos, Bucks, and Mammies: An Interpretive History of Blacks in American Films* (Bloomsbury Academic, 2001). From *Cohen's Fire Sale* (1907), one of the first American silent film comedies to feature Jews and to do so in a way that played into numerous antisemitic stereotypes—the Jewish merchant as physically menacing and dishonest, to the increasing use of antisemitic imagery and tropes in contemporary politics, there is a long history of performative antisemitism in the arts. In April 2020, *Laughter After,* a volume edited by David Slucki and Avinoam Patt, added to this body of scholarship with articles describing well-known comedy films, such as *The Great Dictator* and *To Be or Not to Be* and recent productions (including those by Sarah Silverman, Amy Schumer, and Larry David). I hope to complement the scholarship of Pearlstein and Slucki with breadth and depth. This monograph would be the first of its kind to offer an analysis of well over a hundred comedic productions from the 1930s to the present that represent Hitler, the Third Reich, and the Holocaust through humor.

I organize the book both thematically and chronologically so that there can be two types of analysis—a synchronous/compare and contrast method as well as an investigation of change over time. More importantly, I propose a model that might help guide audiences and reviewers in their assessments of comedy films in this area. Looking to Mikhail Bakhtin's work on satire and carnival and Dan Sperber and Deirdre Wilson's writing about relevance theory, I consider three elements foundational here—purpose, relevance, and originality. Sperber and Wilson see something as relevant if it contains helpful (i.e., accurate and essential) information for a listener that takes minimal time to process.[33] So, for instance, if a comedy speaks to an issue of the time and does so in a way that is easy to decode, it may have a higher relevance. Bakhtin, who survived persecution and exile under Stalin, also believed that comedy and laughter had revolutionary potential, and he took issue with humor that had no purpose beyond itself. Insults, barbs, or abuse, as scholar Grant Julin notes, "destroy and degrade without reviving, leaving only 'bare cynicism and insult.'"[34] Of particular interest for Bakhtin, who wrote about François Rabelais' Renaissance epic, *Gargantua and Pantagruel,* were what he saw as two purposeful tropes of renewal—namely the carnival, with its collective and regenerative laughter, and the grotesque, with its exaggerated focus on the human body and all its functions—particularly the reproductive and excretory. Bakhtin's theories appear throughout this book as a guidepost, and in line with the ideas advanced above, I view an effective comedy as one that should make us laugh and be germane in form and content. It should advance some kind of message, and it should do so in a way that either conveys new information or conveys that information in a new or different way.

Regarding purpose, I found the model developed by writers and philosophers from the British website *Book of Life* also to be helpful. *Book of Life* is an online publication of an entity known as the "School of Life," a London-based organization founded by philosopher Alain de Botton and run by several writers and artists. It appears to be a forum for more popular rather than academic discourse about ideas and society, but its delineation of the purposes of comedy, I felt, was on the mark. The authors of that section entitled

"What Is Comedy For?" advance the notion that comedy is therapy for despair, powerlessness, and losing perspective.[35] Other scholars echo these sentiments. John Morreall argues that comedy "serves as a sword, a spiritual weapon, against the oppressors," and Ruth Wisse adds that joking is a way of freeing "some truth from within a punishing system of lies."[36] English professors Dustin Griffin and Frederick Peter Lock, who focus on satire specifically, believe that although the medium might not have the power to topple regimes or change attitudes, it "consolidates and strengthens" existing critiques, keeping up the "spirit of its own side."[37]

I was already thinking along similar lines, and I would add that comedy can serve as a way of engaging in a discourse about memory, an extension of the idea that comedy is therapy for despair but in a different temporal context. Comedies as solace often showcase some aspect of defiance or resistance during the Holocaust, while comedies that deal with the postwar era present a different kind of mediation—a way to confront memory and work through trauma. I also see that comedy can serve as a warning sign or commentary about contemporary society, but this could be subsumed under the category of offering perspective. I put forward that comedies that might be effective in the orbit of the "Holocaust Kingdom" are those that provide relevant information about life and death either in the past, present, or future; that break new ground (that is to say, that they set or transgress boundaries, to paraphrase Larry Charles); and that serve a purpose or multiple purposes. Here, I mean that comedies should capture the essential dynamic of the Nazi system of oppression, empower or heal its victims, function as a window into memory and trauma, serve as a warning for the future, or keep those who can never grasp the real horror of genocide from losing perspective. I would suggest that when a comedy makes us laugh and hits on the fronts of purpose, relevance, and originality, revealing layers of truths, there is a greater likelihood that it will be both funny and incisive.

Using this broad model as a framework, in chapter 1, I engage in a comparison of well-known comedies *The Great Dictator, To Be or Not to Be, The Producers, Jakob the Liar, Life Is Beautiful, Train of Life, Everything Is Illuminated, Inglourious Basterds, Look Who's Back,* and *Jojo Rabbit,* I thought it would be odd to intersperse these films through succeeding chapters because so much has already been written on them, and it would seem derivative and diminish their specialness. Through a synthetic analysis in one space, I can achieve multiple goals; I can convey to the reader a sense of change over time; I can cull out shared narrative devices and tropes; I can compare productions that have multiple versions (such as *To Be or Not to Be* and *Jakob the Liar*); I can put my analytical framing to the test, assessing the place of the films as examples of empowerment/comfort/memory/warning/ and perspective; and finally, I can uncover the qualities of these films that have made them more successful than others in representing the Holocaust comically.

In chapter 2, I explore the evolution in different platforms and contexts of comic portrayals of Adolf Hitler. Specifically, I focus on the earliest depictions in American films and cartoons (from the Three Stooges' *You Natzy Spy* to Bugs Bunny's *Herr Meets Hare*) through more recent comedic films and television productions, such as the cult films *Son of Hitler* from the 1970s and *Snide and Prejudice,* from the 1990s, German films like *Mein Führer* and *100 Years of Adolf Hitler,* the Israeli show *The Jews are Coming (Ha-Yehudim Baim),* the Australian series *Danger 5,* the Russian comedy, *Hitler Goes Kaput,* and the controversial British productions, *Heil Honey I'm Home* and *A Kitten For Hitler*. Wartime productions existed in a world in which a Nazi victory was a serious possibility, and although Hitler has retained his place as a villain of history, he has benefited from a normalization that has come with the passage of time. In addition, there is now such an excess of Hitler comedy across so many platforms that he has become more of a stand-in for tastelessness than anything else.

In chapter 3, I focus on comic representations of the Third Reich's system of oppression, the German occupation of Europe, and the concentration camps. The chapter asks the difficult question about how (or whether) comedies can be a part of a discourse about this particular aspect of the Nazi era, and the films under consideration include *Once Upon a Honeymoon, Me and the Colonel, The Two of Us, Monsignor Batignole, Goebbels and Geduldig, My Mother's Courage* and, the Brazilian performance piece, *Holoclownsto,* Unlike Hitler comedies, which are in abundance and have had wider acceptance, films with comedic frameworks about the concentration camps are understandably rare. Two of the earliest films that attempted to go down this path came in the 1970s, and they feature prominently in the analysis of this chapter. They are Lina Wertmüller's *Seven Beauties* and Jerry Lewis' *The Day the Clown Cried,* which was never released in cinemas. The shooting script for the latter is available on the Internet, and the Library of Congress has dailies from the film, but these remain inaccessible to researchers. This chapter relies on the theories of fantasy, carnival, and the grotesque from the likes of Bakhtin as well as Hayden White and Eli Pfefferkorn, who view fantasy narratives as helpful in representing a world where the unthinkable became real.[38]

Chapter 4 deals with Holocaust comedies and memory. Unlike the previous chapters, which include films made during the era of the Third Reich and World War II, the films for this chapter are set primarily in the postwar period, and they explore how those in the present remember the past. They are also among the most purposeful and perhaps least comedic of the films in the book, pointing to how, if used with greater subtlety, comedy can play a constructive role either as therapeutic or as an access point to broader, more serious discussions about the Holocaust. For this chapter, the question is how comedic films and television productions aid Holocaust memory work. Here, the writing of Lawrence Langer on survivor memory and the theories of collective memory from Maurice Halbwachs and Oren Baruch Stier are constructive.[39] In his 1992 book, *Holocaust Testimonies: The Ruins of Memory*, Langer devised multiple memory archetypes, which he felt captured the diverse ways in which survivors confronted their trauma, and many of the characters in the movies under analysis demonstrate these.[40] For Halbwachs, who taught sociology at the Sorbonne and who died in Buchenwald in 1945, and Stier, currently a professor at Florida International University, collective memory is the product of multiple, repeat engagements with, and constructions of, ideas about the past. The memory that emerges from this past has power and purpose; it can create and reinforce identities and act as a means to work through trauma. The question for this chapter is: How have films with comedic or semi-comedic frameworks on the subject of Holocaust memory been a part of this mediation of identity and working through? Among the films and productions here that will be compared and contrasted are: *Harold and Maude, Enemies, A Love Story, This Must Be the Place*, the Israeli film *Mr. Kaplan*, the British television series *Fawlty Towers*, the British films *Wondrous Oblivion* and *Genghis Cohn*, the German films, *The Nasty Girl (Das Schreckliche Mädchen)* and *The Bloom of Yesterday (Die Blumen von Gestern)*, the Norwegian production, *Mendel*, Deb Filler's autobiographical one-woman show, *Punch Me in the Stomach*, and the two Amazon Prime series—*Transparent* and *Hunters*, The latter deals with a team of Nazi hunters whose purpose is to torture and execute Nazis hiding in the United States in the 1970s. This series seems to counter decades of philosophy, if not centuries of teaching within Judaism, espoused by survivors such as Viktor Frankl, Emil Fackenheim, and Gerda Weissmann-Klein, who insisted that to beat the Nazis, one has to retain a moral code and not take on the qualities of their oppressors, but as we shall see upon closer viewing, the showrunners' intentions resist easy categorization.

Finally, chapter 5 showcases Holocaust and Third Reich comedy as satire—a warning or contemporary social commentary, using the model of satire developed by New York University Emeritus Professor of English, Dustin Griffin, whose book *Satire: A Critical Reintroduction* repositions satire as a rhetorical system of play and provocation rather than of moral substitution.[41] Productions here consist of Sarah Silverman's performance piece, *Jesus Is Magic*, the Netflix comedy *Historical Roasts*, German films such as *The Parrot (Der Papagei)* and *Terror 2000*, the two *Borat* films, and episodes of *South Park, Robot Chicken, The Amy Schumer Show*, and *Nathan For You*. Much of the chapter centers on the "Survivor" episode from Larry David's show, *Curb Your Enthusiasm,* which, as I mentioned before, sets up a comic scenario of misdirection when a Holocaust survivor confronts a veteran of the television series, *Survivor*. Each production could be seen as a race to the bottom, and therefore engaging the question about limits and applying Griffin's model and my analysis of the purpose and direction of satire will be a critical focus for this chapter.

The question that I posed at the beginning of the chapter—whether it is appropriate to engage the topic of the Holocaust through comedy—is not easily answered, and it is one that that is sure to arouse passions, but comedy is a legitimate site of inquiry in the humanities, and as we shall see, many of the films and television shows that I investigate, regardless of genre or type of comedy, attempt to elicit laughter as therapy that takes the form of restoration or defiance on the part of victims. The laughter that comes through evokes the grotesque juxtaposition of the masks that adorn the cover of this manuscript. They are an apt metaphor for the kind of comedy we will encounter in the chapters ahead. It is the laughter of ghosts. Haunted laughter.

NOTES

1. *Transparent,* Amazon Instant Video, directed by Jill Soloway, Season 5, Episode 1, 1:34–1:41. *Transparent's* Jay Duplass went on to appear in the Netflix series, *The Chair,* as a dysfunctional professor who is fired after briefly giving a Nazi salute while lecturing about fascism and absurdism.

2. Mary Oster, "Louis C. K. Jokes In Israel," *The Jewish News of Northern California,* 2 December 2019, in https://www.jweekly.com/2019/12/02/louis-c-k-jokes-in-israel-id-rather-be-in-auschwitz-than-new-york-city/, accessed 22 December 2019.

3. https://variety.com/2017/tv/news/larry-david-snl-monologue-holocaust-1202607500/, accessed 22 December 2019. A year after David's SNL appearance, Sarah Silverman quipped after learning that she had received a star on the Hollywood Walk of Fame: "In a scary time when antisemitic crime is up 57 percent since 2016, it's not lost on me how lucky I am to be given a star and not have to sew it into my clothing." Jenny Singer, "Sarah Silverman: I'm Lucky My 'Walk Of Fame' Star Isn't Getting Sewn Onto My Clothing," 12 November 2018, https://forward.com/schmooze/414047/sarah-silverman-im-lucky-my-walk-of-fame-star-isnt-getting-sewn-onto-my/, accessed 22 December 2019.

4. This essay was eventually published as "I'm a Survivor! The Holocaust and Larry David's Problematic Humor in *Curb Your Enthusiasm,*" *S.I.M.O.N. Shoah: Intervention. Methods. Documentation,* Vol. 5, No. 1 (August 2018): 110–115.

5. "Sacha Baron Cohen Breaks Down *Borat Subsequent Moviefilm's* Cake Scene," *Vanity Fair,* 16 April 2021, https://www.youtube.com/watch?v=mXKzMReDPKE, accessed 19 April 2021.

6. *The Oxford English Dictionary Online,* https://www.oxfordlearnersdictionaries.com/us/definition/english/comedy, accessed 8 March 2021.

7. Linda Francis, "Laughter, the Best Mediation: Humor as Emotion Management in Interaction," *Symbolic Interaction,* Vol. 17, No. 2 (Summer 1994): 152. See also Daniel Berlyne, "Laughter, Humor, and Play," in *the Handbook of Social Psychology,* ed. Lindzey Gardner (Reading, MA: Addison-Wesley, 1968), 795–852.

8. See Henri Bergson, *Laughter: An Essay on the Meaning of the Comic,* trans. Cloudesley Brereton and Fred Rothwell (London: Macmillan, 1911); David H. Monro, "Theories of Humor," in *Writing and Reading Across the Curriculum* 3rd ed., ed. Laurence Behrens and Leonard J. Rosen (Glenview, IL: Scott, Foresman and Company, 1988), 351; and Magda Romanska and Alan Ackerman, ed., *Reader in Comedy: An Anthology of Theory and Criticism* (New York: Methuen, 2016), 221.

9. Sigmund Freud, *Jokes and Their Relation to the Unconscious,* trans. James Strachey (New York: Norton, 1963), and John Morreall, "A New Theory of Laughter," *Philosophical Studies: An International Journal for Philosophy,* Vol. 42, No. 2 (September 1982): 246–248; and Romanska, *Reader in Comedy,* 227.

10. See Roy Eckardt, "Divine Incongruity: Comedy and Tragedy in a Post-Holocaust World," *Theology Today,* Vol. 48, No. 4 (January 1992): 399–412, Immanuel Kant, *Critique of Judgment,* trans. James Creed Meredith (Oxford: Clarendon Press, 1911), and Arthur Schopenhauer, The World as Will and Idea, trans R. B. Haldane and J. Kemp, (London: Routledge, 1907), as well as Lawrence La Fave, et al., "Superiority, Enhanced Self-Esteem, and Perceived Incongruity Humour Theory," in *Humour and Laughter: Theory, Research and Applications,* ed. T. Chapman and H. Foo (London: Wiley, 1976), 63–91.

11. Peter McGraw and Caleb Warren, "Benign Violations," *Psychological Science,* Vol. 21, No. 8 (2010): 1141–1149.

12. Asa Berger, *The Genius of the Jewish Joke* (Northvale, NJ: Jason Aronson, 1993), and Aviva Atlani, "The Ha-Ha Holocaust: Exploring Levity Amidst the Ruins and Beyond in Testimony, Literature and Film," (unpublished thesis, University of Western Ontario, 2014), 56.

13. See Linda Hutcheon, *A Theory of Parody: The Teachings of Twentieth-Century Art Forms* (Champaign-Urbana, IL: University of Illinois Press, 2000), 6.

14. Kerry L. Pfaff, et al., "Authorial Intentions in Understanding Satirical Text," *Poetics,* Vol. 25 (1997): 46. For his part Avner Ziv argues that comedy is more optimistic, while satire is fundamentally a pessimistic genre. Ziv, "Humor as Social Corrective," in *Writing and Reading Across the Curriculum,* ed. Laurence Behrens and Leonard Rosen (Glenview, IL: Scott, Foresman, and Company, 1988). See also, Astrid Klocke, "Subverting Satire: Edgar Hilsenrath's Novel *Der Nazi und der Friseur* and Charlie Chaplin's Film *The Great Dictator,*" *Holocaust and Genocide Studies,* Vol. 22, No. 3 (Winter 2008): 497–513. See her citation of Bruce Lee Janoff, "Beyond Satire: Black Humor in the Novels of John Barth and Joseph Heller," Ph.D. diss., (Ohio University, 1972), 116; and Lance Olsen, *Circus of the Mind in Motion: Postmodernism and the Comic Vision* (Detroit: Wayne State University Press, 1990), 18, 31, 32, 61.

15. Conrad Hyers, *The Spirituality of Comedy: Comic Heroism in a Tragic World* (New Brunswick, NJ: Transaction Press, 1996).

16. Hyers, *Spirituality of Comedy,* 11.

17. Ferne Pearlstein, *The Last Laugh,* Amazon Prime Video, directed by Ferne Pearlstein, Los Angeles: Tangerine Entertainment, 2017.

18. Sander Gilman, "Is Life Beautiful? Can the Shoah be Funny? Some Thoughts on Recent and Older Films," *Critical Inquiry,* Vol. 26, No. 2 (Winter 2000): 284.

19. Freud, *Jokes,* 111–112.

20. See Ruth Wisse, *No Joke: Making Jewish Humor* (Princeton: Princeton University Press, 2013); Elliott Oring, "The People of the Joke: On the Conceptualization of a Jewish Humor," *Western Folklore,* Vol. 42, No. 2 (1983): 267–71; Jeremy Dauber, *Jewish Comedy: A Serious History* (New York: Norton, 2017); See also Friederichs, "Humour as a Way," 10–20; Hillel Halkin, "Why Jews Laugh at Themselves," *Commentary,* 4 January 2006; Sigmund Freud, "The Tendencies of Wit," in *Wit and Its Relation to the Unconscious,* Trans. A. A. Brill (London: Kegan Paul. 1916), 166–167.

21. Wisse, *No Joke,* 10, and Friederichs, "Humour as a Way," 10.

22. See Avner Ziv, *Personality and Sense of Humor* (Springer: London, 1984), and Ziv, "Psycho-social Aspects of Jewish Humor in Israel and in the Diaspora," in *Jewish Humor,* ed. Avner Ziv (New Brunswick, NJ: Transaction, 1997).

23. Des Pres reviewed Tadeusz Borowski's *This Way for the Gas Ladies and Gentleman* (New York: Penguin, 1976); Leslie Epstein's *King of the Jews* (New York: Other Press, 1979); and Art Spiegelman's *Maus: A Survivor's Tale* (New York: Pantheon, 1986). See Terrence Des Pres, "Holocaust Laughter," in *Writing and the Holocaust,* ed. Berel Lang (New York: Holmes and Meier, 1988), 216–233, here 217.

24. Des Pres, 217.

25. Steve Lipman, *Laughter in Hell: Use of Humor During the Holocaust* (New York: Jason Aronson, 1991); Chaya Ostrower, *It Kept Us Alive: Humor During the Holocaust* (Jerusalem: Yad Vashem, 2014); Liat Steir-Livny, *Is it OK to Laugh About it? Holocaust Humour, Satire, and Parody in Israeli Culture* (London: Vallentine Mitchell, 2017); and David Slucki, et al. eds., *Laughter After: Humor and the Holocaust* (Detroit: Wayne State University Press, 2020). To these monographs should be added theses: Aviva Atlani, "The Ha-Ha Holocaust: Exploring Levity Amidst the Ruins and Beyond in Testimony, Literature and Film," (unpublished thesis, University of Western Ontario, 2014); Robin Jedlicka Knepp, "Laughing Together: Comedic Theatre as a Mechanism of Survival during the Holocaust," (unpublished thesis, Virginia Commonwealth University, 2013); Hanni Meirich, "A Laughing Matter? The Role of Humor in Holocaust Narrative," (unpublished thesis, Arizona State University, 2013); and Marie Friederichs, "Humour as a Way of Dealing with the Trauma of the Holocaust: Discussion of the Use of Humour to Approach the Holocaust by Two Members of the Second Generation—Melvin Jules Bukiet and Roberto Benigni," (unpublished thesis, University of Gent, 2014). There are numerous articles and book chapters as well, including Lynn Rapaport, "Laughter and Heartache: The Functions of Humor in Holocaust Tragedy," in *Gray Zones: Ambiguity and Compromise in the Holocaust and its Aftermath,* ed. Jonathan

Petropoulos and John K. Roth (New York: Berghahn, 2012); Whitney Carpenter, "Laughter in a Time of Tragedy: Examining Humor during the Holocaust," *Denison Journal of Religion,* Vol. 9, No. 3 (2010): 1–14; Eyal Zandberg, "Critical Laughter: Humor, Popular Culture and Israeli Holocaust Commemoration," *Media, Culture & Society,* Vol. 28, No. 4 (2006): 561–579; Jaye Berman Montresor, "Parodic Laughter and the Holocaust," *Studies in American Jewish Literature (1981–), Vol. 12, The Changing Mosaic: From Cahan to Malamud, Roth, and Ozick* (University Park, PA: Penn State University Press, 1993), 126–133.

26. Viktor Frankl, *Man's Search for Meaning* (New York: Washington Square Press, 1984), 63.

27. Like Roy Kift, "Comedy in the Holocaust: The Theresienstadt Cabaret," *New Theater Quarterly,* Vol. 48 (1996): 299–308.

28. John Efron, "From Lodz to Tel Aviv: The Yiddish Political Humor of Shimen Dzigan and Yisroel Schumacher," *Jewish Quarterly Review,* Vol. 102, No.1 (2012): 50–79, 61; and Dauber, *Jewish Comedy,* 28.

29. Dauber, *Jewish Comedy,* 27, and Lipman, *Laughter in Hell,* 197, 206.

30. Tadeusz Borowski, *This Way for the Gas Ladies and Gentlemen* (New York: Penguin, 1976); Ruth Klüger, *Weiter Leben* (Berlin: Deutsches Taschenbuch, 1992); Jurek Becker's *Jakob der Lügner* (Frankfurt am Main: Suhrkamp Verlag, 1969); Romain Gary, *The Dance of Genghis Cohn* (New York: Signet, 1967); Jonathan Safran Foer, *Everything Is Illuminated* (New York: Houghton Mifflin, 2002); Jiří Weil, *Mendelssohn is on the Roof* (1959-English Edition: Evanston, IL: Northwestern University Press, 1998); Ladislav Fuks, *Mr. Theodore Mundstock* [1963], trans. Iris Urwin (London: Ballentine, 1969); Edgar Hilsenrath, *The Nazi and the Barber* (New York: Doubleday, 1971); Melvin-Jules Bukiet, *After* (New York: Picador, 1997); Philip Roth, *The Ghost Writer* (New York: Farrar, Straus & Giroux, 1979); Shalom Auslander, *Hope: A Tragedy* (New York: Riverhead Books, 2012); Tova Reich, *My Holocaust* (New York: HarperCollins, 2007). See also, Bram Presser, "7 Strange and Brilliant Holocaust Novels You've Probably Never Even Heard About," https://electricliterature.com/7-strange-and-brilliant-holocaust-novels-youve-probably-never-even-heard-about%EF%BB%BF/, accessed 22 December 2019.

31. Lawrence Baron, *Projecting the Holocaust into the Present: The Changing Focus of Contemporary Holocaust Cinema* (Lanham, MD: Rowman & Littlefield Publishers, 2005), 137, 139, and Atlani, "Ha-ha Holocaust," 126, 127.

32. Valerie Weinstein, *Antisemitism in Film Comedy in Nazi Germany* (Bloomington, IN: Indiana University Press, 2019).

33. Dan Sperber and Deirdre Wilson, *Relevance: Communication and Cognition* (London: Wiley-Blackwell, 1995), 153.

34. Grant Julin, "Satire in a Multi-Cultural World: A Bakhtinian Analysis," *The Routledge Comedy Studies Reader,* ed. Ian Wilkie (London: Routledge, 2020), 268–270, and Mikhail Bakhtin, *Rabelais and His World,* trans. Helene Iswolsky (Bloomington, IN: Indiana University Press, 1984), xviii.

35. "What Is Comedy For?" https://www.theschooloflife.com/thebookoflife/what-is-comedy-for/, accessed 22 December 2019.

36. John Morreall, "Humor in the Holocaust: Its Critical, Cohesive, and Coping Functions," *Holocaust Teacher Resource Center*, 22 November 2001; Wisse, *No Joke,* 178; and Friederichs, "Humour as a Way," 18, 20.

37. Dustin Griffin, *Satire: A Critical Reintroduction* (Lexington, KY: University Press of Kentucky, 1994), 155, and F. P. Lock, *Swift's Tory Politics* (London: Duckworth, 1983), 21.

38. See Eli Pfefferkorn, "The Art of Survival: Romain Gary's *The Dance of Genghis Cohn*," *Modern Language Studies,* Vol. 10, No. 3 (Autumn 1980), and Hayden White, "The Modernist Event," in *Figural Realism: Studies in the Mimesis Effect* (Baltimore, MD: Johns Hopkins University Press, 2000).

39. See Oren Baruch Stier, *Committed to Memory: Cultural Mediations of the Holocaust* (Amherst, MA: University of Massachusetts Press, 2003) and Maurice Halbwachs, *On Collective Memory,* ed. Lewis A. Coser (rev. ed. Chicago: University of Chicago Press, 1992).

40. Lawrence Langer, *Holocaust Testimonies: The Ruins of Memory* (New Haven, CT: Yale University Press, 1991).

41. Griffin, *Satire*.

Chapter 1

Famous Comedies from *The Great Dictator* to *Jojo Rabbit*

This chapter begins the conversation about the use of comedy in the orbit of the Third Reich and the Holocaust. Its focus is on films that are generally well-known to scholars, reviewers, and students of film history. They are: *The Great Dictator, To Be or Not to Be, The Producers, Life Is Beautiful, Train of Life, Jakob the Liar, Everything Is Illuminated, Inglourious Basterds, Look Who's Back,* and *Jojo Rabbit,* Through a comparative analysis, I seek to distinguish these films in terms of their overall purposes, the motivations of their creators, their relevance, and how they crossed existing boundaries and set new ones for the use of comedy as a narrative tool. Although many readers are familiar with the plot lines of the films, I begin this chapter with a summary of each to provide context for the analysis that follows.

THE GREAT DICTATOR

Premiering in New York on 15 October 1940, Charlie Chaplin's *Great Dictator* was a groundbreaking film in numerous ways. It was Chaplin's first all-sound picture and his biggest moneymaker, generating a three-million-dollar profit, and the American Film Institute ranks it as the 37th funniest film of all time. Chaplin plays two roles in the movie, a Jewish barber and Adenoid Hynkel, the dictator of a fictionalized Germany called Tomania. It is noteworthy that Chaplin repurposed his tramp character for the film, from the silent and universal trope that it had been to the voiced representation of Jewish suffering, and that he did so at a time of heightened antisemitism in the United States. At the beginning of the film, the barber is a private in World War I, and he tries to deliver to safety a wounded pilot by the name of Schultz (played by Reginald Gardiner). The private crashes the plane, and while both passengers survive, the private loses his memory and fails to wake up until after Hynkel's takeover of power.

Returning to what is now a Jewish ghetto, the private resumes life as a barber, develops a love interest in his neighbor, Hannah (played by Paulette Goddard), and is nearly lynched by stormtroopers until Commander Schultz, now the head of the ghetto, recognizes him and saves his life. After failing to secure funding for the military from a Jewish financier by the name of Epstein, Hynkel ratchets up the persecution of the Jews, which Schultz protests, resulting in his incarceration in a concentration camp. Escaping, he returns to the ghetto to try to convince the residents to assassinate Hynkel, but he and the barber are arrested and incarcerated yet again, although Hannah and her family escape to the neighboring country of Osterlich. In the meantime, Hynkel, who wants to invade Osterlich, meets with the Mussolini-inspired character of Napaloni (played by Jackie Oakie) in order to work out a plan for the country's takeover, and after some food fighting, they sign an agreement. The Tomanians invade, Hannah's family is harassed, and Schultz and the barber escape from their camp and wind up on the Osterlich border. Police find Hynkel, who for some reason is off duck hunting in a small boat, mistake him for the escaped barber and arrest him, while Schultz and the barber are taken to a victory parade where the barber, now speaking as Chaplin, delivers his famous speech about uniting to protect democracy, ending with the words: "Let us fight to free the world—to do away with national barriers—to do away with greed, with hate and intolerance. Let us fight for a world of reason, a world where science and progress will lead to all men's happiness. Soldiers! In the name of democracy, let us all unite!"[1]

TO BE OR NOT TO BE

Ernst Lubitsch's *To Be or Not to Be,* released in Los Angeles on 19 February 1942, centers on a group of theater actors who find themselves caught up in a web of anti-Nazi intrigue during the early months of the German occupation. The lives of protagonists Josef and Maria Tura (played by Jack Benny and Carole Lombard) are disrupted at a personal level as well as a professional one when Polish pilot Stanislav Sobinksi (played by Robert Stack) develops a love interest in Maria, who tells him to come to her dressing room just as her husband starts the soliloquy from *Hamlet*. As news of the war starts, Sobinski flies to London, where the Polish underground is operating. There, he meets with the leader of the resistance, professor Siletsky (played by Stanley Ridges), who turns out to be a double agent and who holds the names of the families of the Polish resisters. Sobinski discovers this and flies back to Warsaw to warn Maria and intercept Siletsky, who calls on the actress and tries to enlist her to spy for the Nazis, which she pretends to support. Josef arrives home in the middle of this chaos, with Sobinksi in his bed wearing his bathrobe. Maria returns in a panic, she and Sobinski try to figure a way out of the mess, and Josef has to absorb the weight of these multiple affairs. He agrees that he will kill Siletsky and return to deal with the love triangle later—if he returns. He has one of the theater members dress up as a Nazi to convince Siletsky that he has to see Colonel Ehrhardt (played by Sig Ruman) at Gestapo headquarters. Siletsky is driven to the back entrance of the theater, now remade as an office, and he meets with Josef disguised as Ehrhardt. However, Josef blows his cover, forcing Sobinski's men to improvise and kill Siletsky in the theater. Word of the murder reaches the real colonel Ehrhardt so that when Josef has to meet with him the following day, it appears that the jig is up. The colonel and his men put Josef in a room with the corpse, but Josef finds a way out because he has an extra beard, and he finds a shaver and some shaving cream in the bathroom, so he is able to make it look like the corpse was someone impersonating professor Siletsky.

The mistaken identity plot keeps going as shortly after, members of the theater troupe burst into Ehrhardt's office dressed as Nazis and arrest Josef, whom they unmask as the real impostor, leaving Colonel Ehrhardt dumbfounded (and yelling at his adjutant Schultz). That night, at a performance for Nazis at the theater, Hitler makes an appearance, and the troupe manages another mistaken identity sleight of hand to escape. The Jewish actor, Greenberg, tries to flee, but he is surrounded by real Nazis, and then members of the troupe masquerading as Nazis, including one who impersonates Hitler, and they proceed to take Greenberg away after he delivers Shylock's "Hath not a Jew Eyes" speech from *Merchant of Venice*. Colonel Ehrhardt tries to seduce Maria back at her apartment, but the actor dressed up as Hitler barges in and leaves the colonel to think that he is messing around with the Führer's mistress, resulting in yet another misdirection; this time, it is a botched suicide attempt on the part of Ehrhardt, who yells out to Schultz once again for good measure. The troupe (without Greenberg) reaches Scotland by plane, and for his valiant efforts, Josef gets to play *Hamlet* on an English stage, where it is another officer, not Sobinski, who exits at the beginning of the soliloquy. While hewing largely to Lubitsch's script, Mel Brooks' remake from 1983 with wife Anne Bancroft changed several plot points, including the spelling of names and the actual names of the Turas, who become Frederick and Anna Bronski (played by Brooks and Bancroft, respectively—and the name of the character who played Hitler in the original). Brooks adds a musical number at the beginning as well (*Sweet Georgia Brown* in Polish), and he creates a gay assistant for Anna by the name of Sasha, through whom he explores the plight of gay men during both the Nazi period and in the United States of the early 1980s.[2] Both films were modest hits at the box office. The 1942 production made 1.5 million dollars on a budget of 1.2 million, and the 1983 film made thirteen million dollars, four million over its budget. Of *To Be or Not to Be*, Jack Benny said it was the only film that he truly loved.[3]

THE PRODUCERS

Mel Brooks made his screen debut as writer and director on 22 November 1967 with *The Producers,* The production has gone on to have two additional iterations, one as a musical (which ran from April 2001 to April 2007) and a film version of the musical (which came out in December 2005). The original film starred Zero Mostel as Max Bialystock, a shady and fading Broadway producer who finances terrible shows by seducing little old ladies, and Gene Wilder as Leo Bloom, an accountant who finds discrepancies in Bialystock's books and realizes that one "could make more money with a flop than with a hit" if the producer oversells shares of a production. Nathan Lane and Matthew Broderick played Bialystock and Bloom in the 2001 musical. Setting out to make a sure-fire flop, the two come upon a script entitled "Springtime for Hitler," buy the rights to the play from *Stahlhelm*-wearing writer Franz Liebkind (played by Kenneth Mars), enlist the worst director for the project, musical revue queen Roger De Bris (Christopher Hewett), and hire a hippie by the name of LSD (Dick Shawn) to play Hitler. On opening night, the crowd is initially disgusted, and Bialystock and Bloom feel confident that their play will close that night, but once the audience senses that the show is a satire, they start to find it funny, and the scheme falls apart. The show is a hit, and in the words of a congratulatory note—"Hitler will run forever." The two end up in jail without learning much of a lesson as they run the scheme again for their production of "Prisoners of Love."

The musical iteration of *The Producers* changed a couple of plot elements, most notably the role of Hitler. Instead of having a hippie play the Führer, Brooks gives the part to Liebkind, but after he breaks his leg before the show opens, he is replaced by director De Bris, who camps it up. There is also a romantic subplot between Bloom and Ulla, a Swedish secretary (played by Lee Meredith in the 1967 film and Uma Thurman in the 2005 film version), who works for the two producers before the musical's opening. In the original film, Ulla is basically a sex object who dances to music whenever the two are around, but in the 2001 production, she is more of an active agent, and she gets a starring role in "Springtime for Hitler." Interestingly, both films and the musical had very different experiences at the box office, and as we shall see, with critics. The 1967 film was modestly successful, garnering Brooks an Oscar win for Best Original Screenplay and taking in over 1.6 million dollars on a budget of $941,000, but the 2005 film only took in thirty-eight million dollars on its forty-five-million-dollar budget. The musical was the successful incarnation of the story, making millions—a record three million dollars alone in one night, and winning twelve Tony Awards, breaking another record that had stood for three decades when *Hello, Dolly!* won ten.

LIFE IS BEAUTIFUL

Life Is Beautiful, starring, directed, and co-written by Italian comic actor Roberto Benigni, is one of the biggest non-English box office hits, taking in over two hundred million dollars since its release on 20 December 1997. The film won the Academy Award for Best Foreign Language Film, and Benigni won for Best Actor. Set in Tuscany in the 1930s, the first fifty minutes of the film is pure romantic comedy, with Benigni's character, a Jewish waiter by the name of Guido, wooing a betrothed woman by the name of Dora (played by Nicoletta Braschi), whom Guido repeatedly meets by chance. At the end of the first act, Guido and Dora ride out of Dora's engagement party on a horse. The second act begins years later. The couple is married, Guido runs a bookstore, and they have a son, Giosué. Guido, his uncle, and Giosué are set to be deported to a concentration camp, and Dora insists that she will go along as well. Guido convinces his son that they are part of an elaborate game and that if they win one thousand points, they get a tank but only if Giosué does not cry or complain about being hungry. In the camp, Guido gets a message out to Dora over the loudspeaker, and although his uncle is murdered in the gas chamber, Giosué escapes a similar fate by refusing to go with the other kids because he hates taking showers. Guido convinces Giosué to continue the game by showing him German children playing hide and seek. Giosué is mistaken as a German child and brought into SS quarters, where he receives food, but he nearly blows his cover by saying "*grazzi*." Guido, serving as a waiter, steps in and corrects the error by having all the other children repeat the same word. As the Allies close in on the camp, Guido is executed, but American soldiers ride in on a tank, scoop up Giosué, and he is reunited with his mother at the end of the film.

JAKOB THE LIAR

Jakob the Liar differs from the previous films and productions in that it originated as a screenplay but was turned into a novel by East German and Jewish author Jurek Becker in 1969 after production on the film came to a halt in 1966. After the novel became a bestseller, Becker was able to proceed with the movie version, and it appeared in East Germany in December 1974 and West Germany in October 1975. The film was nominated for an Academy Award for Best Foreign Language Film, and although it did not win, it is still the only East German film to have this special distinction. In September 1999, French director Peter Kassovitz came out with another version of the film, which bombed with both critics and the general public, taking in slightly over four million dollars on a forty-five-million-dollar budget. The 1975 version starred Czech actor Vlastimil Brodský as Jakob, while the 1998 film featured Robin Williams in the role, who was nominated for a Golden Raspberry for worst actor.

Having survived the Lodz ghetto and the concentration camps of Ravensbrück and Sachsenhausen, Becker based the story on a tale he remembers his father told about someone who lied about having a radio in the ghetto, which was forbidden by Nazi authorities and punishable by death. The plot of the novel and films centers on protagonist Jakob Heym, who tells other inhabitants of the Lodz ghetto that he has a radio and that Soviet forces are advancing. Jakob hears such a report on a radio in the office of the ghetto commandant after guards force him to go there for violating curfew. Jakob has to keep feeding his fellow ghetto inmates news from the front, but eventually, the lie catches up to him. In the meantime, Jakob takes care of a Jewish girl, Lina, who has escaped from a transport and whose morale is lifted by Jakob's radio reports. She keeps pestering Jakob to see the radio, and to continue the ruse, he has Lina sit in front of a partition while he acts out a fictional radio broadcast. In Frank Beyer's East German production, it appears that Lina sees through the ruse but does not seem to mind because it has so lifted her spirits. Jakob tells her the fairy tale of a princess who became sick because no one could make her a cloud. After a gardener makes her a "cloud" out of cotton, she gets better because that is what she thought clouds were made from. At the end of the novel, the narrator proposes two conclusions—one in which Jakob is killed trying to escape, but the Russians liberate the ghetto and another in which all the ghetto inhabitants are deported to an extermination camp. Beyer's film ends just with the deportation as Jakob retells the fairy tale about the princess and the cloud to Lina. In the Kassovitz version, Jakob is executed in front of the remaining ghetto inhabitants, who are then deported, but then rescued (possibly?) by advancing Russian and American troops.

TRAIN OF LIFE

Train of Life is perhaps the least known of the three late 1990s Holocaust comedies, at least for an American audience, and it was released in between *Life Is Beautiful* and *Jakob the Liar* on 15 September 1998. The film's set-up is that a village idiot named Shlomo (played by Lionel Abelanski) runs to a nearby shtetl to warn the Jews that the Germans are murdering everyone in sight. The elders believe him, and Shlomo suggests they get a train, make it look like a German transport, and deport themselves to Palestine. After some protesting, the rabbi and the members of the Jewish community agree to the plan, even though some of the Jewish residents have to don Nazi garb and learn German. One in particular, by the name of Mordecai (played Jacques Narcy), is selected to be the Nazi commander of the group, and he becomes infatuated with power. Some Jews form a communist faction, while actual partisans scheme but fail to blow up the train on multiple occasions. The convoy nearly misses being hit head-on by another train, and after an additional series of narrow escapes, Mordecai manages to rescue a member who falls into the hands of actual Nazis. Then German soldiers stop their convoy, but they are, in fact, Roma who are undertaking the same plot, and they join together in song and dance. At the film's climax, the train ends up on the Soviet border during a cartoonish bombardment between German and Soviet forces. Shlomo says that most of the passengers stayed in the Soviet Union and became communists, while some, mostly the Roma, went to Palestine, and some, mainly the Jews, went to India. Others went to China and America. As Shlomo narrates this, we see Shlomo talking to the camera as a prisoner in a concentration camp, declaring, "that's the true history of my shtetl . . . well almost the truth."

EVERYTHING IS ILLUMINATED

Also based on a novel, the film *Everything Is Illuminated,* released on 16 September 2005, was the first feature directed by actor Liev Schreiber. It stars Elijah Wood as Jonathan Safran Foer, the author of the semi-autobiographical story from 2002 loosely premised on Foer's journey to Ukraine to discover how his grandfather survived the Holocaust. Although generally praised by critics, it failed at the box office, taking only about 3.6 million dollars on a seven-million-dollar budget. In the film, Jonathan collects and preserves items from his family members, and he keeps these effects in plastic bags pinned to a wall to preserve their memory. After his grandmother on her deathbed shows Jonathan a photograph of his grandfather, Safran, standing next to a mystery woman named Augustina in a Ukrainian shtetl known as Trachimbrod, Jonathan begins his quest (or as his young Ukrainian guide Alex, played by Eugene Hütz, describes it, his "rigid search"). The film has a notably comic tone at the beginning, as Alex serves as Jonathan's translator, despite a tenuous command of English. Alex's love for American culture also runs as deep as it is outdated, and he describes himself as a "premium dancer." His family manages a tourist business for, in his words, "rich Jewish people looking for their dead families." Alex, his antisemitic and allegedly blind grandfather (played by Boris Leskin), his dog (or again in the words of Alex, seeing-eye bitch, Sammy Davis, Jr.) drive Jonathan around the Ukrainian countryside in search of Trachimbrod. The trio ultimately arrives at a house in the middle of a field of sunflowers, and they find an old woman who shows them a host of boxes that consist of mementos of the Jews of Trachimbrod. She says that her name is Lista, that she is Augustina's sister, and that Safran was able to flee somehow before the German occupation. She also recognizes Alex's grandfather as a young Jewish man who survived an execution at the hands of the Nazis. Grandfather commits suicide at the end, Alex realizes his family's true heritage, and Jonathan returns home. Alex and his family bury their grandfather in Trachimbrod according to Jewish tradition, and Jonathan sprinkles soil from the shtetl on his grandfather's grave.

The film departs in a number of ways from the book. For one, the novel features a backstory about the shtetl of Trachimbrod that interweaves between the narrative of the present, but this is absent in the film. Moreover, the Augustina of the novel only thinks she is Lista because she is suffering from dementia. The most significant change, however, concerns Alex's grandfather. In the book, he is a Gentile who, out of fear for his life, turned his Jewish friend over to the Nazis to be executed. The guilt from this revelation better explains the logic behind grandfather's suicide at the end, rather than guilt and shame stemming from self-denial and hiding. Moreover, it appears that Alex and Jonathan have a falling out over the revelation about Alex's grandfather, and Jonathan refuses Alex's pleas for reconciliation.

INGLOURIOUS BASTERDS

Quentin Tarantino's *Inglourious Basterds,* released on 20 August 2009 in the United States, is one of the most profitable World War II satires, taking in over 320 million dollars on a budget of 70 million dollars. The film received much critical praise as well, although many reviewers found, and continue to find, its premise to be offensive. The multilayered plot focuses on a fictional group of American-Jewish soldiers and their non-Jewish lieutenant named Aldo Raine (played by Brad Pitt), who are dropped into German-occupied France in 1944 essentially to commit war crimes against the German army. Because of their terror activities, which involve scalping and bludgeoning German POWs to death, the troupe becomes known as the "bastards" by Hitler and his henchmen. Plot line number two involves a French Jewess, Shoshanna Dreyfus (played by Mélanie Laurent), whose family is murdered, and who's in hiding by Nazis under the command of Nazi SS Colonel Hans

Landa, who holds the nickname "Jew hunter." Austrian actor Christoph Waltz won the Academy Award for Best Supporting Actor for his role as Landa.

Shoshanna escapes the massacre, moves to Paris, and opens a cinema under a false identity. A German war hero, Frederick Zoller, falls for Shoshanna and convinces Propaganda Minister Josef Goebbels to stage the film's premiere about his heroism at Shoshanna's theater. Landa, the head of the security detail, interviews Shoshanna, and there is some suspicion that he recognizes her, but he lets the premiere go forward nevertheless. As the entire Nazi leadership will be at the premiere, Shoshanna plans with her Afro-French boyfriend to blow up the theater and kill everyone inside. Concurrently, there is a British plot to infiltrate the theater with the "bastards" led by Lieutenant Archie Hicox (played by Michael Fassbender). At a basement pub in Paris, Hicox and other bastards meet film star Bridget von Hammersmark (played by Diane Kruger), a spy who also intends to be at the premiere. Other Germans discover that Hicox is undercover, and a gun fight ensues in which everyone but Hammersmark is killed. Landa comes in to investigate the crime scene, and he discovers Hammersmark's shoes as well as a napkin bearing her signature. Raine and other bastards pose as von Hammersmark's Italian guests at the premiere, but Landa sees through the ruse, murders von Hammersmark, and arrests Raine and one of the bastards. (He allows two of them, who have bombs strapped to their feet, to take their seats). While in captivity, Landa strikes a deal with Raine; he will not interfere with their assassination attempt if he receives a pardon and special recognition by the Allies for his role in bringing down Hitler. Shoshanna sets the theater on fire, and the two bastards machine gun everyone else in sight, including Hitler and Goebbels, and then they detonate their bombs. Raine drops off Landa behind enemy lines in the final scene and carves a swastika into his forehead to mark him for the rest of his life.

LOOK WHO'S BACK

Like many of the above productions, David Wnendt's German-language satire from 2015, *Look Who's Back* (*Er is wieder da*), has its origins in a novel. Timur Vermes' book from three years earlier envisions a scenario in which Adolf Hitler is somehow transported to 2012 Berlin on the site of his bunker and then proceeds to become a reality-tv sensation. In the film, which premiered on 8 October 2015, a young video journalist by the name of Fabian Sawatzki (played by Fabian Busch) gets fired from his job at a television studio that produces an offensive variety show called *Whoa Dude* (*Krass Alter* in German). Sawatzki catches a break when a friend who owns a newspaper kiosk introduces him to a person for whom he has been providing shelter—an individual who claims to be Adolf Hitler (played by Oliver Masucci). Thinking that he has found a way back into his old job, Sawatzki takes Hitler on a video journey through Germany, introducing this person he believes to be a Hitler impersonator to various locals, who embrace him to a frightening degree. Along the way, Hitler berates Sawatzki and shoots a small dog for good measure. The two then run out of money, and in order to finish the trip, Sawatzki has Hitler offer to draw caricatures of people.

Returning to the television studio, Sawatzki shows the footage to his former boss, Christoph Sensenbrink (played by Christoph Maria Herbst), who is disgruntled by a female colleague, Katja Bellini (Katja Riemann), who received a promotion over him. Sawatzki gets a lower-rung job at the studio, and Hitler gets a computer and an assistant, Fräulein Franziska Krömeier (Franziska Wulf). Hitler has trouble setting up his email account because his name and phrases like wolf's lair are all taken, and he has to settle on "New Reich Chancellery" as his username. He gets put on *Whoa Dude* and starts his propaganda rants about child poverty and unemployment, and he becomes an overnight sensation. Sensenbrink, however, cannot tolerate Bellini's success, and once he sees footage of Hitler shooting the dog, he has that broadcast over the air, and public outrage ensues. Bellini loses her job, Sensenbrink comes in as the studio head, but ratings sink, and as is typical in the 24-hour news cycle, the general public forgets the incident. In fact, after Hitler is forced to live in Sawatzki's apartment with his mother, where he writes his new manifesto, which Bellini gets published, Hitler once again becomes a great success. Colleagues of Sensenbrink suggest bringing Hitler back because, after all, as one admits, "people just can't stay mad at Hitler for very long." Sensenbrink breaks into the film studio where a film adaptation of his book, *Er ist wieder da,* is underway, and he gets Sawatzki to agree to broadcast the film on Sensenbrink's network. Later, Hitler, Sawatzki, and Fräulein Krömeier go to the latter's apartment, where Krömeier's mother also lives. She proceeds to scream at Hitler to get out—that he killed all of her relatives. Hitler promises that she will never have to worry about British bombs again, but she says, "who said anything about bombs! You gassed them all!" Her granddaughter says that it is all satire, but she looks at Hitler, says, "I know who you are," and screams for him to get out. Shaken, Sawatzki goes back home and looks at his footage of the bunker area where he initially discovered Hitler. To his shock, he sees that there was some kind of supernatural event, and he becomes convinced that he is dealing with the real Hitler, which leads him to be put into a psychiatric hospital. Hitler and Bellini ultimately join forces in a toxic union of ratings-obsessed media and right-wing politics. (In the novel, Sawatzki has a lesser role and remains supportive of Hitler.) Although many critics found the film distasteful and problematic, it was a hit at the box office, taking in over twenty-five million dollars on a small budget of just over three million dollars.

JOJO RABBIT

Finally, there is *Jojo Rabbit,* Taika Waititi's comedy about a Hitler Youth member by the name of Johannes Betzler (played by Roman Griffin Davis), who has an invisible friend in the *Führer* (played by Waititi). Like *Everything Is Illuminated* and *Er ist wieder da, Jojo Rabbit is* an adaptation of a novel, and yet the source text, Christine Leunens' book, *Caging Skies,* from 2004, is darker in tone than the film, and Johannes has neither a nickname nor Hitler as an imaginary buddy. In the film, which appeared on 18 October 2019, "Jojo" goes off to Hitler Youth camp, run by a one-eyed army captain, Klenzendorf (played by Sam Rockwell). There, older boys tease Jojo and give him the name "Jojo Rabbit" after he fails to muster the strength to kill a bunny. Then, after a pep talk from Hitler, he bravely throws a grenade, but it bounces off a tree and blows up at his feet, scarring him for life. (In the book, Johannes' injuries are the result of an air raid). Meanwhile, Jojo's mother, Rosie (played by Scarlett Johansson), distributes anti-Nazi leaflets and, more dangerously, is hiding a Jewish girl named Elsa Korr, a friend of Jojo's deceased older sister, Inge. (New Zealand actress Thomasin McKenzie plays Elsa.) Initially repulsed, Jojo comes around to develop a crush on Elsa, who says she has a boyfriend, which stokes his jealousy. The Gestapo suspects that Rosie is hiding someone in the house, but Elsa attempts to pass as Inge. Klenzendorf sees through the ruse, although he does not say anything. Rosie is ultimately executed for her activities, but American and Soviet forces soon enter the city. Klenzendorf saves Jojo from Soviet troops, who are executing Germans, by saying that Jojo is Jewish. Elsa reveals to Jojo that Nathan has been dead for a year, Jojo professes his love for Elsa, and she says she loves him like a younger brother. Jojo kicks his increasingly quarrelsome Hitler friend out of a window, and after slapping JoJo upon her release from hiding, presumably remedying the wrongs done to her and her family, Elsa takes Jojo by the hand, and the two dance in the streets of their destroyed town. In the book, by contrast, Johannes keeps Elsa captive for years after the end of the war, telling her that the Germans actually won, and it is only once she realizes that this is a lie that she leaves him. The box office returns on the film were favorable, as it took in over ninety million dollars on a budget of over fourteen million dollars. Critics generally praised the film as well; it was nominated for an Academy Award for Best Picture, and Waititi won the Oscar for Best Adapted Screenplay.

It is not easy to compare and contrast these films for a variety of reasons. They appeared in different temporal and spatial contexts, which makes comparisons very much an "apples and oranges" exercise. In addition, they run the gamut of comedic genres from slapstick (*Great Dictator*) to political satire (*Look Who's Back*) to black comedy (*To Be or Not to Be, The Producers, Inglourious Basterds*), with the remaining films somewhere in "comedy-drama" territory (*Life Is Beautiful/Train of Life/Jakob the Liar/ Everything Is Illuminated/Jojo Rabbit*). There is also already a vast literature on some of the films, which presents the challenge of finding an original mode of analysis. However, I would argue that grouping these pictures together in one text and filtering them through a comparative lens may help uncover discursive linkages and reveal the evolution of common tropes over time. Such an approach may also facilitate a clearer contextual understanding of the milieu in which these films appeared, and by delineating and distinguishing purpose, relevance, and originality, a comparative approach might offer insight as to why some of the films succeed or fail as fictional representations.

Let us begin with some essential background about the Holocaust in film. Israeli film historian Ilan Avisar has postulated four phases of the evolution of Holocaust feature films over time—an initial phase of propaganda and newsreels, a second phase of realism using classic Hollywood staging techniques, a third phase of what he calls modernism, which is more discordant in both content and form, and a final, postmodern phase, which appears to abide by few, if any, hard and fast rules.[4] As has been well documented by Avisar and other scholars, such as Ben Urwand and Thomas Doherty,[5] the cinematic depiction of Nazi Germany in the 1930s and 40s was minimal. The first phase of Holocaust representation included propaganda pieces like Leni Riefenstahl's *Triumph of the Will* (1935), the anti-Nazi play *We Will Never Die* (1943), and then after the war, Allied newsreels, such as the gruesome short, entitled *Death Mills*. The realist phase was coterminous with the propaganda phase, but it lasted from the 1930s until the 1960s and featured classics like *The Mortal Storm* (1940), *Diary of Anne Frank* (1959), and *Judgment at Nuremberg* (1961). The French documentary, *Night and Fog (Nuit et Brouillard)* (1955), could be considered the beginning of the so-called modernist phase, with its jarring soundtrack and jump cuts of violent imagery juxtaposed against contemporary footage of Auschwitz. The modernist use of non-traditional scenic styles and focus on suffering rather than heroism continued with films such as Sidney Lumet's *The Pawnbroker* (1964), *Sophie's Choice* (1983), and Claude Lanzmann's *Shoah* (1985).[6]

Feature film productions on the Holocaust reached their numerical peak in the 1990s, the decade of Steven Spielberg's *Schindler's List* (1993) and the establishment of both the United States Holocaust Memorial Museum (in the same year) and the Survivors of the Shoah Visual History Foundation.

"Postmodern" films have characterized much of the cinematic output from the late 1990s to the present, challenging narrative frameworks, reinventing existing iconography, and focusing on memory, especially the "received" memory of the second and third generations. For instance, in *The Grey Zone* (2002), which deals with the Jewish prisoner units in Auschwitz (or *Sonderkommando*) who were forced to work in the gas chamber-crematoria, ambiguity has replaced clarity vis à vis victims and perpetrators. In the Israeli film about revenge against a former Nazi, *The Debt (Ha-Chov)* from 2007, remade with Helen Mirren in 2011, the traumatic memory of the Holocaust has become a surrogate for other national traumas. Comedic narratives have also been a part of the "postmodern" turn in filmmaking about the Holocaust.[7]

Although credited as the first anti-Hitler comedy, Charlie Chaplin's *Great Dictator* premiered several months after the Three Stooges released their short, *You Natzy Spy,* in January 1940. As most who study Hollywood films in the 1930s are aware, there were numerous restraints on filmmaking at the time. A production code limited what could or could not be shown, not only violence and sex but also particular depictions of religion and nationalities. In addition, although most studio heads were of Jewish heritage, they had not only invested much energy in drawing attention away from their Jewishness and toward a homogeneous American identity, but as businessmen, they were also wary of upsetting their markets in Europe, including Nazi Germany. A few films in the 1930s bucked the trend, including Twentieth Century Fox's *House of Rothschild* (1934), which depicted antisemitism in 18th and 19th century Europe and Warner Brothers' *Confessions of a Nazi Spy* (1939).

The Great Dictator emerged in this environment. Indeed, many producers and even some lawmakers did not want the film to be made. Chaplin had been inspired to embark on the film by Hungarian-Jewish film producer Alexander Korda who, in 1937, proposed the story of mistaken identity because both Chaplin's "Tramp" and Hitler sported the same mustache. However, executives from United Artists expressed concern that the film could not pass the censorship office, headed by Joseph Breen, and that it would not be able to be shown in Great Britain. Isolationist Senator Robert Reynolds, a Democrat from North Carolina who served as the chair of the Senate Foreign Relations Committee, sent Breen a letter from a constituent who attacked Chaplin as a "resident alien" who was using the Hollywood film industry to "air his personal antagonism towards a foreign government."[8] Chaplin also received hate mail and threats that cinemas showing the film would be bombed, which led him to ask Harry Bridges, the head of the longshoremen's union for protection.[9]

However, attitudes changed after the Japanese attack on Pearl Harbor and the subsequent German declaration of war on the United States in December 1941. Hollywood partnered with the government to produce hundreds of shorts, features, and documentaries supporting the war effort. Jan-Christopher Horak counts 180 anti-Nazi films between 1939 and 1945, with German exiles involved in about one-third of these productions.[10] *To Be or Not to Be* straddled this transformational moment. Production on the film began in the fall of 1941, before the attack on Pearl Harbor, but it appeared in March 1942, in the early months of the war during which Japanese forces were advancing on several fronts in Southeast Asia. The British had already lost Singapore to the Japanese, and the U.S. teetered on the edge of losing the Philippines. The appearance of *To Be or Not to Be* therefore came at both a more favorable and anxious moment on the American home front. There is an added dimension here of reality that is as tragic as it is incongruous. Although Allied intelligence officials were aware of reports of atrocities committed by German forces against Jews in Eastern Europe at the time, the Allies did not necessarily know that Third Reich was about to embark on a widespread campaign of genocide against Jews throughout all of Nazi-occupied Europe. When *To Be or Not to Be* premiered in the United States, the Nazis had just begun construction on a killing center for this purpose in a forest near the village of Sobibor in eastern Poland, and another killing center to its south in a place called Belzec would begin gassing Jews less than two weeks later.

In the decade after the war, in the wake of the full revelation of Nazi genocidal policy, few filmmakers regarded as legitimate the idea of using satire or comedy to depict the Nazi system of oppression.[11] Broad comedies about the war could find their way into production, but it would not be until the 1960s that filmmakers would revisit the idea of focusing a comedic lens directly on Hitler and the Nazis. This was the context for Mel Brooks' *Producers*, Although Brooks had been doing Hitler routines in the Catskills since the late 1940s, it was not until culture, society, and even law changed in the 1960s that an opportunity presented itself to expand on what it meant to merge comedy with the history of the Third Reich. Literature at the time was replete with unconventional voices like Kurt Vonnegut, and books once deemed obscene, like Henry Miller's *Tropic of Cancer,* found their way into print. In film, the replacement of the Production Code in 1965 with the current rating system had a liberating impact, and this, plus the ground paved by comedians doing "sick" humor like Lenny Bruce and Mort Sahl, provided the opening for Brooks' anarchic debut. As Kirsten Fermaglich notes, *The Producers* was a statement about the times, although the film's messenger was hardly a hippie; Brooks was already forty-one when the movie premiered, and yet his comic sensibility meshed with that of the generation of baby boomers who faced racial discord at home and military service in Vietnam and who were fed up with what they saw as the hypocrisies and sacred cows of their parents' generation. Brooks' use of humor about the Nazi regime, flouting a "significant taboo of American popular culture in the 1960s," was a part of this culture shift.¹² However, A.O. Scott, writing for the *New York Times*, disagrees that Brooks was piercing a taboo as much as preserving it. The taboo was not laughing at Hitler but instead supporting him, and Brooks' characters, Bialystok and Bloom, operate in a world where that would be beyond the pale. As Scott notes, "it never occurs to Max Bialystok that the audience might respond to *Springtime* as satire. . . . The very possibility of an actual, effective, politically empowered Nazi, a Nazi who could pose a real danger, is unthinkable. And the job of *The Producers* is to keep it that way."¹³

Going deeper into the context for *The Producers* reveals some interesting aspects of art imitating life. Brooks based the character of Max Bialystok on a producer by the name of Benjamin Kutcher, with whom Brooks had worked after World War II. According to Brooks' recollections, "Kutcher lived in his office to save money. . . . He would wash his shorts and hang them out over the desk. . . . He would make love to old ladies on the way to the cemetery. He would nail them, and they would give him money."¹⁴ There is a scene at the beginning of the film related to this that happened in real life. This was the moment in which one of the ladies asks Bialystok to whom she should make out her check, and Bialystok says "cash," and she says, "that's a funny name," and he replies, so is *"The Iceman Cometh."*¹⁵ The very premise of the movie is also based on reality; Kutcher habitually raised more money than he needed for his productions, and he pocketed the rest. In January 1962, when asked, Brooks blurted out that his next project would be *Springtime for Hitler*—a parody of the title for a 1934 comedy film, *Springtime for Henry*, Universal executive Lew Wasserman wanted Brooks to substitute Mussolini because everybody hates Hitler, which was precisely Brooks' underlying assumption. "We need that hatred!" he exclaimed.¹⁶ When he pitched the idea to Sidney Glazier, the producer nearly choked on his food and thought he had peed himself, although he had just spilled his coffee.¹⁷

In Europe, at around the same time, the East German-Jewish writer and child Holocaust survivor Jurek Becker abandoned his film project, *Jakob the Liar* (*Jakob der Lügner* in German), and reworked the script into a novel, which he published in 1969. Becker was born in 1937 in Lodz, Poland, where he endured years of confinement in the ghetto during the German occupation. In 1944, he was deported with his mother to the Ravensbrück and then Sachsenhausen concentration camps in Germany. His mother died in the latter camp due to tuberculosis. Becker's father survived Auschwitz and was able to reunite with his son after the war. The two ultimately settled in communist East Germany as Becker's father viewed it as less antisemitic than Poland. Becker pitched the idea for his film to the state-run studio DEFA (*Deutsche Film-Aktiengesellschaft*) in 1963, and two years later, acclaimed director Frank Beyer agreed to participate in the project. Problems quickly arose, however; in July 1966, Beyer released the film, *Spur der Steine* (*Trace of Stones*), in which he criticized socialism, leading to his removal from DEFA, and then he and Becker encountered difficulties trying to film in Kazimierz, the Jewish quarter in Krakow, Poland, where studio heads and government officials objected to the subject matter. Yet the novel became such a bestseller that Becker and Beyer got a second chance to make their film, which DEFA approved in 1974.[18]

Despite the appearance of films such as *Jakob der Lügner* and *The Producers,* and a few others, comedies about the Holocaust were uncommon, even through the 1980s. As Sander Gilman and Lawrence Baron point out, this was due in part to the increased presence of Holocaust history and memory in the American imagination—with the 1978 *Holocaust* miniseries, the creation of the United States Holocaust Memorial Museum, and efforts to educate the general public about the genocide, all of which reinforced a solemn framework for fictional representations in the arts. Gilman noted that when *The Producers* appeared in the 1960s, "the name Hitler was not solely identified with the *Shoah*."[19] By the 1980s, this was not the case, and as Baron convincingly argues, "the use of comedy to depict the worst genocide in the twentieth century seemed too offensive."[20] Brooks did produce his remake of *To Be or Not to Be* during this decade, though, and the popular and critical consensus (mildly supportive) was unlike what Lubitsch encountered with his film.

The 1990s was, in many respects, the apex decade of Holocaust memorialization and representation. As cultural studies scholar Deborah Staines argues: "There was a noted tendency throughout the 1980s and 1990s for cinema to articulate the Holocaust into a public discourse of memory. Indeed, one might almost say that there was a cultural demand on cinema to perform memories of Auschwitz."[21] The embrace of Holocaust memory by "baby boomers" and their concern for preserving the testimonies of survivors, as more and more approached their final years, helped to fuel this unprecedented creative and critical output. The decade witnessed the end of the Cold War, the unification of Germany, the opening of the United States Holocaust Memorial Museum, the establishment of the Survivors of the Shoah Foundation, and the use of Holocaust memory to justify intervening in the ethnic cleansing occurring in Kosovo. All of this culminated in the Declaration of the Stockholm International Forum on the Holocaust in January 2000, in which forty-four countries agreed to promote the importance of Holocaust education, remembrance, and research. In his book *Hi Hitler*, Gavriel Rosenfeld sees this as the peak of a moral-historical approach to the Third Reich, which began to be challenged in earnest at the end of the decade.

Rosenfeld argues that a desire to "normalize" Hitler, the Third Reich, and the Holocaust, which entails moving away from an emphasis on their exceptional place in history, has deep roots and that this phenomenon has grown since 2000. He advances multiple causes for this, including the death of people who lived through the era of the Reich and the war, the rise of the Internet, which has enabled any number of media platforms, a cultural pessimism stemming from the 9/11 attacks and the 2008 Great Recession, the rise of hyper-partisanship in which the left and right compare each other to Nazis and/or communists, and finally, an increase in what he calls "counterfactual thinking."[22] We see this in the many productions that deal with alternative histories (from *Man in the High Castle* to *Inglourious Basterds*), but also in films that have attempted to "humanize" Hitler to a certain extent (e.g., the films *Mein Kampf* from 2009 and *Max* from 2002). Normalization has brought with it a relativization of Hitler and the Nazi terror that competes with, and in some ways has displaced, a normative perspective and more importantly, has opened up the floodgates for any kind of performative treatment of the period where it appears the only rule is to upend what has gone before. *Life Is Beautiful, Train of Life,* and *Jakob the Liar,* appeared in this changing milieu.

When one compares the backgrounds of the directors of these three films, notable distinctions come to light. Two have connections to the Holocaust, either as survivors or children of survivors. Radu Mihăileanu, the director of *Train of Life,* was born in 1958 in Bucharest. His father, who survived internment in Nazi labor camps, changed his name after the war from Mordecai Buchman to Ion Mihăileanu to sound Romanian. In his early twenties, Radu fled the dictatorship of Nicolae Ceaușescu and went to France to become a cinematographer. His first film, *Betrayal (*1993), a critique of political repression in Romania, won the Grand Prix des Amériques at the Montreal Film Festival. *Train of Life* was his second feature. Peter Kassovitz, who directed *Jakob the Liar,* was born in Hungary in 1938. Facing deportation to death camps, his parents hid their son with a Catholic family. Miraculously, all three survived and were able to reunite after the war. Like Mihăileanu in 1980, Kassovitz sought asylum in France in 1956 after the Soviet suppression of the Hungarian uprising, which had contested Moscow's grip on the country. By the time he directed *Jakob the Liar,* Kassovitz had over forty films to his credit, either as a director or writer. Roberto Benigni, by comparison, grew up in a Catholic home, and he spent his twenties breaking into theater and television as a comic actor. He has gone on to receive multiple film awards and honorary degrees, including some not-so-sought-after Golden Raspberry nominations for worst actor (for the 1993 comedy *Son of the Pink Panther* and his 2002 film, *Pinocchio*).

It is at the very least interesting, if not ironic, that Benigni's film has the greater name recognition, given his heritage, but this should be irrelevant. It would be ridiculous to suggest that only filmmakers who are Holocaust survivors or have a Holocaust experience in their family or professional backgrounds should make films (let alone comedies) about the Holocaust. Theodor Adorno argued that no one should write a poem after Auschwitz. So, leaving that line of argumentation aside, it could be, as many reviewers claim, that *Life Is Beautiful* is simply the best of the three films. As Lawrence Baron notes, Mihăileanu's film was rejected at Cannes as disrespectful, while Benigni's won the grand prize. Mihăileanu also faced obstacles raising funds, and he even fielded accusations that his film was antisemitic.[23] Apparently, Benigni was able to get his picture screened after "adopting a recommendation made by the festival director to pitch his story as a fable rather than reality."[24]

Timing, though, could also have played a role in the reception. The fact that *Life Is Beautiful* premiered first (in Europe in 1997, ten months before *Train of Life,* and twenty months before *Jakob the Liar*) made it the one to break new ground. Indeed, many reviewers of *Train of Life* and *Jakob the Liar* frequently set it against *Life Is Beautiful* in their critiques—even though both *Jakob the Liar* and *Train of Life* were in production before the release of Benigni's film. There is the added controversy that in 1996 Mihăileanu had sent Benigni the script to *Train of Life* and wanted him to play Shlomo, but Benigni rejected the offer so that he could concentrate on *Life Is Beautiful,* Although Mihăileanu took issue with similarities in the structure of the two films, particularly the use of narration at the beginning and end of the film, Mihăileanu now refuses to be drawn into a discussion over whether Benigni plagiarized *Train of Life,* preferring to say that they simply made "two very different films."[25] Meanwhile, as we will see in our discussion of the popular and critical responses to the films, Kassovitz encountered a different type of complication: reworking an existing and highly acclaimed film. Although Kassovitz sent Becker scripts to keep him apprised, his widow, Christine, believes that he probably did not read them and at one point pleaded with Duncan Clark, the president of Columbia TriStar, not to make the film "too sweet."[26] Kassovitz's film has the distinction of being the lowest-rated of the films under consideration in this chapter both among critics and the general public.

The "postmodern" and "normalizing" tendencies in Holocaust representation have only become more conspicuous since the trio of Holocaust comedies of the late 1990s. The musical version of *The Producers* appeared in April 2001, *Everything Is Illuminated* came out in 2005, and *Inglourious Basterds* closed out the decade. Commenting on the context for the new version of *The Producers*, Kirsten Fermaglich sees the musical as a statement about how many American Jews, "comfortably ensconced in the American middle class, embraced the outrageous premise of the play as a signal of their triumph over Nazism, their success in the United States, and as a nostalgic reminder of their youth."[27] Replacing a hippie Hitler with a foppish, gay Hitler also reflected a different set of cultural codes. Hippies were not the immediate, cultural factor at the beginning of the millennium as they had been in the 1960s, but LGBT people were increasing in their visibility, and thus by filtering Hitler's representation through gay director Roger De Bris, Brooks transferred "anxieties from the emergence of a proto-fascist subculture of hippies and college radicals in the 1960s to the rapidly expanding visibility and power of gay men and women in American culture in the 1990s."[28] The widespread acclaim for the musical did not carry over to 2005, which was essentially a beat-for-beat, cinematic version of the Broadway show. This struck me as odd, given the rapturous reception of the musical, but Fermaglich suggests that in post-9/11, Iraq War America, anxieties on the part of Jews increased, leading to another culture shift: "The years after 2001 have been uneasy, divided, and anxious ones for Americans and for American Jews, and in this environment, audiences' comfortable assumptions about a Jewish victory over Hitler have been undermined."[29]

Anxiety over the preservation of the history and memory of survivors has persisted as well, and *Everything Is Illuminated* reflects the concern over the ability of the second and third generations to translate their "postmemory," or inherited memory of the Holocaust, into knowledge that is useful both as history and as a way toward reconciliation. *Everything Is Illuminated* grapples with these issues, venturing into territory that is new, literally and metaphorically, by exploring a country (Ukraine) and topics (the fate of the Jews in the country during World War II and how to preserve that history), which few American Jews, or non-Jews for that matter, know or think much about. As the grandchildren and great-grandchildren of the World War II generation become more influential as drivers of culture, issues of intergenerational trauma and the plasticity of memory may feature even more prominently as frameworks for developing original storylines about the Holocaust.

The rise of authoritarianism and antisemitism worldwide since the Great Recession of 2008 has added another rationale for comedies as critiques of contemporary society. David Wnendt, the director of *Look Who's Back,* and Taika Waititi, the director of *Jojo Rabbit,* have spoken about this in interviews about their films. Both the novel and film version of *Look Who's Back* appeared during a period of heightened social tension over refugees fleeing civil war in the Middle East and Africa. By 2015, there were well over twenty million refugees around the globe, in addition to tens of millions of internally displaced people, and at the time of the film's premiere, Germany had taken in nearly one million refugees, more than any other European country.[30]

The reality-tv portion of the film that involved a journey across the country revealed pervasive and increasingly virulent xenophobia, ranging from statements about the intelligence of Africans or the need to protect German "racial purity" to anti-foreigner demonstrations and arson attacks on the homes of asylum seekers. Inspiring Wnendt was Bertolt Brecht's 1941 satire about the rise of Hitler and the Nazi party entitled, *The Resistible Rise of Arturo Ui*, which, in his words, "shows how his rise would not have been possible without normal German people. He did not hypnotize them, they chose to follow him."[31] For Taika Waititi, the context has been the United States in the era of Trump, a time when, as he puts it, " . . . if you're a Nazi, feel free to go down to the town square and have a little rally. . . . "[32]

For film reviewers, this analogy might seem facile and one of many disconnects between reality and the artifice of cinema that problematize comedic efforts to take on Hitler, the Third Reich, and the Holocaust. Interestingly, as of 2020, nearly all of the films considered in this chapter receive high marks from the aggregate review sites, IMDb, Metascore, and Rotten Tomatoes. *Great Dictator* was nominated for multiple Academy Awards; Mel Brooks and Taika Waititi won Oscars for their screenplays; Waltz won for Best Supporting Actor; and *Life Is Beautiful* won the Academy Award for Best Foreign Language Film. The exceptions to the generally positive critical responses are the 2005 version of *The Producers* and the Kassovitz adaptation of *Jakob the Liar*, although there is a wide range even among films where the consensus is favorable. For instance, on Rotten Tomatoes, where the baseline critical score for a good or "fresh" movie is sixty, Beyer's *Jakob der Lügner* gets a perfect one hundred, *Jojo Rabbit* an eighty, and *Train of Life* a sixty-four. Meanwhile, Stroman's *Producers* gets a fifty, and Kassovitz's *Jakob the Liar*, a twenty-nine. The popular reception parallels the critical consensus but is often more generous; *Life Is Beautiful* has a ninety-six rating with audiences, and *Train of Life* scores a ninety-four. Audiences even give *Jakob the Liar* a "fresh" sixty-three. It does not appear that the type or genre of comedy matters much in determining critical or popular acclaim, although the classic films from the 1940s to the 1970s score in the nineties, and the film here with the lowest score is Kassovitz' *Jakob the Liar*, perhaps the most dramatic of the comedies. Yet sentiments are not immutable, and a film's initial negative reaction might become more positive over time. This has been the case with *To Be or Not to Be*, which currently holds a score of ninety-eight on Rotten Tomatoes.

Clearly, there has been an evolution in the structure and content of films dealing with the Holocaust over the past seventy years, and certain narrative frameworks, topics, and strategies that may have once been taboo now have greater legitimacy. Ridiculing Hitler has been a longstanding device, which might account for why some critics see it as dated and thus devoid of the power that it once had. Comedic reflections of the world of the ghetto or the concentration camps meanwhile remain more problematic. A comedy that references tragedy and is closer in time to it may never be seen as an appropriate response, and this may account, at least in part, for the negative reviews of *To Be or Not to Be*, which premiered at a dark time in the early months of 1942, as compared to *The Great Dictator*, which came out in 1940, well before the German invasion of Russia and the Japanese attack on Pearl Harbor. Still, comedies closer to an event might also possess a greater relevance or be more courageous and forward-thinking. A glance at reviews of the above films offers an indication of this evolution, not only of content and frameworks but also of critical and popular sensibilities.

Some contemporary and later reviewers found the slapstick portions of *The Great Dictator* dated[33] or simply unfunny. For instance, Thomas J. Fitzmorris, the reviewer for *America*, referred to Chaplin's comedy as "pantomimic nonsense."[34] Theodor Adorno said in 1962 that the film lost its "satirical force" and became "offensive in the scene in which a Jewish girl hits one storm trooper over the head with a pan without being torn to pieces."[35] For Adorno, Chaplin short-sold reality for political commitment, which for him undercut the film's impact.[36] Yet many were equally repelled by Chaplin's political messaging. When *The Great Dictator* appeared, concerns ran high over increasing U.S. involvement in the war, and many critics viewed Chaplin's speech at the end as incendiary. John O'Hara, writing for *Newsweek*, labeled the speech a harangue.[37] In his review in *Commonweal*, Philip Hartung lamented that Chaplin had forgotten "George M. Cohan's sage advice: 'Always leave 'em laughing.'"[38] Thomas J. Fitzmorris declared that "Chaplin has forsaken pantomime in the interests of propaganda . . ."[39] Even worse, he saw hints of Stalinism in Chaplin's rhetoric because of lines like: "Let us fight to free the world—to do away with national barriers" and "Soldiers—in the name of democracy, let us all unite," which evoked Marx and Engels' famous phrase about workers. This is a stunning read of a text that makes references to the Gospel of Luke, democracy, and the creation of a world "where science and progress will lead to all men's happiness," something which sounds much more in line with 19th-century liberalism than anything else. In the documentary about Chaplin and Hitler, *The Tramp and the Dictator* (2002), historian Arthur Schlesinger described Chaplin's speech as mawkish but admitted that its reception has improved over the decades, and most filmmakers today regard the closing speech as a classic moment of cinema.[40] Director Sidney Lumet, who called the film a miracle, said that the speech brought him to tears.[41] One of the more prominent voices supporting the film at the time of its release was the *New York Times* critic Bosley Crowther, who hailed it as "a superb accomplishment."[42]

When he reviewed *To Be or Not to Be,* however, Crowther was much more critical, calling it "callous and macabre," adding that "one has the strange feeling that Mr. Lubitsch is a Nero, fiddling while Rome burns."[43] There seems to be a shared theme in assessing contemporaneous reviews that the film was funny but in poor taste. Writing for the *New York Daily News*, Kate Cameron gave the film 3 ½ stars and said that while the film has "some deliciously funny moments . . . the background . . . is a bit too grim for joking."[44] As I have suggested before, some of the discomfort with *To Be or Not to Be* may have been due to both the timing of the film and its focus—away from Hitler and toward his victims, which might have come across as trivializing, even though the characters in the theatre troupe resist the Nazis and the occupation of Poland in their own way.

Scholars who have analyzed *The Great Dictator* and *To Be or Not to Be* have pointed to the use of irony in language, spoken and physical, to strip Hitler and the Nazis of power. Chaplin's German gobbledygook in the two public speeches he gives as Hynkel is about sound, not content, probably reflecting the few German words Chaplin knew like *Sauerkraut*, *Hund* (dog), *Sekt* (champagne?), and *Strafen* (punishment). Chaplin's word choice makes Hynkel look like a lunatic, and the calm, English translation of the garble as an indictment of the people listening to the speeches who heard something reasonable or appealing. Adrian Daub, professor of comparative literature at Stanford, sees in the Hynkel speeches "a hysterical acting out, a mere excretion of sound rather than lexical language," and that the incongruousness of the translations "is meant to suggest that if the Phooey were to be translated faithfully, the full extent of his inhumanity might slip out."[45]

The Hitlers in Lubitsch's *To Be or Not to Be* do not have many words to say but are a part of the film's numerous moments of misdirection. In the 1942 film, the character Bronski, an actor in the troupe, makes a "Heil Myself" joke in the opening sequence. He reappears during the scene in which Greenberg recites Shylock's soliloquy and then again in Maria's apartment, where a stunned Colonel Ehrhardt tries but fails to commit suicide believing that he has just made a sexual advance on the Führer's mistress. Brooks also used the "Heil Myself" line in his version of *To Be or Not to Be* at the beginning of the film and then at the end of Greenberg's soliloquy. Then, in the 2000 musical version of *The Producers,* the line is the central lyric for gay director Roger De Bris' entrance as the Führer midway through the song "Springtime for Hitler," when he sings "Heil myself, Heil to me, I'm the Kraut who's out to change our history." Lubitsch and Brooks present Nazi officials as stupid, tightly wound, and obsessively self-referential. This comes through with Colonel Ehrhardt's unctuous response to being called "concentration camp Ehrhardt," his complete bungling of the set-up of Tura/Siletsky, and the dynamic between him and Captain Schultz. Similar to how the repeated use of the phrase "Heil Myself" follows Hitler's narcissism to its absurd conclusion, Lubitsch also parodied the utterance of "Heil Hitler" as the slavish greeting that it was among his adjutants. Nazism, in the words of Germanist Gerd Gemünden, relied on "performance to exert its powers,"[46] and Lubitsch subverted that by having the film's many Nazis often resort to the phrase in a Pavlovian way when they sense that they are in trouble. There is a scene that is reminiscent of this in *Jojo Rabbit,* Thus, in several comedic efforts from the past seventy years, beginning with the films of Chaplin and Lubitsch, and as we will see in the next chapter, continuing with dozens of other filmmakers, the myth of Hitler as an almost transcendent, all-powerful leader is contested with a rendering of the Führer as hysterical, effeminate, or narcissistic. Having his Nazi adjutants appear as cowardly and officious, if not the banality of evil then the stupidity of evil, achieves the same purpose.

More problematic is the insertion of "noble" German characters in *The Great Dictator* and then later in *Jojo Rabbi* (for instance, Commander Schultz in *Dictator* and Captain Klenzendorf in *Jojo,* in addition to Jojo's mother, Rosie). Not all Germans were Nazis, to be sure, but the distinction can also feed a skewed remembering of history and play into normalization. Yad Vashem recognizes only a few hundred Germans for their efforts to rescue Jews during the Third Reich—out of a total population of eighty million, so while there were German resisters and heroes, they were the exceptions. Viewing resistance as more widespread might reify the notion that Nazis hijacked German politics, society, and culture and terrorized or brainwashed ordinary Germans, which is a throwback to how many German historians wrote about the period in the immediate years after the war, and it goes against almost everything that modern scholarship about the functioning of the Reich has revealed since then.

Some scholars have found Chaplin and Lubitsch's representation of Jews even more troubling in their respective films. Adrian Daub sees the Jews in *The Great Dictator* as "stand-ins" for his left-leaning take on the Enlightenment. There is, in his assessment, little that marks Jews as "culturally or socially distinct," and even the written language on the signs in the ghetto are out of place, written not in Yiddish or Hebrew but rather in Esperanto, the universal language invented by the Polish-Jewish ophthalmologist Ludwig Zamenhof in the late 19th century as a tool to facilitate international communication and understanding. For Daub, the "subsumption of *The Great Dictators'* Jews into the 'little people' of Chaplin's pop socialism rendered the film incapable of addressing the particular problem of the Nazi persecution of Jews."[47]

The criticism of Lubitsch's film is more about absence.[48] Except for the character of Greenberg, the central theatre troupe comprises Polish non-Jews, and this is preserved in Brooks' 1983 remake. There are thus two layers to this effacement, with two Jewish comedians (Brooks and Benny) masquerading as Poles who then masquerade as Nazis. Benny's father was so appalled with this that he walked out of the film's premiere, although after being persuaded by his son to stick with the film, he went on to see it over forty times.[49] There is thus a different way of looking at the issue of absence in this case. Richard McCormick points out that in Lubitsch's films, "identities . . . are rarely what they seem; characters often need to indulge in masquerade or passing. Identities are something about which his characters are usually insecure: they need to overcome their identities, or they must compensate for them by taking on other identities."[50] McCormick adds that *To Be or Not to Be* was the first Lubitsch film to include an openly Jewish character in Greenberg and that he was played by a German-Jewish émigré, Felix Bressart.[51] We do not know what happens to Greenberg after he recites Shylock's soliloquy and is carted off by members of the theater troupe dressed as Nazis, and he is not with Benny's Tura at the end of the film. According to Joel Rosenberg, to have Greenberg present "would have diminished the aura of ever-present danger against which the comedy of the film gains its peculiar force and perpetuated a lie about the situation of the Jews."[52] Gerd Gemünden also suggests that that other members of the cast, even Benny's Tura, or Brooks' Bronski for that matter, "can be seen as assimilated Jews trying to camouflage their origins."[53] Gemünden notes that the name Tura is linguistically close to Torah and that Benny's subtle Jewish humor "was well-known to contemporary viewers," so that the joke is that "'we' know that Tura/Benny is Jewish but the Nazis don't."[54] Far from being erased by Lubitsch, Jews are at the center both of deconstructing Nazi performativity and criticizing the broader erasure of Jewish characters in Hollywood films of the time.

If we return to my main focus on the purpose of comedy in this area, and if we look at Chaplin and Lubitsch's intentions, then the position of scholars who look favorably on their work becomes all the more reasonable. Chaplin and Lubitsch thought that they could both rob Hitler and the Nazis of agency and lift Allied audiences out of despair through laughter and by presenting narratives of resistance. Despite coming from different backgrounds—for Chaplin, it was the grinding poverty of south London, and for Lubitsch, the experience of being a Jew in Germany,[55] both felt compelled to speak out against oppression. Chaplin initially held the attitude that it was "more effective to laugh at those fellows who are putting humanity to the goose-step."[56] With the revelations of the extent of the genocide, Chaplin later expressed reservations about the film, but he insisted that he was "determined to ridicule [the Nazis'] mystic bilge about a pure-blooded race. . . . "[57] For his part, Lubitsch wrote a response to the *New York Times* review of *To Be of Not to Be* that made similar points:

> I admit ... that I have not resorted to the methods usually employed ... to depict Nazi terror. No actual torture chamber is photographed, no flogging is shown, no close-ups of excited Nazis using their whips and rolling their eyes in lust. My Nazis are different; they passed that stage long ago. Brutality, flogging, and torture have become their daily routine. They talk about it the same way as a salesman referring to the sale of a handbag. Their humor is built around concentration camps, around the sufferings of their victims.[58]

I read into these statements an ambivalence rather than a rejection of the films, as well as a continuation of the kind of thoughtfulness that both Chaplin and Lubitsch brought to their work from the very beginning. The two films might not stand the test of time as laugh-out-loud comedies, given how culturally specific comedic sensibilities are, but they have a power and an authenticity that other films may lack due to the commitment of purpose of their creators. Although, as political cartoonist David Low has argued: "no dictator was ever inconvenienced or even displeased by pictures showing his terrible exercise of power ... it is damaging to have the idea propagated that he is a fool, especially if the idea takes root among his own people."[59] Satire such as this might not topple a regime, but it can sustain popular outrage, provide a "moral" victory, and, in the words of scholar Dustin Griffin, "maintain the momentum of a political movement toward political victory."[60] Lubitsch continued to defend his film using this very logic:

> It seemed to me that the only way to get people to hear about the miseries of Poland was to make a comedy. Audiences would feel sympathy and admiration for people who could still laugh in their tragedy. ... What is the only picture that is still remembered from the last war? It's not Griffith's *Hearts of the World*, or any of those sad ones. It's Chaplin's *Shoulder Arms*.[61]

When *The Producers* had its run in 1967/68, as Brooks recalls, "The Jews were horrified. I received resentful letters of protest, saying things like: 'How can you make jokes about Hitler? The man murdered six million Jews.'"[62] The film gave reviewers pause as well, but many critics praised it. Roger Ebert dubbed it one of the funniest movies ever made, and Gene Shalit said people would be rolling in the aisles.[63] However, Renata Adler, a critic for the *New York Times*, was one of the more conflicted voices. She described *The Producers* as a "violently mixed bag ... shoddy and gross and cruel ... [but] funny in an entirely unexpected way."[64] Fast forward forty to fifty years, and there is a continuity of sorts with reviewers of *Inglourious Basterds* and *Jojo Rabbit* echoing some of these same mixed feelings. Paul Byrnes, in the *Sydney Morning Herald*, praised *Inglourious* as "naughty, apocalyptic fun," while Dana Stevens, for *Slate*, criticized Tarantino's "juvenile delight in shocking the audience," and Manohla Dargis of the *New York Times* called it "repellent," arguing that even if the film is a statement about Tarantino's love of film, he had "polluted" that love.[65] Jonathan Rosenbaum went further and declared *Inglourious Basterds* to be "akin to Holocaust denial."[66] Meanwhile, a decade later, Bill Goodykoontz, the reviewer for the *Arizona Republic*, began his largely positive assessment of *Jojo Rabbit* with the words, "Too Soon?"[67] Writing for *The Washington Post*, Ann Hornaday described the film as an "audacious high-wire act: a satire in which a buffoonish Adolf Hitler delivers some of the funniest moments."[68]

Although reviewers like Rosenbaum thought that Tarantino had crossed the line with his film, one of the differences in the negative reviews of contemporary pieces like *Look Who's Back* and *Jojo Rabbit* is the critique that they do not go far enough, that they are too safe with their subject matter. Boyd van Hoeij, writing for *The Hollywood Reporter*, argued that *Look Who's Back* "doesn't dig deep enough nor generates sufficient belly laughs to become more than another Hitler-themed curiosity further afield . . . The film doesn't . . . suggest something meaningful about either contemporary German society or whether Hitler's ideas and methods could potentially take root again beyond some ultra-niche groups."[69] Richard Brody from *The New Yorker* said of *Jojo Rabbit* that "making fun of Hitler . . . is both easy and pointless, because he poses no threat; Waititi is kicking a dead bull."[70] *Vanity Fair's* K. Austin Collins insisted that "wielding the *Führer's* image humorously isn't automatically satire; there's a bar to clear. . . . The key isn't just to make us laugh—it's to *reveal* something new."[71]

I disagree with the assessment about *Look Who's Back*, Although political satires about the dangers of neo-Nazism have gone before, such as Helmut Dietl's *Schtonk!*, Ralf Huettner's TV production, *The Parrot (Der Papagai)*, and Christoph Schlingensief's *Terror 2000—Intensivstation Deutschland*, all from 1992—*Look Who's Back* does reveal much about the persistence of right-wing and authoritarian leanings in contemporary German politics. The film's deviations from the novel give it a focus and greater tragic and comic urgency. Bringing the Sawatzki character to the fore and making him the "straight man" who increasingly figures out the truth about Hitler and then is institutionalized for it, both generates laughs and reinforces the key message of the film, which is that German society is losing its collective mind by ignoring or labeling as crazy people who speak out against fascism and its media enablers. The plot point about Hitler shooting the terrier who bites him, followed by the public outcry at this revelation and then the rehabilitation that ensues, shows that for some people, anything goes.

Sperber and Wilson contend that a phenomenon has higher relevance when it creates more "positive cognitive effects," meaning that it offers information that helps an individual better process his or her understanding of a current environment and that the effort to decode this information to obtain any positive cognitive effect is not demanding. The more steps one has to go through to process information that may not be helpful, the less relevant an utterance, circumstance, or phenomenon may be.[72] *Jojo Rabbit* does not cross into new enough territory or operate on a level of criticism that provides helpful and transparent information about the current political world, and I would argue that it would have been more provocative, radical, and perhaps funnier for Waititi to make a movie about the era of Trump—the twice-impeached, quasi-authoritarian twitter president who once said that he could shoot someone on Fifth Avenue and not lose any voters. Waititi is doing something like that with his comedy, *Reservation Dogs,* about indigenous teenagers from Oklahoma doing everything to get to California. The comedy, both a reference to stray animals on indigenous reservations and a nod to Tarantino's 1992 mob film, *Reservoir Dogs,* is original, as the first to feature an almost entirely Native American cast and crew, and relevant, by contributing to the movement to empower marginalized populations.

Comparing the motives and purposes of Brooks, Tarantino, Wnendt, and Waititi again reveals much continuity but also discrepancies, which shed light on the disconnect between creators and some critics and cinema-goers. In interviews, Brooks, Wnendt, and Waititi frame their choice to write a comedy about Hitler as an act of resistance or social criticism. Discussing the premiere of the 2005 film version of *The Producers* in Germany, Brooks stood by his claim that "by using the medium of comedy, we can try to rob Hitler of his posthumous power and myths."[73] In his memoirs, *All About Me,* published in 2021, Brooks elaborated by saying, "the way you bring down Hitler and his ideology is not by getting on a soapbox with him, but if you can reduce him to something laughable, you win. That's my job."[74] Wnendt, for his part, used the film as a vehicle to uncover "a feeling of deep discontent in the population, where people of every social status demonstrated how they were against foreigners."[75] Finally, Waititi argued that he aimed to dismantle regimes "built on intolerance and hate."[76] Tarantino's motives are perhaps the most challenging to evaluate. In an interview with *TimeOut*, the director said that "what makes me sit down to start writing is a genre that I'm interested in tackling. But once I start, I explode the borders of that genre."[77] When asked if he were making a point about how cinema usually treats World War II, he responded that "a point could be made, though that's not necessarily what I was trying to get across to everyone in the multiplex. On the one hand, I'm making a revisionist history of the war, but I'm also dealing with characters who deal with revisionist histories of the war."[78] He went on to say:

> I'm also looking at the tragedy of genocide. I'm dealing with the Jewish genocide in Europe, but my Jews are going native and taking the roles of American Indians—another genocide. Then there's a "King Kong" metaphor about the

slave trade, that's another genocide. And Germany wasn't always the bad guy.... And this goes against all the ponderous, anti-war, violin-music diatribes that we've seen in war movies since the '80s. I'm not trying to be pissy about the movies of the past 30 years. It's just that there's been a one-note concentration on victimization.[79]

One could take away from such a statement that what matters more to Tarantino in making a story about the Holocaust is subverting its narrative than shedding new light on it.[80] This aligns with Griffin's assessment that "there is little evidence that a satirist is typically motivated by clearly articulated political principles, or even by what might now be called political ideology.... The satirist's primary goal *as writer* is not to declare political principles but to respond to a particular occasion and write good satire."[81] Brooks, Wnendt, and Waititi come across as more thoughtful (although not ideological) in their efforts to deflate Hitler or to critique contemporary society, and although I would have preferred a different vehicle for Waititi or a closer adaptation of the novel, Tarantino's motives are the more self-evidently shallow. It seems as if his primary impulse is deconstruction for the sake of deconstruction, a kind of gleeful nihilism hardwired into a vast and deep knowledge of all things cinema. Critics who objected to *Inglourious Basterds* might have been more forgiving if Tarantino had paid deference to the seriousness of subjects such as war or genocide, but his tone is too cavalier. Although most critics praised the film and it won an Academy Award, those who dislike it feel a revulsion both toward the way Tarantino has framed his purpose, as an irreverent inversion of tropes, as well as the result of that inversion, which some saw as turning Jews into villains and Germans into victims.

It is important to note that the above films generally focus on Hitler and the Nazis, and even if they confront the persecution of the Jews as well, they do not situate their worlds in the ghettos, killing fields, or concentration camps. This remains more challenging territory for filmmakers to represent through a comic narrative. *Everything Is Illuminated* does this to a certain extent, but it is set in the present, and its comedy recedes as it becomes more of a lesson about memory, which is a more recent field of inquiry in Holocaust studies. Some critics did not like Schreiber's adaptation, particularly the way he changed the character arc of the grandfather, but most found it to be a thoughtful musing about how "we are all connected"[82] and how the history of the Holocaust will be preserved by subsequent generations. Schreiber himself has said that the death of his grandfather and a realization of the importance of memory led him to want to turn Foer's novel into a film. In his words, "I was worried that I was losing things too important to lose and that was the beginning of writing and the kind of obsessive-compulsive thing of collecting mementos of places to remember places and people."[83]

In the film, when Augustine's sister, Lista, who is actually Augustine in the novel, presents Jonathan with Augustine's wedding ring and says that the ring does not exist for him but rather that he exists for it, she is speaking directly to the issue of how the third generation and beyond must be proper custodians of memory. This is a core challenge of Holocaust "postmemory"—taking pieces of memories of trauma that one does not share and constructing them in such a way as to preserve their historicity and deeper ethical truths. Francisco Collado-Rodriquez argues that the novel's "use of two narratives serves to evaluate the power of fiction as an ethical instrument" and that the dual diegesis results both in a surfacing of "repressed trauma" and a positioning of characters and readers as "non-referential witnesses" to these traumatic events.[84] There is the question, which is absent in the film, but which is very much a part of the book, about whether or not third-generation descendants of survivors can forgive once they hold a fuller view and appreciation of the memory that has been illuminated. In the film, Alex's family responds to this illumination by returning to Judaism, and Jonathan and Alex remain friends (presumably), while in the book, it is not clear that this is possible.[85] The way Schreiber changed the arc of the grandfather clears the way for this in the film, but the revelation in the book presents too high a hurdle to overcome for Jonathan. In all of this, what strikes me is the dissimilarity between Schreiber's framing of the connection between memory and history and Tarantino's in *Inglourious Basterds*. The former uses the film as both an exhortation to remember and a lamentation on the danger of forgetting, while the latter sees memory as plastic and useful as a tool to create alternative histories.

Perhaps the most difficult of the comic films to assess are the ones that focus on the "Holocaust Kingdom" of the camps and ghettos, and the trio of films from the 1990s (*Life Is Beautiful, Train of Life,* and *Jakob the Liar*) remain highly polarizing, with vocal supporters and detractors. As the only Holocaust comedy to ever receive an Academy Award in the picture category (admittedly in the International Feature Film section), *Life Is Beautiful* director Benigni continues to have many advocates. In her review of the film, Janet Maslin said it works because "Mr. Benigni can be heart-rending without a trace of the maudlin."[86] Even many Holocaust scholars, such as Michael Berenbaum and David Myers, support the film. Berenbaum, former director of the Survivors of the Shoah Visual History Foundation, called Benigni's use of humor masterful, and Myers, director of the UCLA Center for Jewish Studies, said that the "movie's absurdist approach captures its own truth about the Shoah."[87] Others like UCLA professor Saul Friedländer were cautious: "A true work of art requires symbolization, but what if there is no conceivable symbol that is greater than the reality?" Friedlander asked. "How can you write great fiction when the truth is infinitely stronger than the imagination?"[88] More negative reviewers, like *Slate's* David Edelstein (who said the film made him want to throw up)[89] and scholars like Kobi Niv, have taken issue with the film's basic premise, jarring change of tone, and construction of yet another invisible Jew in Guido. Niv goes so far as to equate Guido to Judas, while Giosué is Jesus,[90] and while Sander Gilman sees the former's death as a logical, if not necessary, conclusion to the story, Niv attributes antisemitic motives in the erasure of "the Jew."[91]

Commentary by Benigni about why he made the film has helped his cause to a certain extent. Gilman recounts an interview when Benigni initially rejected the idea of doing such a film because it would be like "Donald Duck in an extermination camp."[92] However, he warmed to the project once he saw it as a way of honoring his father, who was incarcerated in a German labor camp, and who injected humor into his stories about his time there as a way of shielding his children from the actual horrors of the camp.[93] Moreover, unlike Tarantino, Benigni has acknowledged that he remained "apprehensive" because "you can't do comedy with the Holocaust," but he believes that *Life* "isn't a comedy about the Holocaust." In his words, "it's a comedian who makes a film about the Holocaust. A comedian in an extreme situation. I made it basically because it is a love story . . . I hoped I had the sensitivity not to offend anyone":[94] In another interview, he defends himself by saying, "to laugh, to cry comes from the same point of the soul, no? I'm a storyteller: the crux of the matter is to reach beauty, poetry; it doesn't matter if that is comedy or tragedy. They're the same if you reach the beauty."[95]

When I first saw the film, I was moved by how far Guido would go to protect his child, but I found the slapstick first hour (and the repeated "*bon giorno principesas*") to be tonally off-putting. Maurizio Viano says that the abrupt change "helps its viewers to imagine what many Italian Jews must have felt, the eruption of absurdity and the transformation of one reality into its opposite,"[96] but this could have been accomplished by shortening the humorous courtship portion of the film and expanding the storyline about life under fascism during the war but before the deportations. I felt in 1998, and continue to feel today, that instead of having the camp be an Auschwitz derivative, it would have been more interesting and provocative to have it be an Italian-German camp like Fossoli di Carpi, which had Italian and then German guards. That may have been a more dangerous choice for Benigni, but it might have prompted a necessary discussion about the role of Italian officials in the persecution of the Jews.

The fantasy narratives of *Train of Life* and *Jakob the Liar* also provide striking contrasts to *Life Is Beautiful,* for where Benigni ultimately presents a happy ending in the wake of tragedy, Mihăileanu, Becker, and director Beyer offer fantasy as a temporary distraction from horror. The use of diegesis frames all three texts, but in *Train of Life*, the narrator's story is an outright lie, and in *Jakob the Liar*, the narrator is a nameless survivor who tells the story about a character who lied. In both cases, the lies are tactics to alleviate trauma, which Mihăileanu and Becker foreground more than Benigni, even in his camp narrative, at least until his character is killed. As Sander Gilman suggests, Benigni employs almost without irony tropes of comedy and heroism, which Mihăileanu and Becker turn on their heads. In *Jakob the Liar*, Jakob is the "schlemiel who cannot avoid the randomness of the world in which he exists but can, through simple actions, attempt to ameliorate its suffering. Benigni, too, attempts to use these images. But, unlike Becker, who is self-consciously using this vocabulary as an antidote to the heroic, Benigni simply uses them for their own worth, for their own value."[97]

At the same time, reviewers were more critical of both *Train of Life* and *Jakob the Liar*, although they preferred the former to the latter. In his review in the *New York Times*, Stephen Holden, for instance, praised Mihăileanu's "comic buoyancy."[98] Some of the more negative criticism undoubtedly stemmed from what one could call "Holocaust comedy" fatigue or a sense that Mihăileanu and Kassovitz's films were derivative. Owen Gleiberman's review for *Entertainment Weekly* bears this out:

> *Train of Life* isn't as tedious as *Jakob the Liar* (where Robin Williams paraded around in his schmattes as if they were the Pope's robes), but, if anything, it's even more insufferable. Set in 1941, it follows a village of Eastern European Jews who launch a plan to evade the Nazis by getting hold of a train and faking their own deportation. The amazing thing is, they bring it off with a bluster and enthusiasm that would shame Mickey Rooney and Judy Garland.
>
> Except that this is shtetl-shtick bluster: Every raucous peasant dance is interspersed with a theatrically pained moan to heaven. A few of the Jews have to pose as Nazis, and the scenes where they outwit the bumbling Third Reich soldiers are so awkward and unbelievable that I ended up wishing Mel Brooks and Jerry Lewis would just team up and make the Holocaust comedy to end all Holocaust comedies: *Springtime for the Day Hitler Cried*.[99]

The irony is that of all the comic films under consideration here, the two that are the most dramatic and advance the darkest conclusions are the ones that critics seem to like the least. These are films, too, where the directors approach their topics with just as much sensitivity and thoughtfulness as Benigni and certainly more than Tarantino. Mihăileanu justified the film's warped sense of humor as the product of the history of the Jewish people, which, in his words, has brought Jews "to the edge of madness . . . the invisible chain that holds us Jews together, down through the centuries, is a combination of religion, humor and the permanent tragedy we have no choice but to undergo."[100] Kassovitz evinced a similar sense of desperation and incongruity in an interview to *Film-Philosophy:* "This is one thing you can learn from the Holocaust: you can keep your humanity even when the situation is desperate. Actually, there is not really hope. The hope is that you will not lose your humanity."[101] And Jurek Becker was thinking on multiple levels when he began engaging the story in the first place:

> I had the desire to meditate upon the question of what role hope plays in the lives of people. Whether it is sufficient for survival, or whether it is only helpful when it spurs people into action . . . I was also preoccupied with the question whether lying is a purely cognitive theoretical category or whether it also has a moral dimension. I wanted to know if there is a level at which the rules of logic become unimportant and obsolete and are replaced by the rules of morality. . . . What I also wanted . . . was to write a story about the value of storytelling, above all in times of misery; whether it can help people survive or distract them from the worries, they would have been better off taking care of.[102]

The level of intellectual engagement and purpose undergirding both *Train of Life* and *Jakob the Liar* at the very least parallels that of the films of Benigni and Tarantino, and one could argue that Mihăileanu and Kassovitz are humbler in acknowledging the power of film to create memory and knowledge and to uplift and wound at the same time. And yet, the result was, at least in the case of Kassovitz's film, critical rejection, which bears exploring because it goes counter to what my expectations would be given my hypothesis that strong purpose/thought/execution behind a comic story about the Holocaust would result in a strong performance piece.

As I suggested above, *Jakob the Liar* and *Train of Life* probably lost points for originality and relevance by appearing after *Life Is Beautiful,* Robin Williams put it best when he said in an interview that: "It's like you can have twenty-five buddy movies or guys who are blowing each other away, but another Jewish film, 'Oh God, one a year is enough, thank you.' Please."[103] It also bears noting that *Train of Life* does have a generally favorable consensus, although it is less than most of the other films in this chapter, and here, execution might be the reason. The film feels bizarre in parts, but once we realize at the end that the entire story is the imagining of a disturbed mind, then its strange, almost cartoonish tone makes more sense. The issues with Kassovitz's *Jakob the Liar* go deeper and center on performer, performance, and narrative, but here I agree with scholars like Jennifer Bjornstad and Ilona Klein that the criticism is unjustified.[104] Many reviewers aimed their fire directly at Williams himself. James Berardinelli for *ReelViews* argued the actor was "seriously miscast,"[105] and Janet Maslin, trying to be more diplomatic, thought that the film did not bring out his "best."[106] John Hartl for the *Seattle Times* even suggested that Williams was trying to "cash in" on the success of Benigni's film.[107] To be fair, a handful of reviewers, like Bob Graham for the *San Francisco Chronicle* and David Hunter for the *Hollywood Reporter,* praised Williams.[108] Like these critics, as well as Sander Gilman, I found Williams to be restrained in his comedy and powerful in the dramatic sequences. He is certainly not a slapstick character like Benigni's Guido, and he compares favorably to Vlastimil Brodský's long-suffering Jakob in the East German film. I have to think that part of the critical rejection here was an afterglow effect of the negative response to Williams' film, *Patch Adams,* released in December 1998, about the real-life doctor who dresses up as a clown to cheer up his patients.[109]

In Pól Ó. Dochartaigh's assessment, the problem with Kassovitz's version of *Jakob the Liar* was more about the story than any single performance.[110] Dochartaigh contends that Kassovitz "Americanized" Becker's text in two instances, with the insertion of a subplot about resistance, in which Jakob leads a group of ghetto fighters, and with the ending, which features Soviet and American forces, along with the Andrews Sisters, liberating the deportees. This ending seemingly parallels that of the novel, where Becker's narrator envisions two possibilities for the ghetto inhabitants—one where they all perish in an extermination camp and a second in which they are liberated. However, the text's narrator also distinguishes an "invented" from a "true" conclusion, and he ends the story with the latter—with the Jews on a train bound for death, which is closer to Beyer's film and closer in spirit to the book. *Train of Life's* ending also operates on the same level. Perhaps if Kassovitz had been more faithful to the novel, critics would have been more generous, but Kassovitz's emphasis on hope, even over truth, was what guided him in his journey, and he admits that the novel was darker and that Becker did not "pretend that there is any hope."[111]

In conclusion, I return to the hypothesis that there are guiding theories and criteria that can help assess the quality and efficacy of comedy films about Hitler and the Holocaust. The films I have evaluated in this chapter are generally well-known, and as the sources consulted demonstrate, scholars have been analyzing many of them for decades. They are also, for the most part, critically acclaimed and popular. The reasons for that are legion—quality writing, directing, acting—the basic ingredients for successful filmmaking, and as comedies, they are funny or at least have moments of comedic relief. But they also meet a number of the criteria I advance in the introduction—criteria of purpose, relevance, and originality. They reveal layers of truth and begin conversations about those layers. *The Great Dictator* and *To Be or Not to Be* cover nearly all of these fronts. They capture the essence of Hitler and the Nazi system of oppression; they aim to uplift and empower; and they serve as a warning and critique of contemporary society. *The Producers,* I would argue, is more of a commentary on the times in which it was filmed, even if Brooks sees it as a way of lampooning the Nazis. Its power is heightened through the mocking of the two worlds that should never be joined: Broadway and Nazi propaganda. The three comedies of the late 1990s, *Life Is Beautiful, Train of Life,* and *Jakob the Liar,* depict ghetto and camp life, but the close appearance of three films about the same universe impacted their reception, as did the darker nature of the latter two films and the casting and plot choices of the third. The films of the post 9/11 era, meanwhile, have fulfilled some of the purposes outlined above as well, and many have original frameworks. *Everything Is Illuminated* is the one film whose purpose relates to memory, and *Look Who's Back* serves as a chilling warning about the reactionary potential of German politics.

Three of the films continue to vex me. *Inglourious Basterds* operates in an original, alternative world, and it also effectively portrays, through the character of Hans Landa, the dynamic of the Nazi terror, but director Tarantino has not been the most tactful messenger in articulating his purpose. Gavriel Rosenfeld believes that Tarantino has little investment in history and that he operates at an aesthetic level to get, in his own words, "a laugh at things that aren't really funny."[112] This accounts for much of the visceral reaction among critics and scholars against the film. *Jojo Rabbit* also depicts the Nazi terror dynamic, and many reviewers hold it in high regard, but the film, for me, feels oddly irrelevant. Meanwhile, *Jakob the Liar,* a film with a thoughtful director coming at the subject with a thoughtful aim and purpose, missed the target for most critics. One could see it as the reverse of *Springtime for Hitler,* a case of everything going wrong despite having the right ingredients. Although I think the film is much better than critics give it credit for, a different set of actors and a script that more closely fits the dark ending of the novel might have made a difference. Was the Kassovitz version just poorly done, or was it too liminal and ambivalent a film—not dark enough like *Train of Life* or as whimsical as *Life Is Beautiful?* It will be interesting to see if the Williams-Kassovitz version of *Jakob the Liar* experiences a critical reevaluation over time, like *To Be or Not to Be* has done.

Therefore, my hypothetical model has explanatory power in assessing the effectiveness of the above films, but it is not all-predictive. Subtle changes in casting or writing can make a significant difference, as can the timing of a film. In addition, it appears that the notion that films of this sort must deliver "something new" is not a deal-breaker as long as there are elements of "newness" in them, that is to say, that they upend certain tropes (victims and perpetrators, for instance), and in the words of scholar Grant Julin in his analysis of Bakhtin and satire, they approach the subject with a humor that is "ambivalent; while humiliating and mortifying," they at the same time revive and renew.[113]

NOTES

1. *The Great Dictator,* directed by Charlie Chaplin. Los Angeles: Charlie Chaplin Productions 1940, DVD.
2. It is important to note that Brooks did not write the updated screenplay or direct the film. Alan Johnson was the director, and Ronny Graham and Thomas Meehan wrote the screenplay.
3. Jack Benny, "The Role I Liked Best," *Saturday Evening Post,* 13 March 1948, 148.
4. Ilan Avisar, Screening the Holocaust: Cinema's Images of the Unimaginable (Bloomington, IN: Indiana University Press, 1988) and Avisar, "Historicizing the Holocaust in Film," in *Performing Difference: Representations of the Other in Film and Theater,* ed. Jonathan Friedman (Lanham, MD: University Press of America, 2008).
5. Urwand, *Collaboration: Hollywood's Pact with Hitler* (Cambridge, MA: Belknap, 2013) and Doherty, *Hollywood and Hitler, 1933–1939* (New York: Columbia University Press, 2013). These fine books follow the recent publication by Lawrence Baron, *Projecting The Holocaust Into The Present: The Changing Focus of Contemporary Holocaust Cinema* (Lanham, MD: Rowman and Littlefield, 2005), Terri Ginsberg, *Holocaust Film: The Political Aesthetics of Ideology* (Newcastle, UK: Cambridge Scholars, 2007), Toby Haggith, and Joanna Newman, eds., *The Holocaust and the Moving Image: Representations in Film and Television Since 1933* (London: Wallflower, 2005), and Joshua Hirsch, *Afterimage: Film, Trauma, and the Holocaust* (Philadelphia: Temple University Press, 2003). See also Miriam Borenstein, "Heroes, Victims, and Villains: Character Inversion in Holocaust Cinema," (unpublished thesis, West Chester University, 2009). Each of these books owes much to the works by Judith Doneson, *The Holocaust in American Film* (Philadelphia: Jewish Publication Society, 1987) and Annette Insdorf, *Indelible Shadows: Film and the Holocaust* (New York: Random House, 1983).
6. See especially, Margaret Olin, "Lanzmann's *Shoah* and the Topography of the Holocaust Film," *Representations,* No. 57 (Winter 1997): 1–23.
7. See Janet Ward, "Holocaust Film in the Post 9/11 Era: New Directions in Staging and Emplotment," *Pacific Coast Philology,* Vol. 39 (2004): 29–41.
8. Gerald Gardiner, *The Censorship Papers* (New York: Dodd Mead, 1988), 126, 127, and Robert Cole, "Anglo-American Anti-fascist Film Propaganda in a Time of Neutrality: *The Great Dictator*, 1940," *Historical Journal of Film, Radio and Television,* Vol. 21, No. 2 (2001): 144.
9. Charles Chaplin, *My Autobiography* (New York: Plume, 1992 edition), 387, 392.
10. David Meerse, "To Reassure a Nation: Hollywood Presents World War II," *Film and History,* Vol. 6, No. 4 (1976): 82, and Horak, *Anti-Nazi-Filme der deutschsprachigen Emigration von Hollywood 1939–1945* (Münster: Maks, 1985).
11. Baron, *Projecting the Holocaust,* 136.
12. Kirsten Fermaglich, "Mel Brooks' *The Producers*: Tracing American Jewish Culture Through Comedy, 1967–2007," *American Studies,* Vol. 48, No. 4 (Winter 2007): 61.

13. A.O. Scott, "When We Laugh at Nazis, Maybe the Joke's on Us," *New York Times*, 16 October 2019, https://www.nytimes.com/2019/10/16/movies/the-producers-jojo-rabbit.html, accessed 15 February 2020.

14. Dale Sherman, *Mel Brooks FAQ* (Montclair, NJ: Applause Theatre and Cinema Books, 2018), 14.

15. Sherman, *Mel Brooks*, 14.

16. Sherman, *Mel Brooks*, 92.

17. Sherman, *Mel Brooks*, 92, and Timothy White, "'Producers' Producer: The Man Behind a Classic," *Billboard Magazine*, 26 April 1997.

18. Gilman, "Is Life Beautiful? Can the Shoah Be Funny? Some Thoughts on Recent and Older Films," *Critical Inquiry*, Vol. 26, No. 2 (Winter 2000): 295, and Pól Ó. Dochartaigh, "Americanizing the Holocaust: The Case of *Jakob the Liar*," *The Modern Language Review*, Vol. 101, No. 2 (April 2006): 460.

19. Sander Gilman, "Is Life Beautiful? Can the Shoah Be Funny? Or the Frontier Between Acceptable and Unacceptable Representations of the Holocaust in some Newer and Older Films," in *Jewish Frontiers: Essays on Bodies, Histories, and Identities* (New York: Palgrave Macmillan, 2003), 74, and Baron, *Projecting the Holocaust*, 136–138.

20. Baron, *Projecting the Holocaust*, 138.

21. Deborah Staines, "Knowledge, Memory, and Justice: Some Grey Areas in Contemporary Holocaust Research," *Journal of Contemporary History*, Vol. 42, No. 4 (October 2007): 657, 658.

22. Gavriel Rosenfeld, *Hi Hitler! How the Nazi Past is Being Normalized in Contemporary Culture* (Cambridge: Cambridge University Press, 2015), 15, 25–27.

23. Stefan Steinberg, "'Not to banalise, not to rewrite, but to keep the discussion going': Radu Mihăileanu's *Train of Life*," World Socialist WebSite, 26 November 1998. https://www.wsws.org/en/articles/1998/11/trai-n26.html, accessed 24 January 2020.

24. Baron, *Projecting the Holocaust*, 152.

25. Baron, *Projecting the Holocaust*, 152, 153, Anne Thompson, "The Evolution 'Life,'" *Premiere Magazine* (April 1999): 1–2, and Stefan Steinberg, "'Not to banalise, not to rewrite," https://www.wsws.org/en/articles/1998/11/trai-n26.html, accessed 24 January 2020.

26. Telephone conversation between Pól Ó. Dochartaigh and Christine Becker, 23 February 2005, cited in Pól Ó. Dochartaigh, "Americanizing the Holocaust," 469.

27. Fermaglich, "Tracing American Jewish Culture," 60.

28. Fermaglich, "Tracing American Jewish Culture," 72.

29. Fermaglich, "Tracing American Jewish Culture," 81.

30. https://www.unhcr.org/en-us/figures-at-a-glance.html, and "Are refugee numbers the highest ever?" 14 August 2018, https://www.unhcr.org/blogs/statistics-refugee-numbers-highest-ever/, both accessed 27 January 1945.

31. Kate Connolly, "David Wnendt on Filming *Look Who's Back*: 'Our idea was to see how people react to Hitler,'" 6 October 2015, https://www.theguardian.com/film/2015/oct/06/hitler-look-whos-back-director-david-wnendt-interview, accessed 27 January 1945.

32. Noel King, NPR Interview with Taika Waititi, 18 October 2019, https://www.npr.org/2019/10/18/771219868/director-taika-waititi-on-jojo-rabbit, accessed 27 January 1945.

33. Franz Hoellering, Review of *The Great Dictator*, 26 October 1949, *The Nation*, 401.

34. Thomas J. Fitzmorris, Review of *The Great Dictator*, *America*, 2 November 1940, 111.

35. Theodor W. Adorno, "Commitment," *Notes to Literature*, vol. 2, ed. Rolf Tiedemann, trans. Shierry Weber Nicholsen (New York: Columbia University Press, 1992), 76–94, and Gerd Gemünden, "Space out of Joint: Ernst Lubitsch's *To Be or Not to Be*," *New German Critique*, Vol. 89 (Spring - Summer, 2003): 59–80.

36. Adorno, "Commitment," 76–94.

37. John O'Hara, "Charley, Charley," *Newsweek*, 28 October 1940, 333.

38. Philip Hartung, "That Funny Little Man Again," *Commonweal*, 8 November 1940, 80, 81.

39. Thomas J. Fitzmorris, Review of *The Great Dictator*, *America*, 2 November 1940, 111.

40. Scholar Astrid Klocke, in her comparison of *The Great Dictator* with Edgar Hilsenrath's novel *The Nazi and the Barber*, concludes that it was not Chaplin's activism but his optimism that was the problem, which, seemingly to her preference, Hilsenrath rejected as a viable perspective in the wake of the Holocaust. Astrid Klocke, "Subverting Satire: Edgar Hilsenrath's Novel Der Nazi und der Friseur and Charlie Chaplin's Film *The Great Dictator*," *Holocaust and Genocide Studies*, Vol. 22, no. 3 (Winter 2008): 497–513.

41. *The Tramp and the Dictator* (London: The British Broadcasting Company, 2002), 47:44–49:00.

42. Bosley Crowther, review of *The Great Dictator*, *New York Times*, 16 October 1940.

43. Bosley Crowther, review of *To Be or Not to Be*, *New York Times*, 7 March 1942.

44. Kate Cameron, review of *To Be or Not to Be*, *New York Daily News*, 7 March 1942. The reviewer for *Time* magazine wrote that "*To Be or Not to Be* is a very funny comedy, salted to taste with melodrama and satire," 16 March 1942, and writers for *Variety* and *Morning Telegraph* echoed a similar sentiment. See Scott Eyman, *Ernst Lubitsch: Laughter in Paradise* (New York: Simon & Schuster, 1993), 301.

45. Adrian Daub, "'Hannah Can You Hear Me?" Chaplin's *Great Dictator*, "Schtonk," and The Vicissitudes of Voice," *Criticism*, Vol. 51, No. 3 (Summer 2009): 459, 462.

46. Gerd Gemünden, "Space out of Joint: Ernst Lubitsch's *To Be or Not to Be*," *New German Critique*, Vol. 89 (Spring – Summer, 2003): 59–80

47. Daub, "'Hannah Can You Hear Me?' 462.

48. Sander Gilman, "Is Life Beautiful?" *Critical Inquiry*, Vol. 26, No. 2 (Winter, 2000): 287.

49. Jack and Joan Benny, *Sunday Nights at Seven: The Jack Benny Story* (New York: G.K. Hall, 1991), 232.

50. Richard McCormick, "Transnational Jewish Comedy: Sex and Politics in the Films of Ernst Lubitsch—From Berlin to Hollywood," in *Three Way Street: Jews, Germans, and the Transnational*, ed. Jay Howard Geller and Leslie Morris (Ann Arbor, MI: University of Michigan Press, 2016), 189.

51. McCormick, "Transnational Jewish Comedy," 188.

52. Joel Rosenberg, "Shylock's Revenge: The Doubly Vanished Jew in Ernst Lubitsch's *To Be or Not to Be*," *Prooftexts*, Vol. 16 (1996): 235.

53. Gemünden, "Space out of Joint," 70.

54. Gemünden, "Space out of Joint," 70.

55. Chaplin came to the United States in 1910, Lubitsch in 1922—years before the rise of Hitler. Richard McCormick argues that Lubitsch's position "made him sensitive to social distinctions around class, gender, and ethnicity, and I would argue further that this sensitivity informs his films, along with a sympathy for underdogs, outsiders, and the marginalized. In comedy, the genre at which he was most successful throughout his career, Lubitsch's humor usually turns on such social distinctions, which he often satirizes. Such jokes seem, at their core, to allude to very painful social and political discrimination." McCormick, "Transnational Jewish Comedy: Sex and Politics in the Films of Ernst Lubitsch—From Berlin to Hollywood," in *Three Way Street: Jews, Germans, and the Transnational*, ed. Jay Howard Geller and Leslie Morris (Ann Arbor, MI: University of Michigan Press, 2016), 173, 174.

56. Jeffrey Vance, *Chaplin: Genius of the Cinema* (New York: Harry N. Abrams, 2003), 236. Stephen J. Whitfield, "Humor and the Holocaust," in *Laughter After*, 109.

57. Chaplin, *My Autobiography*, 387.

58. Eyman, *Ernst Lubitsch*, 302.

59. David Low, *Autobiography* (London: Simon & Schuster 1957), 253, and Cole, "Anglo-American Anti-fascist Film Propaganda," 145.

60. Dustin Griffin, *Satire: A Critical Reintroduction*, 155.

61. Eyman, *Ernst Lubitsch*, 302.

62. *Der Spiegel* interview with Mel Brooks, 16 March 2006, https://www.spiegel.de/international/spiegel/spiegel-interview-with-mel-brooks-with-comedy-we-can-rob-hitler-of-his-posthumous-power-a-406268.html, accessed 31 January 2020, and Mel Brooks, *All About Me: My Remarkable Life in Show Business* (New York: Random House, 2021), 184.

63. Sherman, *Mel Brooks*, 111.

64. Renata Adler, "*The Producers* at Fine Arts," *New York Times*, 19 March 1968, 38.

65. Paul Byrnes, Review of *Inglourious Basterds*, *Sydney Morning Herald*, 24 August 2009, https://www.smh.com.au/entertainment/movies/inglourious-basterds-20090824-gdtp1a.html, accessed 31 January 2020; Dana Stevens, "The Good, The Bad, and the Nazis: Review of *Inglourious Basterds*," *Slate*, 20 August 2009, https://slate.com/culture/2009/08/quentin-tarantino-s-inglourious-basterds.html, accessed 31 January 2020; and Manohla Dargis, "Tarantino: Avengers in Nazi Movieland," *The New York Times*, 20 August 2009, https://www.nytimes.com/2009/08/21/movies/21inglourious.html?searchResultPosition=5, accessed 31 January 2020.

66. https://www.jonathanrosenbaum.net/2019/05/16606/, accessed 31 January 2020, and Walters, "Debating Inglourious Basterds," 19.

67. Bill Goodykoontz, "Hitler in a Coming-of-Age Film? *Jojo Rabbit* Pulls it off in Grand Style," *Arizona Republic,* 23 October 2019, https://www.azcentral.com/story/entertainment/movies/billgoodykoontz/2019/10/23/movie-review-jojo-rabbit-works-hitler-into-coming-age-story/4066342002/, accessed 31 January 2020.

68. Ann Hornaday, "A Comedy about Nazis That's Actually Funny? Yes. But *Jojo Rabbit* is Also Deadly Serious." *Washington Post,* 23 October 2019, https://www.washingtonpost.com/goingoutguide/movies/a-comedy-about-nazis-thats-actually-funny-yes-but-jojo-rabbit-is-also-deadly-serious/2019/10/23/9847e6d0-f113-11e9-89eb-ec56cd414732_story.html?arc404=true, accessed 31 January 2020.

69. Boyd van Hoeij, Review of *Er ist wieder da* (*Look Who's Back*), 14 January 2016, https://www.hollywoodreporter.com/review/look-whos-back-er-ist-851346, accessed 31 January 2020.

70. Richard Brody, "Springtime for Nazis: How the Satire of *Jojo Rabbit* Backfires," *The New Yorker,* 22 October 2019, https://www.newyorker.com/culture/the-front-row/springtime-for-nazis-how-the-satire-of-jojo-rabbit-backfires, accessed 31 January 2020.

71. K. Austin Collins, "It's Possible to Make a Good Comedy About Hitler—But *Jojo Rabbit* Isn't It," *Vanity Fair,* 10 September 2019, https://www.vanityfair.com/hollywood/2019/09/jojo-rabbit-movie-review-taika-waititi-hitler, accessed 31 January 2020. A similar sentiment can be found in John Semley's "*Jojo Rabbit's* Satire Fail," *The New Republic,* 17 October 2019, https://newrepublic.com/article/155415/jojo-rabbits-satire-fail, accessed 31 January 2020.

72. Sperber and Wilson, *Relevance,* 125 145, 108 265.

73. *Der Spiegel* interview with Mel Brooks, 16 March 2006, https://www.spiegel.de/international/spiegel/spiegel-interview-with-mel-brooks-with-comedy-we-can-rob-hitler-of-his-posthumous-power-a-406268.html, accessed 5 February 2020.

74. Brooks, *All About Me,* 184.

75. Kate Connolly, "David Wnendt on Filming *Look Who's Back*: 'Our Idea Was to See How People React to Hitler,'" *The Guardian,* 6 October 2015, https://www.theguardian.com/film/2015/oct/06/hitler-look-whos-back-director-david-wnendt-interview, accessed 5 February 2020.

76. Interview by Noel King for NPR with Taika Waititi, 18 October 2019, https://www.npr.org/2019/10/18/771219868/director-taika-waititi-on-jojo-rabbit, accessed 5 February 2020.

77. Interview with Quentin Tarantino *TimeOut,* https://www.timeout.com/london/film/quentin-tarantino-interview-1, accessed 5 February 2020.

78. Interview with Quentin Tarantino, *TimeOut.*

79. Interview with Quentin Tarantino, *TimeOut.*

80. Quote from Ben Walters, "Debating Inglourious Basterds," *Film Quarterly,* Vol. 63, No. 2 (Winter 2009): 21.

81. Griffin, *Satire: A Reintroduction,* 150.

82. See G. Allen Johnson, review of *Everything Is Illuminated,* https://www.sfgate.com/movies/article/FILM-CLIPS-Also-opening-Friday-2567750.php, 23 September 2005, accessed 5 February 2020. In his review, Roger Ebert said that the film "grows in reflection. The first time I saw it, I was hurtling down the tracks of a goofy ethnic

comedy when suddenly we entered dark and dangerous territory. I admired the film but did not sufficiently appreciate its arc. I went to see it again at the Toronto Film Festival, feeling that I had missed some notes, had been distracted by Jonathan's eyeglasses and other relative irrelevancements (as Alex might say). The second time, I was more aware of the journey Schreiber was taking us on, and why it is necessary to begin where he begins in order to get where he's going." https://www.rogerebert.com/reviews/everything-is-illuminated-2005, accessed 5 February 2020. For an example of a negative review, see David Edelstein's "Adapt This: *Everything Is Illuminated* and *Thumbsucker* are Lost in Translation," *Slate*, 16 September 2005, https://slate.com/culture/2005/09/adapt-this-everything-is-illuminated-and-thumbsucker-lost-in-translation.html, accessed 5 February 2020.

83. Paul Fischer, "Good Omens for Schreiber," 15 September 2005, http://www.filmmonthly.com/Profiles/Articles/LievSchreiber/LievSchreiber.html, accessed 5 February 2020, and Interview with Live Schreiber, "Even the Sunflowers are Illuminated," *New York Times*, 18 September 2005, https://www.nytimes.com/2005/09/18/movies/even-the-sunflowers-are-illuminated.html, accessed 5 February 2020.

84. Francisco Collado-Rodriguez, "Ethics in the Second Degree: Trauma and Dual Narratives in Jonathan Safran Foer's *Everything Is Illuminated*," *Journal of Modern Literature*, Vol. 32, No. 1 (Fall 2008): 58.

85. Menachem Feuer and Sue-Ann Weissmark see an internalization of ambiguity as the key to reconciliation, which Jonathan in the novel lacks. Feuer, "Almost Friends: Post-Holocaust Comedy, Tragedy, and Friendship in Jonathan Safran Foer's *Everything Is Illuminated*," *Shofar*, Vol. 25, No. 2 (Winter 2007): 24–48, and Sue-Ann Weissmark, *Justice Matters: Legacies of the Holocaust and World War II* (London: Oxford University Press, 2004).

86. Janet Maslin, "Giving a Human (and Humorous) Face to Rearing a Boy Under Fascism: *Life Is Beautiful*," *New York Times*, 23 October 1998, https://www.nytimes.com/1998/10/23/movies/film-review-giving-a-human-and-humorous-face-to-rearing-a-boy-under-fascism.html?searchResultPosition=2, accessed 6 February 2020.

87. Tom Tugend, "Jewish Community Generally Happy with 'Life," *Los Angeles Times*, 30 October 1998, https://www.latimes.com/archives/la-xpm-1998-oct-30-ca-37417-story.html, accessed 6 February 2020.

88. Tugend, "Jewish Community."

89. David Edelstein, "White and Dark: The Scary Power of Skinhead Art," *Slate*, 1 November 1998, https://slate.com/culture/1998/11/white-and-dark.html, accessed 6 February 2020.

90. Kobi Niv, *Life is Beautiful, But Not for Jews* (Lanham, MD: Scarecrow Press, 2003).

91. Gilman, "Is Life Beautiful?" 303.

92. "Life Is Beautiful: An Interview with Roberto Benigni," Interview by Prairie Miller, http://allmovie.com/cg/x.dll?UID=8:20:451AM&Pp=avg&sql=, as cited in Gilman, 293.

93. Bülent Diken, Carsten Bagge Laustsen, "The Ghost of Auschwitz," *Journal for Cultural Research*, Vol. 9, No. 1 (January 2005): 83. Benigni also credits as inspiration survivor Rubino Romeo Salmoni's memoir, *In the End, I Beat Hitler* and its anecdotes laced with black humor. See Salmoni, *He derrotado a Hitler: memorias de un prisionero de Auschwitz* (Spain: Confluencias, 2013).

94. Interview with Roberto Benigni, co-writer/director of *Life Is Beautiful*, The Movie Show, Episode 42, 1998, https://www.sbs.com.au/movies/video/11676227599/Life-Is-Beautiful-Roberto-Benigni-interview, accessed 10 February 2020.

95. Brian Logan, "Does this man really think the Holocaust was a big joke? Brian Logan meets Roberto Benigni - director and star of *Life Is Beautiful*," *The Guardian*, 29 January 1999, https://www.theguardian.com/culture/1999/jan/29/awardsandprizes, accessed 10 February 2020.

96. Maurizio Viano, "*Life Is Beautiful*: Reception, Allegory, and Holocaust Laughter," *Jewish Social Studies*, New Series, Vol. 5, No. 3 (Spring–Summer, 1999): 55

97. Gilman, "Is Life Beautiful?" 303.

98. Stephen Holden, review of *Train of Life*, *New York Times*, 3 November 1999.

99. Owen Gleiberman, review of *Train of Life*, *Entertainment Weekly*, 12 November 1999.

100. Mihăileanu as cited in Jon Morris, "Against the Comfort of Catharsis: Teaching Trauma and the Sobering Lesson of *Train De Vie*," *Transformations: The Journal of Inclusive Scholarship and Pedagogy*, Vol. 16, No. 2, Teaching through Testimony (Fall 2005): 40.

101. Marty Fairbairn, "The Ethics of Representation: A Review of *Jakob the Liar;* An Interview with Peter Kassovitz Report from the Toronto International Film Festival," *Film-Philosophy*, Vol. 3, No. 1 (1999).

102. Jurek Becker, *My Father, The Germans, and I: Essays, Lectures, Interviews*, ed. Christine Becker (London: Seagull Books, 2010), 40.

103. Alan Riding, "An Oft-Told Tale? Not by His Lights," *New York Times*, 19 September 1999, https://www.nytimes.com/1999/09/19/movies/film-an-oft-told-tale-not-by-his-lights.html, accessed 14 February 2020.

104. Klein argues: "It is in their endings that these two films truly intersect, and the endings help explain why *Jakob the Liar* flopped at American box offices while *Life Is Beautiful* became an international success. For both films the central issue is truth vs. falsehood, and both posit pervasive questions as to who is lying and who is telling the truth. Jakob, in Robin Williams' remake of the film, dies a liar: i.e., he does not reveal the truth about the radio before being hanged by the Nazis in very public circumstances. Paradoxically, it is this same Jakob, nicknamed 'the Liar,' who ultimately does give film audiences some true information about life in the ghetto, antisemitism, despair, resilience, and the cattle cars. However, at the same time, the film also offers a more convenient (revisionist) dual ending for its audience. Such antithetical duplicity forces a conscious choice on the viewer's part, a choice between historical reality and a more comforting and reassuring falsified ending. *Life Is Beautiful*, on the other hand, ends its bittersweet story line on one false, sugar-coated survival note. Benigni's audience is never given a chance to decide for itself. See Ilona Klein, 'Life Is Beautiful, Or Is It?' Asked *Jakob the Liar*," *Rocky Mountain Review*, Vol. 64, No.

1 (SPRING 2010): 26; and Jennifer Bjornstad, "East Berlin to Hollywood: Literary Resistance in Jurek Becker's *Jakob Der Lügner*," *The Journal of the Midwest Modern Language Association*, Vol. 41, No. 1 (Spring, 2008): 56–66

105. James Berardinelli, review of *Jakob the Liar,* for *ReelViews,* cited on Rotten Tomatoes, https://www.rottentomatoes.com/m/jakob_the_liar/reviews?type=top_critics&sort=, accessed 14 February 2020.

106. Janet Maslin, "*Jakob the Liar:* A Flicker of Hope Sustains the Ghetto," *New York Times,* 24 September 1999.

107. John Hartl, review of *Jakob the Liar,* for *The Seattle Times,* cited on Rotten Tomatoes, https://www.rottentomatoes.com/m/jakob_the_liar/reviews?type=top_critics&sort=&page=2, accessed 14 February 2020.

108. See Rotten Tomatoes: https://www.rottentomatoes.com/m/jakob_the_liar/reviews?type=top_critics&sort=, https://www.rottentomatoes.com/m/jakob_the_liar/reviews?type=top_critics&sort=&page=2, accessed 14 February 2020.

109. As a thought experiment, I ceded the point about the choice of Williams in the lead role, and I racked my brain trying to think of other big-name actors at the time who could have played the role of Jakob. I could only come up with Dustin Hoffman, but he too might have fallen victim to the comparisons with Benigni in *Life Is Beautiful.*

110. See Dochartaigh, "Americanizing the Holocaust."

111. Fairbairn, Interview with Kassovitz.

112. Rosenfeld, *Hi Hitler,* 285, and Jordana Horn, "Glorious Bastard," *Forward,* 21 August 2009, https://forward.com/culture/112638/glorious-bastard/, accessed 15 May 2021.

113. Julin, "Satire in a Multi-Cultural World," 265, and his quoting of Bakhtin, *Rabelais and His World,* 16.

Chapter 2

Comedy Films and TV Shows about Hitler

Few historical villains have as pervasive a cultural presence as Adolf Hitler. In the past decade, impersonations of the "Führer" have been everywhere, in films, television, and especially on the Internet, where the "Hitler meme," an image with funny captions that people share on various platforms, has become something of a defining artifact of the early 21st century. A cursory Internet search for Hitler memes yields over forty-five million hits. By comparison, Mao and Marx memes return about six million each, and Stalin memes only yield about 2.7 million hits. In addition, performers of Jewish descent or identification, such as Taika Waititi, Gilbert Gottfried, and even Sarah Silverman, have had their say as Hitler either on the big screen or on television. This overexposure may have the effect of keeping Hitler in the headlines, but like anything in the law of diminishing returns, it makes Hitler comedy less funny, which also diminishes the relevance of that comedy.

In this chapter, I explore the evolution in different platforms and contexts of comic portrayals of Adolf Hitler. Specifically, I focus on the earliest depictions in American films and cartoons (from the Three Stooges to Bugs Bunny) through comedic films and television productions of the present day (including German films like *Mein Führer* and the Australian series *Danger 5*). Here again, I intend to uncover common devices and tropes and evaluate their effectiveness as representations when set against my model of purpose-relevance-originality. The films I consider do not share uniform purposes; the humor in wartime productions was directed toward disempowering Hitler and empowering his victims, while later filmmakers have used Hitler as a symbol of terror to critique contemporary politics. For others, Hitler has become a vessel to re-appropriate and reinvent cultural elements from the past. This appears to be a trend in the current employment of his persona. Filmmakers have constructed numerous caricatures of the "Führer"—Hitler as a buffoon, as the devil, as a ranting lunatic, as a criminal mastermind, or they have infantilized Hitler by constructing child characters to take on his role. However, a vast swath of Hitler references in popular media appears to serve no purpose at all, which only accelerates the process of normalizing Hitler and reducing the impact of his malevolence.

HITLER CARTOONS AND COMEDIES, 1933–1945

Hitler comedies were part of the critique against fascism from within Europe in the 1930s and '40s. Performers and artists who used comedy to take on Hitler understood the danger he posed to freedom and were more explicitly at peace with a Manichean view of the German leader as evil personified. German visual artist John Heartfield published anti-Hitler caricatures in the socialist *Arbeiter Illustrierte Zeitung* (*Worker Illustrated Newspaper*), even before Hitler's appointment as chancellor in 1933. Heartfield continued publishing such imagery in exile in Czechoslovakia before he fled to London in advance of the German occupation. In 1938, the famous Anglo-Irish playwright George Bernard Shaw premiered his satire *Geneva,* a send-up of Hitler, Mussolini, and Generalissimo Francisco Franco, at the Teatr Polski in Warsaw.

In the United States, however, multiple forces worked against any cinematic representation of Hitler, let alone a comedic one. There were economic considerations, as Germany and Italy constituted the market for thirty percent of overseas profits, estimated at over two million dollars.[1] The isolationist political climate, enforced by aggressive congressional investigations into "pro-war propaganda," and a surge of antisemitism in the United States also made many Jewish studio moguls reluctant to produce anti-Hitler films and draw attention to their Jewishness. Moreover, the 1927 Production Code contained explicit provisions against depicting public figures in an "unfavorable light," and the creation of the Production Code Administration in 1934, which gave the Code teeth, prevented the release of any film which did not bear its certificate of approval. A documentary entitled *Hitler's Reign of Terror* and a feature, *Are We Civilized?,* appeared that year to expose the dangers of Nazism, but because of their content, they could not secure a wide release. Historian Michael Birdwell argues that as a Polish Jewish immigrant, Harry Warner favored more anti-Nazi films from the Warner Brothers' catalog, but constraints from the Code, fears of exacerbating already high levels of antisemitism, and opposition from his younger brother Jack, who was born in Canada, forestalled this until closer to the war.[2] Indeed, it was not until the Warner Brothers' film, *Confessions of a Nazi Spy* (1939), starring Edward G. Robinson, that American audiences would see another overtly anti-Nazi feature film.

Before these films, the first visual encounters American audiences had of Hitler were through newsreels and two cartoons, *Cubby's World Flight* (released on 25 August 1933, directed by Hugh Harman and Rudolf Ising and distributed by Van Beuren Studios) and *Bosko's Picture Show* (released on 18 September 1933, directed by Hugh Harman and Fritz Freleng and distributed by Warner Brothers). Cartoons and shorts operated under the radar of the Production Code and the U.S. government, and as a result, animators and comics had greater leeway. Gerald Nye, a Republican senator from North Dakota who helped secure passage of laws that forced the United States into a policy of neutrality during the 1930s and who was one of the leading investigators into what Congress viewed as pro-war propaganda, admitted as much when he said that only "quality" pictures, or those made for $250,000 or more, would be investigated.[3] According to historian Dan Morlan, this attitude allowed cartoons and shorts an enormous degree of latitude and the opportunity to reach thousands of viewers. He argues that acts like the Three Stooges were "'getting away with murder' at a time when even the slightest hint of anti-Nazi sentiment in a feature film was sure to draw the wrath of the isolationists."[4] Michael Schull and David Wilt point out that cartoons were very much a part of the double-feature experience for adults until the 1960s and should be evaluated as historical documents of mass popular culture.[5] They estimate that nearly three hundred animated shorts touched on the war crisis in some way from 1939 to 1945.[6]

In *Cubby's World Flight* and *Bosko's Picture Show,* the main characters Cubby the bear and Bosko were not editorial or political characters by any stretch, but rather the product of a desire by Walt Disney's competitors in animation, Harman and Ising, the Van Beuren Studios, and Leon Schlesinger's *Merrie Melodies* and *Looney Tunes* series (which were distributed through Warner Brothers) to capitalize on alternatives to Oswald the Rabbit and Mickey Mouse. The Bosko character is particularly problematic; although Ising insisted that Bosko "was supposed to be an inkspot sort of thing," he looks either like a caricature of an African American boy or a white boy in blackface. Ising has admitted that although he did not think of Bosko as human, "we had him behave like a little boy."[7]

Both cartoons feature brief depictions of Hitler. In *Cubby's World Flight,* the character Cubby Bear flies across the globe, and at one point, Hitler, holding a beer stein, and German President Paul von Hindenburg, wave at him. In *Bosko's Picture Show*, Bosko plays the organ as a series of mock newsreels flash on the screen. In one of these, the announcer tells of a "Famous Screen Lover on European Vacation." The screen cuts to a cartoon Hitler in lederhosen wielding an ax and running after a character that is a composite of a German Jew and comedian Jimmy Durante, the Italian and Catholic comedian whose large nose was one of his trademarks. While the Durante character keeps repeating, "Am I mortified," the announcer says he has the "lead by a nose!" It is revealing that this first feature image of Hitler references his antisemitism with an antisemitic trope, which has resulted in the scene being cut in later versions on television.[8]

Cartoons from Disney and Warner Brothers became a major forum for anti-Nazi messaging, but before the U.S. involvement in World War II, they were few in number, and their criticisms were more oblique. Some have suggested that Disney, in particular, harbored Nazi sympathies as he attended meetings of the German American Bund and hosted Hitler's propagandist Leni Riefenstahl in 1938, one month after *Kristallnacht*. Richard Huemer, a Disney animator, said that Disney was "definitely to the right" and that he could not tolerate anyone "tinged with a little pink."[9] At the same time, as media scholar Tracy Mollet points out, Riefenstahl had doubts about Disney's true sympathies, and historian Neal Gabler, in his biography of Disney, concluded that his politics "were marked by confusion or neutrality."[10]

While this may be true, some efforts predated the U.S. entry into the war. For instance, the Disney cartoon entitled *The Three Wolves* was released in 1936, and it featured a big bad wolf character speaking English with a decidedly German accent; in a later cartoon, *The Thrifty Pig*, which was released in Canada weeks before Pearl Harbor, the big bad wolf morphed outright into a Nazi, complete with a swastika armband.[11] In this effort, other pre-war cartoons by Disney and Warner Brothers included *Donald's Better Self* from 1938 and *What Price Porky*, from the same year, which saw Donald Duck and Porky Pig lending support for intervention against global fascism.[12]

Once the U.S. entered the war, Disney and Warner Brothers lined up squarely behind the allied campaign and produced some classic anti-Nazi cartoons. The most famous of these is perhaps Disney's *Der Führer's Face*, released on 1 January 1943, which won the Academy Award for Best Animated Short at the 15th Academy Awards. Disney benefited from receiving government contracts for animated shorts, and he went on to produce over thirty animated features between 1941 and 1945, which enabled the studio to remain solvent after the box office failure of *Fantasia*, The other notable anti-Nazi cartoons were *Education for Death*, released on 15 January 1943, and *Reason and Emotion*, released on 27 August 1943. Leon Schlesinger's animation studio, which had its cartoons distributed through Warner Brothers until he sold his operation in 1944, also produced numerous anti-Nazi cartoons, including *The Ducktators* (1 August 1942), *Daffy the Commando* (20 November 1943), (*Russian Rhapsody* (20 May 1944), and *Herr Meets Hare* (13 January 1945).[13]

The Disney cartoons share a darker tone, and although there is humor in each, it is buried under more didactic and ominous messaging. *Der Führer's Face* features Donald Duck as a peon in the Nazi state living in a house that looks like Hitler. Donald is roused to work by the eponymous title song, which was a hit record by Spike Jones. The hysterical speed of the armament work (*a la* Chaplin in *Modern Times*) overwhelms Donald to the point where he starts to hallucinate. The images of artillery shells coming alive and beating the poor duck on the head are much creepier than anything in the Warner Brothers' cartoons, but that has always been a part of the Disney mystique, and the sequence is evocative of similar segments in *Dumbo*. All ends well, though, as Donald awakens from this nightmare back in the safe confines of the United States, and he ends by hugging a miniature Statue of Liberty and proclaiming how glad he is to be a citizen of the USA.[14] *Education for Death* is an even darker exposé of Nazi indoctrination. Loosely based on a book by Gregor Ziemer, an American educator in Berlin who fled the city in 1939, *Education for Death* centers on a German boy, Hans, who is nearly murdered because of a childhood sickness, which he overcomes, and then is turned into a ruthless killing machine. In one scene, which shows continuity up to *Jojo Rabbit,* Hans is in class where his teacher has drawn on the chalkboard a rabbit being eaten by a fox. He wants to elicit the proper lesson from the drawing, that only the strong survive, but Hans feels sorry for the rabbit and is mocked and punished by his teacher until he parrots the correct message. The only humorous portion of the short is a parody of *Sleeping Beauty* when a scrawny Hitler dressed as a knight rescues a very rotund Brunhilde, who represents Germany. In *Reason and Emotion,* another short that appears to have a contemporary link, this time to the Disney-Pixar film *Inside Out,* the message is that there needs to be a balance between both sides of the human psyche. Hitler symbolizes the danger posed to the world when reason is destroyed and replaced by the emotion of fear. Because of their content and tone, it took Disney until 2004 to release the cartoons on DVD.

The four Schlesinger/Warner cartoons, *The Ducktators*, *Daffy the Commando*, *Russian Rhapsody*, and *Herr Meets Hare,* are by contrast much zanier and lighter. Tracey Mollet argues that because the Warner Brothers' films are less "realist," that is to say, the Axis villains are drawn either as animals or caricatures in outlandish situations, they come across as less of a threat and are more easily ridiculed than in the Disney films.[15] In *Daffy the Commando* and *Herr Meets Hare,* Daffy Duck and Bugs Bunny—frequently enemies themselves—torment and outsmart their Nazi foes. In the case of *Daffy the Commando,* the villain is Commander von Vultur, whose main concern is preventing American commandos from parachuting behind enemy lines. Von Vultur has a lackey by the name of Schultz, which must have been taken directly from *To Be or Not to Be* because anytime anything bad happens, Von Vultur yells out, "Schultz!!!" very much like Colonel Ehrhardt in the Lubitsch film. Daffy winds up being fired out of a cannon, and he lands on a podium where Hitler is delivering one of his speeches.[16] The German spoken in the cartoon is closer to actual German than in other shorts or films like *The Great Dictator,* and the cartoon makes hay of this. At one point, Daffy is in a phone booth while Von Vultur waits outside. Daffy says in German, "*Kannst du nicht sehen diese Telefon ist busy? Bleiben sie ruhig!*" He holds a sign for the audience, "Can't you see the telephone is busy? Wait your turn!" (He then asks for a nickel, again in German). Then at the end, as Hitler exclaims, "*Ach, du Lieber! Mein Herr! Mein Pupkin! Mein Milch! Mein Heineken!*" Daffy hits him over the head, prompting Hitler to yell out, "Schultz!!" In *Herr Meets Hare,* one of the last of Warner Brothers' war cartoons, Bugs Bunny harasses Hermann Goering and uses for the first time the line that has since become a classic—"I knew I shoulda made that left turn at Albuquerque!" The cartoon also has Goering utter a line from the song *Der Führer's Face,* The sequence where Bugs dresses as Brunhilde and Goering as Siegfried is also a precursor to the famous 1957 cartoon, *What's Opera Doc?,* which features Bugs again as Brunhilde, but this time, Elmer Fudd as Siegfried. Although Bugs is captured, stuffed into a bag, and delivered to Hitler by Goering, the Axis leaders freak out when Bugs emerges as Stalin.

In *Ducktators,* two bad ducks (Hitler and Tojo) and a bad goose (Mussolini) constitute a menace who refuse to listen to a peace-loving dove, clearly a symbol of the United States. The dove ultimately fights back and wins; the three bad birds are stuffed and mounted on his mantle. (This ending did not appear in subsequent versions of the cartoon. In fact, because of its racist depictions of the Japanese leader, the cartoon has only rarely appeared on television. This is also the case for the Bugs Bunny cartoon from 1944 entitled *Bugs Bunny Nips the Nips*; Hitler is the main character in *Russian Rhapsody;* here, he is furious that German bombers have been unable to hit Moscow, and so he takes it on himself to fly a mission. He is beset by "gremlins" (all caricatures of the cartoons' animators) who dismantle the plane and torment Hitler as he crashes to the ground. The short was the first to feature a cartoon image of Stalin.

What stands out in the wartime anti-Nazi cartoons from Disney and Warner Brothers is an originality, relevance, and clarity of purpose that can vie with any of the studios' classic pieces of animation. In an article in the *New York Times* from 7 February 1943, entitled "Donald Duck's Disney," writer Theodore Strauss offered a bemused commentary:

> Who would have thought in the dim primordial past of five years that one day Donald Duck would be giving the retort perfect to Herr Doktor Goebbels? Not Mr. D. and hardly, one suspects, Dr. Goebbels; and least of all Walt Disney, who has a paternal interest in "the duck" and more vehement interest in the Nazi mouthpiece. But there it is. Donald, who used to be just another noisy neighbor,

has by some odd token of fate become a sort of ambassador-at-large, a salesman of the American Way.[17]

In the same article, Strauss quoted Disney:

> the war has taught us that people who won't look at a book will look at a film. It's shown that you can take knowledge out of a dusty tome somewhere and wrap up the effort of many teachers in one can of film. You can show that film to any audience, and twenty minutes later, it has learned something—a new idea, or an item of important information—and it at least has stimulated further interest in study.... Mass education is coming. It's coming because it's a necessity. Democracy's ability to survive depends on the ability of its individuals to appreciate their duties as citizens and to comprehend the complex problems of the changing world we live in.[18]

The Warner films differed in their more madcap sensibility; in fact, in interviews, Fritz Freleng has said that what distinguished Warner from Disney animators was the desire to be as "silly as we could—rather than as artistic as we could," but their humor which deflated the Nazis and raised morale was just as purposeful.[19]

As for "live-action" representations of Hitler from Hollywood, it was not Charlie Chaplin's *The Great Dictator* that led the way. As early as November 1933, the Marx Brothers were having their say about militarism and corrupt leadership in Leo McCarey's *Duck Soup*. The film's scenario involves a wacky politician, Rufus T. Firefly, played by Groucho Marx, who is installed to run a bankrupt country called Freedonia. Trentino, a sinister ambassador from a neighboring country, wants war and commissions two spies, played by Chico and Harpo Marx, to infiltrate Firefly's government. The film features all of the classic Marx Brothers dialogue and antics, with lines about gas attacks being thwarted with bicarbonate of soda, and everything devolves into mayhem and a food flight at the end, with Groucho and the other brothers wearing different and increasingly bizarre military uniforms as the war with Trentino reaches its crescendo. The film did not receive the kind of critical or popular acclaim it holds today, and even Groucho was lukewarm about the production, insisting that "we were just four Jews trying to get a laugh."[20] However, director McCarey described the film as a cautionary tale against ignoring the dangers of hypernationalism, and the film was subversive enough to get banned in Mussolini's Italy.[21] It is recognized today as a classic of American film comedy, and its narrative structure and plot devices reappear in subsequent anti-Hitler satires.

In January 1939, the Three Stooges (Moe and Curly Howard and Larry Fine) released the short *Three Little Sew and Sews,* which centered on villains trying to steal American submarine secrets. Although the antagonists are not identified as Germans, their names (Count Alfred Gehrol and Olga) are a give-a-way. The Stooges bumble their way to rooting out the plot, but Curly accidentally blows everyone up in the end.[22] A year after *Sew and Sews* and months before the premiere of *The Great Dictator*, the Stooges came out with their own anti-Hitler spoof, the 18-minute short, *You Natzy Spy*, which hit theaters on 19 January 1940. By then, producer Jules White and writers Felix Adler and Clyde Bruckman had come to the conclusion that Germany had become "the unwholesome center of human affairs" and that Hitler was a "simultaneously fearsome and absurd figure who begged to be stripped bare via lampoon."[23]

There are noticeable parallels between *You Natzy Spy* and *Duck Soup*—the inane leader installed by moneyed elites, the use of spies, and slapstick fighting. And even though the setting has changed, the name of the country, Moronika, is in the same language orbit of wordplay as the Marx Brothers' Freedonia. It is just more transparently silly. Arms manufacturers at the beginning of *You Natzy Spy* (with the names of Ixnay, Onay, and Amscray) bemoan that they have netted only five million dollars and need more profit. The only way to do that is to start a war, but the king, Hermann the Sixth and Seven Eighths (a Kaiser Wilhelm II type), wants peace, so they decide to overthrow him and install a dictator who is stupid enough to do their bidding. They find their man in paper hanger Moe Hailstone, who, along with fellow painters Curly Gallstone and Larry Pebble, leads the new regime. Moe plays the role of Hitler, the first American actor to appear on screen as the Nazi leader, although technically Chaplin was shooting his film months before. Curly is a combination of Goering and Mussolini, and Larry gets the post as minister of propaganda. Typical of the kinds of jokes in the film, Larry asks what propaganda is, and Curly responds that a "popaganda marries a mommaganda, and they raise a lot of little goslings," which leads Moe to strangle Curly. The three stand on a balcony, and Hailstone delivers a rousing speech, declaring that the new country's motto will be "Moronika for Morons," parodying the "Germany for Germans" line of the Nazis. Moe promises hamburgers and eggs every Thursday, and the audience cheers and applauds but only when Larry holds up a sign. Moe also insists that Moronika must extend its neighbors a helping hand, and he amps that up, saying that "we'll extend two helping hands and help ourselves to our neighbors." Once in the office, Moe sentences a citizen who has been caught with a chicken to be put into a "concentrated camp" because he cannot explain which came first, the chicken or the egg, and then he changes his mind and wants the prisoner to be thrown to the lions. But the country does not have lions—only tigers, giants, and cubs (a bad baseball reference lost on German viewers). Meanwhile, the king's daughter (played by Lorna Gray) poses as spy Mattie Herring who plots to overthrow Hailstone. She escapes, and Hailstone seeks action before

Herring raises an army with her father. He decides that the smartest course of action is to take over the country of South Starvania as a distraction. In the Munich-like conference that ensues, fistfights break out, and Curly subdues the Starvanian diplomats by hitting them in the head with golf balls. A mob storms the palace, and the Stooges flee to a room that Curly has locked them into, but it turns out it is a lion's den, and the lions pursue the three to a corner off-screen and eat them.[24]

In July 1941, the Stooges came out with the first of only two sequels they made for Columbia—*I'll Never Heil Again,* a play on the Tommy Dorsey/Frank Sinatra song, "I'll Never Sing Again."[25] The Stooges are back from the dead (or they just never die). Moe now sports a Hitler mustache throughout the entire film, and Gilda, the daughter of King Hermann, concocts a plan to pose as an astrologer to Hailstone and plant a bomb inside a billiard ball to kill him. Gilda shows Moe and the other two their fate; they are tied to a rotisserie by their allies, and then she plants the bomb on the office pool table—because, of course, there is an office pool table. More punching and poking follow, as does a conference of all the Axis, or in this case "Axel," powers, which includes a delegate by the name of Bey of Rum, named after bay rum, an aftershave, which represents Turkey—even though the Turks were neutral in World War II. Then, fisticuffs ensue over a globe, and the Axels are dispatched, but when Curly's character, now known as Field Marshall Herring, just as in *The Great Dictator,* smashes the globe over Moe's head, more in-fighting occurs, and Curly throws the billiard ball-bomb to the ground blowing everyone up. The king returns to power, and the heads of the Stooges are mounted on a mantelpiece. There is the story that during the filming of *I'll Never Heil Again,* Moe was running late for his daughter's birthday and that he kept his Hitler costume on, which resulted in Hollywood police stations being inundated by reports of the Führer in Hollywood.[26]

The third Hitler short by the Stooges was *Higher than a Kite,* released on 30 July 1943. In this film, the Stooges play mechanics in the Royal Air Force who want to see action and wind up stuck in a bomb dropped on Germany. Moe and Curly find disguises as German officers, while Larry poses as a woman. (They repurpose the name Moronica for his character here.) Parodies of general Erwin Rommel and Hermann Göring show up, as Bommel and Boring, the latter on a scooter; they flirt with Larry and then have their invasion plans stolen. Before this, however, Moe and Curly use the invasion map as a checkerboard and move the pieces around to such an extent that Boring exclaims, "What is this? The 28th Division in the Red Sea? Und the Afrika Korps in the North Pole?"[27] The Stooges escape in the end as Larry (Moronica) knocks Boring through the floor, and Moe knocks out Bommel because he cannot stop saluting a photo of Hitler that Curly has stuck to his rear. A bulldog wearing a U.S. marine coat proceeds to latch onto Curly's behind at the film's end.

The Devil with Hitler is a short film released on 22 October 1942 from Hal Roach's Studios as part of his Streamliners' series of comedy featurettes. Roach, famous for his *Our Gang* and *Laurel and Hardy* productions, had a wartime transformation in many ways, similar to Walt Disney. Like the famous animator, in the 1930s, Roach did not seem to have a problem working with fascists. He also met with Leni Riefenstahl and attempted a business partnership with Mussolini's son, Vittorio, an enterprise thwarted by the activism of the Hollywood Anti-Nazi League. Beginning in September 1941 and continuing through the period of American involvement in the war, Roach embraced the anti-fascist media blitz. *Devil* is the first of Roach's anti-Nazi comedies, the second being *That Nazty Nuisance (aka The Last Three).* The plot of *The Devil with Hitler* centers on the dilemma of Satan (played by Alan Mowbray) trying to keep his job as the leader of hell as the other demonic minions on hell's board of directors want Hitler instead. Satan gets the board to agree that if Hitler does one good deed, Satan can keep his job. The slapstick that ensures sees Hitler (played by Bobby Watson), Mussolini (Joe Devlin), and a Japanese diplomat Suki Yaki (George Stone) involved in one farcical scene after another. (There are a fair number of scenes of Hitler getting struck in the rear by flying objects.) Two civilians, Walter and Linda, are set to be executed, and Satan tries to convince Hitler to release them, but he refuses. While Hitler takes the afternoon to paint a masterpiece, Satan locks him in his studio, impersonates the Führer, and gets Walter and Linda released. Hitler falls off his painting ledge, and a bucket of paint lands on his head, prompting him to call out for help; actually, he starts a rant against everyone else. Although the real Hitler is rescued by S.S. guards, Satan initially convinces them that he is an impostor, and he nearly gets Walter and Linda on a train to safety. Hitler promises Mussolini and Suki Yaki Italy and the Pacific, respectively, and they vouch for his authenticity. Running after Satan, they end up in an armory, where more bombing and rocket-flying insanity ensues. (This scene evokes a part in *Duck Soup* in which a shell comes through a window, seemingly with a mind of its own.) Hitler agrees to release Walter and Linda in return for his life, but he is blown up and winds up punished for eternity in hell as Satan retains his job as lord of the underworld.

Watson and Devlin reprised their roles as Hitler and Mussolini in the sequel, *That Nazty Nuisance,* which premiered on 28 May 1943. This time, Hitler sets off to the fictional Asian island of Norom to sign a treaty with a mysterious leader known as Paj Mub (Ian Keith). Mussolini and Suki Yaki (now played by Johnny Arthur) crash the trip as well. At the same time, an American ship has been sunk by a German submarine, and its crew has landed on Norom. The crew members investigate the island, and a seaman by the name of Benson meets a young woman, Kela, who happens to be the assistant of a drunk magician slated to perform for Paj Mub—because why not? Benson takes the magician's place, amuses Paj Mub by turning Suki Yaki into an orangutan, and then everyone leaves on the German sub, which the Americans proceed to take over. Fearing for their lives, Hitler, Mussolini, and Suki Yaki squeeze themselves into the torpedo shafts and get blasted back to Norom.

While the Roach and Stooge films feature ample sight gags, bottom jokes, and groaning wordplay (Norom is Moron, etc.), there are some glaring contrasts. The Roach films are for one much more openly racist in their portrayal and language about the Japanese; the fact that Paj Mub is "Bum Jap" spelled backward is merely the tip of this iceberg. Roach's films were also produced and released well after the U.S. entry into the war, at a time when such films were not only tolerated but demanded for the war effort. That Roach remained an apologist for Mussolini further complicates any evaluation of his comic shorts. An article from *Motion Picture Herald* dated 2 October 1937 has Roach describing Mussolini as "the only square politician I've ever seen."[28] Thomas Doherty, in his book *Hollywood and Hitler,* reports that Roach doubled down on his engagement with Mussolini's son by insisting that he did it "on the advice of one of the most prominent Jews abroad . . . who thought it would do more good for the situation concerning Jews over there than anything that possibly could be done."[29] In another biography, Roach admitted with a tinge of antisemitism that " . . . there was a problem from the very beginning . . . since the motion picture industry is a Jewish business . . . ."[30] Another of Roach's biographers, Harjinder Singh, quotes Roach as saying, "history has been very unfair to Mussolini," and recalls that he believed the conspiracy theory that Hitler murdered the Italian dictator.[31]

By contrast, the Jewish Stooges not only were at the forefront of anti-Hitler comedy, but they frequently inserted Yiddish or Hebrew wherever they could to add to their humor. In *You Natzy Spy,* they shout the word, "*Beblach*," which is Yiddish for beans; they say, "Shalom Aleichem," Hebrew for "Peace be unto you"; and Moe yells multiple times in garbled rants "*in pupik gehabt haben*," Yiddish for "I've had it in the belly button." He also declares that he is going to start a "*blintzkrieg*," to which Curly responds, "oh goodie, I just love blintzes, especially with sour *krieg!*" The Stooges use of language, therefore, differs from that of Chaplin, who spoke largely in gibberish and employed signage in Esperanto, in that while both forms were purposeful, the Stooges added the irony of Jewish actors delivering messaging through a spoken language of the Jews as part of their subversion. The Stooges recognized the importance of their anti-Hitler comedies so much so that Larry and Moe regarded *You Natzy Spy* as their favorite short out of the hundreds that they did.[32]

POSTWAR HITLER COMEDIES IN THE UNITED STATES, GREAT BRITAIN, AND GERMANY, 1945–2010

After the war, as the scope of the crimes of the Nazi regime came into full view, films about Hitler and the Third Reich tended to hew to a moralist perspective. Some of the key dramatic features included Georg Wilhelm Pabst's *The Last Days (Der Letzte Akt,* 1955) and Ennio di Concini's *Hitler: The Last Ten Days* (1973), both of which chronicled Hitler's demise in his bunker. Other films included Joachim Fest's *Hitler: A Career (Hitler—Eine Karriere,* 1977), Hans-Jürgen Syberberg's *Our Hitler (Hitler-Ein Film aus Deutschland,* 1978), and Marvin Chomsky's *Inside the Third Reich* (1982).[33] Yet there were some comedic-fantasy representations of Hitler before *The Producers* in 1967, mostly in the realm of science fiction. Nazis were villains in zombie films from the early 1940s (in *King of the Zombies,* released in May 1941) through the 1950s and '60s (in *Creature with the Atom Brain,* July 1955, *She Demons,* March 1958, and *The Frozen Dead,* from October 1966). There have been ninety-four Nazi zombie films from the 1940s to the present day, although over seventy have been produced in the past twenty years.[34] The first of these to focus on Hitler specifically was the sci-fi comedy, *Madmen from Mandoras,* from 1963, lengthened and released on television in 1968 as *They Saved Hitler's Brain,* In the film, Nazis have preserved Hitler's head in a jar but are thwarted in their plan to revive the Reich.[35] Episodes of *The Twilight Zone* in the 1960s also featured plots about Hitler.[36] Although the creators of these productions might have intended to take down Hitler as their wartime era predecessors did, they helped foster normalization well before the current proliferation of "funny" Hitler films and memes. It was one thing to reduce Hitler to a joke during the years of the Reich and the war when it could serve as a morale booster or temporary distraction, but in the postwar years, with memory the source of his historical construction, the desire to skewer Hitler comedically had to be set against the real possibility that the collective memory of him would become so denuded as to diminish the impact of his evil. The comedies and comic sketches about Hitler from the 1960s through the 1970s and beyond demonstrate this peril.

For instance, Rod Amateau's 1979 cult film, *Son of Hitler,* serves as a warning about the dangers of neo-Nazism and a cautionary tale about film's role in the balance between moralism and relativism vis-à-vis Hitler. In the film, Amateau, best known as a television producer on shows like *The Dukes of Hazzard,* cast Bud Cort (of *Harold and Maude* fame) as Willi Katzenmacher, the Führer's long-lost son, who lives as a woodcarver in the mountains unaware of his lineage. Peter Cushing, fresh off his stint as Grand Moff Tarkin in *Star Wars,* plays a version of that character as the Nazi

Heinrich Haussner, who seeks a restoration of the Third Reich. For him, the only way to do this is to find Hitler's long-lost descendant. When Willi realizes who he is, he starts dressing like a Nazi, which gets him thrown out of a McDonald's and then hit by a car. He finds himself hospitalized in a psychiatric ward until Haussner and his men kidnap him and prop him up as the leader of their revolution. At first, Willi delivers a speech that suggests he possesses his father's charisma, but in the end, his oratory becomes more like Chaplin's at the end of *The Great Dictator,* which leads to a brawl, a police shootout, and ultimately, Haussner's demise (by suicide). Willi goes back to the asylum, which is now made up to look like the interior of his mountain cottage.

The film is a low-budget, low-quality effort, one that might have been funnier if it had gone to extremes in developing Cushing's character, or it might have been more narratively relevant if it had magnified its self-reflectivity, like another contemporary parody, the movie *Airplane,* but it does prefigure films, such as Michael Verhoeven's *The Nasty Girl* (from 1990) and Christoph Schlingensief's *Terror 2000,* from 1992, both of which warn about the revival of fascism. This impulse behind *Son of Hitler* can be inferred in a later, unrelated interview with director Amateau, who, expounding on his overall world view, amplifies the idea that comedy should advance a moralistic framework in which antagonists are frustrated and denied their ambitions. In his words:

> Every time the Dukes of Hazzard beat the Boss, every time George Jefferson learns a lesson, the audience is reassured that the prevailing values are intact.... By promulgating this myth that if you do anything wrong, you'll be caught within thirty to sixty minutes—depending on the network—you perpetuate at least a sense of morality and order. Even if it's not true.[37]

It is instructive that Amateau ends here, believing that moralism is necessary even if it does not reflect reality. This statement has broad ramifications beyond a discussion of something both as silly and serious as anti-Hitler comedy. A world that only aspires to morality but has lost it would be, as I will repeatedly argue, one that can easily laugh off Hitler and then embrace another version of him. This, to me, is the core conundrum of anti-Hitler comedy, namely how comics can be funny, possibly ridiculous, and therefore potentially relativizing, and at the same time be preachy—which so often kills the humor. There is no easy answer for this.

In the 1970s, Carol Burnett, in her American variety show, and the British comedians Spike Mulligan and Monty Python occasionally ventured into Hitler comedy for their sketches, and the results were almost always hilarious and original yet wildly divergent in terms of their relevance and purpose. I would argue that the Pythons found a way to thread the needle of creating something funny, outrageous, and multi-purposed, all without being either sanctimonious or dismissive about Nazism. The first Hitler skit on the Carol Burnett show aired on 29 November 1972 as a "play within a play"—a skit for an imaginary series "Non-Violent Theater" called "The Plot to Hurt Hitler." More of a send-up of violence on television, the skit featured Burnett as a spy and Carl Reiner and Harvey Korman as eye-patch-wearing German officers trying to find ways to injure the Führer. (Korman delivers one of the series' classic lines, "Heinz, you have mother's eye.") Their suggestions range from giving Hitler a hickey, which they reject as too violent, to putting a note on his back that says, "kick me" and sending a photo of it to *Reader's Digest,* The second, more famous sketch, "The Interrogator," which aired on 23 February 1974, centered on the torture of an American POW played by Lyle Waggoner by Nazi Germany's best interrogator, Wolfgang Schweinhund, played by Tim Conway. The torture consists of Conway tormenting Waggoner with a puppet of Hitler singing in a high pitch German-inflected accent all three verses of "I've Been Workin' on the Railroad." Waggoner apparently did not know that Conway was going to use a puppet and could not keep a straight face throughout the entire skit.[38]

The Hitler humor in Spike Milligan and Monty Python's series is similarly absurdist. Milligan, whose work in the *Goon Show* and *Q* influenced generations of comedians from the members of Python down to the likes of Eddie Izzard, would occasionally appear as Hitler in ridiculous situations. In one skit, he plays Hitler with a guitar, singing songs by famous singers of the time like Kenneth McKellar, Anne Shelton, and George Formby. After a couple of seconds of each song, he gets hit with a pie in the face. In the Monty Python sketch, "Mr. Hilter and the North Minehead By-Election," written by John Cleese and Michael Palin, which aired on 7 January 1970, Hitler, Himmler, and von Ribbentrop are hiding out in a remote bed and breakfast planning a return to politics by running in a local election. They have changed their names (Hilter, Bimmler, and Ron Vibbentrop), and no one is any wiser even though they repeatedly blow their cover. Bimmler, in particular, played by Palin, cannot help blurting out the truth:

> How do you do there squire, also I am not Minehead lad but I in Peterborough, Lincolnshire was given birth to, but stay in Peterborough Lincolnshire house all during war, owing to nasty running sores, and was unable to go in the streets play football or go to Nürnberg. I am retired vindow cleaner and pacifist, without doing war crimes *(hurriedly corrects himself)* tch, and am glad England win World Cup - Bobby Charlton, Martin Peters - and eating lots of chips and fish and hole in the toads, and Dundee cakes on Piccadilly line. Don't you know old chap I was head of Gestapo for ten years. Five years! No, no, nein, I was not head of Gestapo at all. . . . I make joke.[39]

Hitler (Hilter), played by Cleese, gives a speech from a small balcony in front of a bemused peasant while Von Ribbentrop plays the sounds of cheers through a wind-up Victrola. Hitler also utters the shocking line when his plan to hire bombers by the hour is revealed: "If he opens his big mouth again . . . it's lampshade time!"[40]

Each skit elicits laughs for their own reasons, and some are more original than others in the sense that they say something new; Milligan's pie-in-the-face routine, for instance, relies on well-worn physical comedy, but it is funny because he has Hitler mouthing songs by contemporary singers from the U.K. Evaluating the relevance and purpose of the skits is more of a challenge given the different levels of commentary by their creators. In discussing the "Interrogator" skit, Tim Conway focused on the improvisational nature of the joke: "I like to have that leeway to be able to do things like that. Sometimes they'd just put up a cue card that said, 'savor, savor, savor' on it, meaning that we needed to stretch, and I could just do my thing."[41] Meanwhile, Milligan, Reiner, and Korman were veterans of the war, and Reiner has spoken about the antisemitism he encountered in basic training.[42] Milligan wrote numerous war memoirs, including *Adolf Hitler: My Part in His Downfall* and *Mussolini: My Part in His Downfall*,[43] replete with comic tales of service and camaraderie of his battery unit.[44] But it is Michael Palin, in more than one interview, who offers specific commentary about the boundaries and the purpose of Hitler satire:

> Hitler was a taboo character for quite some time, and being interested in pushing against taboos, Hitler was among the first to be, how shall we say, re-presented.[45]
>
> [in another interview]: I think we were attacking more the establishment version of the war, this dreadful waste of human life, which tends to be nothing to do with the officers who'd ordered people into battle in the first case. In a way, I think we felt, well, this is fair game, and also it was tinged with silliness. . . . Anything could be thrown into the mix, of course, and sketches had to have—they had to be about something.[46]
>
> [referring to the book *Er ist wieder* da]. . . . There's a long tradition of laughing at Hitler. That was what we were asked to do during the war. . . . There was no controversy when we did the Python sketch. It was a piece of surrealistic, totally absurd comedy. . . . But if it's just comedy and makes [Hitler] look absurd, that's fine.[47]

It is difficult to construct any deep understanding of motivation from these quotes, but among the veterans and even the members of Python, there is a level of observation and a recognition of the need for some kind of commentary behind and beyond the joke. The Minehead skit is noteworthy because of its layered purpose and timeliness, tackling historical memory and the "tabooization" of Hitler and envisioning the most incongruous of scenarios in which, through a vacancy in Parliament, Hitler would attempt a political comeback in 1970 through a by-election in the unassuming confines of Minehead in southwestern England. By sending up Nazis, small-town life, by-elections, and the Hitler taboo all at once, forcing a clash of competing texts of knowledge—of history, memory, and politics—the skit offers a multilayered satire of the past and present.

Although perhaps not the lowest point, a low point in the history of Hitler comedy came in September 1990 with the British pilot series, *Heil Honey I'm Home!* A convergence of trivialization, bad taste, and humorlessness, the comedy was a parody of American sitcoms from the 1950s and 60s, except it was set in Germany in the late 1930s. Hitler and Eva Braun, speaking American English, live in an apartment and are irritated by their Jewish neighbors, Arny and Rosa Goldenstein. In the pilot, the Hitlers try to keep it a secret from the Goldensteins that British Prime Minister Neville Chamberlain is coming for dinner, but the secret gets out, and the Goldensteins crash the dinner party. The parody is as grating as it is broad. Eva admonishes her husband, and he says, "I've been a very, very bad Hitler." Then he tries charming her with lines like "here comes the tickle monster." The Goldensteins get thrown out of the Hitlers' apartment for revealing the Führer's plans to invade everywhere. Chamberlain admonishes Hitler, who reluctantly agrees to sign a peace agreement, saying, "Would a naughty Hitler sign this piece of paper? Now am I a nice Führer or what?" There is a conga line at one point, and at the end, once Chamberlain has left (with the Goldenstein's homely niece Ruth), Hitler admits his plan to not abide by the agreement, confiding to Eva "So how about that babe—you're living with one slick Führer here?" She responds: "Mr. Sausage!" Hitler replies: "Hoochie Coochie girl."[48] It is even more awful than it looks on print. Hayim Pinner, secretary-general of the Board of Deputies of British Jews, decried the pilot as both trivializing and unfunny, and David Hawkes, a professor of English at Arizona State University, said that the show "disastrously exceeded" the limits of irony.[49]

Unlike the skits by Carol Burnett, Spike Milligan, and the Pythons, who retained Hitler's villainy at the heart of their irony, in *Heil Honey I'm Home,* that is almost completely gone. Hitler is no menace, just a misunderstood, bumbling husband like Ricky Ricardo in *I Love Lucy* or Darrin Stephens in *Bewitched,* Eliminating the tension between Hitler's evil and the banality of the situation lessens the incongruity, which in turn renders the comedy unfunny. The show's creator Geoff Atkinson had a purpose in mind, insisting that it is necessary to debunk and destroy fascists through satire, but he admits that the show did not deliver. "There's an awful lot I'd do differently. . . . The slapsticky stuff made it . . . dumb. It's not clever, it's not subtle, it's not smart, it's just dumb."[50]

Another example of the dive into the ridiculous from around the same time as *Heil Honey I'm Home* is Christoph Schlingensief's experimental hour-long West German comedy-drama, *100 Years of Adolf Hitler—The Last Hour in the Führer Bunker (100 Jahre Adolf Hitler—Die Letzte Stunde im Führerbunker)*. This film was the first of his "German Trilogy," which included *The German Chainsaw Massacre—The First Hour of the Reunification (Das Deutsche Kettensägenmassaker)*, from 1990, and *Terror 2000 –Germany out of Control (Intensivstation Deutschland)*, from 1992. Shot in black in white in the Bergstrasse Bunker in Hagen, south of Dortmund, *100 Years* is a surreal mixture of Fellini and Fassbinder that centers on the final moments of Hitler, Eva Braun, Goebbels, et al.; yet with the exception of Hitler's mustache, which ends up on Eva's face, there is nothing remotely historical about the production. The actors wander around aimlessly in the bunker in clothes from the 1980s, they ruminate while on the toilet, Hitler gets drugged, Eva has multiple orgasms and eventually marries Martha Goebbels, who dies while giving birth to a stuffed baby doll, and then they set Blondie, Hitler's dog, on fire. One might see unpacking all of this insanity as challenging (if not pointless), but the world of arts and letters has had only high regard for the style of filmmaking pioneered by Schlingensief, who died of lung cancer in 2010 at the age of forty-nine. Upon the director's death, Nobel Prize Laureate Elfriede Jelinek called Schlingensief "one of the greatest artists who ever lived . . . He has coined a new genre that has been removed from each classification. There will be nobody like him."[51] In their collection of essays on the director, scholars Tara Forrest and Anna Teresa Scheer argued that "by rooting the existence of Neo-Nazism in high society's refusal to engage directly with the continued fascination with Hitler, and by subsequently making a film about fascism in the mode of a trash horror mockumentary, Schlingensief suggests that coming to terms with the past is not only a matter of politics but a matter of taste as well."[52] Schlingensief had this to say about his motivation:

> I think Nazis were always an interesting theme for me because I also found camps so interesting . . . obviously, I liked to watch Pasolini's films. I liked Sodom . . . they were films that presumed to have people in their grip and to confine them . . . and from there to build Nationalism. Aesthetically, that was, for me, eerily appealing: humans under observation, humans in camps, humans in their little nests. Or maybe like me here now in my little cancer room.[53]

Regardless of how I feel about *100 Years of Adolf Hitler* from an evaluative standpoint, as a matter of analysis, the film is a revealing document of its time, exposing much about West Germany in the 1980s, similar to how the humor of Monty Python shed light on Britain in the 1970s. This is perhaps the key importance of Schlingensief's body of work, especially his "Germany

Trilogy." In adopting a framework of surrealist "unpleasure," the film owes much to French, Italian, and West German counter-cinema of the period. The film also reflects the turn in West German politics that brought re-energized conservatives to power whose questioning of the narrative of guilt about Hitler and the Holocaust that underpinned West German civic culture since the end of the war was now out in the open. In May 1985, Chancellor Helmut Kohl and U.S. President Reagan stirred controversy by visiting a German military cemetery in Bitburg, where S.S. soldiers were buried. Some German scholars (like Ernst Nolte) began suggesting that the communists were worse than the Nazis or were the impetus for fascism, and historians engaged in a bitter debate about this "past that would not pass away." Following German reunification in 1990, concerns remained over whether German leaders would continue to emphasize commitment to memory and education about the Holocaust as a key element of citizenship, and Schlingensief's films lay bare this anxiety.

One of the more prominent German films of the past twenty years to present a complex version of Hitler is Oliver Hirschbiegel's *Downfall (Der Untergang)*, from September 2004, another portrait of the last days of Hitler that has the distinction of being Germany's highest-grossing film of all time. In addition to its 85 million dollar haul, what made Hirschbiegel's presentation of Hitler different and controversial was that it was intended to present him as "humane . . . friendly, even courteous" in order to show that "the most inhuman things can emerge from a human being."[54] Hirschbiegel's overall intentions were more far-reaching than that. In interviews, he expressed the desire to create "a new national identity," asserting that with his film, it would be "easier for me to say that I am German and that I am not embarrassed about it."[55]

Bruno Ganz's portrayal did something else as well. In August 2006, a parody emerged on YouTube of the scene in which Hitler screams at his generals over the failure of a final counterattack against the Soviets. This first "Hitler Rant" retained the German language, but the subtitles involved Hitler complaining about the Microsoft video game, *Flight Simulator X,* Since then, thousands of "Hitler Rants" have appeared—each more nonsensical than the next, including Hitler ranting about everything from *Harry Potter* to Bernie Sanders. There have been Hitler rants even in Israel, and while reactions there are decidedly mixed, as Liat Steir-Livny points out, they attract thousands of viewers. One of these, from 2016, had over 200,000 hits; it involved Hitler complaining about the lack of parking places in Tel Aviv.[56] The "Hitler Rants" have given rise to a cottage industry of Hitler memes, music videos, and Internet trends, like cats and houses that look like Hitler. One of the best-known Hitler music videos is the German animated short by Walter Moer and Thomas Pigor, entitled "I'm sitting in my Bunker (*Ich hock in meinem Bonker*)." The cartoon features Hitler sitting naked on a toilet and musing about how the war is no fun anymore. A female chorus sings, "Adolf, you old Nazi pig, surrender!" but Hitler, now in his bathtub with his dog, Blondie, playing with miniature rubber duck-Hitlers, insists that he will never do that. Meanwhile, outside the graffitied bunker, which has "Nazis Out!" spray-painted on it, the entire city of Berlin lies in ruins.[57] Director Hirschbiegel has spoken favorably of these productions, believing them to be an extension of the film itself: "The point of the film was to kick these terrible people off the throne that made them demons, making them real and their actions into reality . . . I think it's only fair if now it's taken as part of our history and used for whatever purposes people like."[58] Although there is no stopping the Internet, as the satire *Look Who's Back* demonstrates, the danger of such a comic saturation is, as I see it, the end of history, or at the very least the upending of history—where Hitler becomes yet again the attractive face of the disgruntled everyman, at least for those whose only source of information is YouTube, Snapchat, and TikTok.

Another comic German film about Hitler's demise in this period between *Downfall* and *Look Who's Back* is Dani Levy's *Mein Führer—The Truly Truest Truth about Adolf Hitler (Die wirklich wahrste Wahrheit über Adolf Hitler)*. Released on 11 January 2007, the film stars Helge Schneider as Hitler and Ulrich Mühe as Israel Grünbaum, an individual who was once, in this scenario, Hitler's acting coach. Late in the war, with defeat looming and Hitler depressed, propaganda minister Josef Goebbels releases Grünbaum and his wife and children from Sachsenhausen concentration camp so that Grünbaum can lift Hitler out of his depression and bring out his old self so he can give one last rousing speech to a crowd in Berlin. The Swiss-born Levy, whose mother was a Holocaust survivor, already had a comedy about Jewish identity under his belt at the time. This was *Go for Zucker (Alles auf Zucker)*, from 2004, which focused on a secular Jew from communist East Germany forced to reconcile with his Orthodox brother. That film received mixed but generally favorable reviews as both funny and insightful. *Mein Führer*, as many critics noted, suffers from not knowing what kind of film it wants to be.[59] Moments of comedy, like when Grünbaum accidentally knocks Hitler out during an early training session designed to loosen him up through faux boxing, or when Grünbaum has Hitler get on all fours and bark (which leads Blondie to start humping the Führer) precede and are offset by moments of brutality, usually visited on Grünbaum himself. Revelations about the trauma inflicted on a young Hitler by his father come through, again in a way that makes Hitler seem more pitiable than laughable. Developing a friendship with his mentor, Hitler comes to admit to Grünbaum that the "Final Solution" was not his idea and that he had other plans. The most bizarre scene comes when Hitler goes to where Grünbaum is staying looking for comfort, and he falls asleep between the actor and his wife, who is thwarted by her husband from smothering Hitler with a pillow. As all of this unfolds, Goebbels plans to blow up Hitler during his climactic speech and blame Grünbaum. In the end, not only does Hitler accidentally get his mustache shaven off (which has to be replaced), he loses his voice after berating his hairdresser, who made the mistake. Grünbaum provides Hitler's voice during his speech to the crowd, but in a moment that parallels Chaplin's final speech in *Great Dictator,* he decides to have Hitler say almost unimaginable things: "I'm a bed-wetter, a drug addict. I can't get an erection! I was beaten by my father so often that I torture defenseless people as I was once tortured myself."[60] Grünbaum is shot, and the bomb planted by Goebbels goes off, although the audience does not know if Hitler survives or not.

Levy has credited *Downfall* as the inspiration for his film, saying that he wanted to parody Hirschbiegel's humanistic portrayal of Hitler, but Levy and his film are a mess of contradictions. On the one hand, Levy has said that he did not want to give "this cynical, psychological wreck of a person the honour of a realistic portrayal," but on the other hand, he wanted his film to create an "unexpected closeness to Hitler" that would spark emotions like "empathy [or even] . . . pity."[61] I think here again the model of purpose/relevance/originality might be instructive in assessing why *Mein Führer* did not quite work. Although purposeful—as a rejection of what Levy says was Hirschbiegel's presentation of Hitler's self-representation at face value—the film was not original enough in its humor or alternate narrative framework. Nor did it put forward the kind of relevant commentary that would come a few years later with *Look Who's Back.*

"POSTMODERNISM" AND METADISCURSIVE HITLER COMEDIES, FROM THE 1990S TO THE PRESENT

Popular media culture from the past twenty to thirty years has experienced a number of changes, but two developments stand out as informative here. One is a pattern of reworking existing cultural references and tropes, a development that has been reinforced in linguistics and philosophy with their emphasis on language and codes as the basis of knowledge. Deconstructing or reinventing the past has been a by-product of this development. The second revolution has been technological—the rise of platforms like the Internet that enable global, popular participation in the construction of culture and history. Scholars call this the phenomenon of postmodernism, and what has flowed from this—historicization, relativization, "visual and narrative reconstruction," as Sabine Hake calls it, all the way down to shock comedy and reality television, have become a dominant part of the global cultural imagination.[62] The ramifications for comedies about Hitler is that practically anything goes, and often it is a race to the bottom without any acknowledgment of history or context.

Postmodernism, comedy, and animation converged in 1997 in the infamous cartoon series by Trey Parker and Matt Stone, *South Park,* This intentionally poorly drawn, anarchic, cultural-mash-up centering on four kids in the mountain town of the show's name, has taken potshots at everything from racism to Islam, and on more than one occasion, the show has featured segments and episodes of Hitler. In the seventh episode of the first season, one of the boys, Eric Cartman, the antagonist of the group, who is as large as he is obnoxious (or as he would say, "big-boned"), dresses up as Hitler during Halloween and freaks everyone out—his Jewish friend, Kyle, and the African-American school chef (aka, "Chef"). The school principal makes matters worse by having Cartman watch videos of the Nazis, which Cartman disturbingly likes, and then dress up as a ghost, which makes Cartman look like a member of the Ku Klux Klan.[63] In March 2004, Parker and Stone devoted an entire episode to Cartman as Hitler in their parody of Mel Gibson's *The Passion of the Christ,* entitled "Passion of the Jew." In this episode, Cartman, dressed as Hitler, organizes a group of Christians who think they are in a pro-*Passion* fan club but who are pawns in Cartman's plot, which is genocide. He says at one point—"now we all know why we are here—and we know what needs to be done—It's best we don't talk about it until we have most of them on the trains heading to the camps . . . " A woman in the group asks her husband, "What does that mean, sweetie," which generates this response—"We owe this little boy and Mel Gibson our thanks for this revolution of spirituality."[64] Cartmen gets the people to march to the center of town, shouting *"Wir müssen die Juden ausrotten,"* which they do not know means "We must exterminate the Jews." (They think they are quoting a line from the film in Aramaic.) Meanwhile, Kyle seeks reassurance from his rabbi, and Stan and Kenny track down Mel Gibson to demand their money back because they thought the film was terrible. It turns out that Gibson is a nut-case masochist with a fetish for torture who chases Stan and Kenny back to South Park, where everyone in the town gets an unvarnished view of Gibson as a raving lunatic who smears excrement everywhere and ultimately ends up defecating on Cartman. Kyle says, "I feel so much better about being Jewish now that I know that Mel Gibson is just some wacko douche."[65]

Surprisingly, the episode did not generate the kind of controversy that one would have expected. That could have been due to the medium, again reflecting a reality that cartoons are not taken as seriously as live-action features, or it could have been the timing of the episode's appearance; by 2004, the shock of *South Park* had worn off. In fact, in her review for the *New York Times,*

Virginia Heffernan intimated just that when she said the episode proved, "the show's still got it or that it's made a comeback or that it's better than ever."⁶⁶ Yet even the associate national director for the Anti-Defamation League, Kenneth Jacobson, praised the episode. He saw the message of the show to be that *The Passion* is "no way to teach Christianity," constructing a defense around what he saw as the show's purpose.⁶⁷ So while Cartman's portrayal of Hitler might be an example of normalization, Hitler was not the focus of the episode. The broader intention was to shine a spotlight on antisemitism. Indeed, although Parker and Stone have often given more emphasis to what they see as a disturbing torture fetish on the part of Gibson, rather than his antisemitism, the duo believes that they were ahead of the curve on the director, and they regard the episode as their most "prescient": "We did the Mel Gibson episode after *Passion of the Christ* came out, and there was that huge national debate on whether he was an antisemite. It wasn't obvious. . . . Then, like, two years later, he's bitching at a cop in Malibu, calling him a Jew. We're like, O.K., good; we were right about that one."⁶⁸ To bring in my model here, *South Park* serves as an example of how comedy can be successful if it is funny, multilayered, purposeful, germane, and original. What keeps *South Park* going after over twenty years is its relevance and ability to mix satire, meta-discursive criticism of satire, and Bakhtin's ethos of carnival in unpredictable ways.⁶⁹

Between *South Park,* the proliferation of reality television, and the rise of platforms like Amazon, Netflix, YouTube, and others, popular entertainment has a wider palette of expression, choice of content, and degree of audience participation than ever before. There is far too much that can ever be absorbed, and while some of it is substantial, as I have already laid out with the numerous Internet sites and memes about Hitler, this oversaturation narrows the terrain of originality, which has left some to go to troubling places with their comedy. Hitler and the Nazis continue to be parodied by American comedians like Sarah Silverman and in American skit comedy shows like *Robot Chicken, Family Guy, Saturday Night Live, Key and Peele, The Britishes,* and Israeli comedies, like *The Jews Are Coming (Ha-Yehudim Baim).* There has been a comedy about turning psychiatric patients into Nazis (*Snide and Prejudice,* 1997), a mockumentary (*100 Years of Evil,* from Sweden in 2010), a Russian spoof (*Hitler Goes Kaput,* from 2011), a campy action series (*Danger 5,* from Australia, 2012 and 2015), and even a film from the legendary avant-garde filmmaker, Ken Russell (*A Kitten for Hitler,* from 2007). While the results are often amusing, their purposes, relevance, and originality are at best uneven.

The second season of Seth Green's stop-motion animated series *Robot Chicken,* from 2006, features a short vignette, "Lil' Hitler," which sets up a scenario of Hitler as a schoolboy who wants the desks of his fellow students who happen to be Polish and Czech, while an American kid sits back drinking a soda saying "not my problem," until a Japanese student knocks his soda off his desk, prompting him to say, "now, it's my problem!"[70] The skit is funny both because of its setting and because it is a lesson in World War II in thirty seconds. Sadly, Green's commentary about the segment is cursory and tangential. He references Alex Borstein, the actress who voices the character of Lois, the wife on the cartoon *Family Guy*, who claims that it is Jewish writers who write the overwhelming majority of Hitler jokes, which they have to reject because there are too many of them. Green says that the "Lil' Hitler" sketch was written by, in his words, "Doug, our resident Jew."[71] This is a case where artist commentary weakens the case for a particular performance piece. One could conceive of a scenario where a professor might use the skit in a class as both an example of satire and history and as an anticipatory set for a more substantial discussion about the war. However, commentary about the skit by Green and his fellow animators is so flippant and superficial that it confirms that anything in a postmodern context, no matter how trivial, can be re-appropriated and infused with significance.

Similar issues bedevil the episode "Road to Germany" from Seth MacFarlane's cartoon series *Family Guy*, which aired on 19 October 2008. Owing much to *South Park*, the show is a parody of *All in the Family*, but with its own twist. The family at the center of the show are the Griffins—Peter, the Archie Bunker type, Lois, his long-suffering wife, their children, Chris, Meg, and Stewie (who is an infant but who speaks like an adult with an English accent), and their dog, Brian, who also talks and drinks alcohol. With plenty of offensive jokes, non-sequiturs, and cultural references, the show fits again within the meta-discursive trend pioneered by *South Park*. In the episode "Road to Germany," one of the Griffin's Jewish neighbors, Mort, is visiting but has to use the bathroom, and he accidentally mistakes a time machine in Stewie's room as a toilet. He is blasted back to Warsaw in 1939, and Stewie and Brian realize this and go back in time to try to rescue him. The three hijack a Nazi submarine bound for England, but then they fly with an RAF squadron to land in Germany to find some uranium for their time travel pad in order to return to the future. If this sounds like the 1985 film *Back to the Future*, it is no accident; there is an actual *Back to the Future* moment during the earlier escape involving Nazis getting covered in manure. In Berlin, Stewie dresses up as Hitler, the group finds uranium, and when confronted by the real Hitler, they are offered freedom if they can perform a song and dance number, which Mort abruptly interrupts as the group activates the time pad and disappears.

Although the executive producer of the show, David A. Goodman, who is Jewish, feared getting kicked out of his synagogue because of the episode,[72] *Family Guy* was nominated for an Emmy for Best Comedy Series in 2009, in part because of "Road to Germany." Like the commentary offered by Green and his fellow writers on *Robot Chicken,* though, the discussion by MacFarlane et al. about "Road" is similarly too cute for its own good. They make comments like, "We have a hard time making fun of the Jewish people . . . so we saved up all of our jokes for this show," and they mention two jokes in particular that did not survive in editing. One comes before Stewie, Brian, and Mort hijack the submarine. Mort says that he does not want to go because he is claustrophobic, to which Stewie responds, "just think how you'll feel when your whole family is packed into a bar of soap."[73] Another quip, cut from the film, was a sign outside Berlin listing its population as ten million, crossed out with four million written over it (to refer to the decline in the population of six million). In the absence of a discussion about the meaning or purpose of the show, one is left to divine intentions, and what is left is an occasionally humorous, often frenetic cultural jamboree.[74]

By contrast, Sarah Silverman's appearance as Hitler on a March 2016 episode of *Conan,* Conan O'Brian's comedy talk show, works better because it is a part of her longstanding use of transgressive comedy both to engage taboo conversations, to lay bare hypocrisies, and more importantly to tackle political threats. Her Hitler bit was designed as both a contemporary political critique of the xenophobic and quasi-authoritarian inclinations of Donald Trump and a warning about the rise of the radical right in the United States. Silverman does not attempt a German accent for the impression but keeps her own voice and intonation, so as both a physical and aural performance by a Jewish woman, it presents a dual take-down of the Führer. Conan asks Silverman's Hitler what he thinks of journalists comparing him and Trump. She then shifts into a discussion about genitalia, emasculating both Trump and Hitler in the process. Silverman responds, "Ninety percent of what this guy says, I mean this guy gets it—it's just I don't like the way he says it. It's crass. What kind of person talks about his penis size on national television? I'm sure Donald Trump has a big penis. I famously have a micro penis. That's what makes a tyrant." After Conan says, "I'm very sorry to hear about your micro penis," to which Silverman's Hitler responds, "If I had a gold filling every time I hear that. . . . Oh, I can't believe Hitler went there."[75]

Because they could serve as a springboard for a discussion about Nazi foreign policy, Hitler's worldview, or commentary about society and politics, both Silverman's bit and "Lil' Hitler" succeed as insightful comedy, and there have been plenty of skits from the past decade that have mined the Hitler trope for these purposes. A *Saturday Night Live* skit from 2010 called "Timecrowave" ridiculed consumers and technology by displaying a device that uses time travel to reheat food with a side effect that causes changes in the space-time continuum, like allowing, in one sequence, the Nazis to win World War II. The 2014 skit from the show *Key and Peele*, entitled

"Awesome Hitler Story," featured Ty Burrell from the sitcom *Modern Family* as a Nazi officer who is repeatedly thwarted by an underling from finishing his tale. The junior officer, played by Jordan Peele, tries to warn his superior that an American soldier shot by Nazis, played by Keegan-Michael Key, is only playing dead. Burrell's officer gets so annoyed that he shoots Peele and then finishes up his story with other Nazis as Peele and Key's characters both play dead. The story, by the way, is not that awesome, which is the essence of the joke. Burrell just happened to bump into Hitler at a store, and the two were buying bread and cheese at the same time.[76] This evokes, in a way, Nazi officiousness or the banality of evil. In "The Charming Mr. Hitler," the first episode of CollegeHumor and DirectTV's 2014 parody of *Downton Abbey,* entitled *The Britishes,* Hitler visits the noble family and wows everyone with his charisma. One of the ladies of the house responds to his desire to "see ze world—Poland, France, and zen push into Greece and northern Africa, maybe try to fit Russia in," with the ironic quip, "Oh Hitler, you really are the devil himself!"[77] The skit is funny because it assumes knowledge about Hitler's villainy and an audience's expectations about how one would react to it in the real world, and then it presents the opposite behavior, making the skit as much a satire of British aristocrats as a send-up of Hitler. In the end, these bits, however short and trifling, are entertaining and often informative, and therefore purposeful, even if their creators might resist that label and if a purpose is grafted on after the fact.

Philippe Mora's 1997 film, *Snide and Prejudice,* also probes the links between Hitler as a figure of history and Hitler as a symbol of present-day political dangers in its focus on psychiatric patients in Los Angeles who think they are major historical personalities. One patient in particular, Michael Davidson, played by Angus Macfadyen, thinks he is Hitler, and the head of the hospital, Dr. Sam Cohen, a Jewish psychiatrist played by René Auberjonois, uses a form of therapy designed to shock patients out of their delusions by forcing them to relive aspects of their personas' lives. For Michael, this means re-enacting episodes from Hitler's life, from early childhood through adulthood, and the movie is more a chronological journey of Hitler's rise to power than anything else. There are few laugh-out-loud moments, although rock drummer Mick Fleetwood makes a strange appearance as a patient who thinks he is Pablo Picasso, and there is a 1990s self-aware utilization of interviews of Auberjonois' character of Dr. Cohen, clearly intended as Jewish for added irony. Macfadyen's performance is noteworthy as well, especially as he captures in English, but with a German accent, Hitler's many idiosyncratic movements and way of talking. The poses he strikes throughout the film recall the photos taken in 1927 by Heinrich Hoffmann of Hitler, who used them to hone his public speeches. Director Mora, whose French-Jewish parents managed to escape the German occupation and survive the war, says that he loved "the device of staging [the film] as re-enactment, simultaneously getting info across and parodying documentaries that do ridiculous and false re-enactments."[78] Like *Son of Hitler* and other experimental efforts, the problem with *Snide and Prejudice* is that it does not maximize the potential of its form or content. There is an insufficient exploration of the dangers of a personality such as Hitler's, nor do we gain much insight into how such a mindset is constructed. Indeed, there is no breakthrough moment or resolution at the end; Michael still believes that he is Hitler. The satirizing of documentaries is interesting, but the real promise of the film lies in its ability to offer commentary about the existing threat of fascism and the psychology of those who believe in it. At one point, Michael, as Hitler, utters a line that is eerily relevant for American politics in the age of Donald Trump: "The more social chaos I can create, the more people will join for security."[79]

Satires from Israel, meanwhile, often flirt with even more incendiary material. Any comedy about Hitler or the Holocaust in Israel is bound to be more dangerous, and it has only been in recent years that either topic has been fodder for comedians. The show *The Jews are Coming* (*Ha-Yehudim Baim*), which began in 2014, is a Monty Python-esque sketch group that has poked fun at everything from the binding of Isaac to the Holocaust. In 2016, they aired a skit entitled "Final Solution 2.0," about a group of Nazis who gather to plan the next phase of their genocidal scheme, which is to deny Israel a single point at the Eurovision song contest.[80] Another episode envisioned Jews from 1933 Germany talking about why Hitler is such an attractive candidate, dismissing everything about his ideology, his actions, and his entire essence to justify their support. A skit from 2015 featured a benign Hitler trying to gain entry into the Vienna Academy of Art with pictures of flowers, and the professors try to elicit rage in the young Hitler by berating him. He resists at first saying things like "All my works are about kitties," but the professors press on with more offensive insults, like "I banged your sister!" Finally, Hitler is pushed overboard to the point where his buried personality emerges, and he threatens the professors that he is going to blow them all up. Satisfied that they have tapped into his passion, they reject him for admission, and one professor sends him on his way, saying, "Now take this anger and channel it somewhere.... I promise that in a few years everybody will know the name.... What is it?" Hitler responds, "Adolf Shickelgruber." The faculty's last recommendation is that he change his name to "something catchier."[81]

The Jews are Coming has a following in Israel, and their use of Israelis pretending to be Germans or even Nazis speaking in Hebrew is the ultimate inversion and inside joke. Shoshana Razel and Gordon Guedalia have written favorably about the show in *The Jewish Standard,* declaring that it is "something to smile about," and Esther Kustanowicz, for *The Jewish Daily*

Forward, sees in the show a "deep passion for uncovering tradition and taking ownership of Jewish history."[82] Showrunners Asaf Baizer and Natali Marcus, unlike others who plow forward without any thought about history, insist that they approach their humor "with grave respect and with much thought," and Baizer has mentioned as a key influence his partisan grandfather who fought in the forests in Belarus during the war. In his words, he was "one of the funniest people I ever met. His humor was offbeat, hard-hitting, and irreverent."[83] Not all Israelis are enamored of the production, though, and many, particularly on the religious right, find it reprehensible. Yet, by my standard of purpose, relevance, and originality, it does appear that the *Jews are Coming* troupe has hit on a successful formula for delivering a type of comedy that resonates with Israelis. Liat Steir-Livny says that the purpose of their humor is not to offend or be distasteful for the sake of it but rather to serve as a defense mechanism among Jewish Israelis suffering secondary traumatic stress, who seek ways to lessen reactions of tension and anxiety not only about the Holocaust but about the existential threats that they continue to feel about their national security.[84]

If *The Jews are Coming* functions as a collective outlet and commentary on issues specific to Judaism, the Swedish mockumentary *100 Years of Evil*, released on 29 November 2010, uses Hitler as a window into what to believe about media in an age of limitless access to unfiltered information. The film evokes the "found footage" premise of *The Blair Witch Project* (1999) and Woody Allen's *Zelig* (1983), about a man who was able to morph into the people he meets. In *100 Years of Evil*, a fictional historian from Sweden by the name of Skule Antonsen and a Spanish filmmaker, Idelfonso Elizalde, investigate documents and film footage around an individual named Adolf Munchenhauser, whom they believe to be Hitler. They trace this individual, brought from Germany after World War II to a mysterious camp in Nevada for German prisoners of war, all the way to drag shows in New York, to Cuba, Mt. Rushmore, and Bismarck, North Dakota, where Munchenhauser allegedly helped to initiate the building of a rocket destined for the moon. Skule and Idelfonso discover a corporation known as Cryoputsch, which has been keeping Munchenhauser in a frozen state until he can be revived in the future. Skule tries to sabotage the effort in the end, but his fate and whereabouts remain unknown. The actual directors of the film, Erik Eger and Magnus Oliv, have said that what drove them to the topic was the idea that there are "forces behind the media and the news to make us believe almost anything. And, of course, what we believe makes us into who we are. And we just felt a need to do something on this theme. And it evolved into this crazy story about Adolf Munchenhauser, who might have been Adolf Hitler, we don't know."[85] The film garnered mixed reviews, some positive for the premise, but Justine

Smith, in her review, felt that the film "suffers due to its length and adhering far too closely to the model it is mocking. . . . There is no real certainty as to what aspect of society is being satirized either . . . ."[86] When I watched the film, I felt the same level of waning interest with each locale shift. When the conspiracy storyline about Cryoputsch enters the picture, the historicity underlying the believability of the film goes out the window. It might have been better to have Munchenhauser and Skule's fate remain a mystery with no traces or clues. That is what feeds conspiracy theories and would make the film itself a meta-discourse on the phenomenon.

A comparable, alternative-universe exploration about Hitler came from Russia in 2011 in Marius Weisberg's *Hitler Goes Kaput (Gitler Kaput)*, a movie so polarizing that many Russian critics wanted it banned. For context, most films from Eastern Europe about Hitler, the Third Reich, and World War II, during and after communist rule, have aimed to reinforce national narratives of resistance and heroism.[87] Moreover, some of the first films about the Nazi concentration camps and the systematic mass murder of the Jews came from Soviet Russia—Aleksandr Macheret's *Bog Soldiers (Bolotnye soldaty*, from 1938) and Mark Donskoi's *The Unvanquished (Nepokorennye*, or *The Taras Family,* from 1945). After the war, the Holocaust practically disappeared from Soviet cinema, and one can only speculate about the reasons—longstanding antisemitism, the politics of the Arab-Israeli conflict where the Soviet Union stood on the side of Arab countries, the belief that emphasizing Jewish victims did not align with socialist ideology, or the desire to emphasize heroic war stories about Soviet citizens (like the popular television series from 1973 about a Soviet spy in Nazi Germany, entitled *Seventeen Moments of Spring (Semnadtsat' mgnoveniy vesny)*. Films about the Holocaust have reappeared in Russia after the fall of communism, such as the 2018 film *Sobibor,* but Holocaust education has difficulty competing with the existing national narrative about the war.

It is even rarer to see a comedy about the war or Hitler from Russia. Leonid Bykov's film, *Only Old Men Are Going to Battle (V boy idut odni "stariki,"* from 1973), about members of a fighter squadron who are also in a musical group, has comedic elements, but it is by and large a dramatic work. *Hitler Goes Kaput* is truly the first, and perhaps, the last of its kind from Russia. Despite negative reviews for its poor production quality, the film operates very much within the semiotic world of postmodern "counter-cinema," with its use of contemporary music (from the likes of Britney Spears) and other anachronisms (such as the incorporation of discos, laptops, FaceTime, and an African-American character named 50 Schilling a la 50 cent, who is Hitler's D.J., all in a film ostensibly set in 1945). The film also has Hitler snorting cocaine after getting it from a Hitler-shaped cocaine Pez dispenser, which I believe is a first in cinema. The plot of the film, if one can call it that, allegedly pays homage to *Seventeen Moments of Spring,* by centering on a Soviet spy, by the name of Alexander Isaevich ("Shura") Osechkin, played by Pavel Derevyanko, but the film is a bizarre and aimless trip. Shura has a love interest in Zina, a Soviet radio operator, played by Anna Semenovich, who gets captured and then rescued. Shura and Zina manage to tie up Hitler and Eva Braun, steal their clothes, and get out of Germany. There is also mud wrestling. Director Weisberg, who was born in Moscow, insists that his films are "hard to watch in intellectual circles" and that it is his right to "independently define the framework of taste and vulgarity."[88] To me, the film evoked Schlingensief's cinema of "unpleasure," except with less, or less clear, commentary about contemporary politics. The cultural mashups are intentionally decontextualized, which is interesting from a structural point of view, but there is little else behind that—no substance, no real story. There is originality, perhaps of narrative form, but little relevance and even less purpose of content.

Another show that is nearly all meta-discourse and past-referencing is the Australian action-comedy *Danger 5,* whose two seasons (2012 and 2015) revolve around a team of hero-spies fighting Hitler and the Nazis. The early 1960s is the setting for season one, while season two is set in the 1980s or early 90s. The show parodies both the content and forms of these eras in their storylines. Season one, for instance, mixes tropes from James Bond as well as the puppet series, *The Thunderbirds,* and the cinematography, sets, acting, dialogue, editing, and even voice synchronization (which is slightly off), all combine to create the impression of a low-budget action film from the 1960s. Season two, by contrast, takes its inspiration from *Miami Vice,* with its grittier tone and soundtrack, and also *The Mighty Morphin' Power Rangers,* but the super-agents somehow do not appear to age over the decades. The team consists of Tucker, a neurotic Australian, Jackson, an overbearing American, Claire, a Cambridge-educated genius, Ilse, a Russian spy who only speaks Russian (but whom everyone understands), and Pierre, a Mediterranean sort whose main interest is mixed drinks. The leader of the team is Colonel Chestbridge, an individual who has the head of a bird, for some unknown reason, who repeatedly insults Claire, also for reasons unknown but most likely to parody the sexism of the time, and who ends each mission assignment with the command to kill Hitler, which the group in every episode, until the last one, fails to do. Hitler's henchmen, Goering, Goebbels, and Himmler, make appearances in various episodes, only to be dispatched by the team. Their criminal conspiracies in season one, in episodes like "I Danced for Hitler" and "Fresh Meat for Hitler's Sex Kitchen," include creating giant lizard Nazis, creating robot Nazis, stealing all of the great monuments of the world to make one giant Nazi monument, and spreading a sexually transmitted disease that turns everyone into Nazis. There are also many talking Nazi dog puppets. Season two tops this by having Hitler enter high school (as "Johnny Hitler," a sort of Ferris Bueller character), die and kill Satan, come back as a zombie, and then, in a nod to *Back to the Future,* alter the space-time continuum so that the Nazis win World War II. Hitler is only vanquished after the team combines forces into one giant Power Ranger and blasts him into space.

During the first episode, I found myself laughing out loud because of all the nonsense, particularly the German-inflected puppet dogs. Colonel Chestbridge's escalating series of insults thrown at Claire were also amusing. However, as with *100 Years of Evil,* the repeated story beats wear thin in the first season, and things go downhill even more quickly in season two, not only because it is more violent but because it dispatches two of the main characters early on—Colonel Chestbridge and Claire, who gets decapitated during her wedding to Tucker in a particularly gruesome scene. (Tucker then keeps Claire's head with him through the rest of the season, which is even more stomach-turning.) Cavan Gallagher noted in his review for *Metro Magazine* that the repeating of tropes in the first season felt like "postmodernism cannibalizing itself."[89] The second season, which had a larger budget and better special effects, left me with an even more negative impression.

Part of that is due to the fact that productions from the early 1960s were more innocent and campier and thus more open to the kind of incongruities that can be set up in a show about a bird-led group of nitwits chasing Hitler and his minions of scantily clad dancing girls. Parodying the 1980s is more of a challenge because it was already a time of greater violence and more openness about sex, both in reality and in film and television, and so the only place to go with satire is to ramp up the sex and violence, which undercuts the evil versus innocence incongruity. But the bigger problem for me again was the issue of purpose. What were showrunners Dario Russo and David Ashby aiming for? In their YouTube and online interviews, the two are circumspect, or they joke around, or they talk about their influences in pulp fiction:

Ashby: . . . Years ago, we went to Melbourne and wound up in a bookshop that had all these various sorts of literature and books, and one of them was a massive collection of men's magazine covers going all the way from the 1930s to the early 70s. The illustrations of these men's magazines which were so outrageous, vivid, surreal . . .

Russo: . . . and stupid! You know, for example, there was a panther with a swastika on its head mauling some chick in a bikini with a big high hairdo in a Nazi torture dungeon . . .

Ashby: . . . and they had all these bitchin' taglines on it that we mimicked with the episode titles ("Kill Men of the Rising Sun," "Hitler's Golden Murder Palace,").

Russo: It was all very provocative material, you know; it got the ball rolling to think, Jesus, this would be a great concept to make a T.V. show about this ludicrous, distinctively 60s tainted World War II in which dinosaurs could potentially factor prominently![90]

These explanations feel more in line with those of Quentin Tarantino; indeed, Ashby and Russo's intentions seem to be to put stuff up on a canvas and mash it all together to get something different. It is not surprising that in a self-aware medium like this, director Russo feels the need to remind reviewers (and critics like myself) that "there's never any misconstruing this isn't a ridiculous show, which exists far outside the realms of reality."[91] But *Danger 5* sheds light on the boundaries of self-referential, postmodern satire. A few episodes might have been amusing, but short of different and unexpected plot turns or narrative structures, the repetition of meta-discourse is not sustainable. As for Hitler, portrayed by Russo's father, but dubbed over in German by another actor, the series inadvertently does more to retain his villainy, which is in some ways a return to moralism, but this again is lessened by the construction of Hitler as a stand-in for cultural re-appropriation.

As is clear from the analysis thus far, it is difficult to create an effective comedy about Hitler that demonstrates a purpose and that is relevant and original, particularly the further we go in time away from the period of the Reich. Contemporary representations of Hitler, in particular, feel like they are the result of metaphorically putting culture in a Cuisinart and pushing purée. And just when it looks like we have either reached a threshold or a bottom, one finds that new, disturbing level. This point came in 2007 in the short film, *A Kitten for Hitler*, the last production by avant-garde filmmaker Ken Russell, whose credits include up to then included the Oscar-nominated adaptation of the D.H. Lawrence novel, *Women in Love* (1969) and The Who's rock opera, *Tommy* (1975). Set in 1941, *A Kitten for Hitler* centers on an American child who thinks that by going to Germany and giving Hitler a kitten for Christmas, the Führer will suddenly become nice. Because Russell could not find a child for the role, he substituted an older gentleman with dwarfism, which only adds to the shock value. Although Adolf and Eva are initially touched by the gesture, especially when the old-man-child shows them his swastika tattoo, but then they notice that the child is wearing a Star of David necklace. The scene cuts to Adolf and Eva in bed, somehow proud of themselves for doing something, and it becomes clear what they have done when they go to turn out the lights. They have killed the child (old man) and turned him into a lampshade. After that comes a cut, and the words "Miracle!" appear across the screen as the lamp and mother are reunited after the war. The president pins a medal of honor on the lampshade as the ghostly image of the old man appears in it.[92]

After I watched the film, I was so perplexed that I had to find out what possibly could have motivated Russell to make what would become his final statement in the performing arts. Here is where my opinion about the value of the film changed. Russell has said that the inspiration for the project came during a discussion about censorship with friend and collaborator Melvyn Bragg:

> Broadly speaking, Melvyn was against it, while I, much to his surprise, was absolutely for it. He then dared me to write a script that I thought should be banned. I accepted the challenge and, a month or so later, sent him a short subject entitled *A Kitten for Hitler*. "Ken," he said, "if ever you make this film, and it is shown, you will be lynched . . . ."[93]

Although the content and the production values of the short are terrible, they are intentionally so in order to present the most obvious, horrific case of trivializing Hitler and the Holocaust. Whether or not the film deserves censorship is a matter for lawyers in different settings to discuss. However, *A Kitten for Hitler*, like Schlingensief's *100 Years of Adolf Hitler*, has value as the absolute anti-matter of Hitler comedy. From the standpoint of structural analysis, both films align with New Wave traditions of alienating audiences and resisting closure. There is an expectation for viewers to be upset because they go beyond oppositions to consensus forms and narratives about Hitler. They use, in the words of scholars Laura Mulvey and Linda Hutcheon, the "destruction of pleasure as a radical weapon" in order "to contest the very possibility of there ever being 'ultimate objects.'"[94] In other words, they force audiences to recognize context and construction of reality as merely discursive, where "the only 'genuine historicity' becomes that which would openly acknowledge its own discursive, contingent identity."[95]

A Kitten for Hitler and *100 Years of Adolf Hitler* are original in that they break new ground in terms of form, although that is not necessarily a positive given their erratic execution and the content they present. But *A Kitten for Hitler* takes counter-cinema truly to its breaking point and reveals why such comedy is problematic, and why, unless there is a combination of purpose/relevance/originality and quality of production, then comedies about Hitler may potentially do more damage to history, memory, and education, and by extension to cinema. Scholars such as Mulvey make a convincing argument that "the satisfaction and reinforcement of the ego that represent the high point of film history must be attacked . . . to make way for a total negation of the ease and plenitude of the narrative fiction film."[96] Russell and Schlingensief's deconstructed narratives serve that purpose, and as Mulvey might suggest, it is not on them to supply a "reconstructed new pleasure."[97] However, to bring in Bakhtin again, if the result is nihilism or a focus merely on process, that is to say, how we collectively and individually perceive Hitler, and there is no meaning beyond that, what then? The absurd and dangerous end of this line of thinking is that Hitler could be a kitten just as a kitten could be Hitler. It would not matter because the only thing that has meaning is how we make meaning. There are no real historical or even moral distinctions, just how we construct them. Why then continue with history, philosophy, or morality, for that matter?

One hundred years have elapsed since Adolf Hitler emerged on the German political scene as the leader of the Nazi Party, and from the earliest days, comedy has been a tool of contesting Hitler, his worldview, and the Nazi state. However, the two periods of comedy—the contemporaneous and post-Hitler years, stand in marked contrast in terms of their purpose and relevance. During the era of the Third Reich and World War II, the stakes were life and death, and so comedy that aimed at "neutering" Hitler and lifting the spirits of those oppressed by his regime was both purposeful and relevant, as well as original, at least in terms of content if not form. As we have seen, comedies and cartoons were at the forefront of Hitler criticism because of the nature of the medium and the activism of artists, writers, and performers. After the war, comic representations of Hitler receded to the margins until the 1960s and 70s, but many of these productions did not go beyond the joke, as it were, apart from the Monty Python skits, which deployed satire as commentary on historical memory and current British politics. Hitler comedy has proliferated since the 1990s in the context of the postmodern arrival of the Internet and the turn toward rule-breaking and reinventing the past. As agents of global mass culture, ordinary people can construct and infuse meaning into existing texts and narratives as never before. However, we have moved from a situation where Hitler comedy as a salve and deflator was once immediate to the point where it is everywhere but vacuous. Hitler remains the villain, fool, and everything in between, but more than that, he has become a symbol not of evil but at best of irony and, at worst, kitsch. As Oren Baruch Stier notes, in his apt quotation from historian Saul Friedländer, this has the effect of evoking a "distinct uneasiness," which I clearly feel, and which "stems . . . from a dissonance between the declared moral and ideological position of the author or the filmmaker, the condemnation of Nazism, and . . . the aesthetic effect . . . "[98]

NOTES

1. Don Morlan, "Slapstick Contributions to WWII Propaganda: The Three Stooges and Abbott and Costello," *Studies in Popular Culture,* Vol. 17, No. 1 (October 1994): 32.

2. Birdwell quotes Jack as saying, "The less you, I, or any Warner talks at this time, the better." Leave it to the president, he thought, because "he isn't a Jew, even though the German agencies say he is." Michael Birdwell, *Celluloid Soldiers: Warner Brothers' Campaign Against the Nazis* (New York: New York University Press, 2000), 31, 32, and his citation of a letter from Jack to Harry Warner, 5 October 1939, 2, Joe Hazen Correspondence File, Jack Warner Collection, University of Southern California.

3. Morlan, "Slapstick Contributions," 35, and David Culbert, ed., *Film Propaganda in America: A Documentary History, Vol II: World War II* (New York: Columbia University Press, 1990), 23.

4. Morlan, "Slapstick Contributions," 35.

5. Michael Shull and David Wilt, *Doing Their Bit: Wartime American Animated Short Films, 1939–1945*, 2nd ed (Jefferson, NC: McFarland, 1987), 9, 10.

6. Shull and Wilt, *Doing Their Bit,* 15.

7. Ising quoted in Steve Schneider, *That's All Folks: The Art of Warner Brothers Animation* (New York: Henry Holt, 1988), 34.

8. https://looneytunes.fandom.com/wiki/Bosko%27s_Picture_Show, accessed 10 March 2020.

9. "From This You Are Making a Living?" An Oral History of Richard Huemer, Interview with Joe Adamson, 1968. American Film Institute Archives, Los Angeles, 134, and Tracey Mollet, *Cartoons in Hard Times: The Animated Shorts of Disney and Warner Brothers in Depression and War 1932–1945* (London: Bloomsbury Academic, 2019), 64.

10. Mollet, *Cartoons in Hard Times,* 64; Leni Riefenstahl, *A Memoir* (New York: St. Martin's Press, 1993), 286; Neal Gabler, *Walt Disney: The Biography* (London: Aurum, 2007), 448.

11. Mollet, *Cartoons in Hard Times,* 69.

12. Mollet, *Cartoons in Hard Times,* 82.

13. The animator duo William Hanna and Joseph Barbera featured a brief image of Hitler in their Tom and Jerry short, *The Lonesome Mouse* from 22 May 1943.

14. Mollet, *Cartoons in Hard Times,* 124.

15. Mollet, *Cartoons in Hard Times,* 160.

16. The 1940 British comedy-musical, *Let George Do It*, directed by Marcel Varnel and starring comic actor George Formby, has a similar scene in which Formby dreams about landing on Hitler during a rally and punching him out. Kevin Flanagan, "The British War Film, 1939–1980: Culture, History, and Genre" (unpublished thesis, University of Pittsburgh, 2015), 12.

17. Theodore Strauss, "Donald Duck's Disney," *New York Times,* 7 February 1943, x3.

18. Strauss, "Donald Duck's Disney," x3.

19. Fritz Freleng, Interview at Reg Hartt's Cineforum, Toronto, Canada, 1980, https://www.youtube.com/watch?v=NbZwISKdfnQ, accessed 14 March 2020.

20. Groucho as quoted by Mark Bourne, "Review: *The Marx Brothers Silver Screen Collection," The DVD Journal,* 2004, http://www.dvdjournal.com/reviews/m/marxbrothers_ssc.shtml, accessed 29 July 2019.

21. Martin Gardner, *The Marx Brothers as Social Critics: Satire and Comic Nihilism in Their Films* (Jefferson, NC: McFarland, 2009), 87.

22. David Hogan, *Three Stooges FAQ* (Milwaukee, WI: Applause Theater and Cinema Books, 2011), 200, 201.

23. Hogan, *Three Stooges,* 202.

24. See *You Natzy Spy,* https://www.youtube.com/watch?v=TClfKwPPAZA, accessed 1 March 2020.

25. Hogan, *Three Stooges FAQ,* 208.

26. Charles River Editors, *The Three Stooges* (New York: CreateSpace, 2014), Kindle Edition, Locations 317 and 330.

27. See *Higher than a Kite,* https://www.youtube.com/watch?v=QoNiPuq-aPA, accessed 1 March 2020.

28. "Hal Roach Announces Big Deal as Mussolini Partner," *Motion Picture Herald,* 2 October 1937, 21, 22. See also Richard Lewis Ward, *A History of the Hal Roach Studios* (Carbondale, IL: Southern Illinois University Press, 2005), 100.

29. Thomas Doherty, *Hollywood and Hitler, 1933–1939* (New York: Columbia University Press, 2013), 135.

30. Craig Calman, *100 Years of Brodies with Hal Roach: The Jaunty Journeys of a Hollywood Motion Picture and Television Pioneer* (Albany, GA: Bear Manor Media, 1973), 216, and Mike Steen, *Hollywood Speaks! An Oral History* (New York: G.P. Putnam's Sons, 1974).

31. Harjinder Singh, *Hollywood Pioneer: The Life and Times of Hal Roach,* (Santa Monica: Leprosy Association of Guru Nanak, 2016). This book is of dubious scholarly quality, given the publisher, but film scholars Josh Kanin and Martin Goldstein, both professors of film at Santa Monica College, apparently vouch for its contents.

32. See https://www.threestooges.com/1940/01/19/you-nazty-spy/, accessed 10 March 2020, and Susie Davidson, "Moe Howard, an Honorable Stooge," *The Forward,* 10 December 2010, https://forward.com/schmooze/133860/friday-film-moe-howard-an-honorable-stooge/, accessed 10 March 2020.

33. Rosenfeld, *Hi Hitler,* 234–240, and Michael Richardson, "Tragedy and Farce: Dani Levy's *Mein Führer,*" in *Hitler: Films from Germany,* ed. Karolin Machtans and Martin A. Ruehl (London: Palgrave Macmillan, 2012), 132, 133.

34. https://en.wikipedia.org/wiki/Nazi_zombies, accessed 19 March 2020.

35. A recent, low-budget short from 2015, entitled *Hitler's Brain and the Robot from Hell,* has a storyline about a robot that goes haywire after having Hitler's brain transplanted into it. https://www.youtube.com/watch?v=hChicEZ9IOQ, accessed 19 March 2020.

36. These episodes include "The Man in the Bottle" (1960) which deals with a man who is granted a wise to be an all-powerful leader and who winds up as Hitler at the end of the war; "He's Alive," (1963), in which Hitler helps a neo-Nazi politician; and "No Time Like the Past" (also from 1963), which centers on a plot to assassinate Hitler.

37. Darrell Y. Hamamoto, "Interview with Television Producer Rod Amateau of *Dukes of Hazzard,*" *The Journal of Popular Film and Television,* Vol. 9, No. 4 (1982): 166–170.

38. Interview with Tim Conway by Claudia Perry, https://www.aislesay.com/PA-CONWAY-Interview.html, accessed 20 March 2020.

39. "Mr. Hilter and the North Minehead By-Election," https://www.ibras.dk/montypython/episode12.htm, accessed 20 March 2020.

40. "Mr. Hilter."

41. Interview with Tim Conway by Claudia Perry.

42. On his Iwo Jima experience, see the interview with Carl Reiner by Conan O'Brien, 12 February 2016, https://www.youtube.com/watch?v=b7cbkm07IWs, accessed 20 March 2020, and the antisemitism he faced in the army, see Reiner's interview for *GI Jews: Jewish Americans in World War II*, https://www.facebook.com/watch/?v=469901016532337, accessed 20 March 2020.

43. Milligan wrote seven war memoirs, including *Adolf Hitler: My Part in his Downfall* (London: Michael Joseph, 1971), *Rommel Gunner Who?* (London: Michael Joseph, 1974), *Monty: His Part in My Victory* (New York: Penguin, 1976), *Mussolini: His Part in My Downfall* (New York: Penguin, 1978), *Where Have All the Bullets Gone?* (New York: Penguin, 1985), *Goodbye Soldier* (New York: 1986), and *Peace Work* (New York: Penguin, 1991).

44. In the fifth memoir of the series, *Where Have All the Bullets Gone?*, Milligan opts for telling jokes as part of his recollection of the German surrender: "Führer Bunker: HITLER IS IN THE KARZI GIVING HIMSELF ONE OF DOCTOR MORRELL'S ENEMAS. ADOLPH: Allez oops! Ahhh! Dat is better. GOEBBELS: Mein Führer, mein Führer. ADOLPH: Dere's only one of me. GOEBBELS: In Italy our troops are running out of legs. ADOLPH: You Schwein, you haff ruined my happy enema . . . ," 162, 163.

45. Lenny Rubenstein, "Monty Python Strikes Again: An Interview with Michael Palin," *Cinéaste*, Vol. 14, No. 2 (1985): 6–9.

46. James Gent, "Michael Palin on *Monty Python's Flying Circus*," Interview, 5 October 2019, http://wearecult.rocks/the-gospel-according-to-michael-palin.

47. Tim Landen, "It's fine to laugh at new Hitler book' says Monty Python star Michael Palin," *Ham and High*, 8 February 2013, https://www.hamhigh.co.uk/news/it-s-fine-to-laugh-at-new-hitler-book-says-monty-python-star-michael-palin-1-1869223, accessed 20 March 2020.

48. The pilot of *Heil Honey I'm Home* can be viewed on YouTube at—https://www.youtube.com/watch?v=mf9jJx0NSjw, accessed 20 March 2020.

49. Jeff Kaye, "The Führer in Britain: New Satellite Service Pins its Hopes on 'Dangerous' Hitler Sitcom," *Los Angeles Times*, 23 October 1990, https://www.latimes.com/archives/la-xpm-1990-10-23-ca-3101-story.html, and David Hawkes, "British Contemporary Comedy," in *Comedy: A Geographic and Historical Guide*, ed. Maurice Charney (Greenwood, CT: Greenwood Publishing Group, 2005), 197.

50. Shirley Li, "Hitler Sitcom Creator Explains Most Controversial TV Pilot Ever Made," *Entertainment Weekly*, 17 April 2017, https://ew.com/tv/2017/04/17/hitler-sitcom-tv-pilot/, accessed 20 March 2020.

51. See the article https://archive.vn/20110710142246/http://www.dld-conference.com/2010/08/christoph-schlingensief-passed.php, accessed 20 March 2020.

52. Tara Forrest and Anna Teresa Scheer, *Christoph Schlingensief: Art Without Borders* (Chicago: University of Chicago Press, 2010), 5–22.

53. Florian Malzacher, "Blurring Boundaries/Changing Perspectives," in *Christoph Schlingensief*, 208.

54. Rosenfeld, *Hi Hitler*, 266, and his citation of John Bendix, "Facing Hitler: German Responses to *Downfall*," *German Politics and Society*, 1 (2007): 76, and Hellmuth Karasek, "Der jämmerlich Dictator," *Der Tagesspiegel*, 11 September 2004.

55. "Hitler ist greifbarer geworden," *Frankfurter Rundschau*, 11 September 2004, www.filmportal.de/node/69095/material/544449, accessed 21 March 2020.

56. Liat Steir-Livny, *Is it OK to Laugh About It*, 152.

57. See *Adolf—Ich hock' in meinem Bunker* at https://www.youtube.com/watch?v=np2ymo0iMfk; Moers is adamant that it is not humor or humanizing Hitler that is the problem but, as he sees it, the continued demonization of Hitler which "allows him to become a cult figure for Neo-Nazis." "New Comic Tests Germany's Ability to Laugh at Hitler," https://www.dw.com/en/new-comic-tests-germans-ability-to-laugh-at-hitler/a-2105221, accessed 21 March 2020.

58. Emma Rosenblum, "The Director of Downfall Speaks Out on All Those Angry YouTube Hitlers," *Vulture*, 15 January 2010, https://www.vulture.com/2010/01/the_director_of_downfall_on_al.html, accessed 20 March 2020.

59. Derek Elley in his review in *Variety* said the film was not laugh-out-loud funny, "*Mein Führer: The Truly Truest Truth About Adolf Hitler*," *Variety*, 17 January 2007; Peter Zander, Henryk Broder, and Harald Peters all echoed this; the film simply was not funny enough. Peter Zander, "Ein Adolf kommt selten allein: An Levys Hitler-Komödie *Mein Führer* entzündet sich eine Debatte. Dabei ist der Film dafür zu harmlos," *Die Welt*, 6 January 2007; Harald Peters, "Hitler, menschlich gesehen: Dani Levy wollte mit *Mein Führer* eine Komödie über Hitler drehen. Und nahm dem Stoff jeden Witz," *Welt am Sonntag*, 7 January 2007, and Henryk Broder, "Der Jud tut gut," *Der Spiegel*, 8 January 2007, and Michael D. Richardson, "Tragedy and Farce: Dani Levy's *Mein Führer*," in Karolin Machtans and Martin A. Ruehl, *Hitler—Films from Germany: History, Cinema, and Politics Since 1945* (New York: Palgrave Macmillan, 2012), 148.

60. *Mein Führer*, DVD, directed by Dani Levy (Berlin: X-Filme, 2007), 1:25, Rosenfeld, *Hi Hitler*, 274, and Michael D. Richardson, "Tragedy and Farce," 146.

61. Thomas Stephens, "Swiss Directs Controversial Führer Farce," 12 January 2007, https://www.swissinfo.ch/eng/swiss-directs-controversial-fuehrer-farce/5661024, and Interview with Dani Levy by Johanna Adorjan, "Dürfen wir über Hitler lachen?," *Frankfurter Allgemeine Sonntagszeitung*, 17 December 2006, 25; see also Rosenfeld, *Hi Hitler*, 276, and Angela Rosenthal and David Bindman, eds., *No Laughing Matter: Visual Humor in Ideas of Race, Nationality, and Ethnicity* (Lebanon, NH: University Press of New England, 2016), 312.

62. Sabine Hake, "Entombing the Nazi Past: On *Downfall* in and Historicism," in *Hitler: Films from Germany*, 119.

63. The is the episode entitled, "Pinkeye," which aired on 29 October 1997.

64. *South Park*, Season 8, Episode 3, "Passion of the Jew," air date 31 March 2004 on Comedy Central (Braniff Productions, 2004).

65. "Passion of the Jew."

66. Virginia Heffernan, "Critic's Notebook: What? Morals in *South Park?*" *New York Times,* 28 April 2004, https://www.nytimes.com/2004/04/28/arts/critic-s-notebook-what-morals-in-south-park.html, accessed 22 March 2020.

67. Max Gross, "*The Passion of the Christ* Fuels Antisemitism—on *South Park,*" *The Forward,* 9 April 2004, https://forward.com/news/israel/5445/e2-80-98the-passion-of-the-christ-e2-80-99-fuels-antisemitism/, accessed 22 March 2020.

68. Andrew Goldman, "The Fogies of *South Park,*" *New York Times,* 23 September 2011, https://www.nytimes.com/2011/09/25/magazine/talk-trey-parker-and-matt-stone-of-south-park.html See Parker and Stone's commentary on the episode here: https://southpark.cc.com/clips/tahx4y/creator-commentary-the-passion-of-the-jew, accessed 22 March 2020.

69. Daniel J. Frim, "Pseudo-Satire and Evasion of Ideological Meaning in *South Park,*" *Studies in Popular Culture*, Vol. 36, No. 2 (Spring 2014): 149–171.

70. See the "Lil Hitler" skit on YouTube at: https://www.youtube.com/watch?v=VHSPP-CzNl0.

71. See the "Commentary for 'Sausage Fest,'" Season 2, Episode 15, *Robot Chicken,* DVD (New York: Cartoon Network, 2007).

72. "TV Preview: Family Guy," *Entertainment Weekly,* 18 August 2007, http://www.ew.com/ew/article/0,,20054572,00.html, accessed 26 March 2020.

73. See the "Commentary for 'Road to Germany,'" Season 7, Episode 3, *Family Guy,* DVD (Los Angeles: 20th Century Fox, 2009).

74. A few years later, MacFarlane caught flak for making a Hitler joke during the reveal of the Oscar nominations before his controversial stint as host, although the criticism was more about the joke falling flat. In discussing the Austrian film Amour, he said, "The last time Austria and Germany co-produced something it was Hitler, but this was much better." Camille Mann, "Seth MacFarlane Gets Backlash for Hitler Joke at Oscar Nominations," *USA Today,* January 11, 2013.

75. Watch the segment on Conan--https://www.youtube.com/watch?v=7DcrmnRijTQ, accessed 25 March 2020.

76. See the "Awesome Hitler Story" skit on YouTube at: https://www.youtube.com/watch?v=izh-j8KUYjs.

77. See "The Charming Mr. Hitler" at: https://www.youtube.com/watch?v=d_1REHxLoqM.

78. http://curnblog.com/2016/05/15/interviewing-philippe-mora-history-hitler-deconstructed/. Interviewing Philippe Mora: History and Hitler Deconstructed. James Curnow / May 15, 2016.

79. *Snide and Prejudice,* DVD, directed by Philippe Mora (Kent, UK: Vine International Pictures, 1997).

80. See "Final Solution 2.0" at: https://www.youtube.com/watch?v=Pp3Qi07nJK4.

81. See "At Vienna's Art Academy" at: https://www.youtube.com/watch?v=f66h1hk5yco.

82. Shoshana Razel and Gordon Guedalia, "And *The Jews are Coming:* Reviewing the New Israeli Comedy Show," *The Jewish Standard,* 26 December 2014, https://jewishstandard.timesofisrael.com/the-jews-are-coming/, and Esther Kustanowitz,

"The Jews are Coming! After a Yearlong Controversy," *The Jewish Daily Forward,* 26 November 2014, https://forward.com/schmooze/209851/the-jews-are-coming-after-a-yearlong-controversy/, both accessed 23 March 2020.

83. Quoted by Razel and Guedalia, "And *The Jews are Coming."*

84. Liat Steir-Livny, *Is it OK to Laugh About It?,* 159.

85. "Exclusive Video Interview: Erik Eger—One Hundred Years of Evil," Fantasia international Film Festival, 25 July 2011, http://www.fantasiafestival.com/blog/interviews/exclusive-video-interview-erik-eger-one-hundred-years-of-evil, accessed 24 March 2020.

86. Justine Smith, "Fantasia 2011: *One Hundred Years of Evil* is a One Joke Film, *Sound on Sight,* 26 July 2011, http://www.soundonsight.org/fantasia-2011-one-hundred-years-of-evil-is-a-one-joke-film, accessed 24 March 2020.

87. The Polish film industry has been especially active in making films about the resistance—both against the Nazis and Soviet forces, and perhaps the most prolific director from Poland was Andrzej Wajda, who made some fifty films between 1951 and his death in 2016, including the first film about the Warsaw Uprising in 1944 (*Kanał*, from 1957) and the Academy Award nominated film, *Katyń*, from 2007, about the Soviet massacre of Polish prisoners of war in 1940. Polish comedies about the war, such as Tadeusz Chmielewski's *How I Unleashed the Second World War (Jak rozpętałem drugą wojnę światową),* have also focused on the resistance and the role of the "everyman," standing up to the Nazis. Films about the Holocaust from eastern European countries continue to emphasize resistance (*In Darkness* from Poland) and *The Third Half* from Macedonia), and some (like 2013's *Ida* from Poland focused on suppression under communism).

88. Interview with Marius Weisberg, 28 June 2019, https://moscsp.ru/en/natalya-bardo-posle-rasstavaniya-s-muzhem-ya-okazalas-na-ulice-v-chuzhoi.html, accessed 30 December 2020.

89. The British sci-fi Comedy *Red Dwarf* also had a couple of Hitler references. In the episode entitled "Meltdown," the space-team lands on a planet of wax-robots who are either villains or good-guys from world history; Hitler is one of the bad robots. In another episode, "Timeslides," crewmembers are able to step into slides and travel back into time. In one, they go back briefly to Nazi Germany and accidentally steal a briefcase that contains a bomb intended to blow up Hitler. Cavan Gallagher, "Return to Retro: *Danger 5,*" *Metro Magazine,* 172 (2012): 114.

90. Kwenton Bellette, "Mission Accomplished! A DANGER(ous) 5 Chat with Creators Dario Russo & David Ashby," *Screen Anarchy,* 26 March 2012, https://screenanarchy.com/2012/03/mission-accomplished-a-dangerous-5-chat-with-creators-dario-russo-david-ashby.html, accessed 25 March 2020.

91. Monica Tan, "Danger 5 Director Dario Russo on Mocking Hitler (not Kim Jong-un)," *The Guardian,* 28 December 2014, https://www.theguardian.com/tv-and-radio/2014/dec/30/danger-5-director-dario-russo-on-the-tricky-task-of-mocking-world-villains, accessed 25 March 2020.

92. Watch *A Kitten for Hitler* here: https://www.youtube.com/watch?v=fu-KncLqDjs, accessed 25 March 2020.

93. Ken Russell, "My Kitten for Hitler is all in the Best Bad Taste," *The Times of London,* 27 September 2007, https://www.thetimes.co.uk/article/my-kitten-for-hitler-is-all-in-the-best-bad-taste-3877csdd5p9, accessed 25 March 2020.

94. Laura Mulvey, "Visual Pleasure and Narrative Cinema," in *Film and Theory: An Anthology,* ed. Robert Stam and Toby Miller (Oxford: Blackwell Publishers, 2000), 484, 485; and Linda Hutcheon, "The Politics of Postmodernism: Parody and History," *Cultural Critique,* Vol. 5 (Winter 1986–1987): 182.

95. Hutcheon, "Politics of Postmodernism," 182.

96. Mulvey, "Visual Pleasure," 485.

97. Mulvey, "Visual Pleasure," 485.

98. Saul Friedländer, *Reflections on Nazism: An Essay on Kitsch and Death,* trans. Thomas Weyr (New York: Harper and Row, 1984), 217, 218, 228, and Oren Baruch Stier, *Committed to Memory,* 195.

Chapter 3

Contesting the Nazis and Their System of Terror through Humor

As we have seen in the previous chapter, comedic representations of Hitler are problematic, but the opprobrium which they often generate pales in comparison to the outrage expressed at comic depictions of the terror regime which Hitler and his fellow Nazis devised. The danger of trivialization is probably greatest in the intersection of comedy and what Alexander Donat described as the Holocaust Kingdom—the universe of suffering and industrialized mass murder. Here, the question that I raised on the first pages of this book finds its greatest challenge: Can the heart of the Nazi genocide ever be depicted in film or television, let alone comic productions? It is one thing to use satire to ridicule a dictator; it is quite different when focusing on environments of death. *Life Is Beautiful, Jakob the Liar,* and *Train of Life* demonstrate this challenge. The scale of murder is simply too vast, the suffering too great and the medium too artificial and commodifying to be an appropriate forum for representation.

Even in "higher art" genres such as literature, history, and philosophy, writers like Elie Wiesel and Hannah Arendt pointed to what they saw as the inadequacy of the human imagination to capture the universe of the Holocaust. That is why making any film about the genocide, especially a comedic one or one with comedic elements, is so problematic. Irony, incongruity, and tragedy are central to comedy, and they work when set against a set of rules and circumstances that may be inflexible but somehow rational. Comedy cannot work in the world of the concentration camp because that requires the writer to, in the words of Alexander Alvarez, "take the utterly psychopathic as his norm, and make art out of the forces of anti-art."[1] Therefore, even if a comedic film about the Holocaust were revelatory, providing comfort to surviving victims, engaging in an active dialogue within and outside the production about the seriousness of the topic, even leaving a legacy beyond the film in the form of an infrastructure of education, the film might still generate controversy with critics and the general public. This chapter will explore comic films over time in different contexts that have attempted to critique the Nazis' system of terror, highlighting the perils of such endeavors. Some of the films are about Nazis as "fifth columnists" bent on bringing down the United States from within, others are set in prisoner of war camps, and some are about general resistance to the German occupation. It is difficult to affix a blanket label of comedy to the majority of these films in the sense that they are intended to generate laughs. Few are of the slapstick type that we encountered in the last chapter about Hitler. Some are very dark, and if they are comedic at all, it is only in the sense that they present satirical or absurdist narratives.

Central to this chapter are two productions from the 1970s which set their stories in concentration camps. These are Lina Wertmüller's *Seven Beauties* and Jerry Lewis' *The Day the Clown Cried,* The films illustrate the dual challenge of defining what constitutes a comedic film about the Holocaust and of producing a performance piece about the genocide using comedic tropology. Wertmüller's film was released on 4 May 1975 in France and on 20 December 1975 in Italy, and it went on to receive high acclaim, while Lewis' film from 1972 was never released. One might view *Seven Beauties* and *The Day the Clown Cried* as contemporary opposites in comedic representation; the former is counter-cinema, with violence, absurdity, and "unpleasure" undergirding its tableaux of the concentration camp, and the latter is more in line with the Hollywood tradition of audience identification. However, I would argue that the dynamic is more complex than that; both films are problematic in ways that overlap and depart, and they capture tensions within the narrative strategies of their cinematic reference points. Later comic productions such as *Life Is Beautiful* and those I analyze more closely in this chapter, such as *My Mother's Courage* and *Goebbels and Geduldig,* are heirs to Wertmüller's and Lewis' controversial legacy.

With the intersection of comedy and the world of the concentration camp, my tripartite analytical model of purpose-relevance-originality faces its greatest test as a barometer of effectiveness. One's intention might be purposeful, and disseminating knowledge about ghettos and Nazi camps is certainly relevant. The idea and final product might also be original as a point of craft, but it may still have serious shortcomings. To resolve this problem, I rely on the theories of film scholars, such as Janet Walker and Joshua Hirsch, historian Hayden White, and survivor and academic Eli Pfefferkorn, each of whom confronted the issue of the inadequacy of the human imagination to represent the Holocaust, the fundamental challenge posed by Wiesel and Arendt. Their theories and those about "grotesque realism" from Bakhtin help add nuance to my focus on purpose, originality, and relevance. As I articulated in the introduction—one of the purposes of Holocaust comedy should be to shed light on the system of terror, but how can that be done if the exercise itself is either difficult or impossible, so constrained by language and the limits of imagination? For the scholars above, one solution to this problem is to adopt a fantastical or anti-realist narrative structure (in the vein perhaps of *Life Is Beautiful* or *Train of Life*). Hayden White begins with the premise that the events of the Holocaust lie beyond human "sense-making" capacity; "they cannot be simply forgotten . . . but neither can they be adequately remembered."[2] For White, only a structure that disturbs linear narratives and realism can begin to communicate the trauma of the genocide. Eli Pfefferkorn, writing in defense of Romain Gary's satirical novel, *The Dance of Genghis Cohn*, argued that a literary format that employs and depicts the most grotesque incongruities, that adopts the most extreme metaphorical frameworks, and that self-referentially forces the artist to resist making beauty out of suffering, thus retaining the "brutal terror," "madness" and "chaos" of the genocide, can, in his words, "make it possible for the uninitiated to grasp imaginatively the preposterous fantasies of the Holocaust reality and subsequently to perceive them cognitively."[3] In her analysis of Steven Spielberg's *Saving Private Ryan*, Janet Walker maintained that it was the film's *anti-realism*—its "rapid cutting, special discontinuity, and befuddling alternation between close-ups and wide shots," its use of "fragmentary" and "poetic knowledge"—and not its verisimilitude that conveyed the trauma, and hence realism, of the Omaha beach landing.[4] Joshua Hirsch sees trauma as central to Holocaust films as well but views it as "less a particular experiential content than a form of experience," and that the "discourse of trauma is less about an image or content but more about discovering a form for presenting that content which mimics aspects of PTSD [post-traumatic stress disorder]."[5] Finally, Bakhtin's analysis of François Rabelais use of the grotesque body in satire, specifically how the trope elucidates the mundane, vulgar, sometimes awful, sometimes wonderful aspects of the human form as it connects to life and death, has particular relevance to Wertmüller's film and can even be useful in comparison with Lewis' *Day the Clown Cried*.[6] Applying the above ideas, one might argue that a comedy about the Holocaust set in a camp or killing field or another utterly "unreal" setting of human degradation and mass murder should push the boundaries of form to communicate trauma and to use film discourse to express the "unreality" of the content. In the end, we may find that once we deconstruct a comedic film about the Holocaust Kingdom, one that might on the surface be purposeful, original, or relevant but may have deficiencies in one or more of these areas.

ANTI-NAZI COMEDIES FROM THE
THIRTIES TO THE EIGHTIES

In addition to sending up Hitler and his henchmen, the earliest anti-Nazi films in the United States and Great Britain confronted the danger and terror of fascism through the spy story, a genre which Alfred Hitchcock popularized in Britain throughout the 1930s with such films as *The Man Who Knew Too Much* (1934), *The 39 Steps* (1935), *Sabotage* (1937), and *The Lady Vanishes* (1938). Many of these productions centered on the nefarious deeds of an "unnamed" European country, and they helped to pave the way for the more overtly anti-Nazi productions like *Confessions of a Nazi Spy,* from 1939, starring Edward G. Robinson, *Ten Days in Paris,* Tim Whelan's 1940 classic starring Rex Harrison, and Carole Reed's *Night Train to Munich,* also from 1940 and also starring Harrison and one of the first feature films to depict a concentration camp. As we saw in the previous chapter, the theme of espionage appeared in several anti-Nazi comedies coming out of Hollywood, from those of the Marx Brothers to the Three Stooges, and the device was equally prevalent in British comedies, such as Marcel Varnel's *Let George Do It,* starring ukulele playing George Formby, and Leslie Hiscott's *Lady from Lisbon* (1942), in which Nazi agents steal the Mona Lisa, and a budding South American spy, Tamara (played by Jane Carr), travels to Lisbon to spy for the Germans to get her hands on the painting.

The spy story device had the effect of bringing home the Nazi threat, making more immediate something that could be dismissed as remote. As a literary trope, the spy is different from an enemy; one can see an enemy, but the spy operates in the shadows, almost invisible. A spy could be the neighbor next door, and in fact, so many of the spy narratives of the 1930s and 40s present such a scenario. In doing so, they touch on the primal fear of the unknown, in this case, an unknown villain masquerading as a friend or neighbor. And while a good adventure story in the 1930s was as much about business as it was about storytelling, one of the effects, and some would say benefits, of the spy film was that, alongside newsreels, it could reach a broad audience and help cultivate anti-Nazi sentiment.

A raft of Nazi-themed spy comedies featuring well-known stars came out of Hollywood between January 1942 and April 1943. These were *All Through the Night* (directed by Vincent Sherman, starring Humphrey Bogart, released on 10 January 1942); *Once Upon a Honeymoon* (directed by Leo McCarey, starring Cary Grant and Ginger Rogers, released on 2 November 1942); *Margin for Error* (directed by and starring Otto Preminger, also starring Milton Berle and Joan Bennett, released on 8 January 1943); *They Got Me Covered* (directed by David Butler, starring Bob Hope, Dorothy Lamour, and Preminger again, released on 27 January 1943); and *Air Raid Wardens* (directed by Edward Sedgwick, starring Laurel and Hardy, released on 30 April 1943). The comedies share several qualities in addition to the spy framework. They all are star vehicles that feature an outsider or an underdog American protagonist, a clever but distressed damsel, and sinister Nazis and pro-Nazi spies. Yet their critical and popular receptions, along with their reputations over time, vary wildly, which we will explore. Their broader significance is as cultural texts operating in a particular time during the war when an American and Allied victory was by no means certain. Therefore, their purpose in making audiences laugh was manifold—to lift spirits, instill an urgency to the fight by bringing the danger home, and reinforce a sense of the values that Americans were contesting and promoting.

The storyline of *All Through the Night* is, in a word, convoluted—although that word could be used to describe each of the above spy comedies. One of the more noteworthy aspects of *All Through the Night* is its inadvertent connection to the classic *Casablanca,* which premiered a year later, as Bogart and his co-stars Conrad Veidt and Peter Lorre play similar and similarly villainous or shady characters in both films. In *All Through the Night,* Bogart plays a New York gambler, "Gloves" Donohue, whose baker is murdered by a Nazi sympathizer named Pepi, played by Peter Lorre. Pepi is a Nazi thug by day and piano player by night for torch singer Leda Hamilton, played by Karen Verne.[7] Gloves winds up framed for another murder, which leads him to an underworld of Nazis led by auctioneer Hall Ebbing, played by Conrad Veidt, who is plotting with Pepi and a band of American Nazi supporters to blow up a battleship in New York harbor. Hamilton is only working with the Nazis to save her father, who is imprisoned in Dachau, and when she learns that he has died, she switches sides and is eventually captured by Ebbing. Gloves and his sidekick, Sunshine, played by William Demarest of later *My Three Sons* fame, track down the fifth columnists and pose as two Nazis they happen to knock out. Although they discover the conspiracy, Gloves and Sunshine are put on the spot when they are mistaken for the explosives' experts, whom they dispatched in their fistfight, and they are asked to deliver a report. Bogart gives a diversionary speech in gibberish German,[8] Gloves' gang breaks in to start a ruckus, and Ebbing escapes to fulfill the mission by himself. Gloves tracks him down, and the two end up on a motorboat filled with explosives heading for the battleship. At the last second, Gloves steers the boat off course and jumps overboard; the boat slams into a barge and explodes, killing Ebbing. Gloves finds himself not only exonerated by the police at the end but in line to receive a special commendation.

Once Upon a Honeymoon, meanwhile, was one of many comedies directed by Leo McCarey, who won Best Director in 1937 for *The Awful*

Truth, another romantic comedy starring Cary Grant, and he already had the classic comedy *Duck Soup* from 1933 under his belt. McCarey would go on to direct the famous rom-com *An Affair to Remember* in 1957. In *Once Upon a Honeymoon,* Grant stars as journalist Pat O'Toole, who is on the trail of an Austrian Nazi, Baron von Luber (played by Walter Slezak), engaged to an American cabaret performer, Katie O'Hara (played by Ginger Rogers), who pretends to be a lady of the leisure class with the name of Katherine Butt-Smith (pronounced "byute"). Grant pursues the couple across Czechoslovakia and Poland, where the Baron gets entangled in a plot to sell defective weapons to a Polish general, who is assassinated, and von Luber ends up in prison. Meanwhile, O'Toole and O'Hara fall in love, and after helping a Jewish maid and her children escape Poland (with O'Hara's passport), the two find themselves briefly in a Jewish ghetto before being given exit visas through the help of American diplomats. They ultimately flee to Paris, where O'Hara is commissioned to spy on von Luber, freshly released from jail. He discovers the plot, has O'Hara arrested, and blackmails O'Toole into broadcasting Nazi propaganda. O'Toole rehearses his lines but wants to ad-lib, which the German onlookers in the studio support, saying he needs more "shpontanuity," but he uses the coded phrase "tell it to the Marines," which the Germans do not understand, as a way of saying do not believe a word of the broadcast. In an even more strained turn of events, the Jewish maid whom O'Hara helped to get out of Poland has somehow become the maid at Gestapo Headquarters, and she repays her debt by helping her rescuer escape. O'Toole then delivers the official broadcast and suggests that von Luber is such a great figure in the Nazi party that he is even better than Hitler, which gets the Baron arrested yet again. Like before, mysteriously, he is released, and he winds up on the same boat O'Toole and O'Hara are on bound for the United States. O'Hara and von Luber have one final confrontation, in which the former dispatches the latter by throwing him overboard. At the film's bizarre, semi-comedic, and unresolved ending, O'Hara confesses her crime to O'Toole, who gets the ship's captain to turn around and look for the lost passenger. (McCarey initially supported the idea of letting the Baron drown).[9]

Margin for Error differs from the other films due to its origins; it began as a play written by Clare Boothe Luce, who served in Congress during the war and would become the first female ambassador in U.S. history. The play is based on the true story of a New York police captain of Jewish heritage named Max Finkelstein, who was assigned to protect the German consulate from protesters. The play premiered at the Plymouth Theatre on 3 November 1939, and the film came out a little over three years later.[10] The film's narrative is structured somewhat differently than the play, conveyed as a flashback from the character now known as Moe Finkelstein (played by Milton Berle), who is aboard a ship of fellow soldiers setting off to Europe to fight the Nazis. Moe recounts the story of his post as the bodyguard for the German consul, Karl Baumer (played in both the theatrical production and the film by Otto Preminger). Preminger was not the original choice for Baumer in the film; German actor Rudolf Forster was slated to play him, but he returned to Germany before shooting began, leaving a memo: "Dear Otto—I am leaving to rejoin Adolf." In his memoirs, Preminger found the German note oddly comical.[11] Studio head Darryl Zanuck did not want Preminger on the production after the two had a shouting match during the shoot of a previous film (*Kidnapped*), but he was able to get the job, secretly rewrite the script for *Margin*, and play the part of the German consul, who, in the play and film, has been squandering money earmarked for sabotage. Baumer's secretary, the "good German," Baron Max von Alvenstor (played by Carl Esmond), intends to send the financial report to Berlin. Baumer's wife, Sophia, played by Joan Bennett, also reveals that she hates her husband and only married him to gain her father's release from prison (a plot line analogous to the one in *All Through the Night*). Baumer looks to frame and then dispense with an American Nazi collaborator, Otto Horst (Howard Freeman), who is plotting to blow up a port at the end of a radio broadcast by Hitler. Baumer, Sophia, Horst, and Max gather in the consul's library to listen to the broadcast, and at moments in the speech that are loud and distracting, Baumer is stabbed (by Horst) and then shot (by Sophia). Moe discovers Baumer's corpse and then tries to figure out who killed him. Sophia confesses, and then Max does, but one of the attendees determines that Baumer died from poisoning and that he had switched a glass earmarked for Max during a moment of confusion. Horst is arrested for conspiracy in the foiled bomb plot, and Max and Sophia are exonerated.

There are some interesting deviations between the play and film that speak to the restrictions of the code and the desire to present a clearer contrast of the values at stake. For instance, the play features an exchange between Moe and Baumer (who repeatedly and intentionally mangles the officer's last name) that reveals the consul's antisemitism. He calls Moe a "parasite" and a "lousy, illiterate poverty-stricken pawn of the Ghetto," and Moe responds with the line: "Saay! You got me wrong. I'm really a smart intellectual and an international banker."[12] This attempt to throw Baumer's antisemitism back at him by employing another antisemitic trope is absent in the film. The conclusion of the play, which is about Horst's comeuppance, also differs from the film, which has a dissimilar ending and beginning. The film begins with Moe as an army grunt deployed overseas on a ship where other soldiers torment a draftee with a German accent. Moe starts telling them the tale of Baumer's demise and the heroism of the "good German," Max, who turns out to be the harassed soldier. The lesson here was clear: Nazis were not necessarily synonymous with Germans, and many good Germans could be enlisted into the fight against fascism. This notion would have played well with the hundreds of the thousands of American citizens of German descent, and it provides a stark contrast with the more racialized portrayal of the Japanese in Hollywood films.

Preminger's Baumer was one of several Nazi roles which the Austrian-Jewish émigré took on during his career, the most famous of which was Colonel von Scherbach, the acerbic commandant in Billy Wilder's *Stalag 17*.[13] In the Bob Hope-Dorothy Lamour comedy, *They Got Me Covered,* Preminger played Otto Fauscheim, the leader of a Nazi spy ring who is masterminding a series of terror attacks in Washington, D.C. Preminger has spoken of the role in purely transactional terms: "It was a most profitable assignment," Preminger recalled, "because it went on forever and most of it was cut out."[14] Like *Once Upon a Honeymoon,* the hero of the film, Bob Hope's "Kit" Kittredge, is an American reporter who is fast with the quips. However, unlike Cary Grant's Pat O'Toole, Kit is also a clueless, bumbling idiot. As his paper's Moscow correspondent, Kit loses his job after predicting that Germany would never invade Russia. Kit and his lady friend, Christina Hill (played by Lamour), a stenographer at another newspaper, become aware of the network of spies through one of Kit's informants, who is later murdered. Kit tracks down Otto and his wife Olga at a place he describes as a "cozy little nook . . . when do the bats fly out?" In what is perhaps the film's oddest sequence, the two Nazis trap Kit in a room with a senile Civil War veteran who thinks Kit is a Union spy. But Kit manages to charm him, and he discovers the body of the dead informant. Otto and Olga then conspire to ruin Kit's reputation for good by drugging him and marrying him off to a showgirl in his drugged state. At first, shocked by the news, Christina uncovers the blackmail scheme, although the Nazis seem to be one step ahead as they have the showgirl murdered, kidnap Kit, and try to frame him for the crime. While trying to escape his captors, Kit poses as a mannequin and learns of the Nazis' extensive terror plot. After a climactic fistfight, Christina, her girlfriends, and the Marines arrive to save the day, and Christina and Kit reunite.

In *Air Raid Wardens,* Laurel and Hardy play failed businessmen Stan and Ollie, who wind up sharing store space with a German spy, Eustace Middling (played by Donald Meek). The two try to become air raid wardens in their town, but they are kicked out of the service after a bumbled tryout period. During the war, many communities feared air attacks and appointed air raid wardens to ensure that streets were cleared and lights turned off during drills or in preparation for potential raids. Officials from the federal Office of Civilian Defense and Office of War Information demanded that Laurel and Hardy fail in the film in their attempt to secure posts as wardens. The film's technical advisor also made sure that writers changed the ending of the script, which had originally featured the reinstatement of Laurel and Hardy into the service.[15]

Although Stan and Ollie are down and out throughout the film, they uncover Middling's spy ring and a plot to blow up the town's magnesium plant. There is the requisite capture and escape of the protagonists, complete with a tonally off-putting scene in which Laurel is forced by one of his Nazi captors to shoot an apple off of Hardy's head, with the expectation that he will miss and kill his partner. When Laurel shoots, he hits the apple, causing it to land in the mouth of a portrait of Hitler, which leads to the Pavlovian moment of Nazis saluting the Führer and allowing the heroes to escape. In the end, Stan and Ollie save the magnesium plant and expose Middling as a spy.

Common to each of these films is a presentation of the American cause in the war as not only just but more humane, similar to how Chaplin used words like "unnatural" to describe those who would embrace totalitarianism. This augments the theses of historians like John Bodnar, who argue that World War II films during the conflict used communitarian language to remind audiences that it was "'a people's war,' which would bring about a future with more social justice and individual freedom."[16] It is no coincidence that the male protagonists in the above film comedies were flawed; in fact, it was central to the enterprise. It is Milton Berle's goofy and Jewish Moe who has the last words in the film version of *Margin for Error,* in support of Max, the German fighting for his newly adopted country: "We're all fighting for the same cause, the same peace, the same victory."[17] Leo McCarey claimed that the secret to the success of the heroic representation was "to see the actor as a representative of humanity."[18] By mixing the comedic with the poignant, his male protagonist could sell democratic values in a way that came across as relatable rather than preachy.

Beyond the shared spy plots and character archetypes in each of these films, we see references to the Nazi terror system. In *All Through the Night,* Bogart and Demarest's characters, Gloves and Sunshine, discover a letter that reveals that Hamilton's father was killed in Dachau, which Gloves mispronounces with a "ch" as in chew rather than the guttural "h." References to concentration camps were not unknown in anti-Nazi films, and reporting on Dachau can be found as early as April 1933; the *New York Times* buried a piece on the camp on page ten on April 5 of that year.[19] However, overt imagery of concentration camps in feature films remained problematic and rare through the war years, so the specific articulation of Dachau is noteworthy, as are the ghetto and flight sequences in *Once Upon a Honeymoon,* When O'Hara and O'Toole find themselves trapped in the ghetto, O'Toole looks on mortified and offers an admonition that seems to go beyond the fourth wall: "Now O'Hara, what about these people?" he asks.[20] The scene cuts to the two in a Nazi emigration office, as they are somehow granted the opportunity to leave Poland. They almost open the door to an observation room where Nazi officials determine who is to be sterilized. Glaring at one of the Nazi guards, O'Toole muses: "It used to be the will of God—Hitler doesn't like that. Too many people might be born who wouldn't agree with him." O'Hara then offers a darkly comic rejoinder, pretty cutting for 1942: "It would make better sense if his mother had thought of it."[21]

Comparing the films from the perspective of their critical and popular receptions, we see a notable disparity, based, I would argue at least in part on the degree of the films' purposefulness, relevance, and originality. Each film shares the goal of deflating the Third Reich through humor. *Margin for Error*, as both play and film, was conceived as a rebuttal to National Socialism;[22] Leo McCarey wanted to make a war-related film that mixed serious with comedic elements;[23] and Vincent Sherman said that he wanted to "say a few things that needed to be said about Hitler and Bundists."[24] Even Laurel and Hardy weighed in on their contribution, saying that "we are proud to be permitted to contribute to this truly noble cause for we are all cognizant of the great sacrificial effort the men in the armed forces are making for all of us to bring victory. . . ."[25]

Yet only *All Through the Night,* the first film from the above list to hit cinemas, had a good reception at the time and has aged well over the years, with a one-hundred percent critical mark and seventy percent audience approval on Rotten Tomatoes.[26] In his review of the film for the *New York Times* after its opening, Bosley Crowther hailed *All Through the Night* as a "super-duper action picture."[27] Overall, the film made about $1.3 million in profit for Warner Brothers.[28] By contrast, the other films received either mixed or unfavorable reviews when they came out, and they had uneven success at the box office. Time has not been kind to *Margin for Error,* whose Rotten Tomatoes audience score sits at a lowly seventeen percent.[29] Foster Hirsch, in his 2007 biography of Otto Preminger, had this to say about the production: "Boothe's thin, smart-aleck writing, her drawing-room quips, and her sub-vaudevillian treatment of the Jewish policemen (Yiddish shtick clumsily conceived by a Gentile) are grotesquely mismatched to the gravity of her subject. *Margin for Error* is arrogantly trivial"[30] Meanwhile, although Scott MacGillivray estimates that *Air Raid Wardens* brought in $900,000 and was popular with servicemen,[31] its audience approval on Rotten Tomatoes stands at forty-one percent.[32] In his biography of Laurel and Hardy, Simon Louvish laments that an "air of ineptitude and fatigue hangs over" the film.[33] *Once Upon a Honeymoon* made a small profit of nearly $300,000 for RKO pictures, but the studio lost money on *They Got Me Covered*.[34] The former currently has a fifty-nine percent audience score on Rotten Tomatoes, while the latter receives the highest audience marks of the five films under consideration in this section—at eighty-two percent.[35] It is unclear why this is the case, but it may be due to the charm of star Bob Hope. In his review of the film, Crowther gushed over Hope's performance despite regarding the film's overall story as trite: "Bob ... makes the picture—he and his great big gags. So long as he has them, he's covered—no matter how slight the story is."[36] Still, the contemporary critical mark for *They Got Me Covered* on Rotten Tomatoes is bad, at only twenty percent.[37] Reviews for *Once Upon a Honeymoon* were mixed as well, with critics from the *Hollywood Reporter* and *Variety* approving,[38] and the reporter for the *New York Daily News* and once again Crowther offering blistering critiques because of the film's tone and the incorporation of the ghetto/camp sequence:

> [quoting Crowther] The spectacle of Mr. Grant and Miss Rogers flirting airily amid the ruins of Warsaw is not intellectually enjoyable. But when Mr. McCarey has the Nazis mistake them for Jews and injects a scene of vaudeville burlesque (with a derby pulled down over Mr. Grant's ears) before casting them, momentarily, into a mournful concentration camp, the effort is downright offensive. Mr. McCarey has produced a callous film.[39]

A combination of factors accounts for the yawning gap between the critical and popular responses to the films. The quality of the overall writing in some is lacking, and most of the films are simply not that funny. There are humorous moments, particularly Bogart and Grant's undoing of the Nazis in a way that that they are not in on the joke, and Bob Hope does rifle off a handful of amusing one-liners, but overall, the scenarios in the films are not in the same league as *To Be or Not to Be* or even *The Great Dictator*. *Once Upon a Honeymoon* has the most glaring problem of tone, with its romantic comedy and screwball scenes offset by numerous melancholic and often downright disturbing interludes. The films are relevant in the sense that they tackle a pressing issue of the day; however, some of the humor may have lost relevance in its time. Such was the criticism leveled against *Air Raid Wardens* by Theodore Strauss, who felt that "the Laurel and Hardy style of stumbling idiocy seems considerably less hilarious today than it did in the heyday of two-reel comedies a decade and a half ago."[40] Moreover, as we saw with films like *Jakob the Liar* and *Train of Life,* when films appear in succession utilizing similar storylines, the later ones very often set themselves up for criticism that they are the products of a filmmaker's desire to cash in on a successful formula. These films lose relevance because they are less original, and originality figures to be key here. *All Through the Night* has a tighter story and better dialogue, and although I felt like I was watching *Casablanca* before *Casablanca*, it was also the first out of the gate. Theodore Strauss said it best in his review of *Margin for Error* that, "the script is now painfully dated. The

Nazis certainly are not less villainous, but as they are shown in the film, they are much less interesting. Practically every character and situation has long been a cliché of anti-Nazi films generally."[41]

Similar issues of purpose, relevance, and originality bedevil films that feature anti-Nazi storylines from the postwar years to the present day. In the immediate aftermath of the war and decade thereafter, patriotic war films continued, and some general war comedies emerged, like the navy films, *Mr. Roberts* (1955) and *Operation Petticoat* (1959) and Cary Grant's *I Was a Male War Bride* (1949); Grant also starred in *Operation Petticoat,* Several films depicted the trauma of the war as well, including the Academy Award winner for best picture of 1946, *The Best Years of Our Lives,* and *Home of the Brave* (1949). However, in the postwar era through the 1950s, comedies about Nazis were rare, as we have already discussed in previous chapters, due partly to the widespread exposure of the crimes the Nazis and their allies committed during their reign of terror.[42] Making fun of Nazis in the 1930s and 40s could have been justified as protest, but even here, not all critics agreed, and this was before the disclosure of the full extent of Nazi genocidal policies. After that, to make a comedy about the Third Reich could be seen as making light of its horrific legacy. On many levels, it was difficult after the war to produce any comic film, let alone a critically successful or popular one, with an anti-Nazi storyline. Questions about purpose could legitimately be asked of filmmakers seeking to make a comedy about Nazis when one could argue that there was very little to make fun of, and there were matters that had greater relevance (for instance, the aftereffects and trauma of the war and the new enemy of Soviet communism).

These were the issues two of the few comedies with anti-Nazi plots had to contend with in the postwar era. The Marx Brothers' *Night in Casablanca,* released on 10 May 1946, and Danny Kaye's spy flick, *On the Double,* released on 19 May 1961, lack the immediacy of even the slightest anti-Nazi film released during the war. In the former, Groucho stars as Ronald Kornblow, the third manager of a hotel in Casablanca, who is unaware of a plot by an escaped Nazi, Heinrich Stubel (played by Sig Ruman), to murder the hotel managers so that he can take over the establishment and make off with stolen art treasures hidden in the building. Chico and Harpo play characters designed to add maximum zaniness to the film, and Stubel is thwarted in the end. In *On the Double,* Kaye plays an American soldier by the name of Ernie Williams, who does such good impersonations that he is enlisted to play the role of a British general who fears assassination by the Nazis. Ernie falls for the general's wife, Lady Margaret (played by Dana Wynter), and the two grow closer. After the real general dies in a plane crash, Ernie is kidnapped and taken to Germany, where he manages to escape after changing into different characters, ranging from Marlene Dietrich to Hitler. After foiling a British double agent, Ernie survives and lives happily ever after with Lady Margaret.

Reviews for both films at the time were mixed. Writing for the *New York Times*, Thomas Pryor described the Marx Brothers' humor as "wheezy as an old Model T Ford panting uphill on two cylinders," while James Agee, for *The Nation,* called it "tired."[43] Meanwhile, Bosley Crowther, in his review of *On the Double,* felt that "the plot might have done with more invention. . . ."[44] The two films have not done much better with critics over time, although their popular reception is better than their critical one. On Rotten Tomatoes, *Night in Casablanca* holds fifty-seven percent approval from critics, which is three points shy of a "fresh" rating and a seventy percent rating from audiences.[45] *On the Double* has only an audience rating, which is barely above "fresh" at sixty-one percent.[46]

These assessments reflect not only the middling production values of the films but also problems with their purposes, relevance, and originality. Wayne Koestenbaum, in his biography of Harpo Marx, sees the comedy trio as advancing their Jewishness and contesting Nazism in *Night in Casablanca*, arguing specifically about Harpo that he posed a "cuddly antidote to fascism."[47] Even if we grant that this is what is going on at a subtextual level in the film, its timing is at best "off." Moreover, the film was not explicitly intended as an anti-Nazi satire but rather as a parody of *Casablanca*. The story that Groucho told over the years was that Warner Brothers threatened to sue the Marx Brothers over the use of the word "Casablanca" and that he wrote a letter back threatening a countersuit over the Warner Brothers' name because the Marx Brothers had trademarked the use of the word "brothers" in their name first. In reality, Warner Brothers executives did not sue, but their inquiries into the film resulted in its change from a direct parody to a genre parody. That did not stop the Marx Brothers from exploiting the controversy to maximum effect.[48]

On the Double also has issues of relevance and originality. Although a film like *Judgment at Nuremberg* premiered in the same year, it spoke to issues more relevant to the postwar era, like justice and memory. Director Shavelson said that he had been inspired to make a comedy after hearing about the allied attempt to confuse the Nazis before the D-Day invasion of the Normandy by dispatching a body double of General George Montgomery to Gibraltar.[49] Although D-Day would remain relevant as a box office draw, as attested by the popularity of the film, *The Longest Day,* released in September 1962, the British had already made in 1958 a film about the deception, entitled *I Was Monty's Double*. Even the special effects conceit of *On the Double,* with Kaye playing against himself on split-screen, although challenging to pull off, was not necessarily groundbreaking. Buster Keaton did this back in 1921 in his silent comedy, *Playhouse,* in which he played multiple roles. I refer again to Sperber and Wilson's model of relevance, where relevance is directly related to increases in cognitive effects—more tangibly, insights into life and observable phenomena—and indirectly related to processing time, where "the effort to achieve positive cognitive effects is small."[50] Both *Night and Casablanca* and *On the Double* feel removed from the context they are referencing and through which they seek an increase in cognitive effect. Neither film has an answer to the question about what they were trying to say about life in the world of the late '40s or 1950s. Thomas J. Fitzmorris captured this disconnect from a more relevant context in his review of *Night in Casablanca*:

> Now that the war is officially over, its film value is limited to melodramatic memoirs and to the discovery of surplus Nazis under every bedroom farce. . . . This is the Marx Brothers' turn, with the tenuous story subordinated to their eccentric humors . . . their comedies settle quickly into the formlessness of a renegade review.[51]

In the 1960s, as I have mentioned before, a new generation of filmmakers emerged, seeking to engage audiences more willing to look at World War II in a new light. This was the context for a film like *The Producers*. However, subsequent comedic films that featured Nazis as easy marks, such as George Segal's spoof of the *Maltese Falcon*, *The Black Bird* (from 1975) and *Under the Rainbow* (1981), a fantasy about a Nazi plot during the making of the *Wizard of Oz*, were generally lacking in purpose, relevance, and originality. Notable in this regard was the Jerry Lewis comedy, *Which Way to the Front* (1970), in which Lewis plays a wealthy American playboy who is not allowed to enlist in the army, so he creates his own private force and impersonates a German general to attempt an assassination of Hitler. Although Howard Thompson, writing for the *New York Times,* prefaced his negative review by praising the film's "original idea," he went on to say that "The trouble is that each gag is painstakingly repeated, flattening the pace and squelching the sparkle."[52] Critic Leonard Maltin was less kind, labeling the film a "bomb."[53]

A film that stands out positively regarding postwar anti-Nazi comedy is 1980s *The Blues Brothers,* which features an anti-Nazi storyline that is both hilarious and relevant for the time. While the main plot of the film involves Jake and Elwood Blues, played by John Belushi and Dan Aykroyd respectively, attempting to raise money for the Catholic orphanage in which they were raised, they are hounded by the police, rival musicians, and eventually neo-Nazis, whose rally the Brothers break up by driving their car through their lines. Stuck in traffic as police allow the Nazis to march, Jake delivers one of the film's most memorable quotes: "I hate Illinois Nazis."[54] In the film's climactic moment, the Brothers elude the Nazis and force them to an unfinished section of highway from which they plummet, leading to the film's second funniest line, where the Nazi adjutant turns to Henry Gibson's leading Nazi and declares: "I've always loved you." The film's relevance is heightened here by the fact that in the late 1970s, Nazis had been attempting to march in the Chicago suburb of Skokie and had taken their case to the Supreme Court.

THREE FILMS ABOUT RESCUE

Three dramatic films with comedic undercurrents about contesting Nazi oppression have fared better than some of the above spoofs. They are *Me and the Colonel* (based on the 1944 play by Franz Werfel and Samuel N. Behrman, directed by Peter Glenville and featuring Danny Kaye, released on 26 August 1958) and two French films—*The Two of Us* (*Le vieil homme et l'enfant*, directed and co-written by Claude Berri and released in June 1967), and *Monsieur Batignole* (directed and co-written by actor Gérard Jugnot and released 8 March 2002). Both Berri, who died in 2009, and Jugnot received recognition for their work with multiple nominations for César Awards, the French equivalent to the American Academy Awards. Berri's first film, *Le poulet* (*The Chicken,* from 1962), a short about a boy who tries to save a rooster which his family has brought home, won an Academy Award for Best Short Film, and this opened the door for Berri to do *The Two of Us*. His film, *Jean de Florette,* would go on to win the British Academy Award for Best Picture in 1988. Werfel, for his part, is recognized as one of the most important literary figures of the 20th century. Not only do the three films mentioned above share superior writing and direction, but they also shed new light on aspects of life under Nazi occupation and serve as apt commentaries on collaboration, resistance, and Jewish-Gentile relations. One might argue that it is unfair to compare these films with those intended as slapstick or spoofs, but the three productions share more than just a few comedic moments. Their narrative tones are definitively comedic and light-hearted, and they leave audiences smiling with a happy ending. More importantly, they demonstrate the importance of thoughtfulness in craft and execution,

Werfel's play bore the title *Jakobowsky und der Oberst* (which in English translates as *Jacobowsky and the Colonel*), and the film's original title was *The Best of Enemies* before producers settled on *Me and the Colonel,* The play has had several iterations, appearing as an opera in 1965 and then as a musical, *The Grand Tour,* in 1978. Columbia Pictures paid $350,000 for the rights to the play during its Broadway run in 1944, but as David Koenig notes, production languished, and the film went through numerous fits and starts.[55] Based in part on Werfel's flight from Marseilles and the story of a

Stuttgart banker by the name of S.L. Jacobowicz, who was Werfel's neighbor in Lourdes, and set in German-occupied France at the beginning of the war, the play and film center on a forced partnership between two protagonists, a Polish-Jewish refugee by the name of Samuel Jacobowsky (played in the film by Danny Kaye) and an antisemitic Polish colonel Prokoszny (played by Curt Jürgens).[56] The colonel is on a secret mission to get to London by submarine to deliver important information, but he lacks transport out of Paris. As a Jew fleeing the advancing Germans, Jacobowsky also needs to get out of Paris, and he is able to buy two cars—one that works but does not have gas and another with gas that has been damaged in an accident. Compounding this dilemma is the fact that Jacobowsky cannot drive, but he convinces the colonel to take him along nonetheless. The "buddy road trip" movie that ensues has the colonel detour in the direction of the advancing Germans to rescue his French girlfriend, Suzanne (played by Nicole Maury). The three escape from German officers, but a classic love triangle arises between Suzanne, Jacobowsky, and the colonel, and the two men fight it out. In the play, they have a duel with pistols in their pajamas; in the film, they have a sword fight. All ends well, though, as Jacobowsky and the colonel resolve their differences and make their way to London while Suzanne and the colonel's reliable assistant, Szabuniewicz (played by Akim Tamiroff), remain in France to continue the fight against the Nazis.

The play's backstory is almost as fraught as the relationship between its main characters. The plot emerged out of tales told by Werfel at a dinner party in 1941 hosted by the legendary theatre director, Max Reinhardt. The comic relationship between the two characters intrigued Berhman, who, in his words, "kept thinking: 'Two men in an ambivalent relationship—two men from opposite ends of the earth . . . they hate each other—they party—they miss each other. . . . '"[57] Reinhardt's son, Gottfried, suggested to Werfel that he turn the idea into a play, but after being rebuffed, the junior Reinhardt asked Werfel for his permission to co-author a stage adaptation with Berhman. After the two finished the play's first act, they received a letter from Werfel, who had since changed his mind and declared that he wanted to write the play himself, which prompted Reinhardt and Berhman to threaten a lawsuit. When Werfel presented the play to New York Theatre Guild members, they wanted a co-author to "Americanize" the text, and although Werfel was unhappy, he agreed, wanting above all to see the production come to fruition. In 1943, Werfel worked with playwright Clifford Odets (of *Waiting for Lefty* fame), but that partnership was toxic. Werfel felt that he was "trying to convey the European misery of France to an American deaf-mute by means of sign language."[58] Lawsuits followed from Reinhardt, Berhman, and even the man upon whom the story was based, S.L. Jacobowicz, each of whom wanted compensation. Dropping the Odets version, which featured plot lines that Werfel found absurd, like Jacobowsky carrying a portable record player with him throughout France, Werfel continued rewriting the play with New York Theatre Guild writer Jed Harris, but this was in vain. The Guild did not even offer a response to the draft. Months later, Berhman and director Elia Kazan began rehearsing Berhman's version of the play—all without Werfel's consent. When the play premiered on Broadway in March 1944 at the Martin Beck Theater, the comedy had the clunky tagline: "Original play by Franz Werfel, American play based on same by S.N. Berhman." Werfel considered a lawsuit against the Theatre Guild, but he gave up when it transpired that the play was both a critical and popular success.[59]

The two French films, *The Two of Us* and *Monsieur Batignole,* are revealing windows into historical memory, an issue we will explore in greater length in the next chapter, and even though there are thirty-five years between them, the films demonstrate how antisemitism and the occupation remain powerful and unresolved issues in French society and culture. *The Two of Us* arrived at a time of increasingly critical representations of French life during the Nazi occupation. *The Sorrow and the Pity,* Marcel Ophuls' classic documentary indictment of ordinary French citizens, premiered in 1969, two years after Claude Berri's film. France also has a robust tradition of film comedy, and there were a few comedic productions about the war from the 1960s; Jean Renoir's *The Elusive Corporal* (*Le Caporal épinglé,* from 1962), about a captured French soldier who tries to escape from a German POW camp, Jean-Paul Rappeneau's 1965 romantic comedy starring Catherine Deneuve entitled, *A Matter of Resistance* (*La Vie de château*), and Gérard Oury's 1966 classic, *Don't Look Now . . . We're Being Shot At! (La Grande Vadrouille),* about downed British airmen escaping through occupied France.[60] By the time *Monsieur Batignole* appeared in 2002, it was not as unusual to see more critical and comedic representations of German-occupied France, but unease about how these productions framed the past remained, and anxiety can be triggered about the subject even today, some eighty years later.

Based on Berri's experience in hiding as a child, *The Two of Us* centers on the relationship between an 8-year-old Parisian-Jewish boy by the name of Moshe Langmann (played by Alain Cohen) and an elderly couple living in the countryside, who agrees to shelter the boy although they are unaware of his religion. Moshe's parents give him a new name (Claude Longuet), teach him a bit about Catholicism, and instruct him to hide his circumcision, which presents difficulties during bath time. Claude develops a bond with the paterfamilias, Pépé, played by Michel Simon, even though he is an overt antisemite who believes that Jews have "big, hooked noses like fishhooks—to smell out money; They run faster to the bank than to the front. . . . "[61] At one point, Pépé declares that "France has four enemies—not counting the Huns, who were straightforward. They declared war on us. There are four—The

English, Jews, Freemasons, and Bolsheviks. . . ." Claude tries to soften him up in his many one-on-one interactions by asking things like, "wasn't Jesus a Jew?" and "what did the Jews ever do to you?" which prompts Pépé to answer "nothing. That's all I need."[62] Claude develops anxiety about being Jewish, but Pépé and Mémé (played by Luce Fabiole) console Claude by telling him that he is not a Jews and should not worry; all the while, Pépé and Claude develop a surrogate grandfather-grandchild relationship, and by the end, Pépé is sad to see the boy reunited with his parents. His antisemitism has also ebbed a bit, and there is a hint that maybe he knew that the boy was Jewish all along when he laments about the new situation: "Yesterday it was the Huns, today it's American Negroes. Then it will be the Orientals. They'll turn France into a colony. . . . Don't worry about the Jews. They can't be worse than the others."[63]

Monsieur Batignole has a similar premise—a Jewish child rescued by a middle-aged Frenchman, in this case, the eponymous title character, Edmund Batignole, played by writer-director Gérard Jugnot. Unlike *The Two of Us,* the storyline of *Monsieur Batignole* has some factual bases, but the characters were composites. Batignole, as Jugnot admits, was "a bit of my grandfather, who . . . meant a lot in my life."[64] In the film, the Batignoles take over the Parisian apartment of a Jewish family, the Bernsteins, who are arrested by the Gestapo. One night, while the Batignoles are hosting a party, the young Simon Bernstein (played by Jules Sitruk) returns home, and Batignole, out of guilt, agrees to hide the boy in the servant's quarters on the top floor. The plot then deviates from *The Two of Us* as two cousins join Simon, and Batignole takes it upon himself to leave his family and smuggle the children to safety in Switzerland. They have a couple of close brushes with capture while on the run; at one point, Batignole has to impersonate a doctor to help a German official who has dislocated his knee, and fortunately, he is able to put the joint back into place. At another moment, Batignole is arrested, after a Frenchman overhears Simon talking about Yom Kippur, and in a scene that features language that is the mirror opposite to the words uttered by Pépé in *The Two of Us,* Batignole lies about being Jewish to the French police as a way to launch an attack against antisemitism. In his harangue, he declares:

> You French are assholes, restricting us Jews? The French gave my apartment to a French couple, my furniture was seized, all I owned was stolen! I sold a small painting to get this money, apart from my kids it was the only thing of value! I'm not a butcher—I'm a doctor, a surgeon! I saved tons of idiots like you! I served in the French army to help liberate my country so that you could live freely! I lived here for 50 years, paid my taxes, the state uses my taxes to pay salaries for people like you, and this is the thanks I get! You treat me like a sub-human. Who's the sub-human here?[65]

Batignole is able to get out of the predicament after Simon creates a diversion, and after they flee the village, the group makes it to Switzerland with the help of a sympathetic priest. Rather than let the children go, Batignole chooses to stay at the end, and the audience is informed that they all remained in Switzerland until the end of the war. In addition, unlike the ending of *The Two of Us*, the film's postscript reveals that the children never found their parents.

The two French films were generally well-received by critics, and indeed, Berri won the Gandhi Award, and Simon won for Best Actor at the 1967 Berlin International Film Festival. *Monsieur Batignole* made a profit of $1.5 million at the box office, and Jean-Paul Rouve won the French Academy Award for Best Young Actor in 2002. *Me and the Colonel* fared a bit differently, garnering praise from some critics and derision from others. Kaye won a Golden Globe for his performance, and Philip Hartung gushed over Kaye's "expressive face," in his word, "the face of all the patient, lovable, long-suffering Jacobowskys."[66] Even Bosley Crowther gave a nod to Kaye, saying that "he has the skill and sensitivity to give it a lot of gentle humor and moving sympathy."[67] At the same time, other critics, like Stanley Kauffmann, writing for *The New Republic*, felt that the comedic format was inappropriate for the subject.[68]

At the heart of this tension is the challenge of offering an original and complex representation of Jews, Christians, and their relationship. If the desire is to uncover and contest antisemitism, the question is how to do this in a way that does not offend Gentiles but is still forthright enough to spark a conversation about anti-Jewish prejudice. With *Me and the Colonel,* both the character of Jacobowsky and Kaye's performance create a comfort level, although the invitation into identifying with the character involves playing to stereotypes; Jacobowsky is presented as "fawning, eager to please, [and] cowardly," but the aim is to undo these characteristics by having him become braver at the end. As Herbert Feinstein wrote in 1958 in *Film Quarterly,* Jacobowsky evolves from a "sissy Jew" to a "boxer Jew" by the end, all the while remaining true to his value about living an honorable life. The antisemitic colonel, meanwhile, becomes his friend, confirming, as Feinstein argues, the central idea of the film, which is that "under the pressure of the 'desperate situation,' the myths of stereotypes lose relevance."[69] The same dynamic operates in both *The Two of Us* and *Monsieur Batignole*. As film scholar Charlie Michael argues, French comedies have a deceptive depth of awareness about "their own relevance to a larger conversation, as they thematically and stylistically internalize the very confluence of attitudes that makes comedy such a locus of how a national industry voices its own throes of adaptation to an increasingly global cultural economy."[70]

All three films demonstrate the interplay between personal memory and culture. Both Gerard Jugnot and Claude Berri reference this on numerous occasions. For Jugnot, his family's experience during the war generated questions about bigger issues that he felt compelled to explore. He wanted to know "how I would have conducted myself during the war. Would I have closed my eyes? Opened my heart? You know what you would have done?"[71] In a 1987 interview, Berri said, "I don't think about what is more important, life or movies. . . . In all my life, I am making only one movie, and that movie is my life."[72] Four years later, he described *The Two of Us* as the most interesting of his films because, in his words, "it is my story and touches on themes that go beyond me . . ."[73] In a 1958 interview with Pete Martin for *The Saturday Evening Post*, Danny Kaye remembered being drawn to his project's message of fortitude and reconciliation as well as the immediacy of the character of Jacobowsky: "It's a radical departure for me. . . . I'm not me in the picture, and I've never played this kind of role before . . . Jacobowsky is a Jew who was born in Poland, migrated to Berlin, has lived in Paris, yet with all those migrations, and some of them were extremely hazardous, and in spite of all the persecution, he endured, he managed to stay alive."[74] At bottom, the three films are intimate pieces that aim for emotional connection in the service of wider goals, whether to shed light on antisemitism in everyday life or depict how ordinary people contested the Nazi terror.

At the same time, the films allow cinema-goers, presumably mostly Gentiles, a large degree of comfort. They enable viewers to rally behind the exception—the Gentile hero—no matter how reluctant and flawed he is in a way that may reinforce mythologies and impede a more candid reckoning with antisemitism. Batignole lays bare the pervasive Jew-hatred in France during the occupation, but he, and all the other French citizens who help, offset this, and they become the audience's focus of identification. *The Two of Us'* Pépé might be more honest, but he is also too lovable to hate, and he comes around at the end as well. There is admittedly a fine line to walk here. Cinema is not academia; it is reductionist, and its ability to present multiple realities and complex and often contradictory truths is constrained by numerous factors, chief among them, the limits of time and the desire for some kind of return at the box office. Movies are supposed to reveal a change in a character arc over two hours, and heroes are supposed to win, so both heroes and the films about them are bound to be simplistic. Anything that incorporates comedy, as these films do, risks creating an even greater cushion for audiences to avoid uncomfortable introspection.

THE WORLD OF THE CONCENTRATION CAMP:
SEVEN BEAUTIES **AND** *THE DAY THE CLOWN CRIED*

At this point, I have been discussing comedic or semi-comedic films which have contested some aspect of Nazism or life under Nazi rule, but I have not ventured into the realm of the "terror" and, specifically, the world of the prison camps. As we shall see, films about the Nazi camp system vary widely in tone and structure, but it is telling how some venture into the kind of surrealism suggested at the beginning of this article by theorists like Hayden White. One of the key determinants in this regard is whether the focus is on a prisoner of war camp or a concentration camp. Robert Clary, the French-Jewish actor who survived the Holocaust and who went on to play the French POW, LeBeau, in the 1960s television comedy series *Hogan's Heroes*, has frequently made this distinction when he responds to questions about how and why as a survivor, he could do a show making fun of a German camp. Quoting Clary: "It had nothing to do with my past. I was never a soldier. I was never a prisoner of war. I was in a concentration camp and lucky I survived, which was completely different. We were not human beings . . . and it was acting! It was a part!"[75]

It is revealing to compare Clary's language with that of Otto Preminger and Billy Wilder for his 1953 film, *Stalag 17*, which was the basis for *Hogan's Heroes*. *Stalag 17*'s conflict centers on a group of American prisoners of war who wrongly accuse the central protagonist, Sergeant J.J. Sefton, of being a spy for the Germans. For the film version, Wilder and Edwin Blum revised an earlier stage play to feature a more curmudgeonly anti-hero in Sefton, played originally with reluctance by William Holden, and a new, acerbic character in camp Commandant Colonel von Scherbach, played by Preminger. Wilder, who was born in a Polish town that had been a part of Austria-Hungary, and who was able to flee Germany and make a career in Hollywood after the Nazi takeover, demonstrates not only the tension between a career moment that had a broader connection to the Holocaust but also the difficulty in articulating that tension. In an interview with Cameron Crowe in the 1990s, Wilder claimed that he wanted "to do something better than I did the last time . . . but my life was kind of . . . except for the fact that ¾ of my family was extinguished in Auschwitz, I don't really think that."[76] In his book, Crowe editorializes that Wilder considers this the first inescapably personal question of his interview, and he keeps it at arm's length. The language in Preminger's biography reflected a more transactional pattern with references to his relationship with Wilder and the fact that he initially declined to be in the film until after he read the script, where he was drawn to lines like: "Guten Morgen sergeants. Nasty weather we're having, eh? And I so much hoped could give you a white Christmas, just like the ones you used to know . . ." and "Curtains would do wonders for the barracks. You will not get them!"[77] Preminger saw the film as a work opportunity, and he had a long track record of playing Nazis, so this was well within his wheelhouse.[78]

Other contemporary and later comedic productions about POW life have been able similarly to dissociate reality from fiction. Good examples of this are Jean Renoir's 1962 film, *The Elusive Corporal* (*Le Caporal épinglé*), based on Jacques Perret's book of his prisoner of war experiences, and the 1993 British comedy, *Stalag Luft,* about a German POW camp taken over by British soldiers who pose as Germans. In this fantasy-comedy, the British officer leading the ruse, played by Stephen Fry, actually starts to behave like his captors. Yet when it comes to the realm of the concentration camp, the representational challenges present an almost insurmountable barrier. Clearly, there were important differences between prisoner of war camps and killing centers like Auschwitz, but the conditions in German POW camps, even for Americans, involved terror, privation, death, and disease, and in one particular camp outside of Frankfurt, Stalag IX-B, over a thousand Soviet POWs died. Hundreds of American soldiers, mainly Jewish POWs, were transferred to the concentration camp at Berga, where forty-seven died. So, there is an amount of relativization going on here to allow one type of representation to be acceptable even in a comedic format, while another remains beyond the pale.

Between 1940 and 1970, there were over thirty feature films about the Nazi genocide against the Jews, eleven between 1945 and 1950, seven in the decade of the 1950s, and fifteen from the 1960s. There were also twenty-one documentaries in this same period—ten between 1945 and 1947, one in the 1950s (Alain Resnais' *Night and Fog—Nuit et Brouillard*), and ten in the 1960s. Ten of the documentaries dealt directly with the concentration camp experience or included scenes of that universe, and several of the feature films did as well. I have already mentioned Carol Reed's *Night Train to Munich,* which was the first film to set a storyline in a concentration camp; other productions that followed after the war include the Soviet film, *The Unvanquished* (1945), which was the first to depict the mass murder of Jews in German-occupied Soviet territory, Orson Welles' *The Stranger* (1946), which presented captured footage of the camps, and Wanda Jakubowska's *The Last Stage* (*Ostatni Etap*), partially filmed on location in Auschwitz. Edward Dmytryk's *Young Lions* (1958) features a subplot about the liberation of a concentration camp, and imagery of death camps punctuates Stanley Kramer's *Judgment at Nuremberg* (1961), Sidney Lumet's *The Pawnbroker* (1965), and Gillo Pontecorvo's 1960 film, *Kapo,* about a teenage Jewish girl who, along with her family, is sent to a concentration camp, and who becomes a camp foreman.

Although this list may give the impression that the concentration camp had a multi-dimensional treatment in film in the years after the war, it appears, to me, to be more fragmented and oblique—a kind of presentation that happens more in flashbacks in those who have suffered trauma and who wish to avoid it but who are unable to. The concentration camp's film "chronotope"— Bakhtin's concept of the literary use of time and space—remained diffuse and incomplete certainly well into the 1970s, and some might have thought that the world of the concentration camp was a fundamentally unrepresentable, if not unknowable space. Between the absence of a reference and the moral quandary of setting such representation in a comedy, it is remarkable that Jerry Lewis' *The Day the Clown Cried* (from 1972) and Lina Wertmüller's *Seven Beauties (Pasqualino Settebellezze)* from 1975 ever made it beyond a pitch session. Lewis' film was never completed, but Wertmüller's went on to win accolades; on Rotten Tomatoes, *Seven Beauties* currently has a seventy-one percent fresh rating among critics and an eighty-eight percent audience rating, and the film received multiple nominations for awards.[79] Vincent Canby of the *New York Times* hailed it as "Wertmüller's finest, "and Roger Ebert praised her "virtuoso style" and "mastery of filmmaking."[80] Wertmüller was the first woman nominated for an Academy Award for Best Director.

What follows is an analysis of the two films, their contexts, reference points, storylines, and tropes, and an assessment of why one is held in such high regard when the other never saw the light of day. Is this a fair comparison? One is a finished film; the other is not. One has a production sheen, overdubbed dialogue, professional sound, music, editing, while the other exists in the form of dailies—with no dialogue, music, or editing coverage. Any comparison is, from an evaluative standpoint, an "unfair fight." For this reason, I cannot reasonably pass judgment on the quality of the films, but I can analyze their texts, narrative structures, contexts, and the intentions of their creators to ascertain as best I can the reasons for the wildly divergent assessments of the films and their legacies. The two pieces may have more in common than many have argued, and they are in many respects companion pieces from a time in which filmmakers were operating in the dark when it came to representing the killing centers and concentration camps.

The plot of *The Day the Clown Cried* underwent alterations from the initial to the final shooting script, but it follows the story of Helmut Doork, a German tramp clown past his prime, who causes an accident during a performance and is to be fired from his circus troupe. At a bar, despondent and drunk, he starts mouthing off against Hitler, which leads to his arrest and incarceration in a concentration camp. Doork befriends a prisoner in the camp, a German pastor named Johann Keltner (played by Ulf Palme). Their fellow inmates relentlessly harass both, and one prisoner, Galt, is especially menacing. After the camp receives a transport of Jewish prisoners, including children, Doork is goaded into performing for them, but his act is embarrassing, and the other prisoners once again mock him, and Galt kicks mud in Doork's face, which elicits laughter from the Jewish children. Sensing that he might have his mojo back, Doork mugs for the kids, and he starts giving clandestine performances until camp officials shut him down. During a soccer match among the inmates, Doork steals away a moment to go over to the children, and he lets his guard down to do another performance, which camp officials see. The guard hits Doork, but when he gets up and pretends that it is just part of the act, another SS officer steps in and beats him with a club, and then he beats Keltner to death when he tries to intervene to save Doork. Another prisoner who charges at the officer is shot at point-blank range. As the guards carry off Doork, he remains defiant by waving back at the children and making faces and funny movements with his feet. To keep the children distracted and quiet as they are to be deported to their deaths, Doork gets to continue his interaction with children inside a boxcar. However, Doork is left in the car by accident when it departs, and he panics but then realizes that soothing the children is more important. Upon arrival at the new camp, Doork is taken to the camp's commandant, who accuses Doork of trying to escape. He gives Doork a way out of his predicament by agreeing to spare his life if he escorts the children into a building which Doork realizes is a gas chamber. He makes the choice, and one by one, he leads the kids into the building like it is another circus act. When the last girl to enter reaches for his hand, he initially hesitates, but then he has an epiphany, and he takes her hand, and in words from the script, "looks back at the sergeant and the guards and smiles a smile he hasn't exposed possibly his lifetime . . . and he enters the doorway and into the room with her."[81]

Trouble began on the production of *The Day the Clown Cried* almost from the beginning. Belgian producer Nathan Wachsberger had on option on the script by writers Joan O'Brien (who had created the John Forsythe TV show *To Rome with Love*) and Charles Denton (TV critic for *Los Angeles Examiner*). Initially, the film was to be directed in Europe by Loel Minardi, whose work at the time included the bizarre 1964 film, *Sinderella and the Golden Bra*. Wachsberger wanted Lewis for the film, however, and although the comic's initial reaction was "fear," he agreed. Shooting started in Stockholm on 5 April 1972, with a cast of Swedish actors that included Ulf Palme and Sven Lindberg and the French comedian Pierre Etaix. The problem was that Wachsberger's option had apparently expired, and then the producer went AWOL. Money ran out, Lewis shut down the production, which led Wachsberger to sue for breach of contract, and ultimately Lewis had to put his own money into the film. To make matters worse, Lewis developed an addiction to Percodan, which left the director, in the words of actor Lindberg, "not in good order." Neither O'Brien nor Denton would reissue production rights even after (or especially after) Lewis showed them scenes and pleaded with them. For O'Brien, the film was a "disaster." She objected to Lewis' sympathetic transformation of the protagonist, to whom she and Denton had originally given the name of Karl Schmidt and whom they had intended as an arrogant loser.[82]

Seven Beauties, meanwhile, opts for a narrative form that is surreal, and a protagonist, Pasqualino Settebellezze (played by Giancarlo Giannini), whose relationship with the audience is more about alienation than sympathy. The title sequence sets the tone and reveals Wertmüller's intention to comment about both past and present, with a montage of archival footage from World War II playing over the 1975 pop song from Enzo Jannucci, entitled "*Quelli che* [Those Who] and its lyrics such as: "Those who believe that Baby Jesus is Santa Claus as a young man, oh yeah! . . . Those who lose wars by the skin of their teeth . . . oh yeah . . . Those who, those who cannot believe it even now that the earth is round, oh yeah!"[83] Pasqualino bears the "Seven Beauties" moniker out of irony; he has seven homely sisters, and he fashions himself as a kind of swarthy, good-looking gangster. The family is also fatherless, and so he serves as the moral guardian to his mother and siblings. When one of his sisters, Concettina, runs afoul of Pasqualino's notion of honor by degrading herself first in a burlesque theater and then by working in a brothel with her hoodlum fiancé by the name of Totonno, Pasqualino resolves to murder his sister's lover. He has to make the killing look like self-defense, but when he sneaks into Totonno's apartment and wakes his victim up, he accidentally discharges his weapon, which results in Totonno's death. Pasqualino then opts to dismember Totonno's corpse and dispose of the remains in three suitcases, which he plans to lose in three separate cities. His plot is foiled, and following a farcical chase, the police apprehend the now-infamous "Monster of Naples." Reluctantly pleading insanity, Pasqualino is given a twelve-year sentence in a psychiatric asylum. While in transit, he meets a fellow prisoner, a socialist, who received a twenty-eight-year sentence just for thinking. Pasqualino's political indifference and tacit support for Mussolini comes through in this sequence as he says: "I rather liked him . . . he gave us great roads, created an empire . . ."[84] At the asylum, Pasqualino undergoes electroshock therapy after he rapes a female patient, and although he is discharged and put into service in the Italian army because of the support of the hospital's female doctor, who initially found him charming, Pasqualino winds up in a German concentration camp after he deserts his post. He is there with another deserter, Francesco (played by Piero Di Iorio), whom Pasqualino met while trying to evade capture in the forest. The film actually begins with the sequence of the two watching an execution of Jews at the hands of German forces. It is here that we get the essence of Pasqualino's character when he says, "what could we have done? It would have been useless suicide?" Francesco, for his part, responds that "in the face of certain things, you have got to say no, instead I said yes to Mussolini, and duty, and all that crap. . . . I kill like an idiot, for no reason." And Pasqualino says, "I killed for a woman . . ."[85]

The film then flashes back to the beginning up to the point where he kills Totonno, and it is this use of non-linear time that is one of the key distinctions between *Seven Beauties* and *The Day the Clown Cried*. Chronological time is lost, and memory becomes a device to advance a point about the evolution of Pasqualino's values. After the accidental murder of Totonno, we have a cut to the episodes of Pasqualino and Francesco to the point where they are captured, and then the first images of the concentration camp with its tableaux of naked men covered in dust and surrounded by German guards in a large warehouse-like structure. While in the concentration camp, Francesco plots rebellion, in contrast to Pasqualino, who, relying on the memory of advice about women from his mother, seeks to get out of the camp by seducing its hideous female commandant, Hilde (played by American actress Shirley Stoler). It is at this point that the audience learns about the storyline about Pasqualino's arrest and incarceration for killing and hacking up of Totonno, Pasqualino's rape of the female inmate in the asylum, and his willingness to volunteer for the army as a condition of his release. The degradation that he inflicted on other people he now has to endure himself in the camp. After scenes of sex in odd, green lighting that are at once comical and sickening, the commandant makes Pasqualino a block leader in charge of choosing six prisoners for execution. Francesco wants to be one of these prisoners, and when he rebels, the guards make Pasqualino shoot his friend, which he does again reluctantly, like his first killing, but this time, it is because Francesco asked him to do it, and so it has become an act of mercy. The camera pans up on the tableaux of prisoners shrouded in gray dust and then cuts to bombed-out buildings. Pasqualino has survived the camp but at what cost? His siblings and mother, even his love, Carolina, have become prostitutes, and all he has left is to have children, in his words, "many children, twenty, thirty. . . . It's a matter of self-defense . . . look at the crowds out there; soon, they'll be murdering each other, families slaughtered for an apple." When his mother says that it is not helpful to dwell on past miseries, that he's alive, Pasqualino, looking in a mirror to evoke a distortion, rejoins ironically, "Yes, I'm alive." [86]

Except for their foray into the world of Holocaust comedy, Lewis and Wertmüller shared little in the way of pedigree and reference points, but their careers took interesting trajectories of ebbing and flowing, and there may have been more similarities between the two, at least in this respect, than meets the eye. Lewis started as a stand-up comedian, and he became a Hollywood comic icon, doing some forty comedies like *The Nutty Professor* (1963) and *The Ladies Man* (1961) before he embarked on *The Day the Clown Cried,* After its aborted production, Lewis did not come out with another film until 1980s *Hardly Working,* which did well at the box office, but which critics hated. His pairing with Robert De Niro in Martin Scorsese's satire about fame and obsession, *The King of Comedy* (from 1983), did better with critics but poorly with audiences.[87] Lewis worked on or appeared in over a dozen films after that one, with the final production appearing in 2016, a year before his death at age ninety-one. Titled *Max Rose,* the film portrays Lewis as an aging jazz pianist. Wertmüller, for her part, had a background in theatre, had served as the assistant director on Federico Fellini's 8 ½ (1963), and was beginning to establish herself within the new wave of Italian film comedy, the *Commedia all'Italiana.* In fact, *Seven Beauties* is one of numerous comedies about sex, gender roles, and politics, which she directed in this period with Giancarlo Giannini as the star (such as *The Seduction of Mimi* [1972], *Love and Anarchy* [1973], and *Swept Away* [1974].) *Seven Beauties* also fits squarely within the trend of Italian anti-fascist porno films from the mid-70s such as Liliana Cavani's *The Night Porter* (1974) and Pier Paolo Pasolini's infamous, *Salò, or the 120 Days of Sodom* (1975). Wertmüller became such a darling of the American art film scene that Italian critics began denigrating her as "Santa Lina di New York." One critic, quoted by Darrah O'Donoghue, in a 2018 article in *Cineaste,* offered this particularly cutting review of *Swept Away*: "We have to grant one merit to Lina Wertmüller: she is consistent. Her films get worse and worse; there is a gradual progression from film to film. It would be admirable if it were not so deplorable."[88] After *Seven Beauties,* Wertmüller made a couple more films with Giannini—the romance drama *Night Full of Rain,* from 1978, starring Candice Bergen, and the thriller from the same year, *Blood Feud,* that paired Giannini with Sophia Loren. However, by the 1980s, a bit of the luster had worn off. Wertmüller continued to direct plays and films into the 2000s, yet as evidenced by her last feature film in 2004, entitled *Too Much Romance . . . It's Time for Stuffed Peppers*, starring Sophia Loren once again, there was little to compare with her reception a generation earlier. I would argue that a cursory account of the lives and work of both Lewis and Wertmüller shows that their experiences intersected, at least metaphorically, in ways beyond Holocaust filmography.

Moreover, while statements from the two about motivation reveal dissimilarities of tone and language, they also show purpose, even if that was political for Wertmüller and reverential for Lewis. The latter, who lost thirty-five pounds for the role, has been quoted as saying that the film was a way "to show we don't have to tremble and give up in the darkness. . . . [The clown] would teach us this lesson.[89] However, he was more scattershot in his co-authored memoir from 1982, at one point recounting how haunted he was by the climactic moment of *The Day the Clown Cried* ("something you don't forget"), but then adding the head-scratcher: "My bag is comedy—you're asking me if I'm prepared to deliver helpless kids into a gas chamber? Some laugh. . . . Give me some time. I just might do it . . ."[90] Thirty years later, in an interview given for an as yet unfinished autobiographical documentary, Lewis described his first encounter with the script in a way that was even more offhand: " I Just flipped though the script and said—Holy Jesus Christ—I said I'm going to make that movie. . ."[91] Wertmüller, by contrast, has been more "on message" about the purpose of humor in her films: "I love grotesque poetry, and I think my films have that style, which combines humor and drama, irony and cynicism, comedy and tragedy. . ."[92] She has gone on to say that her "first aim was to underline the background of my characters by using irony and a sense of humor in order to describe vices and defects of human beings. I've always thought that irony and humor are appropriate and effective keys to approach political topics in a film, even if your story is tragic and very serious. My grotesque stories could not exist without the combination of humor and tragedy."[93] Regarding *Seven Beauties,* she makes similar points and takes aim at the mawkish:

> Nobody has dared to portray the world of the concentration camp in a grotesque way. . . . It took a lot of courage to make this film, but also a great passion . . . the grotesque is a very visual phenomenon. In our time, the grotesque has become very rare, including irony. In our time there is a tendency to be sentimental. We live very badly in this post, post, post-romantic time.[94]

What are we to make of these decontextualized quotes? On the surface, it makes it look like Wertmüller possesses a consistency, if not an ideology, behind her body of work, whereas Lewis' statements signal a potential mismatch between subject matter and filmmaker. Although for years, Lewis remained committed to finishing the film, in 2016, a year before his death, he recognized his limitations in this regard: "I was ashamed of the work, and I was grateful for the power I had to contain it all and never let anybody see it. It was bad. Bad. Bad. It could have been wonderful, but I slipped up. I didn't quite get it. It'll never be seen . . ."[95]

Despite this admission from Lewis, neither film is as universally venerated nor condemned as one might think. Wertmüller had her fair share of detractors, from Polish-American author Jerzy Kosinski, who dubbed *Seven Beauties* a "cartoon trying to be a tragedy," to camp survivor and psychologist Bruno Bettelheim, who felt that the film "robs survivorship of all meaning. It makes seeing the film an experience that degrades."[96] And although several people who have seen dailies of *The Day the Clown Cried* have not liked it, including Joan O'Brien, comedian Harry Shearer, and the television producer of Lewis' telethon, Josh White, recent reviewers have offered more favorable perspectives.[97] French film critic Jean Michel Frodon, who saw prints of *The Day the Clown Cried* in the early 2000s, called the film "daring," and "meaningful," a film that is more than just a story about a clown during the Holocaust, but rather about a "man who has dedicated his life to making people laugh and is questioning what it is to make people laugh."[98] Frodon offered generous praise for Lewis' performance choices as well:

> [H]e is kind of at a distance to his own performance because he despises the situation. It is insulting for him to have to perform under these conditions. And then, while there is this very bizarre interaction with the prisoners, there are also the children, who are beyond the barbed wire [in another part of the camp]. And the evolution of his understanding of what he's generating for these audiences—the prisoners and the children, and also the German guards—is very interesting. For me, one of the many elements that draw such negative reaction to the film in the U.S. is that this performance is very far from what is expected from him. There is this idea in the U.S. that we know what he is supposed to do as a comedian—and that is not what he does here . . . there are very long scenes where his expression almost totally dissolves, which is very different from what he used to do in his previous films. It's as if he doesn't know how to react. And then when he starts to perform again, he's pretty much like a robot. It's a very rare style of performance for him, compared to what he used to do. Especially in his facial work.[99]

New Yorker film critic Richard Brody insists that "if these clips suggest anything of the rest of the film, any tastelessness, sentimentality, or clumsiness of Lewis' effort would be beside the point. He was working . . . in a self-inflicted state of moral shock and attempting the impossible."[100]

Paul Boussac's *Semiotics of Clowns and Clowning* and Bakhtin's ideas of the clown and grotesque in his analysis of Rabelais' *Gargantua and Pantagruel* offer further assistance in a comparative analysis of the two films. I would argue that protagonists in both are clowns; one is overtly so, and the other, Wertmüller's Pasqualino, is a clown without the make-up. Boussac outlines the main clown archetypes as the whiteface, auguste, and tramp. The former is the intelligent clown, the second is the de-stabilizer, and the third, a uniquely American variant, is always down on his luck. Lewis' Doork is a tramp clown, while Pasqualino is more of the auguste clown, and this analogy works even better when we see that in Boussac's theory, physical danger and death are ever-present with the auguste clown. Boussac sees clown acts as beginning with the disruption of the established order, and this happens in both *The Day the Clown Cried* and *Seven Beauties*, Doork's mistake causes mayhem in the circus, leading to the events that will lead to his incarceration, and Pasqualino's life comes crashing down with the accidental shooting of Totonno. For Boussac, "clown acts always hinge on a transformation of situation or status."[101] The purpose of this is to uncover through humor aspects of life that are absurd, problematic, or evil. For Bakhtin, the clown is "elected by all the people and mocked by all the people." He ridicules and suffers at the same time, and the "abuse and thrashing" which he experiences is the equivalent "to a metamorphosis."[102] The outward purpose of Lewis' clown in the film is to bring comfort to the children in an environment of death, but his performance also brings about his death, and in this irony, reveals Doork's deeper purpose, to sacrifice his happiness for others—to exist outside himself. Pasqualino, by contrast, survives his ordeal, but he is shaken and weary at the end of the film, with very little left to hold on to apart from procreation. While Doork's purpose is to substitute the other for his ego, Pasqualino's purpose is to exist beyond the film—as a critique of political cowardice, toxic masculinity, and modernity itself. Apropos of these, according to Boussac, clowns "disclose the conventionality of the laws and the taboos that sustain them," and clowns "straddle a dangerous line between the permitted and the forbidden, the moral and the immoral."[103]

Both films also engage two tropes of comedy upon which Bakhtin placed great emphasis in his book on Rabelais—that of the carnival and the grotesque. For Bakhtin, in medieval and Renaissance Europe, the folk carnival was the people's "second life," a world that represented escape and the potential for social change. The performance of the carnival was collective and earthly focused—as distinct from the sacred space of the church, even if carnivals were linked to its various feast celebrations. Carnival aimed at an exaggerated representation of the human body—the grotesque—to lower "all that is high, spiritual, ideal, abstract" and to offer an alternative read of individual and societal birth, life, and death. This meant fixing on the "lower stratum of the body, the life of the belly and the reproductive organs . . . acts of defecation and copulation, conception, pregnancy, and birth . . ."[104] In Bakhtin's mind, carnival, degradation, and the grotesque were not vulgar, but rather regenerative: "Grotesque realism knows no other lower level; it is the fruitful earth and the womb. It is always conceiving."[105] When, after his multiple performances, Doork is physically assaulted, first by fellow inmates and then by camp guards, he experiences rebirths of sorts as his final destiny becomes clearer, and this is in line with Bakhtin's contention that degradation means "contact with earth as an element that swallows up and gives birth at the same time."[106] To degrade, therefore, is to "bury, to sow, and to kill simultaneously, in order to bring forth something more and better."[107]

Carnival and the grotesque pervade *Seven Beauties,* from the burlesque show at the beginning and the dismemberment of Totonno to the scene of sex between Pasqualino and camp commandant, Hilde. Wertmüller's film is all about the world of the grotesque—a world in which, according to Bakhtin, "the body copulates, defecates, overeats, and men's speech is flooded with genitals, bellies, defecations, urine, disease, the nose, the mouth, and the cut-up corpse."[108] When Wertmüller has Pasqualino at the end of the film talk about having dozens of children, removing any other purpose to life than reproduction, she echoes discussions in Rabelais about the strength of the female genitalia, where the point is that "military power and strength are helpless against the material bodily procreative principle."[109]

Carnival's collective laughter is universal, too, which means that while the audience is intended to laugh at the images on the screen, and while, for instance, members of the audience at the burlesque laugh at Concettina, the laughter is also directed at those who laugh. The entire world, fictional and real, is the target of laughter that is both derisive and reviving.[110] The kind of laughter Wertmüller was aiming for fit within the trend of the carnival and grotesque: In her words, "We must laugh about ourselves, and other people, too, all the time, knowing that other people are also ourselves. It is a sign of great civilization because it is a sign of self-criticism, from discussion, from polemic, from the vitality that these bring to our search for a new society."[111]

Both films also advance a carnivalesque and grotesque image of hell. Bakhtin saw that "the image of the netherworld . . . affirmed earth and its lower stratum as the fertile womb, where death meets birth and a new life springs forth."[112] In *Seven Beauties,* Pasqualino's concentration camp experiences bridge sex and death, and his survival and fecund desire at the end become signifiers of what Bakhtin sees as "immortality linked with the body, with earthly life."[113] Pasqualino, the character, could identify with, if not quote directly from, Bakhtin, the theorist, when the latter writes that what interested Rabelais was "the perpetuation of human culture and of the seed, the name, the deeds of men. He is not satisfied with the static survival of the soul departing from the senile body for another world. He wants to see himself, his old age and senility, flowering in the new youth of his son, grandson, and great-grandson."[114] At the same time, Doork's multiple carnival performances—the catastrophic one at the beginning, the ones for the children in the camp, and the final march into the gas chamber—represent not only stages of the descent into hell but also empowerment. Ultimately, *The Day the Clown Cried* and *Seven Beauties* present two distinct chronotopes of the hell of the concentration camp. Wertmüller's vision operates on multiple levels and is perhaps the more relevant or immediate in form for its time because of its surrealism and emphasis on estrangement, but that does not necessarily render invalid Lewis' simpler, more naturalistic and sentimental approach. The actions of the fictional characters in both films represent a shared striving to defeat what in Bakhtin's eyes is the "extreme projection of gloomy seriousness" and to transform it into a "symbol of the defeat of fear by laughter."[115]

The Day the Clown Cried retains a particular aura of mystery, too, and part of the reason for this, I believe, lies with the unfinished nature of the work. This lends the film a kind of ur-text quality that enables it to be completed and reinvented by anyone, and some have attempted to do just that. Comic actor Patton Oswalt led readings of a pared-down version of the script until these were shut down, and an incarnation of the film consisting of dailies mixed with reconstructed scenes with new actors existed on YouTube for a while, until it, too, was blocked. All of this has added to the film's mystique, but it has also reinforced a negative bias against it. The reporting of the Oswalt readings, for instance, features familiar quotes about the film, particularly Harry Shearer's quip that it was like a "black velvet painting of Auschwitz," and even the readings themselves seemed to be mocking rather than revising.[116] There may never be a reboot or completion of the original film, and researchers may never have access to the silent dailies at the Library of Congress, yet in so many ways, its existence as a fragment is an apt parallel to the fragments of survivor memory and the challenges of imagination in a world after Auschwitz. Lewis does not get the credit that he deserves for at least attempting to break new ground, and indeed, one could argue that *Life Is Beautiful* and *Train of Life* are the beneficiaries of what Lewis started and which Wertmüller was able to finish.

Three productions in addition to *Life Is Beautiful* and *Train of Life* owe at least a partial debt to the work of Lewis and Wertmüller. They are the Brazilian clown pantomime from 2011 entitled *Holoclownsto* and the German productions *Goebbels and Geduldig* (from 2001, directed by Kai Wessel) and *My Mother's Courage* (from 1995, directed by Michael Verhoeven). Once more, we are dealing with a comparison that is not entirely symmetrical; *Holoclownsto* is a play, Wessel's film was made-for-television, and Verhoeven's was a feature film based on a theatrical production. This was by Hungarian writer George Tabori, who wrote the play about his mother, Elsa. The three productions are by and large lesser known, at least outside niche or scholarly circles, certainly lesser known than Benigni's *Life Is Beautiful,* and they again demonstrate the promise and peril of comedic portrayals of the Nazi terror system. They can each claim some positive critical appeal; *Holoclownsto* won the Latin UK Award for best theatrical production in 2013; *Goebbels and Geduldig* won a bronze medal for best screenplay and silver for best director at the 2001 New York Film Festival;[117] and *My Mother's Courage* won for outstanding feature film at the German Film Awards in 1996.[118] From the perspective of my analytical model and use of Bakhtin's ideas and the ideas of theorists like Hayden White, the three films uncover fascinating continuities to the films of Lewis and Wertmüller. For one, there is the use of the clown motif and, especially with *My Mother's Courage*, narrative disruptions, including multiple diegesis and breaks in linear time to convey unreality within reality.

The storylines of *Holoclownsto, Goebbels and Geduldig,* and *My Mother's Courage* either feature directly or intimate a clown figure whose world is thrown into chaos. In *Holoclownsto,* the six members of the Brazilian performance group, Troupp Pas D'Argent (Troupe with No Money), play tramp clowns who are being deported to their deaths. The set consists of three mobile walls which rotate and represent the exterior and interior of a cattle car and the inside of a gas chamber. While in the train car, and through silent pantomime, the clowns commiserate, commune, and quarrel; the space might be of a particular time, but what the scenarios reveal about human relationships is intended as universal. At the end of the play, when one clown is murdered by a guard and the rest of the clowns are gassed, the message of needing to be there for one another before we die comes through, although I am ambivalent about the scene, which admittedly I only was able to view on YouTube, and I might have experienced it differently in the setting of a theater.

A different truism about fate comes through in *Goebbels and Geduldig,* which screenwriter Peter Steinbach and director Kai Wessel conceived as an ironic morality play whose text could stimulate new conversations about the Third Reich among ordinary Germans.[119] Ulrich Mühe, who would go on to feature in the comedy-drama, *Mein Führer,* six years later, stars in the double roles of Joseph Goebbels and the fictional "clown," Harry Geduldig, a Jewish lookalike of the Nazi Propaganda Minister, who is unaware of the existence of his *Doppelgänger.* Once Goebbels finds out about Geduldig, however, he intends to murder him, but when the two meet in the prison ward, Geduldig engineers his escape, and he spends the rest of the film pretending to be Goebbels, while the latter languishes in jail, trying fruitlessly to convince everyone that his impostor is on the loose. Throughout his misadventures, Geduldig meets Hitler and Eva Braun (played by Katja Riemann, who would feature in the satire, *Look Who's* Back), and he is revealed as a fake after a successful evening of lovemaking with his wife, Magda. More importantly, he guides his real love interest to safety out of the country before being blown up in an assassination attempt of the real Goebbels. For me, the film evoked another German film, *Genghis Cohn* (from 1993), which deals with a more supernatural tale of revenge by a Jew against a Nazi. But the clown connection is clear, although unlike the tramps of *Holoclownsto,* Geduldig's character is more of an auguste clown who disrupts his imaginary world and exacts retribution. Even his demise at the end suggests agency, and the "living death" that Goebbels must endure at his hand—denied his identity and regarded as insane for the rest of his life, becomes the metaphorical fate worse than death.

In *My Mother's Courage,* writer George Tabori pays homage to Bertolt Brecht's 1939 production, *Mutter Courage und ihre Kinder* (*Mother Courage and Her Children*), but he and director Michael Verhoeven create a sweeter analog to both Brecht's play and *Seven Beauties,* retaining the edifice of fantasy, but offering a more likable protagonist in Tabori's mother, Elsa, played in the film by British actress Pauline Collins, and a much happier ending than either Wertmüller's film or Brecht's play, where the mother, a war profiteer, loses her children. Tabori's story is based on his mother's account of how she was arrested off the streets of Budapest in the summer of 1944, put on a train to Auschwitz, and managed to escape by convincing an SS guard that she had a protective Red Cross pass. The story is almost too unbelievable to be true, and Tabori has only added to its inscrutability by confessing to inserting, in his words, "some lies."[120] The tale, which "oscillates between the fictitious, the forged, the lie, and the truth, which 'is always pain,'" defamiliarizes us and our expectations of a realistic portrayal.[121] For Tabori, the production is less about history but rather how memories are created, retrieved, and expressed. Verhoeven, director of other films about historical memory and the Reich, notably *The Nasty Girl* (*Das schreckliche Mädchen*, from 1990, which we will explore in chapter 5), conveys a similar impression. To him, *My Mother's Courage* is a reflection—a performance—because "dimensions of this horror, of this truth, are so unimaginable" they cannot ever be truthfully reproduced.[122] Hence, Tabori makes multiple appearances in the film and breaks the "fourth wall," and there are juxtapositions of chronotope—from Budapest 1944 to Berlin in the 1990s.

Here again, the clown analogy and references to the grotesque are appropriate. In the beginning sequence, Elsa is arrested by two dimwitted, retired police officers with health problems who have to take her to the train station by tram. As the three try to push onto the moving vehicle, only Elsa is able to make it on board, and as the tram pulls away, the two cops yell at her to wait at the next stop, which she does. They are the auguste clowns to her "whiteface." The line-up at the train station and then the sequences aboard the train itself are both comic and grotesque. They feature Hungarian fascists of the Arrow Cross flinging purses, an orthodox Jew stealing the hat from another Jew because he has lost his hat, another man who is worried that he will not be able to return a library book, and another who has to go to the bathroom. Again, it would be too "on-the-nose-fantastic" if it were not so real, which is, of course, Tabori and Verhoeven's point: the story must be "deliberately theatrical: [in their eyes], everybody knows every moment in this film that it is only art, this is acting, nobody is suffering."[123] When the SS officer, for an unknown reason, agrees to take Elsa into his car and allows her to escape, he first recounts the story of how Christians from his village killed a Jewish tailor and then served his body and blood during mass, which is a major tonal shift in the film beyond the grotesque to the sickening, and then chronological time comes undone again as Elsa gets off the train and she exits a Berlin train station in the 1990s. The film's chronotope switches back to Budapest in 1944, and the tone becomes comical again as she makes it back to her sister's flat. Her family wonders where she has been all day and takes her to task for holding up their card game. As in all clown tales, the "whiteface's" disrupted world returns to normal—except that another disruption is inevitable, and in this case, it is the tragic reality that only Elsa will survive the war. Her sister, Martha, and the bulk of the Tabori family were murdered during the German occupation of Hungary. Therefore, what Tabori did in *My Mother's Courage* was to use an individual story as an intertext to create a new framework and language for exploring the Holocaust.

CONCLUSION

This chapter has covered a vast expanse of time and media representation of what Claude Lanzmann believed was the essence of the *Shoah*—"death itself," and it parallels Lanzmann's belief that what he had done in his documentary was to make "a fiction of the real."[124] He claims he did so to make the "unbearable bearable," and as we have seen, this basic motivation undergirds several of the comedic productions that we have so far encountered. There is a vast body of comedic performance that has offered commentary on the Nazi terror, in many ways a broadening of the Hitler satires we explored in chapter 2, with all the accompanying perils of relativization and normalization. The desire to comedically neuter or render ridiculous both Hitler and the Nazis runs almost essentially on the same track. Moving beyond that subject into the realm of antisemitism and the concentration camps is where we see the greatest challenge to performance and the greatest chasm between vision and vocabulary. Productions on the subject of the actual genocide—the mass murder—attempt the near-impossible. They seek a textual approach through a genre that many perceive as inappropriate and distasteful, and the earliest filmmakers who made an effort in this regard operated in a time not even a generation removed from the genocide, a time in which existing texts and reference points were both raw and fragmentary. It is striking that any films about this particular aspect of the Holocaust have been made at all, and not surprising that one, Jerry Lewis' *Day the Clown Cried*, remains unfinished—a testament to this difficult, if not virtually unachievable task.

NOTES

1. Alexander Alvarez, "The Literature of the Holocaust," *Commentary*, 38 (1964): 66.

2. Hayden White, "The Modernist Event," 69 and Susannah Radstone, "Cinema and Memory," in *Memory: Histories, Theories, and Debates,* ed. Susannah Radstone and Bill Schwarz (New York: Fordham University Press, 2014), 332.

3. Eli Pfefferkorn, "The Art of Survival: Romain Gary's *The Dance of Genghis Cohn,*" 77, 84.

4. Janet Walker, "The Vicissitudes of Traumatic Memory and the Postmodern History Film," in *Trauma and Cinema: Cross-Cultural Explorations,* ed. E. Ann Kaplan and Ban Wang (Hong Kong: Hong Kong University Press, 2004), 124.

5. Joshua Hirsch, "Post-Traumatic Cinema and the Holocaust Documentary," in *Trauma and Cinema,* 101.

6. See Mikhail Bakhtin, *Rabelais and His World* (trans. Bloomington, IN: Indiana University Press, 1984).

7. George Raft and Olivia de Havilland were originally sought after for the roles of Gloves and Leda Hamilton, but Raft did not like the character and de Havilland was busy on another film with Paramount, *Hold Back the Dawn.* See Stephen Youngkin, *The Lost One: A Life of Peter Lorre* (Lexington, KY: University of Kentucky Press, 2005), 524.

8. Although producer Hall Wallis wanted to cut out the double-talk, test audiences liked it, and so he kept the dialogue. Another point of drama behind the scenes involved Conrad Veidt, who, after being confronted with quick script changes said to director Sherman, "You are a terrible man. I don't think I'll ever work with you again." See Vincent Sherman, *Studio Affairs: My Life as a Film Director* (Lexington, KY: University of Kentucky Press, 1996), 103, 104.

9. Wes Gehring, *Leo McCarey: From Marx to McCarthy* (Lanham, MD: Scarecrow Press, 2005), 178.

10. Tragically, and for reasons that were unrelated to his assignment, Finkelstein committed suicide in 1940. "Captain of Police, Accused, Ends Life," *New York Times,* 4 May 1940, 32.

11. Preminger would further assert that he was not "really as horrible as all these stories make [him] out to be. They probably came from the fact that [he] played some Nazis." Gerald Pratley, *The Cinema of Otto Preminger* (New York: Castle Books, 1971), 33, 50

12. Clare Boothe Luce, *Margin for Error: A Satirical Melodrama* (New York: Random House, 1940), 55.

13. Preminger's first Nazi role was as Major Diessen in the 1942 drama, *The Pied Piper.*

14. Chris Fujiwara, *The World and Its Double, The Life and Work of Otto Preminger* (New York: Farrar, Straus, and Giroux, 2008), 46

15. Scott MacGillivray, *Laurel and Hardy from the Forties Forward* (Bloomington, IN: iUniverse, 2009), 76, 84.

16. John Bodnar, "*Saving Private Ryan* and Postwar Memory in America," *The American Historical Review,* Vol. 106, No. 3 (June 2001): 806.

17. *Margin for Error,* DVD, directed by Otto Preminger (Los Angeles, CA: Twentieth Century Fox, 1943).

18. Gehring, *Leo McCarey,* 176.

19. See "Nazis to Hold 5000 in Camp at Dachau," *New York Times*, 5 April 1933, 10.

20. *Once Upon a Honeymoon,* DVD, directed by Leo McCarey (Los Angeles, CA: RKO Pictures, 1942).

21. *Once Upon a Honeymoon,*

22. Henry Luce, "Introduction," in Clare Boothe Luce, *Margin for Error: A Satirical Melodrama,* vii–xx.

23. Gehring, *Leo McCarey,* 176.

24. Sherman, *Studio Affairs,* 98.

25. Charles River Editors, *Laurel and Hardy and Abbott and Costello: America's Most Popular Comedy Duos* (Scotts Valley, CA: Create Space, 2014), Kindle Edition, location 508.

26. See https://www.rottentomatoes.com/m/all_through_the_night, accessed 10 October 2020.

27. Bosley Crowther, "The Screen: *All Through the Night* Action Film About Gangsters and Nazi Spies, With Humphrey Bogart, Opens at the Strand," *New York Times,* 24 January 1942, 13.

28. See Warner Brothers' financial report in The William Shaefer Ledger, from Appendix 1, *Historical Journal of Film, Radio and Television* (1995), 15.

29. https://www.rottentomatoes.com/m/margin-for-error, accessed 10 October 2020.

30. Foster Hirsch, *Otto Preminger: The Man Who Would Be King* (New York: Knopf, 2007), Kindle Edition, location 1635.

31. MacGillivray, *Laurel and Hardy from the Forties Forward,* 84.

32. https://www.rottentomatoes.com/m/air_raid_wardens, accessed 10 October 2020.

33. Simon Louvish, *Stan and Ollie: The Roots of Comedy: The Double Life of Laurel and Hardy* (New York: Thomas Dunne, 2002), 408.

34. See Richard B. Jewell, *Slow Fade to Black: The Decline of RKO Radio Pictures* (Berkeley, CA: University of California Press, 2016), 11, 17.

35. https://www.rottentomatoes.com/m/once_upon_a_honeymoon, and https://www.rottentomatoes.com/m/they_got_me_covered, both accessed 10 October 2020.

36. Bosley Crowther, "*They Got Me Covered*, With Dorothy Lamour and Bob Hope Starred in Spy-Comedy, Arrives at the Music Hall," *New York Times,* 5 March 1943, 20.

37. https://www.rottentomatoes.com/m/they_got_me_covered, accessed 10 October 2020.

38. *Hollywood Reporter,* 2 November 1942, 3, and *Variety,* 4 November 1942.

39. See the *New York Daily News,* 13 November 1942, 52, and Crowther, "*Once Upon a Honeymoon,* With Ginger Rogers, Cary Grant, Opens at Music Hall," 13 November 1942, 28. Philip Hartung, writing for *Commonweal,* echoed Crowther's sentiment: " . . . it is the underlying note of tragedy that makes the light-hearted humor seem too irresponsible." *Commonweal,* 4 December 1942, 177.

40. Theodore Strauss, "The Screen: Where Hilarity Reigns," *The New York Times,* 5 April 1943, 15.

41. Theodore Strauss, "*Margin for Error*, With Joan Bennett and Milton Berle, Opens at Globe—*Lucky Jordan* at Rialto," *The New York Times,* 25 January 1943, 10.

42. Kevin Flanagan makes clear that the drop in comedies was not just a phenomenon of Hollywood. As he notes, war comedies in Britain also all but disappeared for a decade after the war. He sees the film *Private's Progress,* from 1956, about the misadventures of a British conscript, as the beginning of the reappearance of comedies about World War II. Flanagan, "The British War Film, 1939–1980: Culture, History, and Genre," 111.

43. Agee went further to say the it was "unnecessary to urge anyone who has ever enjoyed them [the Marx Brothers] to see *A Night in Casablanca,*" *The Nation,* May 1946, 636; See Thomas M. Pryor, "The Screen; *A Night in Casablanca,* With Marx Brothers, at Globe—*Our Hearts Were Growing Up* and *Sirocco* Also Arrive," *New York Times,* 12 August 1946, 17. For his part Philip Hartung had a more positive review of the film: "If you like 'em, the Marxes are better than an apple a day," *Commonweal,* 15 June 1946, 217.

44. Bosley Crowther, "Comedian Runs Wild in *On the Double,*" *New York Times,* 20 May 1961, 12.

45. See https://www.rottentomatoes.com/m/night_in_casablanca, accessed 24 October 2020.

46. See, https://www.rottentomatoes.com/m/on-the-double, accessed 24 October 2020.

47. Koestenbaum writes, "I will lean on the Nazi theme; Harpo leans on it, too. Harpo was a comic genius before the Third Reich came along, but the Third Reich gave Harpo's anarchy extra pointedness." See *The Jewish Standard,* 28 June 2013, and the chapter in his book, "The Bubble-Blowing Demarcator Tickles Totality: *A Night in Casablanca,*" in Koestenbaum, *The Anatomy of Harpo Marx* (Berkeley, CA: University of California Press, 2012), 184, 188.

48. Martin Gardner, *The Marx Brothers as Social Critics: Satire and Comic Nihilism in Their Films* (Jefferson, NC: McFarland, 2009), 158. See also Simon Louvish, *Monkey Business: The Lives and Legends of the Marx Brothers* (New York: Thomas Dunne Books, 2000)

49. Melville Shavelson, *How to Succeed in Hollywood Without Really Trying. P.S. You Can't* (Los Angeles: MGM Studios, 1974), 83. David Koenig, *Danny Kaye: King of Jesters* (Irvine, CA: Bonaventure Press, 2012), Martin Gottfried, *Nobody's Fool—The Lives of Danny Kaye* (New York: Simon & Schuster, 1994), 241, and https://www.historynet.com/the-full-monty.htm, accessed 24 October 2020.

50. Sperber and Wilson, *Relevance,* 265.

51. Thomas J. Fitzmorris, "Review of *Night in Casablanca,*" *America,* 4 May 1946, 102.

52. Howard Thompson, "Film: Jerry Lewis at War: *Which Way to Front?* on Local Screens," *New York Times,* 5 September 1970, 10.

53. Leonard Maltin, *Leonard Maltin's Movie Guide* (New York City & London: Plume, 2008), 1533.

54. *The Blues Brothers,* DVD, directed by John Landis (Los Angeles, CA: Universal Studios, 1980).

55. David Koenig, *Danny Kaye-King of Jesters,* 186.

56. Peter Stephan Jungk, *Franz Werfel: A Life in Prague, Vienna, and Hollywood* (New York: Fromm International, 1991), 206.

57. S.N. Behrman, *Jacobowsky and the Colonel* (New York: Random House, 1944), viii.

58. Jungk, *Franz Werfel*, 210.

59. Jungk, *Franz Werfel*, 212–217.

60. See Charlie Michael, *Cultural Politics of a Transnational Cinema* (Edinburgh: Edinburgh University Press, 2009), 181.

61. *The Two of Us* (Le vieil homme et l'enfant), DVD, directed by Claude Berri (Paris: Valoria, 1967), 51:56.

62. *The Two of Us*, 53:44–54:07.

63. *The Two of Us*, 1:25:18–1:25:48.

64. Interview with Gérard Jugnot by Denis Rodi, 31 October 2002, https://www.cineman.ch/fr/interview/jugnot-gerard/41/, accessed 21 November 2020.

65. *Monsieur Batignole*, DVD, directed by Gérard Jugnot (Paris: RF2K Productions, 2002), 1:28.

66. Philip Hartung, "*Me and the Colonel*," *The Commonweal*, 19 September 1958, 616.

67. Bosley Crowther, "Danny Kaye and the Colonel: *Jacobowsky* is Star's Latest Surprise Adaptation of Stage Hit, Has Dual Premiere," *New York Times*, 27 August 1958, 33.

68. Stanley Kauffmann, "Funny?" *The New Republic*, 13 October 1958, 21.

69. Herbert Feinstein, "*Me and the Colonel*," *Film Quarterly*, Vol. 12, No. 2 (Winter 1958): 51–53.

70. Michael, *Cultural Politics*, 209.

71. Interview with Gérard Jugnot by Denis Rodi.

72. As cited by David Sterritt, "*The Two of Us:* War and Peace," *The Criterion Collection*, 11 June 2007, https://www.criterion.com/current/posts/585-the-two-of-us-war-and-peace, accessed 21 November 2020.

73. Interview with Claude Berri by M. Burviana, *Sequences*, Vol. 152 (June 1991): 34, 35.

74. Pete Martin, "I Call on Danny Kaye," *Saturday Evening Post*, 9 August 1958, 56. See also David Koenig, *Danny Kaye*, 187, and Martin Gottfried, *Nobody's Fool*, 235.

75. See *Robert Clary, A-5714 A Memoir of Liberation*, DVD, directed by Budd Margolis (Kent, Ohio: Kent State University Productions, 1984), and Robert Clary interview on Televisionacademy.com Interviews, https://www.youtube.com/watch?v=IvJl2u-z8zs.

76. Cameron Crowe, *Conversations with Billy Wilder* (New York: Knopf, 1999), 20. Journalist David Denby wrote in a 1990 essay that Wilder's interest in the film lay in "proving the essential rightness of the realist who sees through everything." Denby, "Always Making Wisecrackers," *Premiere*, 4 November 1990, 48, 49. See also, Ed Sikov, *On Sunset Boulevard: The Life and Times of Billy Wilder* (New York: Hyperion, 1998), 341.

77. See Sikov, *On Sunset Boulevard*, 342.

78. Foster Hirsch, *Otto Preminger: The Man Who Would Be King* (New York: Knopf, 2007), Kindle Version, location 3363.

79. https://www.rottentomatoes.com/m/seven_beauties, accessed 16 December 2020.

80. Vincent Canby, "*Seven Beauties*, Wertmuller's Finest," *New York Times,* 22 January 1976, 41, and Roger Ebert, "Review of *Seven Beauties,*" 16 April 1976, https://www.rogerebert.com/reviews/seven-beauties-1976, accessed 16 December 2020.

81. Jerry Lewis, *The Day the Clown Cried,* "Final Shooting Script," March 1972, 108.

82. See especially Bruce Handy, "Jerry Goes to Death Camp!" *Spy Magazine,* May 1992, 40, 42, 44.

83. Enzo Jannucci, "Quelli Che," track #2, *Quelli Che . . . ,* Impala/RCA, 1975, CD.

84. *Seven Beauties* directed by Lina Wertmüller. Rome: Medusa Distribuzione 1975, DVD, 1:14:22.

85. *Seven Beauties,* 09:20.

86. *Seven Beauties,* 1:54:41.

87. *King of Comedy's* critical reception has increased with time. Roger Ebert's review from 1983 captured the feeling about the film: It is "frustrating to watch, unpleasant to remember, and, in its own way, quite effective." https://www.rogerebert.com/reviews/the-king-of-comedy-1983, accessed 24 December 2020.

88. Darragh O'Donoghue, *"Laughter in the Dark: The Black Comedy of Lina Wertmüller,"* Cinéaste, 22 September 2018, 15

89. Handey, "Jerry Goes to Death Camp," 42.

90. Jerry Lewis and Herb Gluck, *Jerry Lewis in Person* (New York: Athenaeum, 1982), 279, 280. Lewis' language is even more problematic in Shawn Levy's, *King of Comedy: The Life and Art of Jerry Lewis* (New York: St. Martin's, 1991), 379, 380: He quotes Lewis as saying that he was "terrified of directing the last scene. I had been 113 days on the picture, with only three hours of sleep a night. I had been without my family. I was exhausted, beaten. When I thought of doing that scene, I was paralyzed." A page later, Lewis is quoted as calling out an assistant and an extra. Apparently, he became particularly upset at a young Swedish girl who looked into the camera—"There's the little cunt . . . watch her eyes. There. See it? Fucking following the camera. . . . I told her to keep her fucking eyes to the front. That it wasn't a beauty pageant!"

91. https://www.youtube.com/watch?v=Y2CdfppsqKQ, interview with Jerry Lewis for tracesfilms projects, November 2012, accessed 20 December 2020.

92. https://www.criterion.com/current/posts/4498-grotesque-poetry-a-conversation-with-lina-wertm-ller, Hillary Weston, "Grotesque Poetry: A Conversation with Lina Wertmüller," 12 April 2017, Criterion Collection, accessed 20 December 2020.

93. https://www.rogerebert.com/interviews/screw-the-rich-checking-in-with-lina-wertmuller, Charles Bramesco, "Screw the Rich: Checking in with Lina Wertmüller," 13 April 2017, accessed 20 December 2020. See also the interviews of Wertmüller in Wolfgang Jacobsen, et al., *Lina Wertmüller* (Munich: Carl Hanser Verlag, 1988).

94. She adds a personal dimension as well to her choice of theme: "That I deal so intensively with camps, Nazis and fascists has its roots elsewhere. I was in the middle of puberty when I first heard about the concentration camps and their function. That was a shock from which a sensitive person cannot really recover. Even today, I have not got out of the vicious circle that plagues my imagination in this regard." Wertmüller as quoted in Wolfgang Jacobsen, et al., *Lina Wertmüller*, 42, 63.

95. Lewis' statements about the fate of the film have changed over time: In 1982 he said, "I can release [the film] 10 years from now, and it will hold up. One way or another, I'll get it done. The picture must be seen." See Gluck and Lewis, *Jerry Lewis*, 283. He echoed this sentiment in 2012, insisting that "You had to not run from it, but I did run from it—to do it correctly—you need about 30 hours from me. . . . I know I've got 30 hours in me . . ." https://www.youtube.com/watch?v=Y2CdfppsqKQ But in 2016, his position had changed, and he seemed to internalize the views of some of his harshest critics: https://www.youtube.com/watch?v=jbZIyXNRxos, "Story of Day the Clown Cried—BBC South Today," 4 January 2016, accessed 20 December 2020.

96. Jerzy Kosinski, "*Seven Beauties*—A Cartoon Trying to Be a Tragedy," *New York Times*, 7 March 1976, Section D, 1, and Bruno Bettelheim, "Surviving," *New Yorker*, 2 August 1976, 31. See also, Ralph Tutt, "*Seven Beauties* and the Beast: Bettelheim, Wertmüller, and the Uses of Enchantment," *Literature/Film Quarterly*, Vol. 17, No. 3 (1989): 193–201.

97. Handy, "Jerry Goes to Death Camp," 42, 43, 44.

98. Bruce Handy, "The French Film Critic Who Saw Jerry Lewis' Infamous Holocaust Movie and Loved It," *Vanity Fair*, 21 August 2017, https://www.vanityfair.com/hollywood/2017/08/jerry-lewis-day-the-clown-cried-holocaust-movie-review, accessed 21 December 2020.

99. Handy, "The French Film Critic."

100. Richard Brody, "A Glimpse of *The Day the Clown Cried*," *New Yorker*, 13 August 2013, https://www.newyorker.com/culture/richard-brody/a-glimpse-of-the-day-the-clown-cried, accessed 21 December 2020. Even film legend Jean Luc Godard praised Lewis and the concept of the film in a 1980 interview with Dick Cavett. See the interview at the 20:55 mark, https://www.youtube.com/watch?v=xsfAnCwxYFA, accessed 21 December 2020.

101. Paul Boussac, *The Semiotics of Clowns and Clowning: Rituals of Transgression and the Theory of Laughter* (London: Bloomsbury, Academic), 174.

102. Mikhail Bakhtin, *Rabelais and His World*, trans. Helene Iswolsky (Bloomington, IN: Indiana University Press, 1984), 197.

103. Boussac, *The Semiotics of Clowns*, 174, 178, 180.

104. Bakhtin, *Rabelais and His World*, 18–19, 21.

105. Bakhtin, *Rabelais and His World*, 21.

106. Bakhtin, *Rabelais and His World*, 21.

107. Bakhtin, *Rabelais and His World*, 21.

108. Bakhtin, *Rabelais and His World*, 319.

109. Bakhtin, *Rabelais and His World*, 312. The discussion of the strength of female genitalia comes from Rabelais, *Gargantua and Pantagruel*, Book Two, Chapter Fifteen.

110. Bakhtin, *Rabelais and His World*, 11.

111. Quoted in Peter Biskind, "Interview with Lina Wertmüller," in *Women and the Cinema*, ed. Karyn Kay and Gerald Peary (New York: Dutton, 1976), 330, and Josette Déléas, "Lina Wertmüller: The Grotesque in *Seven Beauties*," in *Women Filmmakers: Refocusing*, ed. Jacqueline Levitin, Judith Plessis, and Valerie Raoul (London: Routledge, 2003), 161.

112. Bakhtin, *Rabelais and His World*, 394.

113. Bakhtin, *Rabelais and His World*, 405.

114. Bakhtin, *Rabelais and His World*, 405.

115. Bakhtin, *Rabelais and His World*, 395.

116. Patton Oswalt, "Patton Oswalt On the Time He Enlisted Bob Odenkirk and David Cross to Perform Jerry Lewis's Holocaust Clown Screenplay," *Vulture*, 15 December 2014, https://www.vulture.com/2014/12/patton-oswalt-the-day-the-clown-didnt-cry-jerry-lewis.html, accessed 22 December 2020.

117. Some German critics found the film "unfunny" and thought that it should have taken more risks. Mark Landler, writing for *New York Times*, described the film as "leaden." See, Landler, "The All-Too-Human Hitler, on Your Big Screen," *New York Times*, 15 September 2004, https://www.nytimes.com/2004/09/15/world/europe/the-alltoohuman-hitler-on-your-big-screen.html, accessed 28 December 2020. See also, Tony Czuczka, "Germany's First Satirical Film on Nazis Earns Poor Reviews," *Pittsburgh Post-Gazette*, 30 November 2002, 32, https://news.google.com/newspapers?nid=1129&dat=20021130&id=6CQxAAAAIBAJ&sjid=u3ADAAAAIBAJ&pg=2173,7702629, accessed 28 December 2020.

118. *My Mother's Courage* garnered much praise among US critics: J. Hoberman, for the *Village Voice*, said: *My Mother's Courage* shows that blue skies and sunshine can be as devastating as night and fog." And Stanley Kaufmann, for the *New Republic*, declared that this was "a film about the Holocaust that, after the few memorable films on the subject and the flood of lesser ones, [that] needs to be seen." See http://www.jewishfilm.org/Catalogue/films/mymotherscourage.htm, accessed 28 December 2020.

119. See the interview with Steinbach in, "German Comedy About Nazis: A Breakthrough or Tasteless?" Jewish Telegraphic Agency, 22 November 2002, https://www.jta.org/2002/11/22/archive/arts-culture-german-comedy-about-nazis-a-breakthrough-or-tasteless, accessed 24 December 2020; and Jochen Müller, "Interview mit Kai Wessel zu *Goebbels und Geduldig*," *Blickpunkt: Film*, 20 November 2002, https://beta.blickpunktfilm.de/details/124559, accessed 24 December 2020.

120. Anat Feinberg, *Embodied Memory: The Theatre of George Tabori* (Iowa City, IA: University of Iowa Press, 1999), 226.

121. Feinberg, *Embodied Memory*, 235.

122. As quoted in Annette Innsdorf, "The Moral Minefield That Won't Go Away," *New York Times*, 31 August 1997, Section 2, Page 9.

123. Hans-Bernhard Moeller, "Bridges between New German Cinema and Today's Generation of Political Filmmakers: An Interview with Michael Verhoeven," *Journal of Film and Video*, Vol. 62 (Spring/Summer 2010): 7.

124. Lanzmann as quoted in Daniel Lewis, "Claude Lanzmann, Epic Chronicler of the Holocaust, Dies at 92," *New York Times,* 5 July 2018, https://www.nytimes.com/2018/07/05/obituaries/claude-lanzmann-dead.html, accessed 4 January 2020.

Chapter 4

Memory, Trauma, and Comedy

In this chapter, I examine films and television productions that take place primarily in the postwar era and that deal with how the Third Reich, World War II, and the Holocaust are remembered. We have already seen how Hitler and his reign of terror generate memories that have become reference points for satire and how this satire can be aimed at both past and present. We have also seen how Holocaust memory has been applied in comedic contexts—again to serve the purpose of survivor healing, and we have encountered the limitations of language and genre in this regard, where the utilization of fantastic narratives has been an uneven strategy to bridge the gap between the desire to tell a story in a particular way and the difficulties of doing so. A focus on memory can be just as problematic, but what we encountered in the first chapter with a film like *Everything Is Illuminated* is an example of a production that is able to thread the needle of being light-hearted and funny in parts while enabling darker truths to emerge.

As Oren Baruch Stier aptly states in the opening paragraph of his 2003 manuscript, "memory matters."[1] It is undeniable that in the past generation, the interest in memory as both an academic pursuit and element of popular culture has become nearly ubiquitous. In Stier's words, "Turn on the television, open a newspaper or magazine, and you will likely find, before too long, some mention of the impact the past has made and continues to make on the present."[2] A useful complement to Stier's work is Iwona Irwin-Zarecka's book from 1994, *Frames of Remembrance,* in which she points to the power of traumatic and tragic experiences which, "by their very nature engender a great deal of memory work, both on the part of those who were there and those concerned with securing remembrance."[3] Memory work as history, therapy, and identity has thus become deeply embedded in our diverse social and cultural landscapes. The proliferation of Holocaust memorials and museums since the 1990s, with the loss of survivors and eyewitnesses, confirms this trend on a specific level. The discussion here will involve how comedic films and television shows can shed light on the multiple aspects and uses of memory and remembrance. I will investigate comic representations of both collective and individual memory and the ways in which memory, in this case, humorous memories, can be used to construct identity, impact citizenship, serve the cause of retribution, or address survivor trauma. Multiple analytical models exist to help with such an investigation, and I will apply them where relevant.

Both Stier and Zarecka owe much of their theorizing to French sociologist Emile Durkheim and his student, Maurice Halbwachs. Writing at the beginning of the 20th Century, Durkheim argued that each society uses the past to create social cohesion and identity—a collective consciousness, and Halbwachs took that further to develop the notion of collective memory, a body of thoughts and remembrances about the past, reinforced by institutional rites of commemoration, that serve the purpose of social continuity. Individual and group memories are conditioned by an engagement with other individuals, texts, rituals, and memorial sites. This engagement creates an imagined past that reflects and shapes the values of the present.[4] Scholars have refined Halbwach's theories over the past twenty years by adding processes of forgetting, revising, and reworking memory over time, and some, like James Young, prefer the concept of "collected" rather than collective memory, where memories are "gathered into common memorial spaces and assigned common meaning,"[5] but the conclusion of Durkheim and Halbwachs, that memory is a social phenomenon, remains well agreed upon. Sites of Holocaust memory, and memories of the war in general, whether they are museums, memorials, or monuments, emerge, to quote Oren Stier, "at points of rupture in order to counteract forgetfulness."[6]

In this chapter, I argue that film is an equally important medium for, and generator of, collective memory, and by extension, collective identity. Through cinema's visual sharing and processing, in the words of Irwin-Zarecka, "a community of memory is created . . ."[7] People begin to "feel a sense of bonding with others solely because of a shared experience."[8] Films play a role in constructing one's individual and collective sense of self-belonging and membership in one's culture. They are often one's first and, occasionally, only window into what it means to be a member of a particular national community. Films use collective memory to delineate heroes and villains, to reinforce to the "home" audiences that they are the "good guys." We see in the evolution of World War II films how historical experience has impacted the representation of national origins; while Germans and Japanese remain villains, and Americans, Russians, the British, and the French, are heroes, this general framework has never been static or uncontested, and it has gone through multiple eras of revision. Regarding Holocaust memory, as a "universal moral touchstone," in the words of sociologist David Inglis, it too reinforces and mirrors national solidarity and has been subject to modification and abuse.⁹ As I have laid out since my introduction, we are living through an era of an inversion and of anxiety about this inversion—wherein victims are often presented as perpetrators and vice versa, and comedy has been a part of this phenomenon.

The comedic films I analyze at the beginning of this chapter come from different national contexts, and they use, to varying degrees, Holocaust memory and the memories of World War II in the services of diverse national imaginations. American films incorporate tropes that speak to common memories about the war that are distinct from tropes used in French, Italian, German, and British films. This is interesting from the perspective of an international comparison and also from a historical exploration of how memories evolve. Irwin-Zarecka argues that "while the passage of time makes dealing with the past easier in that one is no longer compelled to question one's own parents, the presence of that past becomes a great deal more pronounced, more widespread, as it were. The moral challenge, too, addresses itself, albeit in different forms, to a great deal more people."¹⁰ War films are closely tied to concepts like heroism, patriotism, and even basic ideas of citizenship, and we will see how these have been subjected to revision and reinvention, with results that have often destabilized a collective consensus.

The other aspect of memory, the individual-psychological dimension dealing with trauma, also has a body of theory and literature that will help to guide my analysis. Scholars such as Lawrence Langer and Joshua Hirsch have addressed different aspects of trauma, whether it is in relation to survivor memory (for Langer) or film (for Hirsch), and their research has helped to shed light on both psychology and history—on the actual trauma and the processes by which survivors have attempted to confront their trauma—so much so that the idea of using their analyses in a discussion of comedy might seem inapposite. I would argue, however, that there is great relevance to their work on a project dealing with comedy and Holocaust, given that comedy is one tactic for engaging all manner of trauma. In films and survivor testimonies about the Holocaust, trauma can come through in both the narrative itself and the form of that narrative. Langer, in his pathbreaking book *Holocaust Testimonies,* created archetypes of memory to help readers delineate the language of survivors. These archetypes included—"Deep Memory," where survivors battle their trauma by attempting to bury it, "Anguished Memory," where survivors doubt or have difficulty creating narratives about their stories, "Humiliated Memory," where there is only shame expressed by survivors about their experiences, "Tainted Memory," where the emphasis is on survival no matter the cost, even to one's value system, and finally, "Unheroic Memory," similar to "Tainted Memory," where survivors see only a "diminished self"—no agency and no salvation.¹¹ While these categories may serve to essentialize, rather than highlight nuance and complexity, we will encounter them in many of the films in this chapter, some coming through multiple times in the same character.

Holocaust trauma has been a part of the cinematic landscape since at least the 1960s, exemplified by films such as *The Pawnbroker, Shoah,* and, from the past twenty years, *The Grey Zone* and *Son of Saul*. In his book, *Afterimage: Film, Trauma, and the Holocaust,* Joshua Hirsch contends that the purpose of film *vis-à-vis* discourses of trauma is "to guard against the tendency of mainstream culture to neutralize discourses that challenge the status quo—that confront the public with unpleasant realities that are not amenable to quick, easy, or commodifiable solutions."[12] This fulfills, as Hirsch notes, Nietzsche's criterion for the "most effective form of collective memory: 'If something is to stay in the memory, it must be burned in: Only that which never ceases to hurt stays in the memory.'"[13] And when we speak of trauma, we mean both peri- and post-traumatic phases—the trauma at the time of the event and the trauma of reliving through memory. Many of the films that we have so far encountered have peritraumatic storylines, but only a handful have placed trauma at the center of both their content and their narrative structure, with the exception perhaps of *Train of Life* and *Seven Beauties,* and maybe, if we acknowledge their fantasy elements, *Holoclownsto* and *My Mother's Courage,* There have been films with disturbing formats about Hitler, but these do not address victim trauma—even if they intend to disturb, and in some ways traumatize, the viewer. I concluded in the previous chapter that a more daunting, if not potentially effective path for films confronting the Holocaust from a comedic perspective would involve crafting stories and frameworks about trauma that alienate or otherwise negatively impact an audience. As Cathy Caruth argues in her book on traumatic memory: "In order to encounter historical trauma on the level of the Holocaust, one must be open to experiencing a textually mediated form of trauma."[14] The attempt to process an almost unknowable level of pain through film requires engagement with it in a story and a format that can evoke, in the words of Hirsch, "aspects of PTSD."[15]

As with the productions we have already explored, issues of purpose, relevance, and originality continue to be important as criteria in evaluating effectiveness. Although not determinative in every case, these criteria often help to distinguish effective from ineffective cinematic efforts. Generally, I have observed that a higher quality product results when there is depth, seriousness, and multiplicity of purpose, relevance in theme, narrative style, social commentary, and originality in structure and delivery. Unlike in previous chapters, particularly chapters 2 and 3, where many of the films I analyzed and evaluated fell short in many areas, ranging from production values to purpose, there is perhaps the greatest consistency of quality filmmaking in this chapter. Several films have received multiple awards and praise from critics, although most did not do well at the box office, and only a few, such as *Crimes and Misdemeanors, Harold and Maude,* and *Enemies, A Love Story,* have any name recognition beyond independent circles. There are some critical misfires here as well, including *The Tollbooth, Getting Away with Murder,* and *Adam Resurrected,* and even *Harold and Maude's* critical reception was initially mixed. I will explore the reasons for this, but I would argue that where there was critical success and corresponding popular shortcoming, the focus on trauma was partly responsible. Trauma and memory stories may serve to weed out more frivolous endeavors and establish relevance at a time in which memory work has become a major part of academic discussions about the Holocaust, but the focus on psychological wounding and individuals who may not be heroic or accessible to a general audience complicates the already formidable task of turning out viewers to a film about genocide. A comedy about Holocaust trauma, one that can both invite and repel a different set of viewers, brings into the mix an additional set of challenges and conversations—whether these are about tone and respect or the myriad other issues that we have seen arise when worlds as opposite as the Holocaust and comedy collide.

COMEDY AND MEMORY IN DIFFERENT NATIONAL CONTEXTS

I begin this chapter with an international comparison of comedic films which address aspects of postwar collective historical memory in nations that counted among the victims, perpetrators, bystanders, and resisters. The productions come from different places and times in the postwar era; from the United States (Debra Kirschner's 2004 film, *The Tollbooth* and Woody Allen's *Crimes and Misdemeanors* (1989); from Argentina (Daniel Burman's 2004 *Lost Embrace*); from Italy (Luciano Salce's 1961 classic, *The Fascist* [*Il Federale*]); from France (Jacques Audiard's 1996 film, *Self-Made Hero* [*Un héros très discret*]); from Great Britain (Paul Morrison's 2003 film, *Wondrous Oblivion,* as well as episodes from two television shows—*Fawlty Towers* and *Misfits);* from Germany (Michael Verhoeven's 1990 film, *The Nasty Girl* [*Das Schreckliche Mädchen*] and Chris Kraus' 2016 *The Bloom of Yesterday* [*Die Blumen von Gestern*]); and finally, from Israel (episodes from the television comedy group, *The Chamber Quintet* [*Ha-Hamishia Hakamerit*] and the 2010 film *The Matchmaker,* directed by Avi Nesher). What unites these disparate offerings is their exploration, to varying degrees, of postwar collective memory and what that memory says about the discourse over collective identity within a particular postwar context. *The Tollbooth, Lost Embrace,* and *Crimes and Misdemeanors* utilize Holocaust memory as an ancillary device that presents backstory or a discussion of values. By contrast, *Self-Made Hero, Wondrous Oblivion, Fawlty Towers, The Nasty Girl, The Bloom of Yesterday,* and *The Matchmaker* foreground a discussion of history and memory in their narratives, and *Il Federale* typifies much of the contradictions and anxieties in postwar Italian cinema about Italy's fascist past.

Debra Kirschner's *The Tollbooth* centers on the character of Sarabeth Cohen (played by Marla Sokoloff), a wannabe artist who is the youngest daughter of a New York Jewish family. Tova Feldshuh and Ronald Guttman play Sarabeth's parents Ruth and Isaac; Idina Menzel plays Sarabeth's pregnant sister Raquel, and Liz Stauber plays her other sister, Becky, who comes out as a lesbian, crushing her parents' dreams. Sarabeth starts dating a Gentile from Pennsylvania, depicted as a white supremacist backwater haven. Her relationship is long-distance—hence the tollbooth reference—and Sarabeth ultimately chooses to focus on her career rather than the relationship. The film is relevant to a discussion of memory here in that Kirschner utilizes the character of Isaac to remind Sarabeth continually of Judaism, antisemitism, and the Holocaust. We learn at the beginning of the film that Sarabeth was named after her two great aunts who died at Auschwitz, and nearly every time Isaac is on screen, he offers a quote or a joke from a Jewish text or personality in a way that reinforces an autobiographical as well as historical memory to preserve Sarabeth's Jewish identity.

Lost Embrace (*El Abrazo Partido*) is one entry in Daniel Burman's semi-autobiographical trilogy set in the Balvanera neighborhood of Buenos Aires. The film tells the story of Ariel Makaroff, played by Daniel Sender, the grandson of Holocaust survivors who is estranged from his father, who is living in Israel and who divorced his mother when Ariel was just a young boy. His mother works in a mall selling lingerie, and the bulk of the film centers on the relationship between Ariel and his mother and the other retailers. One scene, in particular, incorporates a discussion of Holocaust memory, and that is when Ariel, seeking to immigrate to Poland, visits his grandmother to see if she has papers that would support his application to become a Polish citizen. During their discussion, Ariel's grandmother talks about how she used to sing in a club in Warsaw and how, after her escape from Poland and arrival in Argentina, Ariel's grandfather would not let her sing anymore because it was both a reminder of loss and an insult to that memory. Ariel eventually reconciles with his father, who returns at the end of the film after Ariel's mother admits that the reason for their divorce was a brief sexual affair that she had with a fellow retailer.

Finally, Woody Allen's *Crimes and Misdemeanors* focuses on two stories—one about a documentary filmmaker (Clifford Stern, played by Allen) and the other about a prominent ophthalmologist, Judah Rosenthal (Martin Landau), who hires a hitman to murder the woman he is having an affair with (played by Anjelica Huston). Allen's bleak existentialism is on full display in the film; Cliff is hired to make a documentary about his obnoxious television producer brother-in-law, Lester, played by Alan Alda, when all Cliff wants to do is make a film about a philosopher, Louis Levy, who eventually commits suicide. Allen cast New York University psychology professor Martin Bergmann in this role, and he presents in faux-documentary clips a philosophy of life centered on love and small moments, something that seems ostensibly optimistic, but his suicide, plus Judah's ability to escape any kind of punishment or demonstrate remorse or guilt, leaves one with a much grimmer assessment about the human condition. One of the key moments that reflects this is a scene in which Judah goes back to the house in which he grew up and has a vision of a Passover Seder, during which his father, Saul, admonishes his sister Meg over her remarks that God is "mumbo jumbo" and that the lesson of the Holocaust is might makes right. Landau inserts himself into his memory and asks his father—"And if a man commits a crime, if a man kills?" His father responds, "then one way or another he will be punished," but another relative says, "if he's caught," and Meg rejoins, "if he can do it and get away with it, and he chooses not to be bothered by the ethics, then he's home free. Remember, history is written by the winners, and if the Nazis had won, future generations would know the story of World War II quite differently."[16] The conversation in Judah's head might just be a rationalization, but it does not appear at the end of the film that he has or will suffer any consequences for his actions. The only death is of the character who sought meaning and love throughout his life.

Labeling the above films as comedies is a bit of a stretch, but the protagonists (Woody Allen's Cliff, counted alongside Sarabeth and Ariel) are quick-witted, and they often use their wit to defuse tension. *The Tollbooth* and *Lost Embrace* have an Allenesque sensibility, and Daniel Burman has been described as Latin America's Woody Allen.[17] The comedic elements and moments in each film are tools to get the audience to stay with the more abstract material about memory, identity, and morality and the darker storylines about loss and death. As in *Everything Is Illuminated,* the comedy creates a kind of cushioning for viewers, and it both recedes and reappears at points to allow deeper truths to emerge.

The three films also use memory as a device to advance character and plot. In *Crimes and Misdemeanors,* Cliff's competing documentaries preserve the memory of two very different individuals who are in many ways archetypes of humanity—the despicable and the noble. The documentaries symbolize the dilemma of the artist as well. To survive in a world that is only about power and money, the artist has to compromise his or her values—the misdemeanor set against the crimes committed by Judah. In *The Tollbooth* and *Lost Embrace,* memory is constitutive of individual and collective identity, and Kirshner and Burman have spoken to this. "This film is about identity," Kirschner has openly stated: "Sarabeth wants to reject her culture and her parents' values, and yet she is named after two great aunts who died in the Holocaust. . . . In her mind, even her name carries a certain amount of guilt, which as she matures, eventually turns into responsibility."[18] Burman uses similar language for his film: "Let me put it this way, I think my job as a filmmaker is to record the collective memory of a certain community, rather than focus on personal lives and experiences. Ariel is an individual, but his dilemma and way of thinking is always political and a common one among the people of his community and generation."[19] In both films, there is an interplay between memory and identity. The individual memories of the protagonists are initially experienced as a burden or out of alignment with their identities, but throughout *The Tollbooth* and *Lost Embrace,* with the help of other individuals who convey both their personal memories and identities, and the weight of collective ones as well, the protagonists find resolution.

The use of memory in *The Tollbooth,* in particular, calls to mind how Holocaust memory has become Americanized to take "painful memories of a bereaved ethnic community and [apply] them to the most basic of American values."[20] In this process, the Holocaust and Holocaust memory, as distinctly European phenomena, have become conflated with the historical experiences of Jews in the United States, as well as with tropes of American exceptionalism and heroism. Memory of the Holocaust acts as a centripetal force to bind subsequent generations to Jewish history and Judaism, and at the same time, this memory fosters American virtue signaling; the United States is the "hero" of World War II, the standard-bearer of freedom and justice in the world. Together, these discourses provide powerful cultural cohesion. If the appropriation of memory were not problematic enough, the repeated engagement with it has become, to some scholars, a collective fixation or "compulsive repetition." Efraim Sicher cautions that "in the anonymous concrete jungles of industrial urban societies, the past is often a product of the heritage industry that feeds a nostalgia for a lost pastoral innocence . . . and community."[21] Indeed, one of the problems with *The Tollbooth* is Isaac's repeated use of Jewish aphorisms, including quotes from the Talmud, Mel Brooks, and *Fiddler on the Roof,* all designed to keep Sarabeth within the fold. Not only are these references too "on-the-nose," they provide evidence of what Sicher might call performative obsession.

Memory is also a vehicle through which to explore personal ethics in each film, and here is where we find a divergence in messaging. While the tone and moral of *The Tollbooth* and *Lost Embrace* are edgy but hopeful, the lesson of *Crimes and Misdemeanors* is almost Hobbesian. In fact, one could use the discourses of Isaac in *The Tollbooth* and Meg in *Crimes and Misdemeanors* as springboards to discuss strands of American urban Jewish identity—one that is modern but religious, and another that is secular and atheist. Isaac's words of wisdom to Sarabeth and her sisters and Rachel's (often stereotypical) lamentations are evidence of the former, where American Jewish identity is grounded in respect for Jewish traditions, ethics, and creating a Jewish "home." In *Crimes and Misdemeanors,* the particular strand of Jewish thought that wins out is the one that depicts life as Hobbes would as "nasty, brutish, and short." Although scholar David Landry sees a more ambiguous ending to *Crimes,* viewing Judah as leading an empty, meaningless existence and "fighting within himself," filmmaker Allen vigorously disagrees:

> There were a lot of people who felt that Marty (Landau) was haunted and he had to keep telling the story like the ancient Mariner. But that was not it at all. He was in no way haunted. He was just fine. He realized that in a godless universe, you can get away with it, and it doesn't bother him.[22]

Lost Embrace, I would suggest, occupies a middle ground between *The Tollbooth* and *Crimes and Misdemeanors,* The film is not as superficially optimistic as the former nor as dreary as the latter. Instead, its text and characters represent more of the contradictions of life, where reconciliation and happiness are possible and where values matter, but where bad things may continue to happen.

Filtering the three films through my evaluative model of purpose/relevance/originality reveals other differences. *Crimes and Misdemeanors* and *Lost Embrace* are highly regarded films; *Crimes* was nominated for multiple awards, winning the 1990 Writers' Guild of America award for Best Original Screenplay. *Lost Embrace,* too, won over critics[23] and received awards in multiple settings, including Argentina's prestigious Clarin Awards, where it won Best Film, Best Screenplay, and Best Supporting Actress in 2004. However, critics did not like *The Tollbooth,* and it is worth exploring why. Each film demonstrates purpose, but there is a noticeable difference in relevance and originality between the three. *Lost Embrace* and *Crimes and Misdemeanors* operate on multiple levels of social commentary, and there is thick description of a world that feels both real and fresh, while *The Tollbooth* traffics in facile tropes. There are these in *Crimes* as well, and we have seen magical realism again and again in numerous Allen films, but the character of Judah, and his portrayal by Landau, resist easy answers, which *The Tollbooth* seems to offer. *The Tollbooth* and *Crimes and Misdemeanors* are slices of the American Jewish experience (albeit narrow ones, focused on New York), but Allen adds a layer of relevance by offering a satire of the United States in the 1980s—a place morally adrift, smug, and self-satisfied, while the interaction and scenarios in *The Tollbooth* come across as both timeworn and inauthentic for the early 2000s. Jeannette Catsoulis, writing for the *New York Times,* called the dialogue in *The Tollbooth* "oddly dated,"[24] and Ronnie Scheib said the film was a "morass of whiny clichés."[25] *The Tollbooth* has the feel of a production from the late 1980s, not 2004, but even here, it does not stand up well against other films that made similar points about Judaism, family, sex, and memory, like Harvey Fierstein's *Torch Song Trilogy*.

Turning to films and television productions from Europe that are about memories of World War II or that take place during the war, we see that these too are windows into national attitudes and cultural schisms about the past. Italian films, for instance, tend to be critical about fascism in ways that allow Italians to emerge as likable or relatable. In France, the memory of social behavior under German occupation has been a third rail of sorts, pitting a discourse of resistance against one of collaboration. In Britain, Holocaust memory has come through in ways that address particular taboos or issues of class and race in British society. In Germany, where civic culture is built around memory as inoculation, films have often tackled and exposed Holocaust denialism. Finally, there is Israel, where the Holocaust and victim memory are embedded into citizenship and where comedians have given attention to this as relief and social commentary.

Let us begin here with a consideration of war memory and Italian film comedies. Reflecting the devastation wrought by World War II, Italian filmmaking in the first decade after the war has been dubbed "neorealist" for its depiction of everyday life and poverty and the use of non-professional actors. Films, like Roberto Rossellini's *Roma Citta Aperta* (*Rome, Open City*), from 1945, constituted the beginning chapter in a story of postwar memory work in Italy characterized by social anxiety and selective amnesia. As Giacomo Lichtner argues, in his work on Italian cinema since 1945, two postwar stereotypes emerged about Italians in the era of Mussolini. One was that they were fundamentally good and apolitical, and the other was that Italian fascism was "incompetent" and "harmless."[26] In the comedies about the war that helped to constitute the subgenre in postwar Italian film known as the *Commedia all'italiana* (or "Comedy in the Italian way"), these tropes found repeat usage, and they have remained powerful visual reinforcements of a desire to remember the past selectively. From some of the first comedies about the war, such as Carol Borghesio's *How I Lost the War* (*Come persi la Guerra*), from 1947 to Gabriele Salvatores' *Mediterraneo*, from 1991, the bumbling but noble soldier has been a consistent presence in postwar Italian film.

The Fascist (*Il Federale*, 1961), Luciano Salce's acclaimed film within the *Commedia all'italiana*, is very much a part of this tradition. The film tells the story of a fascist, Primo Arcovazzi, played by Ugo Tognazzi, who is assigned to transport to Rome an anti-fascist professor, Erminio Bonafè, played by Georges Wilson. Bonafè escapes from Arcovazzi multiple times, the two are captured by, and then escape from German forces, and they are repeatedly tormented by a girl who at one point steals their clothes. Bonafè saves Arcovazzi's life on a couple of occasions in the film as well, the last time coming at the end of the film after the two finally reach Rome. In a twist of fate, they meet their female bully again, and she offers Arcovazzi a complete "Federale" or fascist uniform, which he takes and proudly wears, only to discover that Rome is now occupied by U.S. troops. While the Americans view Arcovazzi and his pro-fascist outfit as a humorous novelty, Italian residents want to execute him. They give the professor a gun to do the deed, and Bonafè leads Arcovazzi away, letting him go once they are safely out of sight.

The journey of reconciliation in *Il Federale* echoes the storyline of *Me and the Colonel*, but for our discussion, Salce's approach is illustrative of postwar Italian memory work. Salce both criticizes and shies away from criticism of fascism through Arcovazzi, a character who is ultimately likable, and he praises and ridicules the left by portraying Bonafè as honorable but clueless. One could see either apoliticism or moral equivalence in this, but, as Lichtner argues, "*Il Federale* does not equate the mocked. Salce does not question the righteousness of the Resistance . . . [it] is endorsed as a war of liberation."[27] At the same time, while more liberal than neutral, the film avoids the more difficult task of addressing what in Italian society and culture produced fascism in the first place. Here, again in Lichtner's assessment, Italy's "moral compass . . . more than withstands the film's scrutiny."[28] There is a connection here to my earlier criticism of *Life is Beautiful;* I argued that that film would have been more daring and perhaps honest had it set its scenario in an Italian camp, rather than a German one, and shared the villainy between both Germans and Italians, but until Italian filmmakers take that risk, it appears we will be left with stories that are variations on the same theme of disliking fascism but also seeing it as somehow outside the "true" Italian continuum.

The French, meanwhile, have grappled for decades with the German occupation, but unlike their Italian counterparts, some French filmmakers have taken more critical and introspective approaches, most notably Marcel Ophuls, in his 1969 film, *The Sorrow and the Pity (Le Chagrin et la Pitié)*, but also Jean-Pierre Melville's *Army of Shadows* (*L'armée des ombres*), which was released less than a week before Ophul's epic, and whose narrative of resistance is much darker than previous films, peppered by resistance fighters who murder each other or commit suicide. Up to the 1960s, French filmmakers crafted a largely heroic vision of the past in films like René Clément's *Battle of the Rails* (*La bataille du rail*, from 1946) and Robert Bresson's *A Man Escaped* (*Un condamné à mort s'est échappé*, from 1956).[29] The resistance plotline continued into the 1960s, but comedies about the subject also emerged, such as Jean-Paul Rappenau's romantic comedy starring Catherine

Deneuve, *Matter of Resistance* (*La vie de château*, 1965), Jean Renoir's *The Elusive Corporal* (*Le caporal épinglé*, 1962), about a French prisoner of war who tries to escape from a stalag, and Gérard Oury's 1966 comedy about the misadventures of downed British airmen and members of the French resistance, *Don't Look Now . . . We're Being Shot At!* (*La Grande Vadrouille*). The British film from 1974, *Soft Beds, Hard Battles,* starring Peter Sellers, and the television series from the 1980s, *Allo! Allo!* had a similar premise, and comedies about the resistance with happy endings have continued throughout the decades from Gérard Oury's 1982 *Ace of Aces* (*L'as des as*) to Jean-Paul Rappeneau's *Bon Voyage* (2003). At the same time, these films have had to share a space with more critical visions of the past, such as Louis Malle's *Lacombe Lucien* (1974), Claude Berri's, *Uranus* (1990), and the French television series, *A French Village* (*Un village français*), from 2009 to 2017.

Many of the above films merit a separate analysis of French historical memory, but here I choose to focus on one film in particular—Jacques Audiard's *Self-Made Hero* (*Un héros très discret*), released on 15 May 1996, for which Audiard and Alain Le Henry won Best Screenplay at the Cannes Film Festival. The film tells the fictional story of Albert Dehousse, who, after the war, reinvents his wartime history. Played by Mathieu Kassovitz as a sort of non-descript everyman, neither a collaborator nor resister, Albert is egged on by a gay soldier who befriends him and who says that the past is a drag and that he needs a new story. Albert decides that he will pose as a resistance fighter with a heroic record during the German occupation, a ruse that pays dividends at least initially; he gets food and a reprieve on his rent, and other fighters are so convinced by his story that they insist that they were his closest friends during the war and that he invented the phrase, "there are those who discussed the war and those who fought it." Albert receives the rank of lieutenant colonel and is given an intelligence post in French-occupied Baden-Baden, where, after he has a group of French collaborators executed, he gives himself up. Because Albert is so beloved, the army handles the case quickly and quietly, and everything works out for Albert in the end. An epilogue features mock interviews that suggest that he had an illustrious career in government and medicine afterward, with some thinking he was a Soviet agent all along.

I set this film apart from others which I mentioned in the previous paragraph because, in addition to crafting a storyline about how French citizens reacted to resistance and collaboration as well as serving as a reflection of contemporaneous attitudes, *Self-Made Hero* is intentionally about memory and truth, and the mutability of both. One of the implications of this relativization is a loss of accountability, which director Audiard believes persists in French culture, society, and politics and which he sought to highlight through film. In a 1996 interview, Audiard claimed, "It took 40 or 50 years to realize that France did not deserve its place at the victors' table. The main challenge here is to create a situation where the criteria of truth are lost—one by one . . . I was trying to make us examine the basis of our beliefs in any kind of heroism."[30] Audiard's feelings remained largely the same in an interview with the American Film Institute nearly twenty years later: " . . . the generation that was born roughly between 1940 and 1955 in France has been told a historic lie. The big question is what did our parents do during the war? . . . That's something that my generation is saddled with, and perhaps that's the starting point for the exploration."[31]

Anxieties about compromised values and collaborating with the enemy have not been as central as fixations in British historical memory of the war. Rather, it has been the degree of certainty around the idea of British valor that has come in for criticism and ridicule. Films produced in Great Britain during the war, whether they were dramas or comedies, were intended to raise morale, and so they presented largely heroic British characters, although there were some exceptions to what Kevin Flanagan dubs this "pleasure culture of war," such as Alberto Cavalcanti's 1942 film, *Went the Day Well?*, a dark imagining of an English village under German occupation.[32] By the end of the 1950s and into the 1960s and 1970s, there was an increase in critical dramas, like *The Hill* (1965, directed by Sidney Lumet), starring Sean Connery, about a group of British soldiers in a British military prison in Libya, as well as war comedies (notably, *Carry on Sergeant* [1958], the first of 31 such films released between 1958 and 1992, the sitcom *Dad's Army* [1968–1977], Richard Lester's *How I Won the War* [1967], starring John Lennon, and Norman Cohen's 1973 adaptation of Spike Milligan's autobiography, *Adolf Hitler: My Part in His Downfall).*

We have already seen how Milligan and Monty Python were sending up Hitler and the Nazis, and by extension, British war memory, in the early 1970s, and this continued with Python member John Cleese's television series *Fawlty Towers,* which centers on the goofy character of hotel owner Basil Fawlty, played by Cleese. The show, which ran for two seasons, one in 1975 and one in 1979, is perhaps best known for the episode entitled "The Germans," which aired on 24 October 1975. In the episode, Fawlty is knocked out during a fire drill, and he ends up in the hospital. He returns to the hotel prematurely, clearly dazed and confused, to find a group of Germans who are registering. They ask him in German if they can rent a car, and he thinks they are asking for meat (because the word for "rent" in German is *mieten*). Fawlty misidentifies his staff, and tells them "don't mention the war," as he repeatedly does in front of his German guests. When they order their food, Fawlty repeats it back: "That's a Prawn Goebbels, a Herman Goering, and four cold beet salads," prompting one of the German guests to plead, "Will you stop talking about the war," and Fawlty responds, "Me? You started it?" Growing angry, one of the Germans insists, "We did not!" and an exasperated Fawlty yells, "Yes you did, you invaded Poland!" The episode remains highly regarded for its skewering of the rigidity of British memory of World War II, and indeed *TV Guide* ranked it as the twelfth greatest television episode of all time. The phrase "don't mention the war" has wide recognition and has so seeped into the lexicon of popular phrases that it has been used as titles for scholarly books. Cleese even turned the phrase into a song in 2006 at the FIFA World Cup. The episode is also controversial, not for its satirizing of British war memory, but for an unrelated storyline, which features racist language used by one of the show's repeat characters (Major Gowen, who repeatedly uses the "n" word). The episode was removed briefly from UKTV's streaming service in 2020, but it was later reinstated with a warning about language. Cleese has since said that "the Major was an old fossil left over from decades before. We were not supporting his views, we were making fun of them. If they can't see that, if people are too stupid to see that, what can one say?"[33]

Fast forward thirty-six years to the British comic/sci-fi television series, *Misfits,* which ran from 2009 to 2013, about a group of young delinquents sentenced to community service who develop superpowers after an electrical storm. In November 2011, the series featured a Nazi-Hitler-themed episode with a twist. Rather than referencing actual historical memory, the writers proposed an alternate reality through a storyline about time travel. A German-Jewish scientist, who invents a time machine, returns to the past in an attempt to kill Hitler, but he fails, and Hitler acquires the scientist's cell phone, which results in a huge technological breakthrough for Germany, and the Nazis win the war. In the alternative present, Nazis have occupied Britain, and they are on the lookout for misfits with superpowers. However, they are ultimately foiled by the group, who travel back in time and reset history to the original timeline. There is nothing particularly deep or introspective about the episode; in an interview, Lauren Socha, one of the show's actors, responded to the question, "Was it funky fighting Hitler?" by saying, "I loved it . . . knocked him out . . . brilliant."[34]

The episode does evoke some of the concerns that I expressed in chapter 2, and it works just as well as an example of what happens when comedy and cultural artifacts and language of the present intersect to defang Hitler and the Nazis, but the reason I include it here is because of how it presents memory. As with the *Fawlty Towers* episode, the installment of *Misfits* reveals how British comedic approaches to wartime memory differ from their French and Italian counterparts. There is less anxiety about having a fascist regime or the need to recapture some kind of moral center, as in the case of the Italians, or about collaborating with fascists under occupation, in the case of the French.

Rather, the anxiety is over how memory of the war impedes reconciliation (which is the premise of *Fawlty Towers*) or how critical the preservation of wartime memory is to Britain's "normal" present, which is the approach taken in *Misfits*. In its nod to the butterfly effect, the idea that small changes in the space-time continuum can have catastrophic results, the *Misfits* episode is part of a well-worn literary tradition of time-travel narratives (from *The Time Machine* to *Man in the High Castle*), which have been applied, certainly more consciously than this show, as social criticism.[35]

Unlike the comically awkward, almost Freudian presentation of memory in *Fawlty Towers,* the film *Wondrous Oblivion,* from 2003, directed and written by Paul Morrison, presents another dimension to British wartime memory by combing uniquely British referents in its storyline set in the suburbs of London in 1960. The film focuses on a Jewish boy (by the name of David Wiseman, played by Sam Smith) who bonds over a love of cricket with his new neighbors, the Samuels, who are black immigrants from Jamaica. David's parents are Jewish immigrants who had been able to flee Nazi Germany, and there are moments where the film makes overt references to that experience. The racism of the Wiseman's neighbors is on full display, but even the Wisemans themselves are not immune to bigotry as David's parents, Victor and Ruth, tell him to stop socializing with the Samuels even though the father, Dennis (played by Delroy Lindo) has been helping David with his cricket game. A romantic subplot between Dennis and David's mother, Ruth, develops, which comes across as an odd trope of white sexual curiosity and panic, and at the film's climactic moment, the Samuels' apartment is set on fire, evoking *Kristallnacht,* and it leads to another odd moment of white saviorism as David and Victor go in to help rescue the family. Victor admonishes his neighbors for their intolerance, and then days later, David joins the Samuels at their picnic instead of playing at his school's cricket game. Yet in the end, the Wisemans move out of the neighborhood, which, to me, undercuts the movie's dual messages of fighting for what is right and developing harmonious interracial relations. Although the film generally had a warm reception, some critics, like Jeannette Catsoulis, of the *New York Times,* and Derek Elley, for *Variety,* were put off by the way Morrison handled the racism storyline.[36]

The three productions, *Fawlty Towers, Misfits,* and *Wondrous Oblivion,* are disparate in time and format, but they are windows both into British national imagination about the war and its aftermath as well as how that imagination has been either preserved or deconstructed. In *Misfits* and *Wondrous Oblivion,* there is an encounter with memory, and that memory remains a force to inspire moral action. In *Wondrous Oblivion,* Morrison did not necessarily begin with the idea of exploring the memory of historical experiences, such as *Kristallnacht* or the flight of German Jews from Hitler's Germany, starting instead with the premise about a boy who loved cricket but was not any good at it. Historical memory began to enter into the picture as Morrison kept imagining how to construct a story around the cricket motif in a way that would be interesting and relevant. The characters and the storyline about race and racism, which attempts to challenge stereotypes about Jews and Afro-Caribbeans, emerged from this engagement. In *Fawlty Towers*, the approach to memory was threefold—open it up, contest it, and then rebuild it. This meant taking on taboos about how, or even if, one should address the war, as well as the persistence of anti-German attitudes that went beyond the generation responsible for the war. Cleese has argued that the episode was less about the Germans than about "English attitudes to the war and the fact that some people were still hanging on to that rubbish."[37] As writer Sean Braswell notes, in his article on the "Germans" episode, by trying not to mention the war, "Fawlty Towers managed to help the English broach quite a bit."[38]

Yet the need for Germans to preserve memory and continue an honest reckoning with the Nazi past remains pressing, and films from the past generation have attested to this reality. German films critical of the Nazi past came quickly after the war in "rubble films" like Wolfgang Staudte's *The Murderers are Among Us* (*Die Mörder sind unter uns*, from 1946), which addresses Nazi atrocities, and Harold Braun's *Between Yesterday and Tomorrow* (*Zwischen Gestern und Morgen,* 1947), which was the first German film to deal with the Holocaust. In the era of the two Germanies that followed, there were revealing differences that reflected the unique political contexts. Films in West Germany, especially early on in the 1950s and 60s, tended to focus on the experience of ordinary soldiers, and stories of resistance were a staple of West German cinema through the 1980s.[39] By contrast, the focus in East Germany was on the Nazi persecution of communists and socialists, such as Kurt Maetzig's 1955 biopic about the communist leader during the Weimar era, Ernst Thälmann.[40] East Germans also produced films about the ghettos and concentration camps, notably Frank Beyer's *Naked Among Wolves* (*Nackt unter Wölfen,* 1963*)* and *Jakob the Liar*. As Irwin-Zarecka points out, "the unanticipated depth and scope of reaction to the American series *Holocaust,* shown on West German television in 1979, was a sharp reminder of the failures of a long, concerted education effort at exposing the Nazi crimes [in that country.]."[41]

German comedies about the Third Reich are a relatively recent development, although there have been exceptions. In addition to *Jakob the Liar,* there is the West German film *Aren't We Wonderful? (Wir Wunderkinder)* from 1958, directed by Kurt Hoffmann and based on the book by Hugo Hartung, who weaves a semi-humorous tale of two friends whose lives intersect during the Imperial, Weimar, Nazi, and postwar eras. Yet it was not until the 1990s, in the context of the reunification of Germany, that comedies began to appear more frequently, exposing widespread denialism or even support for moving on from the "past that would not pass away." I have already mentioned in this regard Helmut Dietl's *Schtonk!*, Ralf Huettner's TV production, *The Parrot (Der Papagai)*, and Christoph Schlingensief's *Terror 2000—Intensivstation Deutschland*, which all appeared in 1992, and which I will address in chapter 5, as they serve as warnings and commentary about German society and politics. The two films I include in this chapter, while they also say much about contemporary Germany, are anchored to questions about history and memory. They are Michael Verhoeven's *The Nasty Girl (Das Schreckliche Mädchen,* which premiered in February 1990, months before the two Germanies were reunited), and Chris Kraus' *The Bloom of Yesterday (Die Blumen von Gestern* from 2016*).*

Based on the true story of Anja Rosmus, who, as a sixteen-year-old, wrote in the 1970s about her hometown of Passau, in Bavaria, *The Nasty Girl* centers on a teenage German girl, Sonja, played by Lena Stolze, who gradually uncovers the truth about her birthplace and its residents during the Third Reich. Beginning in black and white as a whimsical biography, with sequences showing Sonja as a toddler knocking over her baby brother's carriage while students in a monastery ogle her buxom mother, the film shifts to color and adopts a serious, although still often ironic tone when the storyline moves to the present. Sonja conducts research initially as part of an essay competition, but the task acquires a life of its own beyond that as she uncovers hidden details and obstacles to her research. After winning multiple lawsuits to gain access to incriminating documents, and after escaping physical harm (her home is bombed), Sonja publishes a book revealing that the town's beloved professor, an allegedly anti-Nazi resistance figure, was partially responsible for the incarceration of one of the town's residents in a concentration camp. At the end of the film, the citizens unveil a bust to Sonja in honor of her work, but she sees through the move as a cynical ploy to deflect blame, and she flees the scene.

Kraus' *Bloom of Yesterday* is a romantic comedy about a disgruntled, impotent Holocaust historian (Totila Blumen, played by Lars Eidinger) and his free-spirited intern Zazie Lindeau, played by Adèle Haenel. Zazie is in a relationship with a competing historian, and she initially annoys Totila beyond words. At their initial greeting, Zazie refuses to get into his Mercedes, believing that the company made the gas vans (They did not, but Opel, Renault, Saurer, and Magirus did). Gradually, Totila and Zazie become close, and it is revealed that Totila's grandfather was a Nazi who operated a gas van and most likely murdered Zazie's grandmother. A relationship ensues, with Totila able to have sex, but the additional revelation that Totila had been a neo-Nazi in his youth, leads a pregnant Zazie to break up with him. At the end of the film, the two accidentally meet in an airport, and Totila says that he has broadened his focus to genocide studies (claiming that Native Americans "were exterminated too,") while Zazie introduces Totila to the child that was probably theirs and says that she is in a relationship with an Indian woman. Totila's diegesis near the end carries the lesson of the story for him: "I've spent my whole life searching for life, and now that I've found it, it doesn't seem enough. But what does it matter—desire, longing, greed, as long as such things exist, hearts will beat. We live. If you want something, you have to go beyond yourself, out into the world. No matter how much it sucks."[42]

As films about historical memory, both films are incisive and purposeful, and they received several accolades as a result. *The Nasty Girl* won multiple awards, including Best Non-English film at the BAFTA Awards in 1991, and it was nominated for Best Foreign Language Film at the Oscars in the same year. *The Bloom of Yesterday* won the grand prize at the Tokyo Film Festival in 2016, and two years later, Lars Eidinger won the Austrian Film Award for Best Actor. Solid execution reflected a thoughtfulness of purpose and a desire to cast off for new territory that made a statement about everyday life in the present. Verhoeven, who was born in 1938, has said that what motivated him to make the film was his belief that Germany had come to terms with its past. "When I was a schoolboy in Munich, certain subjects were never taught. A part of history was taboo. We were never told the truth about what happened in Germany during the war."[43] For Kraus, twenty-five years Verhoeven's junior, the task was "to find out what's wrong with our society."[44]

If there were one element of Kraus' film that gave me pause, it was the sexualizing of Holocaust trauma. The relationship between Totila and Zazie is pure "victim-perpetrator" fetishization, and even the characters allude as much to that. I think it is one thing, as I discovered in my research of Holocaust testimonies, to recount stories of survivors who were either sexually abused during the Holocaust or who used sex as a tool of survival, but it is problematic and potentially offensive when it is taken away from this context, where it is already a difficult subject to talk about, and put into a story about two privileged individuals, even if they are of the third generation and psychologically troubled in some way. For me, the more interesting points in the film are the brief utterances or tableaux of memory that reveal incongruities, for instance, when Totila is in an American themed restaurant, and he says, "the only thing I hate more is commercialization of human suffering, as he drinks a milkshake with an American flag in an American diner,"[45] and when Totila and Zazie go to the site of the massacre during the war and a woman comes up to them selling soda and snacks. These are the moments, and *The Nasty Girl* has similar ones, where the banalities of the present collide with an otherworldly past and offer insight into the singular strangeness of the occupation of the Holocaust scholar.

A comparison of the two films demonstrates how much German sensibilities toward Holocaust memory have evolved over the past decades. *The Nasty Girl* raised awareness about the resistance to the truth and the actions put into place to suppress its discovery, while the assumption in *The Bloom of Yesterday* is that mining the truth is a given but that the generation tasked with preserving, evaluating, and disseminating that truth is damaged and in need of its own form of trauma resolution. Gone is the power of a bureaucracy that could place obstacles in the path of truth-seekers and then punish those who resist the constraints, but in its place is a question about the very functioning of the academic infrastructure of Holocaust memory, which is now in the hands of a generation twice removed in time from the event. "Postmemory" pervades each film as the protagonists are, in the words of Marianne Hirsch, "dominated by narratives that preceded their birth [and] whose own belated stories are evacuated by the stories of the previous generation shaped by traumatic events that can be neither understood nor recreated."[46] This inability to experience authentic memory, but to imagine it, is combined in the second and third generations with the burden of being tasked with transforming this memory into history. And while, as Irwin-Zarecka argues, that "the passage of time makes dealing with the past easier in that one is no longer compelled to question one's own parents, the presence of that past becomes a great deal more pronounced, more widespread. . . . The moral challenge, too, addresses itself, albeit in different forms, to a great deal more people."[47] The effect is that the stakes on so many levels are higher; memory and trauma impact more and more people, and the need for precision and therapy is greater, as is the desire to move on from the subject altogether.

In Israel, where Holocaust remembrance is a part of active citizenship, the critique is about the dangers of obsessive victimization and self-righteousness, similar to Great Britain. We saw in chapter two how the troupe, *The Jews are Coming* (*Ha-Yehudim Baim*) have satirized Hitler and the Nazis, and here, I include examples of another comedy group, *The Chamber Quintet* (*Ha-Hamishia Hakamerit*), about which scholars, such as Liat Steir-Livny and Eyal Zandberg, have written extensively. There have been Israeli performers critical of elements of Israeli society before *The Jews are Coming* and *The Chamber Quintet,* most notably Shimen Dzigan, who often pilloried Prime Minister David Ben-Gurion in Yiddish, but the efforts of the two groups, in particular, are recent; like much of the comedy we have encountered so far, it is the product of a younger generation that feels compelled to engage in comedic critique as part of a process of national transformation.

The Chamber Quintet's show ran for five seasons, from 1993 to 1997, and it featured a handful of sketches related to Holocaust memory. One involved an athletic competition in which the Israeli athletes ask to get a head start on the Germans, going so far as to berate the referee, "All you want to do is humiliate us! Haven't the Jewish people suffered enough? Didn't you see *Schindler's List*?" Spielberg's film makes another appearance in a skit that is a parody of Claude Lanzmann's *Shoah,* with a French interviewer interviewing an individual made to appear as a witness or survivor speaking Polish. A voice-over in Hebrew suggests that what is unfolding is a narrative of the Holocaust, while in reality, the individual is just talking about how mean Spielberg was as a director. The group, in this case, does something that is both funny and ingenious; it uses character types and *mise en scène* from a famous Holocaust documentary to satirize the representation of the Holocaust in a famous feature film. Another skit takes place in a travel agency, where the sales-woman describes a trip to Poland that involves visiting concentration camps with a day off for shopping in Warsaw. As Zandberg sees it, the episode criticizes "the Holocaust's 'memorial industry' and rails against the transformation of Holocaust commemoration into a mere commodity."[48] Finally, in another skit, entitled "Ghetto," a man asks a woman for directions, and when she starts to give them, we hear that all the street names have a connection to the Holocaust. She says, "take Warsaw Ghetto Street and then a U-Turn onto Concentration Camp Avenue. Then park at Dachau Square." When the man asks, "Is it nearby?" The woman responds, "Dachau? Dachau is right here. Just around the corner."[49] Although, as Zandberg notes, the Holocaust is only one of many targets for *The Chamber Quintet*, its critique echoes the sentiment advanced by Avraham Burg in his controversial memoir from 2008 entitled, *The Holocaust is Over: We Must Rise from Its Ashes,* and that is that Israel should "not be forever held hostage by memory." The country should "not live in the past but be cured of it."[50] In these snapshots of the Israeli national imagination, we see numerous overlaps and peculiarities, and it is clear that the encounter with Holocaust memory remains difficult and often contentious, and comedic discourses add their own set of dilemmas. Holding to traumatic memories to memorialize and to learn from them while at the same time trying to work them through, let them go, and maybe even be able to laugh again lies at the heart of the great challenge. Two Israeli films from the recent past, *The Matchmaker* and *Adam Resurrected,* are examples of working through trauma through comedic cinema.

The Matchmaker (in Hebrew, *Pa-am Ha-eetee* or *Once I Was*), written and directed by Avi Nesher and released in October 2010, is the story of the relationship between survivors and the second generation in Israel. The film begins in Haifa in the 2000s, as the characters of Arik Burstein and his father, a Holocaust survivor, are informed that an individual they knew, Yankele Braiyd, has died. The film switches back to the summer of 1967 to the characters of Arik as a young boy (played by Tuval Shafir) and Yankele (played by Adir Miller), a survivor who works in the shady underworld of Haifa both as a criminal and matchmaker. The two characters meet at the beginning when Yankele approaches Arik and a group of boys and tells them about his matchmaking service, and Arik plays a prank on Yankele, telling him that he has a sister who has flippers for hands. When Yankele goes to his parent's apartment, rather than shooing him away, his father recognizes him from his past and invites him in. Yankele is able to get Arik to work for him as a scout in a low-rent area of Haifa next to a theater owned by a dwarf who survived Mengele's experiments in Auschwitz, named Miss Silvia (played by Bat-El Papura). Arik also gets a job with Yankele's friend Clara (played by Maya Dagan), another survivor dealing with post-traumatic stress. Arik ends up fired by Yankele for not giving him information that he wanted from one of his surveillance jobs, but he starts a gambling racket with Clara, who, along with Yankele, is outed to the police by one of Yankele's disgruntled suitors. Although they stay one step ahead and get rid of any incriminating evidence, with the help of Arik, they realize that they will be under constant surveillance. Arik narrates as Yankele's office is ransacked by the police—"Who knows where it took him back to—in his mind, his memories; how frightening it was for him."[51] A story then appears in the press with lies that Clara is a prostitute, resulting in her death; it is unclear if this is by suicide or natural death. Yankele and Arik reconnect at Clara's funeral, but then the two never see each other again.

Paul Schrader's 2008 film, *Adam Resurrected,* adapted from Yoram Kaniuk's 1971 novel, stars Jeff Goldblum as Adam Stein, a survivor who is a patient in an Israeli psychiatric clinic in the 1960s. A comedian incarcerated in a concentration camp during the Third Reich, Adam survived his imprisonment by being taken in by the camp commandant Klein, played by Willem Dafoe, who remembered his act. Although Klein keeps Adam alive, he does so by making him act like a dog. Adam is also forced to play the violin as his wife is led to the gas chamber. His trauma is so severe—conditioned by degradation, the loss of his family, the overall fear of death, plus survival guilt—that when these come up against his general demeanor as someone who wishes to make people laugh, the result is funny, unnerving, and often violent—sometimes at the same time. Because of his personality, Adam has a following in the asylum, which the doctors appreciate, and he even has an ongoing sexual relationship with one of the nurses. Goldblum delivers lines in ways that only Jeff Goldblum can, eliciting laughter that belies darkness underneath. (For instance, upon Adam's return to the institute, an inmate asks the random question, "Columbus was a Jew?" and Adam responds, "Yes Columbus was definitely a Jew, but also an Italian, so as a matter of fact, I would not trust an Italian and neither should you.")[52] The audience learns that Klein gave Adam his estate in Germany at the end of the war, and Adam discovered that his daughter was alive in Israel. When he goes to reconnect with her, it is revealed that she died, and the family, knowing how Adam survived the camp, rejects him. Adam's trauma is therefore compounded by survivor guilt, and his process of working through is aided only when the doctors introduce him to another patient, a young boy by the name of David, who also behaves like a dog.

The two films are at once very different in tone and yet similar in how they capture different manifestations of survivor PTSD. Nesher's is the quieter character piece, while Schrader's is discordant, veering from Goldblum's shtick to hard-hitting drama. *The Matchmaker* uses tropes of pleasure (romantic comedy, pathos) to reel audiences in, while *Adam Resurrected* goes for the grotesque clown motif in a way that is even less accessible than *Seven Beauties*, This may help to account for their different critical receptions. *The Matchmaker* received glowing reviews, while *Adam Resurrected* was generally disliked.[53] (Owen Gleiberman, in his review for *Entertainment Weekly*, said that it should have been titled, *One Flew Over the Meshuggenuh's Nest)*. Although I would acknowledge that the two films operate in distinct discursive worlds in terms of format, both were pursued to shed light on Holocaust memory and trauma. Nesher had a dual aim in making his film; one was personal, as a way of unpacking the mysteries of his own parents' Holocaust experiences, and the other was broader in terms of commentary about Israel and how survivors have been treated in Israeli society. Nesher's use of dwarfs was key to this particular goal: They served as a metaphor for how Israelis "tended to think about the survivors as freaks."[54] For Schrader, no stranger to controversial psychological films as the writer of *Taxi Driver* and *The Last Temptation of Christ*, the exploration of irony and black humor in *Adam Resurrected* was a project of deep value and interest, but he admits how the film divided Israelis, recounting his reception in Haifa, where many in the audience loved the film while others hated it. One individual came up to Schrader after the screening and said that he had "dishonored Israel."[55]

Despite their different receptions, both films capture two typologies of traumatic memory delineated by Lawrence Langer in his analysis of survivor testimony: tainted memory and humiliated memory. For Langer, tainted memory is a form a memory that "sacrifices purity of vision in the process of recounting, resulting in . . . a narrative strained by the disapproval of the witness' own present moral sensibility, as well as by some of the incidents it relates."[56] It is a form of "self-justification, a painful validation of necessary if not always admirable conduct."[57] Both Clara and Yankele personify this in how they justify or try to reconcile their survival through their behavior in the present. Clara says at one point, "I don't like to talk about 'there'—but I just want you to know that nothing bad goes on here . . ."[58] And Yankele relates to Arik the wartime story of a man who, in order to ensure his survival in hiding with a group of other Jews, murdered a crying newborn but then ended up with the woman whose child he murdered because he had saved her life. "Can you tell if love is good or bad?"[59] Yankele asks rhetorically. For him, finding love for others becomes a way to undo or even give meaning to his tainted memory, and it is not clear whether Yankele and Clara are the man and woman in the story. What is clear, however, is that neither can escape their memories. There is no heroic redemption, only a kind of reactivity, which Langer calls the "impromptu self." The vanishing of the two at the end confirms this; Clara dies, while Yankele disappears without a trace. One survivor loses the battle, while the other just continues to exist using the strategy that enabled him to survive the Holocaust but that engendered the tainted memory in the first place. In *Adam Resurrected*, meanwhile, humiliated memory is everywhere. Langer describes humiliated memory as "pure misery," in which "neither time nor amnesia soothes its gnawing."[60] It is the lowest form of degradation of the individual that never goes away, disputing, in Langer's assessment, the idea "that the invincible human spirit provided an armor invulnerable to Nazi assaults against the self."[61] The survivors in *Adam Resurrected* are an army of humiliated souls, and perhaps that is why it is so difficult to watch and why the moments of humor seem so out of place, but their randomness is central to the trauma narrative. The fact that Adam had been a clown during the pre-Nazi era, whose purpose was to create joy, adds to the tragedy. Humor remains a part of Adam's soul; however, because of the degradation he endured in the camp and then the rejection he met from his family after the war, his sense of humor has become so twisted and distorted that it provides neither relief nor comfort. It is pure self-defense, like the lashing out of an abused animal or child, violent and unpredictable. In the film's climactic moment, Adam escapes the institute, and, tormented by visions of commandant Klein, he resolves to kill himself, only to be stopped by David, who finally engages Adam as a human. Yet even at the end, where both Adam and David are cured (an ending that many critics felt was too tidy), there is at least with Adam an ambivalence about his breakthrough, a feeling that his creative, witty side is gone forever, sacrificed to purge his "besieged self." Many other comedic films about Holocaust memory present characters that illustrate the diverse trauma discourses advanced by Langer, and they merit separate analyses. They include *Harold and Maude, Enemies, A Love Story, Mendel,* and *Transparent.*

TRAUMATIC MEMORY TYPOLOGIES IN COMEDIC FILMS

Released on 29 December 1971 and directed by Hal Ashby and written by Colin Higgins, *Harold and Maude* is the story of a young man, Harold Chasen, played by Bud Cort, who despises his mother and is so obsessed with death that he stages mock suicides, which terrifies the ladies with whom Harold's mother repeatedly tries to set him up. At a funeral, Harold meets a nearly eighty-year-old woman, Maude, played by Ruth Gordon, whose carefree behavior, love of life, and disrespect for the law intrigue him and lead him eventually to fall in love with her, much to Harold's mother's chagrin. She tries to enlist Harold in the military through the help of his uncle, who is a recruitment officer, but he is horrified by Harold's behavior; he and Maude engineer a scene in which Harold pretends to murder Maude as she disrupts their conversation with an antiwar protest. At Maude's eightieth birthday, Harold intends to propose to her, but she takes an overdose of pills, believing eighty to be the right age to die. In the end, we see Harold's car plunging over a cliff, but Harold is not in it; he is playing the banjo which he learned to play during his courtship with Maude—ready to move on and, in the words of Maude, "go and love some more." Higgins, who developed the story as his master's thesis at UCLA, intended Maude to be a composite of his grandmother, a bohemian woman he had known in Australia, and finally a woman he knew who had been in a concentration camp and who was still positive about life. In his words, the lesson of the film is simple: "We're all Harold, and we all want to be Maude . . . we're all repressed and trying to be free, to be ourselves, to be vitally interested in living . . ."[62] This message has resonated over time and with different cultures. Although a flop initially at the box office and with critics (*Variety* said it had all the fun of a burning orphanage),[63] Harold and Maude currently has a reputation as one of the great films of the 1970s, and some people have seen it over one hundred times, coming back to it again and again, not for the dark comedy, but for its life-affirming philosophy.[64]

Including *Harold and Maude* here in a discussion of Holocaust memory is striking for one reason; there is no discussion about the genocide at all during the film, and yet, because of a line or two and one key sequence, a glance by Harold at Maude's arm revealing a concentration camp tattoo, it is evident that the Holocaust frames the entire storyline. It is interesting that director Ashby did not like the shot of the tattoo but kept it in, and it has become perhaps the signature moment in the entire film. I would argue that it is symbolic of Maude's way of confronting what Langer would describe as "deep memory," the memory of trauma buried beneath the surface that bubbles up occasionally like a lava-flow and corrodes the "comforts of common memory."[65] The audience gets a glimpse of these encounters between common and deep memory when we learn of Maude's past as a young revolutionary, and Harold notices her umbrella. Maude tells Harold that when she was a girl, she was taken to the palace in Vienna to a garden party; "I can still see the sunshine, the parasols," she remembers. She was married to a doctor at the university and maintains that she used the umbrella at rallies fighting for liberty, justice, and rights. She almost continues to reveal the entire story when she says, "but that was all before," and then she catches herself, looks away, and moves on—consciously preventing any rush of deep memory.[66] Harold asks, "You don't use the umbrella anymore—no more revolts?" And Maude responds, clearly fighting back tears, "Oh yes, Oh every day. But I don't need the defense anymore. I embrace. Still fighting for the big issues, but now in my small, individual way . . ."[67]

While Maude does espouse a belief in living life to the fullest, she ultimately chooses death, and although this may suggest agency, I think that there is a deeper performative conflict that Maude may not have been able to resolve, and that was her desire and ability to conquer her deep memory. In the case of Harold, his estrangement from his mother, which resulted from an accident in which Harold was presumed dead and to which his mother did not react sympathetically, leaves Harold with a traumatic memory that shapes a desire to be dead rather than alive. Maude's strategy of working through the trauma of the Holocaust by focusing on the preciousness and beauty of life becomes the therapy that Harold needs to rejoin the world of the living. This message comes through clear enough in the scene where Maude's tattoo is revealed. As the two sit in a junkyard by the beach and watch the sunset, Maude offers a (fictional) vignette from the story of Alfred Dreyfus, the French Jewish captain wrongly convicted of treason and imprisoned at the end of the 19th century. She tells Harold that when Dreyfus wrote from Devil's Island, he saw the most glorious birds. Many years later, in Brittany, he realized that they had only been seagulls. Maude concludes, "for me, they will always be glorious birds."[68] The question for me is: Is Maude truly empowered at the end? Harold may be, and it may be due to Maude's words about life, but is Maude? She seems to embody more of the deep memory survivor, suffering from the ebb and flow of trauma. Does she really think life is beautiful? Or is it just a profound irony—that what remains is still darkness and that the only way out—the only way to true agency is through suicide? Or, is it her only way out, but not Harold's? Higgins seems to play it more as though Maude loves life, and he did change the initial ending, which had Harold committing suicide, so the way to make the new ending "earned" would be to have Maude's philosophy authentic and believable, which it could be, even if Maude did not believe it herself. It could be a simple case of seeing the world as one wants it to be instead of seeing it as it is.

Deep memory also pervades *Enemies, A Love Story,* Paul Mazursky's 1989 adaptation of Isaac Bashevis Singer's novel from 1966 about a Holocaust survivor, Herman Broder, and the three women he is either married to or having an affair within the many boroughs of New York City. The film won numerous awards and accolades, including the New York Film Critics' Circle Awards for Best Director, and it remains a favorite with critics, although not necessarily with audiences. Herman, played by Ron Silver in the film, lives in Coney Island with his wife, Yadwiga, a Christian Pole; he married her mostly because she rescued him during the German occupation by keeping him hidden in a hayloft. Herman is also having an affair in the Bronx with another survivor, Masha, played by Lena Olin. Herman tells Yadwiga that he has to travel for work, but this is only a ruse to cover up his affair and his real job, which is as a ghostwriter for an uptown rabbi, played by Alan King. The rabbi is frustrated at Herman because he is difficult to reach, and he asks him to install a telephone, but Herman uses his Holocaust trauma to justify not getting one because that would blow his multiple covers. The rabbi cavalierly, almost callously, dismisses Herman by saying, "I know countless concentration camp survivors—some practically on their way to the oven, but they're doing fine, they drive cars, they have telephones." Because the audience knows Herman's actual reason for refusing the telephone, a potentially negative response that would otherwise have been directed at the rabbi is reduced, and ambivalence heightened, especially when Herman responds with a true statement that covers the lie: "Maybe that's my problem—I was hiding in a barn."[69] While Herman drifts further from Yadwiga, who starts to think that Herman is dishonest and doubles down on her commitment to him by pursuing conversion to Judaism, Herman and Masha's relationship becomes more volatile and fetishistic. At one point during sex, Masha asks Herman if he would still want her if they both died and "were buried in the same plot,"[70] and she came to him in his grave.

Herman's already fragile world comes completely undone when his presumed-dead wife, Tamara, played by Angelica Huston, appears in Manhattan. Herman tells her that he married Yadwiga and is having an affair with another woman, and Tamara is nonplussed, but as the two continue to share the trauma of their near-death experiences, plus the loss of their children, whom they often see in traumatic flashbacks, they become intimate once again. Herman then discovers that Masha was once married and paid for her divorce through prostitution which Masha denies. She and Herman then get married, Tamara stops by Herman's Coney Island apartment, which frightens Yadwiga, who thinks Tamara is a ghost, and Tamara calms everyone down, including Herman, by declaring to Yadwiga that she has nothing to fear and to Herman: "Don't worry she won't divorce you. If she does, you can go to the other one. If she throws you out too, you can come to me."[71] Eventually, Herman's bigamy is discovered (at a party thrown by the rabbi), and, desperate for a way out of his misery, he meets Tamara, who tells him that he is a "lost man . . . one of those people who can't make decisions for themselves."[72] She offers to be his manager so that he can get his life back on track. She says she will find him a job with her uncle but that he has to return to the now pregnant Yadwiga. He does for a while, but he cannot stay away from Masha, and he goes to be with her once more, but Masha reveals that she had sex with her ex-husband, and Herman leaves yet again. The last image we have of Masha is of her looking at herself in a mirror smiling; then we cut to her grave, next to her mother's, signifying that Masha has committed suicide. At the very end, Yadwiga and Tamara are together raising Yadwiga and Herman's daughter, named Masha, and Herman has vanished.

Flashbacks, hallucinations, and nightmares are present throughout the novel and film, as eruptions of deep memory, but there is an additional manifestation of traumatic memory in the narrative, one that Langer has called "anguished memory." He describes it as memory that "stains the desire for graceful aging with the refuse of annihilation zones and slaughter areas."[73] It is "inseparably identified with victims who did not survive, dividing the self between conflicting claims—the need and the inability to recover from the loss."[74] All of the characters in *Enemies, A Love Story*, Herman, Masha, Tamara, and even Yadwiga, to a lesser extent, are forced to deal with the painful aftereffects of anguished memory. Yet only Tamara and Yadwiga remain at the end, which is telling. While one could see in the conclusion a lionizing of strong women or the idea that the "future is feminine," there is also none-too-subtle moralizing against adultery and, I think more problematically, stigmatization of those who lose the battle against anguished memory. The adulteress is reborn figuratively, but rather than allow her to live, no matter how painful her truth or how long her struggle with her anguish may last, Singer requires her to die. It is either the sacrifice needed for expiation or the path forward from the past or both. Singer does not (cannot) deny the reality of the trauma that Herman, Masha, and Tamara have suffered; in fact, even Tamara says to Yadwiga, "I'm not dead. I'm not alive. I'm not dead."[75] But Herman and Masha's anguished memories do not possess their own moral dignity, or at least ambiguity, as Singer telescopes a preference for a heroic or righteous overcoming in the characters of Yadwiga and Tamara. I suggest that the harsh ending may account for the ambivalence towards the film among audiences. Critics loved the ragged conclusion, but audiences, having invested time in the characters of Herman and Masha, probably wanted them to make their lives work somehow—if for no other reason to test Tamara's "managing" skills. That would have been beside the point for Singer, though, who wanted a tale that ended with, as Dorothy Bilik argues, "the recognition of the potential for new life in America," something absent from his European-based novels.[76] Bilik believes that Singer is more supportive of Herman than my reading suggests, but that for him, presenting a type of rogue that he knew so well from the shtetl was key, to quote Singer: "Their illusions were the illusions of mankind. The vandals who murdered millions of these people have destroyed a treasure of individuality that no literature dare try to bring back."[77]

172   *Chapter 4*

    Alexander Røsler's 1997 film, *Mendel,* is a story of both deep memory and postmemory of the second generation. Røsler, who was born in Dachau in 1947, came to Norway in the 1950s, and while the film is fictional, it has an autobiographical imprint. It centers on a nine-year-old boy named Mendel, played by Thomas Jüngling Sørensen, who is the youngest son in a Jewish family that has settled in Norway after the war. Like any child, Mendel is curious and observant, and he wants to know more about what happened to his parents during the war. In the absence of any discussion, Mendel begins using his imagination to create memory. He notices his father's Auschwitz tattoo, and his father will not explain it, but when Mendel writes a number on a friend's arm, his parents lose their tempers. Mendel's older brother teases him because he is permitted to see photos of the war, which only increases Mendel's thirst for knowledge, and he surreptitiously gains access to some of the images, which have the effect of informing and traumatizing him at the same time, giving him nightmares about falling, but they also disconnect him from his family's personal memory. After Mendel sees a photograph of a boy with his hands raised in the Warsaw Ghetto, he imitates that pose during a house fire when Norwegian firemen come in wearing gas masks to evacuate the family. Gradually, the truth comes out about how Mendel's father survived, and Mendel tries to demonstrate bravery and conquer his fear of falling by jumping off a ladder.

    The comedic moments in this otherwise dramatic, coming-of-age movie appear in the form of jokes told by Mendel and Mendel's father, Aron. The first joke comes close to the beginning of the film when Mendel remembers that his family would be driven around by a friendly German man after the war. On one of these rides, Mendel remembers his father asking the man: "Herr Fischer. Have you heard about the two Jews who were to be shot? They are placed against a wall. A soldier blindfolds them. One tears his blindfold off. The other hisses, "Ssshh, don't make any trouble, now."[78] Situating this joke in the context of the Holocaust heightens the incongruity and absurdity of the second Jewish prisoner's response, but it is in joking that Mendel begins his engagement with his parents, their past, and his fears.[79] Mendel eventually takes over as the joke teller in the family, relaying the last two of the film. The final joke is linked to the truth about a photograph, which Mendel's parents keep hidden from him, leading him to believe that the image holds the answer to all of his questions. When he finally sees the photo, which is only a portrait of a man, he is confused and angry, and he tells his brother David that had he been in the camps, he would have resisted. In classic older brother fashion, David dangles Mendel out of a window, which gives Mendel an intimate appreciation of the limits of resistance. It is revealed that the photograph is of David's biological father, who died during the Holocaust, and the boys put the photo on the wall, which signifies the surfacing of deep memory, and it begins the process of integrating Mendel truly into the family and its hidden knowledge.[80] In the film's climax, right before Mendel takes his literal and symbolic leap into the future, he tells his mother the final joke, which serves as a bookend to his father's joke at the beginning of the film:

> Mama, Did you hear about Moishe, who went for a walk and fell into a ravine? At the last moment, he caught hold of a branch and shouted, "Help, help, dear God, help me!" A voice from heaven replied, "Moishe, this is God speaking. Trust me, let go, and I'll catch you." Moishe looks up and shouts back, "I don't dare to." God repeats, "Moishe, this is God, let go, and no harm will come to you." Moishe looks up and shouts, "Hello up there, is there anyone else I could speak to?"[81]

For Aron, jokes are tools of defiance and deflection, tactics to keep deep memory at bay, while for Mendel, jokes provide a way for him to bond with his parents and satisfy his curiosity about his parents' history. In addition, by becoming the teller of jokes, Mendel is able to confront his acquired traumatic postmemory and take control of his fears. He embodies the children of survivors' need to know and their inability to comprehend at the same time. Still, as Jodi Egerton notes, Mendel, in the end, has become a part of the chain of memory transmission, which begins his "entry into the familial and cultural memory . . . [and] leads him to feel at home not only in Norway but also within his family."[82]

Memories of Jewish history and the Holocaust also work their way into Jill Soloway's series *Transparent,* which ran from 2014 to 2019 on Amazon Prime Video. The show starred Jeffrey Tambor as Maura Pfefferman (formerly Mort), a retired political science professor who comes out late in life as transgender to his children. The other major characters are Maura's bisexual daughters Sarah (played by Amy Landecker) and Ali (Gaby Hoffman), and Maura's son, Joshi (Jay Duplass), a music producer who has one failed relationship with women after another, including a rabbi, Rabbi Raquel Fein (played by Kathryn Hahn). Judith Light plays Maura's ex-wife, Shelly, who, as it turns out, knew of Maura's identity while they were married. For Soloway, who wrote for the acclaimed HBO show *Six Feet Under, Transparent* is a personal testament about sexuality and Judaism; her father is also transgender, and, as she says about her Jewishness to the *Jewish Daily Forward*—"We came from Larry David Seinfeld-y 'we are Jewish when it comes to food' people. . . . My parents are the post-Holocaust generation. . . . My mom came from parents who ran from pogroms. Nobody's proud to be Jewish, nobody believes the tradition has anything to offer. It's more 'we're not going to work on Yom Kippur because we have to but don't really know why.'"⁸³ *Transparent's* essential dilemma may be about what it means to be transgender, but the characters' Jewishness, their Jewish milieu, and discourse are foundational, and in Soloway's opinion and to her surprise, representing Jewishness is the more problematic aspect of the series: "'It's more controversial to be Jewy than trans,' she said, pointing to some of the nauseatingly antisemitic comments left on YouTube under the series trailer. 'There are more people saying horrible things about Jews than about trans people. It's crazy.'"⁸⁴

Many of *Transparent's* episodes focus on Jewish life cycle moments, holidays, and religious rituals. For instance, there is a storyline about Ali's aborted bat mitzvah, which created the opportunity for Maura to attend a trans camp for the first time. There is Rabbi Raquel's sermon about the Jews in the wilderness not being able to see the promised land. There is even a Yom Kippur episode with a break-the-fast dinner that degenerates into ugliness. Season two opens with a Jewish wedding between Sarah and her lover Tammy, but unlike previous gay and Jewish films that conclude in this way to affirm such a union, the wedding ends in disaster with Sarah breaking off the relationship, which then leads her to ask forgiveness from Tammy in the awkward beginning of the Yom Kippur episode. Some of the Jewish elements, like the latter, border on the tasteless and stereotypical, and as great as Judith Light is as Shelly, she is straight out of the *yiddishe mama* playbook. In episode five, when rabbi Raquel comes over to visit Shelly, after her current husband Ed, who suffers from dementia, goes missing, she plays yenta to the hilt, asking the rabbi: "Are you married? My Joshi is not married. Maybe you two could meet. He's gorgeous, absolutely gorgeous. How old are you?"⁸⁵

The storylines related to the Holocaust involve the estranged relationship between Maura and her mother, Rose, and the origins of a mysterious ring she passed down. This subplot also features magical realist elements, with characters from the past appearing in visions. In the first season, we learn that the ring came from Rose's sister, Tante Gitl. In the second season, we see in flashbacks that Rose grew up in Berlin when the Nazis came to power, and more importantly, we discover that Tante Gitl was Rose's brother, Gerson, who identified as transgender. Both Gitl and Rose frequented Magnus Hirschfeld's Institute for Sexual Research, which lobbied for sexual equality for LGBT persons and which the Nazis ransacked early on during Hitler's reign of terror. Gitl and Rose's mother objects to the lifestyle and confronts her son as she's dancing half-naked in the Institute ("If you're gonna be a girl, cover your tits. Shameful.")⁸⁶ But she knows the danger they face, and she is able to get a visa for her family to leave the country and join her husband in California. Gitl does not go and is arrested by the Nazis, presumably taken away to a camp to die, while Rose and her mother make their way to Los

Angeles, only to find that the dad has a new wife and family. Rose eventually marries and gets pregnant; while she is in labor, her husband sits in the waiting room saying that he knows he is having a girl and will call her Faye. Rose then gives birth to a boy, Mort, who is destined to become Maura.

Season three continues with both the dark and chaotic tone of the first two seasons, and it begins with Rabbi Raquel preparing a Passover service, talking about self-discovery and making a "break for freedom." The journeys in this season involve Maura's pursuit of gender reassignment surgery, Sarah's erratic behavior (moving from a sadomasochistic fetish life to Rabbi Raquel's synagogue), the suicide of Joshi's former lover, and his reconnecting with his born-again Christian son (leading to Joshi's brief conversion to Christianity), Ali's relationship with her literary theory professor, and finally, Shelly's quest to be heard above all the Pfefferman craziness with her one-woman show, "To Shell and Back." There are moments in this season that are difficult to sit through, and ones that I felt veered into the realm of self-loathing, particularly episode seven, entitled perhaps too obviously "Life Sucks and Then You Die," which features Joshi's conversion to Christianity and a disturbing, profanity-laced tirade by Rabbi Raquel against Sarah after she took her advice and hooked up with the synagogue's young cantor. The audience also gets more backstory, as we learn that Shelly was sexually abused by a teacher when she was in elementary school and that she and Mort hooked up in the 1960s at an art show, where Mort revealed his gender identity, and Shelly took to him nevertheless. Then everyone ends up on a cruise in which Shelly performs her one-woman show, Joshi throws the ashes of his former lover overboard, and Maura comes to terms with the fact that because of a heart problem, she cannot go through with gender reassignment surgery. The Jewishness of season three seems much more conflicted and even negative, offering very little comfort at points, leading to dead ends at others. While the Jewish and LGBT links in history remain prominent and help provide context and understanding for character motivations and plot, the Jewish framework seems to be more about constant questioning and searching for answers that may never come. Season four adds Israel to the mix as the Pfeffermans journey there, find lost relatives, and Ali stays behind to work through her feelings after experiencing the contradictions of life for Jewish Israelis and life for Palestinians.

After Jeffrey Tambor was fired from the show due to accusations of sexual harassment, season five wrapped with a one-episode musical that provoked so many conflicting emotions in me that they need unpacking here. Maura dies at the beginning of the episode, although we never see her, and the family is left to prepare for the funeral. The siblings fight and regroup, and at the end, Joshi gets Rabbi Raquel to bring a Torah so that Ali (now non-binary Ari) can have a "bart mitzvah," something that would be a clear violation of Jewish funeral rites. Yet cremation is as well, and that is what happens to Maura. The episode is actually a series of transgressions, culminating in Shelly's "Joy-a-Caust" finale that evokes the holiday of Purim, which is all about reclaiming joy from tragedy. The finale also calls to mind Bakhtin's carnival, in which "all endings are merely new beginnings."[87] For me, the most impactful LGBT Jewish moment of the entire series, reflecting Judaism's questioning, disdain for easy answers, and seeming preference for chaos, comes in episode six of season one, in which Sarah's ex-husband Leonard comes to the Pfefferman household and starts making a scene over dinner, and Maura intervenes with perhaps the best lines in the series, ones that, in my opinion, get at the heart of what it means to be LGBT and Jewish in the modern world—accepting, conflicted, loving, individualistic, messy:

> This is my family. Leonard, I am so sorry. This is my fault. Honey, I should have called you, and we should've talked. But I didn't do that. And I'm sorry about the Mort and the Maura and the he and the she. I'm just a person. And you're just a person. And here we are. And baby, you need to get in this whirlpool, or you need to get out of it.[88]

The memory types in the above five productions—*Matchmaker, Adam Resurrected, Harold and Maude, Mendel,* and *Transparent*—are both closer in messaging and more multifaceted than one category can capture. The characters often demonstrate multiple forms of Langer's typologies over the course of the films and perhaps even some that he did not identify in his work, but they are still useful analytical tools to help us understand how survivors construct and convey their memories and how the arts reflect this construction. Tainted, humiliated, anguished, and deep memory are reservoirs of narratives both in reality and in the mind of the artist. In Ruth Gordon's Maude, Ron Silver's Herman, Jeff Goldblum's Adam, Adir Miller's Yankele Bride, even Mendel and the children of *Transparent,* these different traumatic memory types become reified through cinema and serve as a bridge of engagement between survivors and the general public. In their human need for love, control, and healing, a need that might never be met or exist alongside other contradictory or even antisocial behaviors, these particular characters share a resistance to easy resolution and redemption, an idea, controversial though it remains, that is at the heart of Langer's analysis of survivor testimony as the "communal wound that cannot heal."[89]

MEMORY AND REVENGE COMEDIES

For many survivors, and their fictional incarnations in cinema, the elusive search for justice is a part of the process of working through trauma, and in the final section of this chapter, I will explore how memory of the Holocaust is incorporated into comedic films and productions about vengeance. These productions situate memory as the catalyst behind character motivation and action; it is memory that drives anger and a desire, not for justice necessarily, where a perpetrator might be brought to trial, but rather for revenge that takes the form of murder. In these five productions, characters and storylines have comedic qualities, which on a surface level provide relief for viewers, but they also serve to humanize both protagonists and antagonists and, more importantly, create the space for a conversation about morality. The five productions I will analyze next, *Getting Away with Murder, Genghis Cohn, This Must Be the Place, Mr. Kaplan,* and *Hunters,* come from different contexts, and they are as irregular in tone as they are in their overall effect and reception. What binds them are questions about ethics and basic human decency and the premise that the desire to avenge murder threatens to turn victim into perpetrator.

Released on 12 April 1996 and written and directed by Harvey Miller, who received an Academy Award nomination for his work on *Private Benjamin, Getting Away with Murder* stars Dan Aykroyd as Jack Lambert, an ethics professor who poisons his neighbor, Max Mueller, played by Jack Lemmon, whom Lambert believes is a Nazi war criminal. Initially, it appears as if there is a case of mistaken identity, which leads Lambert to feel guilty and dump his fiancée and woo Mueller's daughter, Inga, played by Lily Tomlin, but then the truth comes out that Mueller was a Nazi all along. Lambert admits to the crime, but the judge dismisses the case, leaving Lambert with a sense of dissatisfaction that justice was not served. This film is so stunningly off that it has a "zero" rating on Rotten Tomatoes. (For his part, critic Roger Ebert called the film a "sad embarrassment."[90]) To me, *Getting Away with Murder* felt as if it had been created by artificial intelligence or an alien who had surveyed information about the Holocaust, Nazis, Nazi war criminals, and comedy and wrote a screenplay. It is dark but never funny, revelatory about neo-Nazis but lacking an outrageous or grotesque quality to the villains. The creepiest and unintentionally funniest moment of the film comes when Dan Aykroyd and Lily Tomlin's characters have sex. There is so much potential in a film about survivor and perpetrator memory, and there are several moments where incongruities could emerge to provide comedic tension and then relief, but Miller did not explore or imagine these opportunities or even ask the questions: What constitutes true memories? What if one believes a memory so much that he or she thinks it is true, but it turns out to be false? What if one cannot even remember the truth anymore? This is the premise of Atom Egoyan's 2015 thriller, *Remember,* starring Christopher Plummer. I do not know if there is comic material to be mined here, but it might have been a springboard for something deeper or more unexpected.

    An example of this is the made-for-BBC-television feature, *Genghis Cohn*, from November 1993, directed by Australian theater and opera impresario Elijah Moshinsky. The film tells the story of a Jewish comedian (Cohn, played by Antony Sher) who is executed during the Holocaust and who comes back to haunt and possess his executioner, a German known as Otto Schatz, played by Robert Lindsay. We know that we are watching comedy rather than a horror show or melodrama right from the beginning as Cohn narrates: "How do you kill a Jewish comedian? Answer: Same as any comedian. You don't laugh at his jokes!" Cohn carries his sense of humor with him into the concentration camp even to the moment of his death, when he yells to his executioners, "*Kush mir im tokhes! (*Kiss my ass!") The film had its origins in a book from 1968 by French author, Romain Gary, entitled *The Dance of Genghis Cohn,* although there are major differences in structure and plotline between the book and the film. In the book, Cohn has been tormenting Schatz since the war, while in the film, he appears years later, in 1958, when Schatz has established himself as a police chief in a Bavarian town. In the book, a series of murders leads Schatz and Cohn to the Forest of Geist on the trail of the character of Florian, who represents Death, and Baroness Lily Von Pritwitz, a woman with an insatiable sexual appetite, turned on by humanity's lust for killing. The film retains the sexualized murders, but it turns the Baroness, played by Diana Rigg, into a love interest for Schatz, as the film's focus becomes more about the relationship between Schatz and Cohn and, more specifically, what happens to Schatz as the evidence increasingly points to him as the murderer. The transformation of Schatz is perhaps the most significant divergence between book and film; in the book, Schatz and Cohn simply quarrel like an old married couple, but in the film, Cohn exacts retribution for his murder by possessing Schatz and gradually turning him into a Jew, doing so with a light, humorous touch throughout the process. Daniel Craig, of James Bond fame, plays a German police officer investigating the crimes who suspects that Schatz is the killer, but Schatz professes his innocence and claims that he is possessed by a Jew who is turning him Jewish, forcing him to utter anti-Hitler jokes, Yiddish phrases, and say Kaddish, the Jewish prayer for the dead. Only when Schatz agrees to live as a Jew does Cohn leave, and another German is implicated in the murders. In the end, Schatz comes full circle—selling kosher food, beaten up by neo-Nazis, and uttering the phrase, "*kush mir im tokhes,"* which Cohn yelled in Yiddish to Schatz before his execution.

Genghis Cohn appeared in a watershed year for Holocaust memory work. In 1993, both the United States Holocaust Memorial Museum opened, and *Schindler's List* premiered, and memory is the anchor of the drama in both the book and film. When Cohn introduces himself to Schatz in the film, he is initially terrified that he is seeing a ghost, and he blurts out, "Who are you?" Cohn gives a one-word clue, *tokhes*, and Schatz completes the phrase—a phrase which, when first deciphered, not only heightened Schatz's desire to "kill the Jew" but also embedded a personal memory of his victim. On top of this personal dimension of memory, there is a symbolic, collective aspect. In the book, Romain Gary's concern was that Holocaust memory would fade away, while in the film, the fear becomes a neo-Nazi revival, which goes beyond denial of memory. The only antidote to this is a complete transformation of the German mind and spirit, which is what Cohn, as clown-ghost, aims to achieve.

In addition to commentary about memory, the novel and film provide examples of the clown-as-disrupter trope that we have seen on numerous occasions. The difference, in this case, is that the clown is a *dybbuk*, a vengeful spirit out of Eastern European Jewish lore who takes possession of a living person. The haunting in the film is at once literal and metaphorical, symbolic of the "seething presence," in the words of Avery Gordon, of the ghosts of thousands of murdered Jews whose absence and yet nearness is in an inescapable reality in Germany.[91] For Gordon, ghosts also represent the ability to make amends, a "future possibility of hope," which comes through in Schatz's transformation at Cohn's comic hands.[92] More importantly, according to scholar Eli Pfefferkorn, whom I consulted heavily for the previous chapter but whose actual article was on *Genghis Cohn*, the use of the grotesque and fantasy images "familiarizes the unreality of the Holocaust world . . . by their very perverted extravagances, these devices make it possible for the uninitiated to grasp imaginatively the preposterous fantasies of the Holocaust reality and subsequently to perceive them cognitively."[93]

The ghosts are simply figurative in Paolo Sorrentino's 2011 film, *This Must Be The Place,* which stars Sean Penn as Cheyenne, a retired, Goth rock star (in the vein of Robert Smith of the Cure), who is living in Dublin and who goes on a quest to seek revenge against a Nazi, Alois Lange, who persecuted his father in Auschwitz. Cheyenne discovers the truth about Lange after traveling to New York to reconnect with his dying father, with whom Cheyenne has had no relationship since he was a teenager because his father rejected Cheyenne's lifestyle. His father dies before any resolution can happen, but Cheyenne stumbles upon his father's diary, which leads him to the information about Lange, and so begins a journey that takes him to numerous locations across the United States. Cheyenne seeks out a Nazi hunter, played by

Judd Hirsch, and while driving across the country, Cheyenne meets Lange's wife, his granddaughter, and a local entrepreneur (Harry Dean Stanton), who gives Cheyenne the actual whereabouts of the man now going by the name of Peter Smith. Determined to kill Lange, Cheyenne discovers a blind old man living in a trailer in the middle of salt-flats. He learns what happened to his father; Lange apparently had a German shepherd attack and nearly kill him in the camp. After the war, his father's knowledge of Lange's whereabouts led him to send letters to the war criminal, which Lange admits made his life impossible, but it also generated a degree of respect. In his words: "The unrelenting beauty of revenge. An entire life dedicated to avenging a humiliation. That's what I call perseverance. Greatness, even."[94] Cheyenne takes a picture of Lange and tells him that it was an injustice that his father died before he did. He then forces a naked Lange to walk outside of his trailer in the cold. At the very end, we see Cheyenne without his crazy hair and make-up, giving the impression that he has finally moved on from his state of arrested development.

Mr. Kaplan, a film from Uruguay, directed by Álvaro Brechner and released on 6 August 2014, is a similar story about revenge, but it centers on the limits of memory. The main character, Jacob Kaplan, played by Hector Noguera, an elderly survivor living with his family in Montevideo, starts stalking a German man, Julius Reich, played by Rolf Becker, who runs a beach bar and whom Kaplan suspects was once a Nazi camp guard. With the help of an alcoholic former police officer Wilson Contreras (played by Nestor Guzzini), Kaplan goes in search of Reich's identity, and the two find clues that seem to add up after visiting Reich's stripper daughter and sneaking into the wake of a partner of the alleged war criminal. Reich accosts Kaplan on a bus after he reveals that he is aware that he has been under surveillance, but Wilson and Kaplan are able to shoot Reich with a tranquilizer gun and get him to a boat. When he awakes, he is angry that people will not leave him alone; he admits that he was a kapo, a concentration camp work foreman, but that he was not a camp guard. "Who gives a damn about an almost dead kapo? I've been running away like a rat for fifty years. I'm old and tired," he says before jumping overboard.[95] This prompts Kaplan to jump in the water after him in a rescue attempt, but because he cannot swim, Wilson jumps in after him. Reich climbs back on the boat, and then realizing Wilson and Kaplan are gone, he jumps back in the water and saves them both. Afterward, Reich goes into greater detail about his experience, revealing that he had been a prisoner but that he took the position as a foreman as the only way to survive. "But you can't escape the past. It always finds you." Then Reich asks Kaplan, "what's your plan for me?" and as he sits mute, Reich adds, "Did you really jump in without knowing how to swim?"[96] Kaplan returns home to a family worried about his grip on reality, but he seems relieved that the whole affair is over.

In the Amazon series *Hunters,* created by David Weil, vengeance and torture serve as metaphorical salves on the wounds of traumatic memory. The show combines action, thriller, drama, and comedy in a story arc of Nazi hunters operating in New York City in 1977. It stars Al Pacino as Meyer Offerman, a survivor who heads the group, and Logan Lerman as Jonah, whose grandmother is also a survivor and a part of Offerman's team; her murder in the first episode sets Jonah's journey into motion and results in his desire to join the league. The other members of the troupe include survivors Murray and Mindy Markowitz, played by Saul Rubinek and Carole Kane; a Vietnam veteran, Joe Mizushima, played by Louis Ozawa; a young African-American woman named Roxy Jones (played by Tiffany Boone); a former British secret service agent and German-Jewish child refugee known as Sister Harriet (played by Kate Mulvaney); and for comic relief, there is Lonny Flash, an actor and master of disguise, played by Josh Radnor of *How I Met Your Mother* fame. Adding urgency to the efforts of the Hunters is a plot to restore Hitler's Reich by neo-Nazis led by a mysterious woman known as the Colonel (played by *Enemies, A Love* Story's Lena Olin) and facilitated by a deep undercover Nazi who works in the Carter administration (Biff Simpson, played by Dylan Baker). In addition, an FBI officer, Jerrika Hinton, as Millie Morris, discovers both the Nazis' plan and the Hunters group during a murder investigation. Members of the group torture a Leni Riefenstahl character by forcing her to eat horse excrement, and then they torture and murder rocket expert Wernher von Braun. The backstory of the relationship between Offerman and Jonah's grandmother unfolds, and we learn that in the camp, a dangerous romantic competition developed between Offerman and a camp doctor, Wilhelm Zuchs, known as "The Wolf." In the final episode of the first season, we discover that Al Pacino's "Meyer" is actually "The Wolf," and that he killed the real Meyer, underwent plastic surgery after the war, and, out of guilt for his actions, decided to form the Hunters group. Jonah kills Zuchs, and Mizushima is kidnapped and brought to the Colonel in Argentina, where we learn an equally shocking truth: the Colonel is Eva Braun, she is living with a very-much-alive Hitler, and they have four identical-looking Aryan boys.

Leaving aside the critical and popular bomb, *Getting Away with Murder,* the other productions generally rate highly among critics, although most have been failures at the box office. (*Hunters* has the highest popular score compared to the other films on Rotten Tomatoes at sixty-seven percent, and while this constitutes a "fresh" or positive rating, it is only slightly above *This Must Be the Place* and *Mr. Kaplan,* both of which have ratings of fifty-eight, which puts them in the under sixty or "rotten" category).[97] The independent scale of the films cannot be separated from either their context or their subject matter.

Any film from Uruguay will have difficulty gaining traction in the U.S. market, and a film about survivors chasing or possessing Nazis will need splashy production sheen and star power to entice viewers. The Tarantino-esque quality to *Hunters* can partly explain its edge here, as it is able to tackle the moral conundrum of what to do with Nazis who have escaped justice in a way that satisfies primal and commercial urges. It remains to be seen how the storyline of *Hunters* will resolve in the next couple of seasons, but it appears that far from glorifying the violent ends of perpetrators (which may satisfy some audiences), the lesson of the show is closer to the ambiguous or ragged conclusions of *This Must Be the Place* and *Mr. Kaplan,* whose characters are bedeviled by their memories. They (and by extension, we) are commanded never to forget, but what happens when memory becomes a trap and leads to a situation in which victims transform into the very killers they have been pursuing? In the case of *Genghis Cohn,* it is not the Jew who becomes a Nazi, but the Nazi who transforms into a Jew against his will, perhaps a less violent but no less invasive proposition that robs a human being of free will.

A glance at motivations is helpful here and demonstrates the impact of time and place. Gary wrote his novel, *The Dance of Genghis Cohn,* following a trip in 1966 to Warsaw, during which he fainted from a vision of an arm emerging from a sewer grill shaking its fist. For Gary, Genghis reflected two sides of his upbringing—Jewish and Tatar, and one of the aims of the book was to force, in a comical way, a "dance" between Jews and Gentiles to prevent collective amnesia from taking hold among the latter and to bring Gentiles to a true understanding of the suffering inflicted on the Jewish people.[98] Fast forward a generation, and we have a different set of concerns. While anxieties over memory's disappearance remain, in the context of the loss of surviving eyewitnesses, there is simply too much of a Holocaust memory infrastructure to allow that to happen. What exists is an almost contradictory reality of hyper-memorialization and rising authoritarianism (and antisemitism). The motivation is, thus, to dig deeper and ask the question—should we kill first and ask questions later? Sorrentino's desire in *This Must Be the Place* was to "have the main character somebody who did not live that period in the first person—who would have knowledge, but who would be forced to delve into that world and go and seek someone who was a Nazi criminal."[99] In the end, it is the search and ultimately the rejection of the desire to kill the Nazi that gives the character of Cheyenne the ability to find "a new lease on life."[100] In *Mr. Kaplan,* based at least partially on Marco Schwartz's novel, *El Salmo de Kaplan,* director Brechner fashioned a protagonist who had the wrong memory of, and wrong motivation about, the wrong man. Basing the character of Mr. Kaplan at least in part on his grandfather, who fled from Poland to Uruguay in 1939, Brechner said that the desire to be remembered after death, not righteous indignation, is what drives his protagonist, which lowers his moral standing and makes the situation (and ultimate misunderstanding) all the more absurd:

> I think humanity is basically a big misunderstanding. The need to give certain [meaning] to our existence, to feel that we're special, is, in a certain way, ridiculous. That's what happens to Mr. Kaplan. He asks himself, "Why will anyone remember me after I'm gone?" He looks back and does not see anything extraordinary, anything memorable—I cannot think in those terms if it's not in a humorous way. Anguish and anxiety are too big, especially because I do not have any answer to them. Humor helps accept that. It brings some relief to our absurd and ridiculous questions.[101]

With David Weil and Nikki Toscano's *Hunters,* we encounter representation that gives us the closest "yes" answer to the question about whether it is moral to kill Nazis. However, despite the show's excessive violence and bravado mixed with humor (I particularly like the "fucking Jewperheroes" references), there is more ambivalence here than meets the eye, or at least some tension between the two showrunners. Weil, whose grandmother survived Auschwitz and Bergen-Belsen, has said that he wanted to create a show that featured "a Jewish superhero with might, with power, with strength, not just a Jew who is as the media often portrays us, as ineffectual or intellectual only or nebbishy."[102] In another interview, he admits that for him as a Jew, "who wants to reclaim power, to have a voice, to feel mighty in some kind of way, I think this show allows for that catharsis, that wish fulfillment, so to speak."[103] But at what cost? The torture scenes are excruciating, and the executions run counter to the Jewish prohibition against murder. Historians from the Auschwitz Museum have also criticized the show for its depiction of life and death in the concentration camps, including a segment featuring a human chess game in which the Nazis use, and then execute, prisoners as pawns. Museum historians asserted that "artists have a special obligation to tell the truth" about the camp.[104] Both showrunners do not deny this, and co-producer, Nikki Toscano, appears to moderate Weil's desires to go full-on Tarantino:

> I think the biggest thing that I will say about violence, and speaking to what David said earlier, is this idea that throughout the course of the first season and hopefully beyond, this is a show that is asking those questions. It's not just perpetrating violence for violence's sake. It's asking the question, what is the cost of that violence? All the time in the writer's room, a lot of what we were discussing was the idea that, do you become the monster that you're hunting? Do you have to be evil to fight it?[105]

Once we discover that the entire ring is led by a Nazi posing as a Jew, the actions of the survivors can be at least put into a new context, and while not legitimized, explained as yet another form of dehumanization. In this new light, one can reassess how to see these characters and their behavior. Jonah's postmemory becomes poisoned, not from some inherent desire, but because it is manipulated by a psychopath, and I think this is a fitting epithet for someone who murders a person and then goes so far as to alter his physical appearance to become him. The twist is in many ways the flip side of *Genghis Cohn;* here, the Nazi takes over the Jew's memories as his own and for his own twisted ends, and he has successfully brought others to his cause by exploiting their Ids, their basest desires for revenge, and removing any checks on them. Even the way in which Zuchs intends to right his wrong, by continuing to murder people, demonstrates that he is a sociopath who has not shed any of his ideology or his antisocial behavior. Zuchs not only contaminates the memories of individuals, but he does this to the collective memory and ethos of the Jewish people as well, whose greatest quality he says is the "capacity to remember," as he proceeds to corrode this memory from within with phrases like "it's not murder, it's *mitzvah*," and "The Talmud is wrong, living well is not the best revenge; revenge is the best revenge." It is clear that as the show progresses, there will be additional, unexpected moments and plot twists that will confound reviewers and spark discussions about morality, but I suspect that the showrunners will continue to prefer uncertainty to clear-cut answers to the essential question: If revenge and violence are evil, how do we contend with the threat of fascism and antisemitism if they cannot be eliminated by a pervasive campaign of memory and education and traditional forms of justice and politics?

In her one-person, autobiographical stage play, *Punch Me in the Stomach,* New Zealand comic Deb Filler captures the surreal nexus of traumatic and comedic memory. She ends by recounting a trip she took with her father, a survivor of Auschwitz, to the camp. She remembers her father saying, "Listen, thanks for coming with me. I'm glad that you're here. I couldn't have come alone. I don't think I'll be coming back to that place. You like me to buy you a souvenir, darling?" "No, dad," she responds. "I'm going to the toilet." "Don't be too long," her dad cautions, "I got locked in here once before. I don't wanna get locked in again."[106] In this chapter, we have surveyed a diverse array of comedic films about Holocaust memory—films that offer perspectives on the link between collective memory and national identity, films that explore the psychological dimensions of traumatic memories, and films about the frailty and manipulability of memory. To reprise Oren Stier from the beginning, "memory matters." It remains a key focus of academic and creative work about the Holocaust because it addresses multiple questions about who we are as humans—how we move forward from trauma, how we process the past and then create it as history. In the unfinished work that is Holocaust scholarship, memory is everywhere. The films from this chapter are a by-product of this turn in scholarship, and as comedies or comedy dramas, they add another layer of discursive possibility to our exploration of both memory and the Holocaust experience. From Genghis Cohn, Adam Stein, and Lonny Flash's jokes to Harold's fake suicides and Tamara Broder's breezy advice about managing her husband's life, humor orients the tone and the drama of each film. It does so in a way that invites, rather than shocks or preaches, to keep viewers from turning away or leaving the cinema. The films demonstrate, above all, that humor is a part of human discourse, part of life, not something outside it, and that it is one way of communicating and making sense of everything around us, even, and perhaps especially, the painful moments.

NOTES

1. Oren Baruch Stier, *Committed to Memory*, 1.

2. Stier, *Committed to Memory*, 1.

3. Iwona Irwin-Zarecka, *Frames of Remembrance: The Dynamics of Collective Memory* (New Brunswick, NJ: Transaction Press, 1994), 53.

4. See Émile Durkheim, "Preface to the Second Edition," in *The Rules of Sociological Method and Selected Texts on Sociology and its Method*, ed. S. Lukes, and trans. W. D. Halls (New York: Free Press, 1982 [1901]), 34–47, and Barbara Misztal, "Durkheim on Collective Memory," *Journal of Classical Sociology*, Vol. 3, No. 2 (2003): 123–143. See also Maurice Halbwachs, *On Collective Memory*, ed. Lewis A. Coser (Chicago: University of Chicago Press, 1992), 23–25.

5. James Young, *The Texture of Memory: Holocaust Memorials and Meaning* (New Haven, CT: Yale University Press, 1993), xi. See also Barry Schwartz, "Rethinking the Concept of Collective Memory," and Jeffrey Goldfarb, "Against Memory," in *The Routledge International Handbook of Memory Studies*, ed. Anna Lisa Tota and Trever Hagen (London: Routledge, 2016), and James Fentress and Chris Wickham, *Social Memory* (Oxford: Blackwell, 1992).

6. Baruch Stier, *Committed to Memory*, 9.

7. Irwin-Zarecka, *Frames of Remembrance*, 47.

8. Irwin-Zarecka, *Frames of Remembrance*, 47.

9. David Inglis, "Globalization and/of Memory," in *Routledge International Handbook of Memory Studies*, 153, 144.

10. Irwin-Zarecka, *Frames of Remembrance*, 95.

11. Lawrence Langer, *Holocaust Testimonies*, 21, 40, 54, 74–75, 77, 126, 140, 205.

12. Joshua Hirsch, *Afterimage: Film, Trauma, and the Holocaust*, 162.

13. Friedrich Nietzsche, *On the Genealogy of Morals*, trans. Walter Kaufmann, and RJ Hollingdale (New York: Vintage, 1989), 61, and Hirsch, *Afterimage*, 26. See in addition, Laurence J. Kirmayer, "Landscapes of Memory: Trauma, Narrative, and

Dissociation," in *Tense Past: Cultural Essays on Trauma and Memory,* ed. Paul Antze and Michael Lamek (London: Routledge, 1996).

14. Cathy Caruth, *Unclaimed Experience: Trauma, Narrative, and History* (Baltimore, MD: Johns Hopkins University Press, 1996), 2.

15. Hirsch, "Post-Traumatic Cinema and the Holocaust Documentary," in *Trauma and Culture,* ed. Kaplan and Wang, 101.

16. *Crimes and Misdemeanors*, directed by Woody Allen (New York: Jack Rollins & Charles H. Joffe Productions 1989), DVD, 1:10–1:13.

17. Kaori Shoji, "Latin America's 'Woody Allen' on Jewish Life in Argentina," *The Japan Times,* 20 January 2006, https://www.japantimes.co.jp/culture/2006/01/20/films/latin-americas-woody-allenon-jewish-life-in-argentina/#.Xt1Nsud7k2w, accessed 1 February 2021.

18. https://www.thetollboothmovie.com/director, accessed 1 February 2021.

19. 'Kaori Shoji, "Latin America's 'Woody Allen' on Jewish Life in Argentina," *The Japan Times,* 20 January 2006, https://www.japantimes.co.jp/culture/2006/01/20/films/latin-americas-woody-allenon-jewish-life-in-argentina/#.Xt1Nsud7k2w, accessed 1 February 2021. See also Tamara Leah Falicov, *The Cinematic Tango: Contemporary Argentine Film* (New York: Wallflower, 2007).

20. Berenbaum, quoted in Anson Rabinbach, "From Explosion to Erosion: Holocaust Memorialization in America Since Bitburg," *History and Memory,* Vol. 9, Nos. 1 and 2 (Fall 1997): 230, and David Bathrick, "Cinematic Americanization of the Holocaust in Germany: Whose Memory is It?" In *Americanization and Anti-Americanism: The German Encounter with American Culture After 1945* (New York: Berghahn, 2007), 130.

21. Efraim Sicher, "The Future of the Past: Countermemory and Postmemory in Contemporary American Holocaust Narratives," *History and Memory*, Vol. 12, No. 3 (Fall/Winter 2000): 59.

22. David Landry, "Faint Hope-A Theological Interpretation of Woody Allen's *Crimes and Misdemeanors,*" *Journal of Religion and Popular Culture*, Vol. 22, No. 1 (2010): 14, and Eric Lax, *Conversations with Woody Allen: His Films, The Movies, and Moviemaking* (New York: Knopf, 2007), 122.

23. A. O. Scott, film writing for the *New York Times*, said: "*Lost Embrace* never feels strenuous or overdone. The tenderness of the family drama at its center, and the deep, hard-to-articulate feelings of a son for his enigmatic father and his heroically patient mother, emerge with a charming haphazardness. The sly artfulness is apparent only in retrospect. This is a small movie about a small world, but its modesty is part of what makes it durable and satisfying." A. O. Scott, "Resenting an Absent Father, Very Present in the Mind," *New York Times,* 28 January 2005, section E, 8. https://www.nytimes.com/2005/01/28/movies/resenting-an-absent-father-very-present-in-the-mind.html, accessed 6 February 2021.

24. Jeannette Catsoulis, "Coming of Age in a Strange Land," *New York Times,* 3 February 2006, section E, p. 10, https://www.nytimes.com/2006/02/03/movies/coming-of-age-in-a-strange-land.html, accessed 6 February 2021.

25. Ronnie Scheib, "Review of *The Tollbooth,*" *Variety,* 4 November 2004. https://variety.com/2004/film/reviews/tollbooth-2-1200529744/, accessed 6 February 2021.

26. Giacomo Lichtner, *Fascism in Italian Cinema Since 1945: The Politics and Aesthetics of Memory* (New York: Palgrave Macmillan, 2013), 13. See also, Luca Barattoni, "The Aesthetics Emerging After the War," in Barratoni's *Italian Post-Neorealist Cinema* (Edinburgh: Edinburgh University Press, 2012).

27. Lichtner, *Fascism in Italian Cinema*, 115.

28. Lichtner, *Fascism in Italian Cinema*, 115.

29. See Suzanne Langlois, "Images That Matter: The French Resistance in Film, 1944–1946," *French History*, Vol. 11, No. 4 (December 1997): 461–485.

30. Karen Jaehne, "Un héros très discret," (*A Self-Made Hero*), Interview with Jacques Audiard, 1996 Cannes Film Festival, http://www.filmscouts.com/scripts/interview.cfm?File=her-tre, accessed 10 February 2021.

31. Stephen Saito, "AFI Fest '15 Interview: *Dheepan* Director Jacques Audiard on Being the Eternal Outsider," *moveablefest.com*, 8 November 2015, http://moveablefest.com/jacques-audiard-dheepan/, accessed 10 February 2021.

32. Kevin Flanagan, "The British War Film, 1939–1980: Culture, History, and Genre," (unpublished thesis, University of Pittsburgh, 2015), 3, 13, 36.

33. Karl Quinn, Karl, "John Cleese slams UKTV decision to remove *Fawlty Towers* episode as 'stupid,'" *The Sydney Morning Herald*, 12 June 2020, https://www.smh.com.au/culture/tv-and-radio/john-cleese-slams-uktv-decision-to-remove-fawlty-towers-episode-as-stupid-20200612-p5523w.html, accessed 13 February 2021.

34. See the interview with Socha by Digital Spy, "*Misfits*' Kelly: 'Hitler comes back, and I save the day ... obviously," 31 October 2011, https://www.youtube.com/watch?v=x0DGCPSX4Pk, accessed 13 February 2021.

35. Dean Burnett, "Time Travellers: Please Don't Kill Hitler," *The Guardian*, 21 February 2014, https://www.theguardian.com/science/brain-flapping/2014/feb/21/time-travellers-kill-adolf-hitler, accessed 13 February 2021.

36. Catsoulis said that Morrison "serves up prejudice over easy, joining the ranks of too many filmmakers who suggest that sports and sexual flirtation can cure all social ills. We wish." "Prejudice Blossoms When Neighbors Connect," *New York Times*, 3 November 2006, https://www.nytimes.com/2006/11/03/movies/03obli.html, accessed 13 February 2021. For Elley, the problem with the film was the fact that it was over-obviously celebrating solidarity between minorities rather than a broader message. That's a shame, as the picture works best as a pan-human comedy with warm touches, rather than as a finger-wagging lecture." "*Wondrous Oblivion*," *Variety*, 13 August 2003, https://variety.com/2003/film/reviews/wondrous-oblivion-1200539974/, accessed 13 February 2021.

37. Sean Braswell, "*Fawlty Towers* Mentions the War," *OZY*, 20 October 2015, https://www.ozy.com/good-sht/fawlty-towers-mentions-the-war/65267/, accessed 13 February 2021.

38. Braswell, "*Fawlty Towers*," See also Robert Gore Langton, *John Cleese* (London: Essential Books, 1999), 76–77.

39. See for instance, Paul May's 1957 *Der Fuchs von Paris (The Fox of Paris)*, which looks at D-Day from the German perspective, Bernhard Wicki's 1959 film, *Die Brücke (The Bridge)*, also about German army soldiers on the Western Front, Georg Wilhelm Pabst's *Es geschah am 20. Juli (Jackboot Mutinty)*, from 1955, about the

assassination attempt on Hitler's life in 1944, and Helmut Käutner's film, *Des Teufels General (The Devil's General)*, also from 1955 based on the story of General Ernst Udet, who was part of the resistance.

40. The feting of Thälmann in the postwar era stands in contrast to how he was treated during the years of the Reich. Although he was in prison for eleven years until his execution in Buchenwald in 1944, Stalin did nothing to secure his release, and many German communists who fled the Third Reich to the Soviet Union were murdered over the course of Stalin's purges in the 1930s.

41. Irwin-Zarecka, *Frames of Remembrance*, 50.

42. *The Bloom of Yesterday* (*Die Blumen von Gestern*), directed by Chris Kraus. Munich: Dor Film-West Produktionsgesellschaft 2016, DVD.

43. Glenn Collins, "A German Film Director Muses On His Country's Past and Future," *New York Times*, 8 October 1990, Section C, 11.

44. PÖFF interview with Chris Kraus, 21 November 2016, https://www.youtube.com/watch?v=1v3rz2tcOWc, accessed 14 February 2021.

45. *The Bloom of Yesterday*, 38:00.

46. Marianne Hirsch, *Family Frames: Photography, Narrative, and Postmemory* (Cambridge, MA: Harvard University Press, 1997), 22.

47. Zarecka, *Frames of Remembrance*, 95.

48. Eyal Zandberg, "Critical Laughter: Humor, Popular Culture and Israeli Holocaust Commemoration," *Media, Culture, Society*, Vol. 28 (2006): 572.

49. Liat Steir-Livny, "Holocaust Satires on Israeli TV: The Battle against Canonic Memory Agents," *Jednak Ksiazki: Gdanskie Czasopismo Humanistyczne*, No. 6 (2016): 200.

50. Avraham Burg, *The Holocaust is Over: We Must Rise from Its Ashes* (New York: Palgrave Macmillan, 2008), 239.

51. *The Matchmaker*, directed by Avi Nesher. Tel Aviv: Metro Communications 2010, DVD. 1:45–1:46.

52. *Adam Resurrected*, directed by Paul Schrader. Ramat Gan: July August Productions 2008, DVD. 0:06–0:07.

53. See Nicholas Rapold's review, "Amid Unrest, Hope and Glimmers of Romance," *New York Times*, 17 August 2012, Section C, 12, https://www.nytimes.com/2012/08/17/movies/the-matchmaker-by-avi-nesher.html, accessed 20 February 2021, and Roger Ebert, "You don't know what you want. Yankele knows," https://www.rogerebert.com/reviews/the-matchmaker-2012, 12 December 2012, accessed 20 February 2021. *The Matchmaker* won a number of awards in 2010 at the Israeli Academy Awards, including Best Actor for Adir Miller and Best Actress for Maya Dagan. *Adam Resurrected*, meanwhile, holds a 35 percent critical and 44 percent audience rating on Rotten Tomatoes. See, among others, Owen Gleiberman's review in *Entertainment Weekly*, 10 December 2008, https://ew.com/article/2008/12/10/adam-resurrected/, accessed 20 February 2021. Andrew Sarris for *The Observer*, however, recommended the film because, in his words, "there has never been anything like it in the history of cinema as far as I can remember." And Kirk Honeycutt, for *The Hollywood Reporter*, said Schrader "pulls off enough of this impressionistic comedy to provoke passions and arguments anew about a topic that seems done

to death," https://www.rottentomatoes.com/m/adam_resurrected/reviews?type=top_critics, accessed 21 February 2021.

54. Hannah Brown, "Once I Was Avi Nesher: Celebrated Director Discusses Emotional New Film," *The Jerusalem Post,* https://www.jpost.com/arts-and-culture/entertainment/once-i-was-avi-nesher, 25 June 2010, accessed 20 February 2021.

55. George Kouvaros, "Pretending that Life Has No Meaning: Interview with Paul Schrader," *Rouge,* 19 September 2005, http://www.rouge.com.au/11/schrader.html, accessed 20 February 2021. For the recounting of the Haifa premiere, see his interview with Karlovy Vary, "Paul Schrader *Adam Resurrected Interview,*" 26 July 2009, https://www.youtube.com/watch?v=dofnOwWfPxk, accessed 20 February 2021.

56. Langer, *Holocaust Testimonies,* 122.
57. Langer, *Holocaust Testimonies,* 122.
58. *The Matchmaker,* 00:36.
59. *The Matchmaker,* 00:47–00:48
60. Langer, *Holocaust Testimonies,* 77.
61. Langer, *Holocaust Testimonies,* 77.
62. Michael Shedlin, "Review of *Harold and Maude,*" *Film Quarterly,* Vol. 26, No. 1 (Autumn 1972): 53

63. *Variety* staff review of 31 December 1970, https://variety.com/1970/film/reviews/harold-and-maude-1200422491/, accessed 22 February 2021.

64. James Davidson, *Hal Ashby and the Making of Harold and Maude* (Jefferson, NC: McFarland, 2016), 94, 167.

65. Langer, *Holocaust Testimonies,* 9.
66. *Harold and Maude,* directed by Hal Ashby. Los Angeles: Paramount Pictures and Colin Higgins Productions 1971, DVD. 00:41–00:42.
67. *Harold and Maude,* 00:42.
68. *Harold and Maude,* 1:09–1:10.
69. *Enemies, A Love Story,* directed by Paul Mazursky. Los Angeles: Morgan Creek Entertainment 1989, DVD. 00:10–00:11.
70. *Enemies,* 00:23:54.
71. *Enemies,* 1:20:00.
72. *Enemies,* 1:34:00.
73. Langer, *Holocaust Testimonies,* 54.
74. Langer, *Holocaust Testimonies,* 75.
75. *Enemies,* 1:20:00.
76. Dorothy Bilik, "Singer's Diasporan Novel: *Enemies, A Love Story,*" *Studies in American Jewish Literature* No. 1, *Isaac Bashevis Singer: A Reconsideration* (1981): 99.

77. Singer, *Author's Note to A Crown of Feathers* (New York: Farrar, Straus, and Giroux, 1973), 9 as cited in Bilik, "Singer's Diaspoan Novel," 93.

78. *Mendel,* directed by Alexander Røsler. Cologne: Lichtblick Film-und Fernsehproduktion 1997, DVD. 00:2:40–2:52.

79. Jodi H. Egerton, "*Kush mir in tokhes!*": Humor and Hollywood in Holocaust Films of the 1990s," (unpublished thesis, University of Texas at Austin, 2006), 150, 166.

80. Egerton, *"Kush mir,"* 172.

81. *Mendel,* 01:28:00–1:31:00.
82. Egerton, "*Kush mir,*" 145, 176.
83. Debra Nussbaum Cohen, "How Jill Soloway Created *Transparent*—The Jewiest Show Ever," *The Forward,* 21 October 2014, http://forward.com/culture/207407/how-jill-soloway-created-transparent-the-jewiest/#ixzz3wlf4GOGy, accessed 8 January 2016.
84. Nussbaum Cohen, "How Jill Soloway."
85. *Transparent,* Season 1, Episode 5, 15:00.
86. *Transparent,* Season 2, Episode 8, 8:00.
87. Mikhail Bakhtin, *Problems in Dostoevsky's Poetics,* trans. Caryl Emerson (Minneapolis: University of Minnesota Press, 1984), 163.
88. *Transparent,* Season 1, Episode 6, 25:40.
89. Langer, *Holocaust Testimonies,* 204.
90. https://www.rottentomatoes.com/m/getting_away_with_murder, and Roger Ebert's review on https://www.rogerebert.com/reviews/amp/getting-away-with-murder-1996. Both were accessed 25 February 2021.
91. Avery Gordon, *Ghostly Matters: Haunting and the Sociological Imagination* (Minneapolis: University of Minnesota Press, 1997), 8, 14, and Egerton, "*Kush mir,*" 118, 125.
92. Gordon, *Ghostly Matters,* 8, 14, and Egerton, "*Kush mir,*" 118, 125.
93. Eli Pfefferkorn, "The Art of Survival," 84. See also Jonathan Schorsch, " Jewish Ghosts in Germany," *Jewish Social Studies,* Vol. 9, No. 3 (2003): 139–169.
94. *This Must Be the Place,* directed by Paolo Sorrentino. Rome: Indigo Films, 2011, DVD. 01:36:00–01:37:11.
95. *Mr. Kaplan,* directed by Álvaro Brechner. Madrid: Baobab Films, 2014, DVD. 01:24:00–01:25:00.
96. *Mr. Kaplan,* 01:27:00–01:28:00.
97. https://www.rottentomatoes.com/m/this_must_be_the_place, https://www.rottentomatoes.com/m/mr_kaplan, https://www.rottentomatoes.com/tv/hunters-2020, all accessed 27 February 2021. *Mr. Kaplan* won multiple awards including the Uruguayan Film Critics Association Award for Best Picture in 2014. Of *Genghis Cohn,* John O'Connor said that it "walks a conceptual tightrope. It falters here and there, but its grim humor finally glimpses a measure of redemption," *New York Times,* 4 November 1994, Section D, Page 19. A.O. Scott praised *This Must Be the Place:* "Maybe, beneath the stylistic flourishes and bursts of operatic emotion, it is a simple story of psychological struggle, about a man in midlife reckoning with the damage of his past. But to settle on that interpretation is to deny or discount the splendid strangeness of Mr. Sorrentino's vision—and also, therefore, of the curious corners of reality he discovers along the way." "The '80s Are Long Over, Yet the Makeup Remains: *This Must Be the Place,*" *New York Times,* 1 November 2012, https://www.nytimes.com/2012/11/02/movies/this-must-be-the-place-by-paolo-sorrentino-with-sean-penn.html, accessed 27 February 2021. Finally, about *Mr. Kaplan,* Leslie Felperin, writing for *London Review,* praised the "fine comic timing" of the ensemble, https://www.hollywoodreporter.com/review/mr-kaplan-london-review-742477, accessed 27 February 2021, and *Variety's* reviewers called it a "a good-natured

foray into Yiddishkeit humor," https://variety.com/2015/film/festivals/film-review-mr-kaplan-1201405281/, accessed 27 February 2021.

98. Emma Garman, "Great Pretenders: In Romain Gary's Family, Invention was the Necessity of Mother and Son," 31 October 2007, https://www.tabletmag.com/sections/arts-letters/articles/great-pretenders, accessed 27 February 2021. See also, Ralph Schoolcraft, *Romain Gary: The Man Who Sold His Shadow* (Philadelphia: University of Pennsylvania Press, 2002). The warning about lost resonance is gone from the film, as Schatz simply becomes another Jew encountering antisemitism. As Jonathan Schorsch notes, in the book, Schatz says, "The public is saturated. They had enough of the Jewish shtik . . . . they want the Negro shtik and the Vietnam shtik. You can't keep 6 million Jews on the best-seller list forever." This rant signifies for Schorsch how "Germany's crimes against Jews is withered by being cast as a thirst for new exotic cultures . . . The Jewish ghost has won, yet the triumph is Pyrrhic, its haunting powers dismissed by the insatiable longing for ever more fashionable ghosts." Schorsch, "Jewish Ghosts," 143.

99. David Gritten, "Q & A: Sorrentino Talk Sean Penn-Starrer *This Must Be the Place*," 17 October 2012, https://www.indiewire.com/2012/10/q-a-sorrentino-talks-sean-penn-starrer-this-must-be-the-place-201329/, accessed 27 February 2021.

100. Gritten, "Q & A."

101. Pili Valdes, "Meet Alvaro Brechner, Director of Uruguay's Latest Nazi-Hunting Adventure: *Mr. Kaplan*," 29 July 2015, https://remezcla.com/features/film/alvaro-brechner-interview-mr-kaplan/, accessed 27 February 2021.

102. Gabe Friedman, "Murder or Mitzvah? Amazon's *Hunters* Grapples with the Morality of Jews Killing Nazis," 21 February 2020, https://www.jta.org/2020/02/21/culture/murder-or-mitzvah-amazons-hunters-grapples-with-the-morality-of-jews-killing-nazis, accessed 27 February 2021.

103. Danette Chavez, "Interview: *Hunters* Showrunners David Weil and Nikki Toscano on Punching Nazis and the Power of Al Pacino," 17 February 2020, https://tv.avclub.com/hunters-showrunners-david-weil-and-nikki-toscano-on-pun-1841676320, accessed 27 February 2021.

104. Monika Scislowska, "Auschwitz Museum Criticizes Amazon's *Hunters* for Dangerous Depiction of False Events at Holocaust Death Camp," *Time,* 24 February 2020.

105. Chavez interview.

106. *Punch Me in the Stomach,* starring Deb Filler, 9 September 2010, https://www.youtube.com/watch?v=ojj65zvf5C4, accessed 1 March 2021.

Chapter 5

Humor as Social Criticism

In 2004, Larry David's HBO comedy series *Curb Your Enthusiasm* aired an episode entitled "The Survivor," which featured two storylines—one about Hasidic Judaism and one about the Holocaust. The first storyline has David, who plays either a fictitiously offensive or offensively real version of himself, contemplating an affair with a Hasidic female friend, complete with jaw-dropping jokes about Hasidic notions of sex. The second subplot unfolds at a dinner in which a Holocaust survivor and a former contestant on the reality show *Survivor* square off in an escalating war of words. In his writing for the 1990s television comedy, *Seinfeld*, David created a world steeped in Jewish coding, and while much of this was unspoken and subtextual, it surfaced in a handful of episodes, especially the one about the "soup Nazi," who kicks people out of his store for the smallest infraction while ordering, and the episode where Seinfeld is caught necking with his girlfriend during *Schindler's List*, In *Curb Your Enthusiasm*, David more openly and frequently launches comedic assaults on everything Jewish, and many viewers found the "Survivor" episode to be particularly distasteful. My aim in this chapter is to situate the episode within the context of the use of Holocaust humor as satire—as a critique of, or warning about, aspects of the present.

A number of the films that we have covered in this manuscript so far could be labeled as satire, and while I offered a short definition in the introduction, a more thorough delineation is warranted here to amplify the distinction of the films in this chapter. In the *Oxford English Dictionary,* satire is defined as "a poem . . . a novel, film, or other work of art which uses humor, irony, exaggeration, or ridicule to expose and criticize prevailing immorality or foolishness, especially as a form of social or political commentary."[1] Using this definition, films that aimed to take down Nazism in its time, like *The Great Dictator,* could constitute satire, as would later productions that use the subject of Hitler and the Holocaust as a way of criticizing contemporary issues, such as *Look Who's Back* and *The Nasty Girl*. Professor Emeritus of English at New York University, Dustin Griffin, provides an excellent model for this chapter's conceptualization of the use of satire in connection with the Third Reich and Holocaust. In his book, *Satire: A Critical Reintroduction,* Griffin argues that satirists are not necessarily single-minded moralists, nor is satire a "neatly articulated homiletic discourse."[2] Rather, satirists see and direct attention to things that are awry in life, and they use different rhetorical strategies to point these out without necessarily offering closure or a definitive, opposing value system. These rhetorical forms, in Griffin's assessment, include a rhetoric of inquiry, through which a satirist raises questions about a problem, a rhetoric of provocation to expose or "demolish a foolish certainty," a rhetoric of display, which lays out the problem for all to see, and a rhetoric of play, which generates laughter and perhaps even offends, but gets the reader or audience to pause and think about the problem at hand.[3] Absent from this list is a rhetoric of moralism, and indeed Griffin believes, "the reader's interest is not in rediscovering that greed is a bad thing or that deceit is to be avoided but in working through (with the satirist's help) the implications of a given moral position (how far do you have to go in the public defense of virtue), the contradiction between one virtue (justice) and another (forgiveness), or the odd similarities between a vice (brazenness) and a virtue (steadfastness against censure)."[4] Griffin's view of satire as an "open" rather than a closed system, one that resists imposing its own set of values or virtues, does not apply to many of the films we have seen so far, which clearly do that in their contesting of Nazism, Hitler, and the Third Reich. However, for the films in this chapter, whose satires are not necessarily directed at these particular realities but whose satirists use the reality of Nazism and the Holocaust to satirize other realities, there is a greater focus on exposure through inquiry, provocation, and play rather than sermonizing.

I organize this chapter around five manifestations of Holocaust satire, specifically, five groupings of films and television productions from different times and places. The first group includes three films from Germany, *Schtonk!, The Parrot (Der Papagei)*, and *Terror 2000—Germany Out of Control (Intensivstation Deutschland);* each appeared in 1992, just two years after reunification. The second group consists of two animated episodes, one from *South Park,* entitled "Death Camp of Tolerance," and a skit from *Robot Chicken* called "Care Bear Genocide." The third group also comprises satires from the United States and includes the "Survivor" episode from *Curb Your Enthusiasm,* the episode "Wowschwitz," from *The Sarah Silverman Program,* and the skit from *The Amy Schumer Show* entitled, "The Museum of Boyfriend Wardrobe Atrocities." The fourth segment will deal with Sacha Baron Cohen and Larry Charles' *Borat* films, and the final group compares and contrasts Jeffrey Ross' *Historical Roast* of Anne Frank with Nathan Fielder's campaign against designer Taiga for its connection to an incident of Holocaust denial. Each production addresses a contemporary problem or issue through a satirical narrative that either entirely or partially references genocide, the Third Reich, or the Holocaust. It is my goal in this chapter to peel back the layers of this satire to reveal its purpose and, in the process, once again, to help evaluate its effectiveness.

THE 1992 GERMAN SATIRES

In 1983, the German publication, *Stern,* began publishing what its editors promoted as the authentic diaries of Adolf Hitler. These turned out to be forgeries and resulted in humiliation for journalists and historians alike. Writer-director Helmut Dietl satirized this scandal in his 1992 film, *Schtonk!,* a title taken from the nonsense word for revulsion which Charlie Chaplin repeatedly utters in his role as dictator Adenoid Hynkel in *The Great Dictator,* The film's main character is forger Fritz Knobel, played by Uwe Ochsenknecht, who makes and sells phony Nazi collectibles, including a disturbing portrait of Eva Braun in the nude. He comes upon the idea of forging and burying diaries of Hitler and getting a corrupt, right-wing journalist, Hermann Willié (played by Götz George), to dig them up and publish them. Knobel's plan works brilliantly at the beginning, even though he intersperses in the diaries odd quotes such as the following: "The superhuman efforts of recent times are giving me gas in my intestines, and Eva says that I have bad breath."[5] Far from casting doubt on the quote, publisher Dr. Wieland (played by Ulrich Mühe) declares it as "sensational," and editor Pit Kummer (played by Harald Juhnke) adds, "Adolf Hitler as a private person—a person like me and you."[6] Even when Knobel makes a mistake and labels one of the diaries with an FH rather than AH, experts remain nonplussed and instead debate the meaning of the inconsistency, proposing that it means either *Führers Hauptquartier* (in English, the Führer's Main Quarters) or possibly *Führer's Hund* (the Führer's dog). Willié begins to suspect that something is not right about the diaries, but after an independent committee of experts vouches for the handwriting, he doubles down on their authenticity and becomes an even bigger media celebrity when Knobel brings to Willié what he claims are the mixed cremains of Hitler and Eva Braun. Ultimately, Knobel, accompanied by his wife and lover, gets out of the country before Willié is told that the diaries are indeed fake and written by someone with limited "intellectual capacity." Set back but persistent, Willié goes to his publisher to propose an even greater scoop; if the handwriting experts were correct and the diaries were written after the war, that can mean only one thing—that Hitler lives!

There is a connection in personnel between *Schtonk!* and the next production, Ralf Huettner's made-for-TV film, *The Parrot (Der Papagei)*. Harald Juhnke and Veronica Ferres have roles in both. In fact, we see a number of actors reappearing in these satires, from Ulrich Mühe in *Schtonk!*, *Goebbels and Geduldig,* and *Mein Führer,* to Katja Riemann in *Goebbels and Geduldig* and *Look Who's Back*. In *The Parrot,* Juhnke plays Dieter "Did" Stricker, a down-on-his-luck actor selling sausages on the street. When a right-wing activist named Rainer (played by Dominic Raacke) sees Stricker's ability to connect with ordinary people, he convinces him to be a party spokesperson and candidate. Stricker wins over large crowds with his folksy charm and attacks on the government and other elites. He rails against the lack of Bibles in the country, saying that Germans have to go to America to find them in hotels there. However, he becomes increasingly nervous about the party's inclination towards violence, and he decides to turn on the party and become a spy to disclose their true nature. Rainer remains one step ahead and gets Dieter quietly retired to the countryside, where he remains popular but no threat to the party's ascent.

Terror 2000, meanwhile, another entry in Christoph Schlingensief's cinema of "unpleasure," begins with the premise that Germany is out of control ten years after unification. Asylum centers are overflowing, priests are corrupt sexual predators, and murder is everywhere. The film's focus is a refugee center, where two married detectives, Peter and Margret Korn (played by Peter Kern and Margit Castensen), investigate the disappearance of a social worker who was bringing a family to the camp. A wannabe Hitler stages a rally and rails against the camp's degenerates, and stomach-turning violence ensues between refugees and neo-Nazis. As in *100 Years of Adolf Hitler,* Schlingensief choreographs his actors so that they move as a unit performing violent, sexual, and excretory acts along the way. At the end of the film, the detectives discover that the social worker has been killed and that he was also transgender.

What are we to make of these films that are different in so many ways stylistically? The answer is fairly obvious; they converge around the topic of Germany's Nazi past and the threat this poses to the country's democratic future. All three filmmakers, Dietl, Huettner, and Schlingensief, filter their satire as warning through a different cinematic language, but the underlying premise of fascism lurking below the surface in German society is the glue that binds them together. In *Schtonk!,* commercialization, media obsession, and a Hitler fetish galvanize the radical right, although their celebrity darling is brought down somewhat in the end. In *The Parrot*, the celebrity has more ordinary roots, but there is a similar desire in neo-Nazi circles to capitalize on a particular image—that of the everyman—and to exploit it in the media for political gain. Meanwhile, the anti-immigrant and anti-gay themes, characters, and scenarios throughout *Terror 2000* present to audiences a portrait of a Germany that has succumbed to its vilest tendencies.

Although in interviews, Dietl, Huettner, and Schlingensief are often as circumspect as Griffin would expect a satirist to be, they diverge slightly from Griffin's model by more clearly advancing a worldview that is the opposite of the one they are satirizing. They may avoid extensive commentary that might either ruin the joke or undercut their rhetoric of provocation or play, but what they do say speaks volumes about the power of comedy to expose a deadly serious matter, namely the ever-present threat of right-wing radicalism in Germany. Dietl referred to the material he had to work with as a "gift from heaven," providing him with the perfect vehicle to take on Germany's Nazi past and to contribute to a "political awakening."[7] For Huettner, the need to find an entertaining story that expressed truth and a character with whom an audience could empathize was key.[8] He was almost too successful in that regard as Harold Juhnke became unnerved throughout the filming by extras who were so taken with his speeches that they wanted to join an actual right-wing movement.[9] Finally, Schlingensief also saw in his film, *Terror 2000,* a truth about German politics. In a 2009 interview, he comes closest of the three directors to confirming Griffin's thesis about satirical rhetoric, particularly the rhetoric of play, when he admits that "My films were considered scandalous anyway—and I liked playing along with it. It was fun for me because I found the films, to be honest—they really portrayed how Germany was at the time."[10] Each of the films is purposeful, relevant, and original, and although critics generally preferred *Schtonk!*[11] and *The Parrot*, I see the films as complementary and connected almost in a progression: The media exploitation of *Schtonk*! could lead to the rise of neo-Nazi candidates (as in *The Parrot*) which would lead Germany into the kind of depraved, fascistic violence depicted in *Terror 2000.*

"DEATH CAMP OF TOLERANCE" AND "CARE BEAR GENOCIDE"

Death camp of tolerance and care bear genocide. The fact that these words exist together in the English language says all we need to know about the realm of postmodern comedy. I featured the shows *South Park* and *Robot Chicken* in the chapter on Hitler, and they appear again here in the context of a discussion of how comedy about the Holocaust and genocide can serve as a warning or critique of contemporary society. "Death Camp of Tolerance" aired in *South Park's* sixth season in November 2002. Four years later, in June 2006, the 10th episode of Seth Green's *Robot Chicken* featured a skit entitled, "Care Bear Genocide," in which the Care Bears of 1980s cartoon lore commit genocide against their Care Bear Cousins, who consist of animals that are not actually bears. Unlike the 1992 German trilogy above, whose satire is crafted as a warning, *South Park's* "Death Camp of Tolerance" and *Robot Chicken's* "Care Bear Genocide" are more about ridicule to expose collective hypocrisies and self-righteousness.

"Death Camp of Tolerance" centers on the efforts by teacher Mr. Garrison to get fired because he is gay and then to sue the school. His efforts fail because the teachers and parents do not want to appear homophobic, even when his antics become not only inappropriate but illegal. Garrison brings in a chaps-clad individual named "Mr. Slave," into whom he inserts the school gerbil, Lemmiwinks, who goes on a *Lord of the Rings*-style odyssey through the poor man's colon. Stan, Kyle, Cartman, and Butters are outraged by Mr. Garrison's behavior, and after a failed trip to the Museum of Tolerance, they are sent to a place where harsher measures are required: Tolerance Camp. While there, the animation turns into black and white to evoke a film like *Schindler's List,* and a German-accented camp guard welcomes the children by saying: "You are here because you refused to accept the life choices of your fellow man. Well, those days are now over. Here you will vork every hour of every day until you submit to being tolerant of everybody!"[12] In the camp, the children are subject to all manner of horrors, finger painting and making macaroni pictures of "people of all races and sexual orientations getting along." In the meantime, Mr. Garrison is chosen to receive the "Courageous Teacher" Award at the Museum of Tolerance. At the ceremony, Garrison finally calls out the parents for being idiots, and they recognize that the issue is not dislike of gay people but a dislike of the way "this asshole was acting." As punishment, Mr. Garrison and Mr. Slave are sent to the Tolerance Camp, which, not surprisingly, appeals to the latter.

The much shorter skit, "Care Bear Genocide," begins with claymation Care Bears sitting around a table in their castle, griping that their non-bear counterparts are ruining their empire. "Love-a-Lot-Bear," voiced by Melanie Griffith, calls this the "Elephant in the room," in literal reference to one of the cousins who is an elephant. The bears come to a consensus that they need to put their counterparts "to bed." As Bedtime Bear clarifies, "by bed, I mean ethnic, and by time, I mean cleansing."[13] Don Cheadle enters to try to ferret the Care Bear Cousins to a safe hotel (*a la* Hotel Rwanda), but the Care Bears manage to fire off a cannon and blow the front of the hotel and all the Care Bear Cousins to bits. They then celebrate with rainbow cookies until the Great Cloudkeeper appears and, horrified by what he sees, says he is going to turn the place into a "Hell on Earth," by which he means New Jersey. Then we cut to a claymation governor of New Jersey, eating a rainbow cookie and saying that he hopes the audience has enjoyed this re-enactment of New Jersey history.

The two episodes overlap in their sendup of trends and current iconography. In "Care Bear Genocide," it is not just the innocent and cloying care bears that come under fire, but also commercialism and Hollywood's "cause of the moment." The skit goes to another level of metadiscourse when it is revealed as a promotional vehicle for New Jersey. "Death Camp for Tolerance" mines a related set of cultural memories in its use of concentration camp imagery and its broad satire of political correctness, even its strange *Lord of the Rings* metaphor for Lemmiwinks, but here is where the *South Park* episode diverges and enters into more problematic territory. Both shows take a premise to its ridiculous conclusion, but the Care Bears skit is a benign violation in the truest sense of comedy; the only people injured are Care Bear fans (if this is really a thing) and maybe residents of New Jersey, who, I am willing to wager, can take the joke. The "Death Camp" setting in *South Park,* with its death by finger painting and macaroni pictures, is in this same orbit. It is the gay imagery, especially the gerbil-in rectum-storyline, that many found and continue to find troubling.[14] Even some of the show's writers, who were usually in on the joke, were perplexed by a subplot that seemed to amuse Parker and Stone far more than it should have. Indeed, the showrunners' commentary about the episode is almost entirely about Lemmiwinks, which brings me to an important point about satire, namely the direction of the joke.

At whom or what are the jokes of "Death Camp of Tolerance" pointed? Liberal straight whites or gay people? This matters if we define effective satire as aiming its critique at those with privilege and power. At the end of the episode, an exasperated Mr. Garrison chastises the crowd of supporters that his behavior is so outrageous that it should not be acceptable from a teacher, and this is a message that any reasonable person could get behind. However, when he says that tolerance does not necessarily mean acceptance, he, and by extension Parker, move into dicier territory. The *OED* defines tolerance as being "willing to accept something especially opinions or behavior that you may not agree with, or people who are not like you."[15] In Parker's construction of tolerance, hateful attitudes could continue to exist—just repressed—as majority in-groups hold their noses to "tolerate" minorities. That is separate from, but merged into, the show's "don't be an asshole" message, and it is unclear whether there was much of a discussion about the implications of this subtle yet important difference. Philosophy professor Richard Hanley wrote about the episode in his broader collection of essays on *South Park,* and he made the point that to be tolerant means to accept things that one does not like but should—such as gay people—but not necessarily accepting things that you should not have to like—such as jerks.[16] By muddying the message of the satire, Parker undercut the strongest part of the episode, which lie in what Griffin describes as "holding up to scrutiny our idealized images of ourselves—forcing us to admit that such images are forever out of reach, unavailable to us, or even the last things we would really want to attain."[17]

THE HOLOCAUST IN THE HUMOR OF LARRY DAVID, SARAH SILVERMAN, AND AMY SCHUMER

Navigating, more successfully, I would argue, the pitfall of satirical direction are Larry David, Sarah Silverman, and Amy Schumer, each of whom reference Hitler, Nazis, and the Holocaust to make a point about present-day issues. In the first episode of Larry David's *Curb Your Enthusiasm*, David's character, Larry, the retired ex-producer of the show *Seinfeld*, finds himself in trouble by referring to his wife Cheryl as Hitler in a conversation that is overheard by a friend whose relative was a Holocaust survivor. Right away, the audience knows that Larry is an idiot, and whatever humor there is, it is aimed at him. The ninth episode of the fourth season of *Curb Your Enthusiasm,* entitled "The Survivor," which aired on 7 March 2004, pushed the boundaries of this contract with the audience to its breaking point in a story about a Holocaust survivor whom Larry brings to dinner and the comedy of errors that ensues. In an interview with David Remnick for *The New Yorker* in 2014, David described the moment he came up with the idea for the episode: "Well, there's a show on CBS called *Survivor*, a reality show, and then there are Holocaust survivors . . . and one day . . . I heard survivor and thought survivor, and I went, 'Holy Shit!' And my head exploded over how funny that could be. And I thought, I have got to write this and film it as fast as I possibly can because someone's gonna come up with this idea. It's just so obvious, survivor, survivor. How can nobody have done this?"[18] Meanwhile, in 2010, comedian Sarah Silverman ran an episode in season 3 of her television show, *The Sarah Silverman Program,* entitled, "Wowschwitz," which satirized Holocaust memorialization, and in 2015, comedian Amy Schumer featured a skit in her show, *Inside Amy Schumer,* entitled, "The Museum of Boyfriend Wardrobe Atrocities," which operated on a similar level. Both David and Silverman used mistaken identity (among other comedic devices) in their episodes, while Schumer stuck to irony and parody, but all three anchored a satire around the Holocaust to make specific points about our current cultural ecosystem.

In "The Survivor" episode, Larry and his wife Cheryl are preparing their renewal of vows ahead of their 10th anniversary, which sounds innocuous enough. However, as part of a deal he struck with Cheryl, he is allowed a one-time fling with someone before the ten years are up. An opportunity presents itself as a sexy Hasidic woman who works at a laundromat named Anna, played by Gina Gershon, flirts with Larry, and he goes to his rabbi for advice.

Anna bears little resemblance to any Hasidic woman, and the construction of Jewishness in the characters of this plotline problematizes David's satire. (I had originally felt the same way about David's construction of the rabbi character, but Nathan Fielder's show, which we will address in a moment, has forced a revision of that sentiment.) Even if David intended to poke fun at the lack of knowledge about Hasidism on the part of non-religious Jews, the character of Anna would still be outrageous. For instance, although Anna wears a head covering, she smokes, leaves her shirts unbuttoned to reveal cleavage, and is aggressively sexual with Larry, suggesting at one point that while her husband is at shul, she and Larry should have sex. David tackles the requisite urban legend about how Hasidic couples have sex, allegedly through a hole in a sheet, and although he has Anna point out Larry's stupidity when he wraps himself up in said sheet at their hotel room, David has her spout off more profanity than many secular Jews would probably ever use.

The rabbi, meanwhile, not only gives Larry approval for the affair, but he also fuels the Holocaust storyline by asking Larry if he could bring a survivor to the rehearsal dinner for Larry and Cheryl's renewal of vows. The person whom the rabbi brings, Colby, played by Colby Donaldson, is not a Holocaust survivor or a survivor in any sense of the word; he was simply on the reality television show, *Survivor*. The rabbi confuses the survival issue further after Larry asks him about a photo on his desk, and the rabbi says that it was his brother-in-law, who died on September 11, 2001—9/11. As Larry asks him about where he was at ground zero, the rabbi explains that his brother-in-law died uptown—on 57th street, run over by a bike messenger. So, the rabbi is questionable in his morality and more patently clueless than Larry, if that were possible. The humor in these instances—sexual and social—may be funny, but one might see that it also has the potential of reinforcing negative images of Judaism. I would argue that these images threaten to overshadow David's more valuable lampooning of what it means to be a survivor in contemporary American discourse.

Because the rabbi asks to bring a survivor to the dinner, and Larry assumes he meant a Holocaust survivor, Larry feels compelled to have his father invite his friend Solly, who, Larry knows, is also a Holocaust survivor. David sets up a classic comedic scenario based on mistaken identity, and he plays it to the hilt. At dinner, Colby begins by describing the snakes he had to fend off in the Australian outback, and Solly responds: "That's a very interesting story. Let me tell you. I was in a concentration camp! You never even suffered one minute your whole life compared to what I went through!" Colby then starts the downward spiral into comedy oblivion by responding: "Look, I'm saying we spent 42 days trying to survive. We had very little rations. No snacks." To which Solly rejoins: "Snacks, what are you talking, snacks? We didn't eat sometimes for a week for a month?" Colby continues, "I couldn't even work out over there. They certainly didn't have a gym. I wore my sneakers out. The next thing I know, I have a pair of flip-flops! . . . Have you even seen the show?" Solly shouts back, "Did you ever see our show? It was called the Holocaust! You don't know anything about survival. I'm a survivor!" The two then start screaming back and forth, "I'm a survivor," until Solly hits his plate and splashes food on Larry's face and suit, prompting a non sequitur from Larry's mother-in-law, "somebody get a sponge." Larry's befuddled response ending the scene to the disgust of everyone is, "I'm sorry, why don't you get a sponge? What? I just told her to get a sponge?"[19]

In order to make amends, Larry invites Solly to the renewal of vows, but in the car, Solly's glass eye reflects into Larry's face, and his arm movements lead Solly to believe that he's making fun of him, so he gets mad and bumps Cheryl who spills wine on Larry's suit, freshly cleaned after the dinner incident. Solly demands to get out of the car and washes his hands of the whole pathetic lot. In the episode's penultimate scene, the renewal of vows, Larry is incapable of anything positive to say. His vows are an incomprehensible mess ("It's pretty, pretty, pretty, pretty good. And I am your devoted servant. Well, I don't know about servant. You know I'm not a servant, but I'll certainly help you.")[20] When Larry steps on the glass in the custom of Jewish weddings, he does so too quickly, before the rabbi moves his hand away, and this results in a bloody hand injury and a screaming rabbi, and another reference to getting a sponge. In the "climactic" scene of the episode, in which Larry meets up with Anna in a hotel for some afternoon delight, Anna chides Larry about the "sheet myth," and then an earthquake forces the two almost-lovebirds, still wrapped in their bedsheets, out of their room and into the hotel parking lot. There, they see Colby, who is also coincidentally staying at the hotel, and he has the last words of the show: "Larry, hey, we survived!"[21]

Like Larry David, comedian Sarah Silverman has used the Holocaust as a foil to address antisemitism, racism, and what I would call performative memorialization, where ritual visits and commemorations, rather than foundational social change, serve as remedies for prejudice. In the 2005 film of her stand-up routine, *Jesus Is Magic,* Silverman makes all kinds of seemingly random, and to some, offensive jokes about the Holocaust. She recounts that her niece came up to once and said: "'Aunt Sarah, did you know that Hitler killed sixty million Jews?' I corrected her, and I said, 'You know I think he's responsible for killing *six* million Jews.' And she says, 'Oh, yeah. Six million. I knew that. But seriously, auntie, what's the difference?' 'The difference is that sixty million is unforgivable, young lady.' Kids. Try to figure them out; you can't: They're kids."[22] And then there is this: "My nana was a survivor of the Holocaust or—I'm sorry—the alleged Holocaust, and she had the tattoo, the number, and thank God she was at one of the better concentration camps. She had a vanity number; it said, 'Bedazzled,' which is kinda fun."[23] Her point to all of this? To amplify the ridiculousness of people who actually do trivialize the Holocaust. Her humor seems directed outward, but it is similar to Larry David's in that the focus is on the teller, and the aim is to make her look preposterous. As she has said in interviews: "I tend to say the opposite of what I think."[24]

In season three of her television show, *The Sarah Silverman Program*, Silverman ran an episode in 2010 entitled "Wowschwitz," in which she competes with her sister, Laura, in designing a Holocaust memorial. When Laura proposes the idea to Sarah (over breakfast), Sarah says, "why would you make something for something that never happened?" to which Laura responds, "you're not a good Jew." Sarah begs to differ by saying that she thinks she knows what it means to be Jewish, and she proceeds to tell the waitress that her pancakes are "ishy." Laura's cop boyfriend, Jay, interjects that he is not even Jewish but that he "loves the Holocaust . . . loves reading about it . . . the 'thing that happened.'" Sarah finishes by exclaiming, "Yawn Kippur! I'm getting extremely bored and will not tolerate it. Never Again!"[25] The scene is a fast-paced gumbo of reverse slogans, malapropisms, and self-reflective antisemitism that manages to skewer Silverman, self-righteous Jews, and Gentile hypocrites all at the same time. Once we get to the twin unveiling of the memorials, Silverman's premise is stretched beyond ridiculous and into the realm of the surreal. In the promotional video for the two ceremonies, Laura is serious, while Sarah announces that "Auschwitz? You'll be saying Wowschwitz!" At the actual unveiling, Sarah sets up a carnival, complete with a llama and dunk tank. She brings her friend Murray, whom she believes is an Auschwitz survivor, but who in reality was a prison guard and who conspires with another Nazi, played by the clearly-not-Nazi Ed Asner, to steal the memorial's commemorative gold plaque. Upon this reveal, all hell breaks loose, the attendees are held hostage, and Sarah is shot, prompting her belated admission that "Nazis are dicks." But all ends well as she is magically healed because her time-traveling dog had gone back in time and killed Hitler as an art student.

In 2015, comedian Amy Schumer offered her take on Holocaust humor in a skit in her show, *Inside Amy Schumer*, entitled "The Museum of Boyfriend Wardrobe Atrocities," which imagined galleries of men's clothes displayed in such a way as to evoke the experience of going through a Holocaust museum. The visitors listen with headsets to the guided tour, complete with a mock *Schindler's List* soundtrack, as they proceed from room to room, taking in the horror of crushed velvet suits, cargo shorts, and calf-high tube socks. In the "accessories wing," Schumer parodies pastor Martin Niemoeller's speech about not speaking up, as the narrator says, "first, he wore a braided belt, and I said nothing, then came the hat, and I said nothing. Then, he wore that fucking hemp necklace, and I was like, "PEACE!" In the "Hall of Sighs," which features a collage of voices of girlfriends testifying to their boyfriends' terrible fashion choices, a male denier blurts out, "I don't think this many guys wore this stuff. These numbers are exaggerated." The final gallery is the stack of 1500 crocs that represent a relationship that was "real and tangible until poor judgment tore it apart." As the women in the crowd fight back tears, a young girl asks, "did this really happen?" Her mother responds, "It did, Gabby. It did."[26] The girl then transforms into the girl with the red coat from *Schindler's List.*

Like many Jewish comedians in this chapter, and the book for that matter, David, Silverman, and Schumer share a comic sensibility and perspective on the world, one that is never satisfied with the way things are and always griping about how things should be. In her 1996 solo piece, *Oh, Wholly Night and Other Jewish Solecisms*, Deb Margolin offered her take on what binds together a disparate group like Jews: " . . . I think there's definitely an aesthetic, a certain agitation, sense of humor, irony, or self-abrogation that is cultural and that is so Jewish. We're all praying in the same intonation, somehow."[27] With their cynical yet reflexive tone and transgressive behavior, David and Silverman also fit into Conrad Hyers' archetype of the trickster, exposing flaws in society through provocation while directing their jokes inward, making themselves the representation of bad people who need to change. The themes the three comedians address—privilege, memorial overload, and performative solemnity—coalesce into a frightfully accurate condemnation of current values. It is not the Holocaust that Larry David is satirizing, and he certainly is not mocking Holocaust survivors, but rather what journalist Stephen Vider dubs a culture of victimhood that conflates real tragedy and survival with things that no one in their right mind would ever see as tragic or in the realm of surviving. Vider claims that David is sending up "a culture that reveres trauma and the traumatized at the same time it enjoys the *schadenfreude* expressed in 'reality' contests like *Survivor* and mock-reality television."[28] Silverman and Schumer express related concerns about performance as a substitute for real change. As Rachel Shukert notes in her review of Schumer's skit: "After an hour or two [of museum viewing], we emerge, shaken but usually not so badly that we can't congratulate ourselves for our bravery and sense of justice. We reward ourselves with a nice lunch afterward, all for surviving . . . nothing."[29] As for offending people, David quotes Jewish humorist S. J. Perelman on this: "That's the point . . . Perelman said the office of humor is to offend . . ."[30]

THE BORAT FILMS

In their fusion of satire, reality television, and performance art, Larry Charles and Sacha Baron Cohen's *Borat* films push the limits of comedy even further—to the point of endangering the life of the star. Baron Cohen plays Borat Sagdiyev, a Kazakhstani journalist who speaks in mangled English and a mix of Hebrew and Polish to convey the Kazakh language, and who proceeds to disrupt and disturb everything around him. In true method fashion, Baron Cohen does not simply play the character of Borat or others that he has invented, but he becomes them. In promotional interviews for the first film, which premiered in November 2006, entitled *Borat: Cultural Learnings of America for Make Benefit Glorious Nation of Kazakhstan,* Baron Cohen stayed in character, often with embarrassing results. A news anchor in Mississippi was fired when Baron Cohen as Borat created anarchy on the set of an interview, and before the release of the film, he held a press conference outside the Kazakhstani embassy in Washington, D.C., where he called for the bombing of Uzbekistan because it was forcing on Kazakhstan ideas of equality for women and all religions. The first film involves Borat coming to the United States to film a documentary about American culture. Throughout the film, he meets right-wing politicians, runs naked through a hotel, nearly kidnaps his newfound love, Pamela Sue Anderson, and whips up a crowd at a rodeo with racism and antisemitism. (This performance blew his cover and forced him to be whisked away to safety. Baron Cohen faced danger again in the film *Bruno* when he, as the title character—a gay Austrian fashionista—was nearly mauled by a crowd of Hasidic Jews while filming in Jerusalem.) *Borat* was both a critical and popular success, earning Baron Cohen a Golden Globe for Best Actor in a Comedy in 2007.

By the time the sequel arrived in October 2020 as *Borat Subsequent Moviefilm,* Baron Cohen's character was so recognizable that he had to go undercover in his interactions with ordinary Americans. (Kazakhstani officials, appalled at the first film, had a more muted response to the sequel, and in fact, the Kazakhstan Board of Tourism appropriated Borat's signature phrase, "very nice" in its promotional material.[31]) In *Subsequent Moviefilm,* Borat's goal is to offer his daughter, Tutar, played by Bulgarian actress Maria Bakalova, as a bride to U.S. Vice President Mike Pence. Borat once again meets Americans who eagerly reveal their racism, and Bakalova, posing as a journalist, gets prominent politico Rudy Giuliani to come uncomfortably close to sexual assault. Baron Cohen won another Golden Globe for Best Actor in a Comedy, but this time, the film won as well for Best Picture Musical or Comedy.

The film's connection to this chapter and book has to do with Baron Cohen's satirizing of antisemitism and Holocaust history as part of the "cultural learning" exchange between the United States and Kazakhstan. For instance, in the first film, we learn that Kazakhstanis stage what they call the "running of the Jew," which, similar to the running of the bulls, involves townspeople fleeing from other townspeople sporting giant puppet heads fashioned into antisemitic stereotypes of a Jewish man and woman. In the sequel, Borat notes that this ritual has been replaced by Holocaust Remembrance Day, in which Kazakhstan celebrates the guards who ran the camps. During his interaction in the United States, Borat buys a cake on which he has a willing baker write, "Jews will not replace us," the slogan which white supremacists shouted at their infamous rally in Charlottesville, Virginia, in 2017. Later, he is told that the Holocaust never happened, which sends him into a deep depression. His only solution is to commit suicide by going to a synagogue and awaiting the next mass shooting. When he enters the synagogue, dressed in the worst, most antisemitic costume one could imagine, complete with a giant nose and money bag, he is greeted by a Holocaust survivor, Judith Evans. He says, "very nice weather we have been controlling . . . please don't eat me alive."[32] Evans offers Borat a hug, and the two have matzo ball soup together. She tells him that she was in the Holocaust, and he becomes overjoyed that his fear that it did not happen was all for naught. Despite the touching moment on-screen, there was unease among the participants, and Evans' daughter sued Baron Cohen for misuse of her mother's likeness after her death in the summer of 2020. Evans' estate eventually withdrew the suit after they came to understand more clearly the purpose of her inclusion in the film, which was not to make fun of a survivor, but rather, as the scene in the cake shop demonstrated, to criticize antisemitism and Holocaust denial. In fact, Baron Cohen dedicated the film to Evans and issued a statement in which he declared that her life was "a powerful rebuke to those who deny the Holocaust."[33] He also went on to say that he would "continue his advocacy to combat Holocaust denial around the world."[34]

Like David and Silverman's on-screen alter egos, Baron Cohen's *Borat* is a stand-in for everything that Baron Cohen opposes—cultural parochialism, racism, antisemitism, and misogyny. His ability to generate a reality from fiction, to show that "contexts are never total or closed," is a hallmark of his style.[35] Who else could take a signifier such as Kazakhstan and use Hebrew and Polish to signify the language of Kazakhstanis and imbue the place with a reality that it does not truly possess? Baron Cohen's technique may be different compared to David and Silverman, and while he too makes himself the butt of the joke, his way of revealing truths about the outside world is not the same. His trickster approach is not neatly scripted, and in some cases, it is completely unscripted, relying on the willingness of a dupe to let his or her guard down to generate candor in all its ugliness. In a 2019 speech accepting an award for international leadership from the Anti-Defamation League, Baron Cohen admitted that this tactic was central to his comedy: "When Borat got that bar in Arizona to agree that 'Jews control everybody's money and never give it back,' the joke worked because the audience shared the fact that the depiction of Jews as miserly is a conspiracy theory originating in the Middle Ages."[36] Writing about Borat and Jacques Derrida, Cate Blouke has said that meaning comes from a common awareness of what is absent: "we understand written or spoken signs by the spaces between, because they are not *that*."[37] In a separate homage to his mentor, French performer Phillippe Gaulier, Baron Cohen revealed another clue about his comedy; not only is it ironic and metadiscursive, but it owes much to his training as a clown and the pedagogy of play and insults ("brutality" in the words of Lynn Kendrick) that he received at the hands of Gaulier.[38] What this preparation did for Baron Cohen was to sharpen his desire and ability to become a sponge of playful outrageousness that would soak in and wring out the bile around him.

HISTORICAL ROASTS AND *NATHAN FOR YOU*

In this last group, I compare episodes of Jeff Ross' *Historical Roasts* and Nathan Fielder's *Nathan for You,* Both comedians are Jewish (Ross is American, Fielder, Canadian), but aside from their shared ethnicity, the two shows could not be more different. *Historical Roasts* is what it says it is—a comic roast of celebrities from history, shot before a live audience, while *Nathan for You* is a reality TV show in which Fielder, who studied business, proposes terrible ideas to existing and would-be-entrepreneurs. The Jewish backgrounds of the comedians intersect and become relevant in the episodes under analysis here—the roast of Anne Frank and the "Summit Ice" episode—but the point and direction of the humor stand in marked contrast, reflective of the shows' divergent aesthetics.

Ross' Anne Frank episode, which aired on 27 May 2019, features Ross as the emcee, wearing a worn-out suit and an armband with a Jewish star, Rachel Feinstein as Anne, Jon Lovitz as Franklin D. Roosevelt, Mindy Rickles as her dad, roastmaster Don Rickles, Gilbert Gottfried as Adolf Hitler, and Fred Willard as God. To inject a note of purpose to the proceedings, Ross begins by claiming that Anne Frank's diary helped him understand what his uncles fought for in World War II. He goes for relevance by asserting that the Holocaust stands as a symbol not only for the suffering of victims of genocide but for all refugees and asylum seekers, a reference to the migrant families placed in detention centers at the Texas border during the Trump administration. He offers a quote about Jews getting through pain through laughter, and then he jokes: "Please enjoy the roast of Anne Frank, and the end of my career, because after this, I might have to go into hiding for a while." What follows are some funny borscht belt jokes, like Lovitz's FDR riffing on Hitler's alleged monorchidism: "You weren't popular on the social circuit, Hitler. You were only invited to one ball!"[39] Gottfried's Hitler hits back: "We're not so different, you and I. We both enjoy a comfortable chair, and we both never fucked Eleanor Roosevelt!"[40] Fred Willard's God complains about having to pay for parking to be on the show, proceeds to distinguish chosen from lucky in reference to the Jews as the chosen people, and then he takes Hitler's other testicle as punishment.

In contrast to the vaudevillian feel of *Historical Roasts*, Nathan Fielder's *Nathan for You* is all postmodern in its self-aware irony and reversal of the "business rescue" paradigm. One of the ideas that Fielder promoted in 2015 was a response to the discovery that Canadian outfitter Taiga had published a tribute to Holocaust denier Doug Collins in their winter catalog. In his skit, Fielder proposes a line of outerwear called Summit Ice that includes cool-looking windbreakers and Holocaust education on the side. When Fielder goes to an actual rabbi (technically a mohel) for advice, and the rabbi says that his marketing needs more Holocaust imagery, it evoked for me the fictional rabbi in *Curb Your Enthusiasm* and forced me to rethink my assertion that a Jewish spiritual leader would never demonstrate such cluelessness in reality. The unveiling of the display of Fielder's line of jackets is even more offensive than it sounds—complete with a replica of the gate at Auschwitz, mannequin camp prisoners wearing Summit Ice jackets, and an oven with a fake skeleton. Mortified, the store owner simply says that he has no faith in either the competence or judgment of Fielder or his rabbi. The episode ends well, though, as Fielder's parents approve of their new windbreakers, and an ad for the jacket appears with the tagline: "Never Deny Your Courage! Never Deny Your Strength! Never Deny The Holocaust!"[41]

Ross and Fielder had similar intentions of empowerment with their skit, but Fielder went the additional mile both to magnify comedic incongruity and to create a tangible product against antisemitism at the same time. The Anne Frank roast also generated more of a backlash; Talya Zax, writing for *The Forward,* said that the show "may have set out to roast Anne Frank, but what it really ended up damning was history's approach to Frank," and representatives from The Anne Frank House in Amsterdam decried the episode as "tasteless."[42] In an hour-long webcast defending the roast, Ross drew up a statement in which he insisted that his purpose was to "keep Anne Frank's name and story alive," arguing that there are many people who do not know who she was or who confuse her with Helen Keller.[43] Ross brought up Mel Brooks' often used quote about getting revenge through ridicule and maintained that the episode's humor does not come at the expense of Anne but is instead directed at Hitler. It is Anne who has the last word, and it is entirely about the resilience of the Jews, as she says: "Today the Jewish people are thriving more than ever before. In fact, guess what, Hitler: You're being played by a Jew right now, and it's the loudest, most annoying Jew we could find!"[44] One journalist who got this was Niv Hadas, whose praise of the episode in the Israeli newspaper *Haaretz* included a (not ironic) request for it to be shown in schools, arguing that the episode is "sensitive . . . compassionate, funny and historically accurate . . . [doing] everything it can to honor the 6 million using humor."[45] Although one may dispute the historicity of an episode focused on Hitler's testicles, it does at least add weight to Griffin's point that when the satirist's truth is persuasive, it succeeds in "constructing . . . an image that manages to override the 'facts' and in a sense supplant 'history.'"[46] Fielder, by contrast, has received more accolades, and through the sale of his windbreaker, he has been able to raise $150,000 for the Vancouver Holocaust Education Centre. This says something perhaps even more truthful about our commercial-driven existence. Whereas Ross at the beginning of his show acknowledges the gravity of his subject, and Fielder does as well when he discovers the Holocaust denial ad, it is he who responds by creating a commodity of his own, only this time Holocaust iconography, rather than denialism, serves as the marketing gimmick. In an interview from October 2015, Conan O'Brien questioned Fielder on this and the potential use of child labor in making the windbreaker, which prompted Fielder to respond: "Conan, you have to pick your cause."[47] Summit Ice is perhaps the strangest case of making lemonade from lemons, and I am still uneasy about the conflation of the two worlds. Like Trey Parker, whose "Death Camp of Tolerance" episode generates interesting questions that go unanswered, so too does Fielder's effort.

CONCLUSION

What, then, are we to make of these endeavors? What do they tell us about the use of satirical references to the Third Reich and the Holocaust? Each example of satire that I have included in this chapter is purposeful in its own way, each is relevant in the sense that it connects to issues of immediate concern, and each is original and unique in content and occasionally in form and format. I would go further and say that this chapter contains strong examples of comedy; one might argue that they are the most "laugh-out-loud" of all of the productions in this book. Many of the fictional protagonists are tricksters, to use one of Conrad Hyers' comedic archetypes, provoking their antagonists while themselves "getting in and out of tight spots."[48] The use of provocative and playful rhetoric by each comedian also aligns with Griffin's model of satire, and some, particularly Christoph Schlingensief, Larry David, Trey Parker, and perhaps Seth Green, resist offering any value system as a substitute, but this is where we may see a divergence with Griffin's notion of satire as an "open" system. Both Griffin's model and my own analytical framework are helpful, but there are additional, qualitative distinctions, not only between the productions in this chapter but between those and others in previous chapters, which merit exploring and which might not fit neatly within, or be sufficiently explained by either paradigm.

I would argue that what distinguishes the productions in this chapter from chapters where I analyzed skits or shows about Hitler or those that send up historical memory is their rerouting of historical context. Instead of being shows about Hitler, Nazis, or memory, the shows in this chapter are actually about something else. To quote linguist Diana Popa, they introduce "openness to different interpretations of meaning and value that will further initiate a sudden recognition that the world is not as we expect it to be . . ."[49] In her research, Popa concludes that satire, among other things, "facilitates message transmission for current affairs" and "draws attention through exaggeration and emphasis on issues that may otherwise go unnoticed."[50] Their purpose, therefore, is to take issue with something amiss now and to use a historical referent in that objective. The productions either alert viewers about societal and political dangers or engage in an equally important, but perhaps less dire, appraisal of their world. There is more moral certainty expressed in a number of the films and television shows, particularly the German films, where a neo-fascist hellscape is a clear and present danger. Even in the context of North America, where the satire might be "lighter" and more about hypocrisy and stupidity, the stakes are also high, and comedians such as Sacha Baron Cohen, Sarah Silverman, Jeff Ross, and Nathan Fielder validate this in their statements and actions that demonstrate a degree of certitude in their opposition to something in the "world as it is."[51]

Baron Cohen, Fielder, and Parker deconstruct and reconstruct the meaning of that world in different ways, and they reach different destinations. Parker's *modus operandi* is to tear into everyone, which is one thing when he aims his sights at the powerful and more problematic when he goes after the powerless; in fact, when he does this, he risks reinforcing some of the societal ills he takes on in *South Park.*[52] Fielder's bad business ideas are also primarily about deconstruction, and while his activism against Holocaust denialism is commendable, it is not a prime motivator, nor is activism against racism and antisemitism in general, which is the reverse of Baron Cohen. Irony comes first with Fielder, and the fact that we are talking about a show about business in the realm of the Holocaust and that his company still sells merchandise and donates to Holocaust education, raises the question: Is this a good cause but the wrong platform with the wrong spokesperson? It is not that Fielder's intentions are not good, but that we do not know exactly what they are because his whole shtick is to destabilize certainty. Perhaps this is the ultimate confirmation that satire can be an "open" system or any system that the satirist wants it to be. It certainly comports with Griffin's belief that one of satire's pleasures is "the speculation into which its readers are led.... If we stop insisting on the centrality of the moral in satire, then we are readier to see the satirist as a figure struggling for notice in a particular kind of socio-political context."[53]

NOTES

1. https://www.oed.com/viewdictionaryentry/Entry/171207, accessed 7 March 2021.
2. David Griffin, *Satire: A Critical Reintroduction* (Lexington, KY: University Press of Kentucky, 1994), 37.
3. Griffin, *Satire,* 52.
4. Griffin, *Satire,* 38.
5. *Schtonk!*, directed by Helmut Dietl. Cologne: Westdeutscher Rundfunk, 1992, DVD. 00:58:00–00:60:00.
6. *Schtonk!*, 00:60:00.
7. Christopher Keil, "Im Interview: Helmut Dietl," *Süddeutsche Zeitung,* 10 May 2010, https://www.sueddeutsche.de/kultur/im-interview-helmut-dietl-ein-geschenk-des-himmels-1.201910, accessed 8 March 2021. See also, "Helmut Dietl im CINEMA-Interview,"16 March 2018, https://www.cinema.de/stars/news/helmut-dietl-im-cinema-interview-11877_ar.html, accessed 8 March 2021.
8. Simon Kinglsey, "Ralf Huettner-Director," 28 June 2012, https://cineuropa.org/en/interview/222678/, accessed 28 June 2012.
9. Sabine Jaspers, "Einer wie der Juhnke ist gefährlich," https://taz.de/Einer-wie-der-Juhnke-ist-gefaehrlich/!1638983/, accessed 8 March 2021.
10. Florian Malzacher, "Interview with Christoph Schlingensief, 26 February 2009," reprinted online 1 December 2013, https://florianmalzacher.tumblr.com/post/68669508765, accessed 8 March 2021.
11. *Schtonk!* won three categories (film, actor, and director) at the 1993 German Film Awards. Regarding *Terror 2000,* a number of scholars have pointed to Schlingensief's lasting impact on contemporary German cinema, including: Kristen van der Lugt, "An Obscene Reckoning: History and Memory in Schlingsielf's *Deutschlandtrilogie,*" in Forrest and Scheer, *Christoph Schlingensief: Art Without Borders,* 39–56, and David Hughes,"Everything in Excess—Christoph Schlingensief and the Crisis of the German Left," *The Germanic Review: Literature, Culture, Theory*, Vol. 81, No. 4 (2006): 317–339. Even Stephen Holden, writing for *The New York Times,* who called *Terror 2000* a "shapeless, hysterical mess," praised Schlingensief's style, saying: "If a Keystone Kops film were written by William S. Burroughs, peopled with characters from George Grosz by way of Russ Meyer and directed in a style that suggests Jean-Luc Godard on speed, you would have a movie

with the style and mood of *Terror 2000* . . . This slam-bang comedy lampooning neo-Nazism and xenophobia in contemporary Germany wallows in ridiculously fake gore and grotesque sexual couplings. The director Christoph Schlingensief's idea of how to film a shooting is to show a gun aimed at someone's face and a moment later to have that face doused with a bucket of entrails. Holden, "Absurdist Spoof of Nazism: *Terror 2000,*" *New York Times,* 18 November 1994, section 3, p 20, https://www.nytimes.com/1994/11/18/movies/film-review-absurdist-spoof-of-nazism.html, accessed 8 March 2021.

12. *South Park*, season 6, episode 14 "Death Camp of Tolerance," directed by Trey Parker, aired November 20, 2002, on Comedy Central (Braniff Productions, 2004).

13. "Care Bear Genocide," Season 2, Episode 10, *Robot Chicken,* DVD (New York: Cartoon Network, 2007)

14. Bob Chipman, writing for *Screen Rant,* said this about the episode: "Over a decade later, divorced from the 'it's funny because every other media entity is passionately on the other side of this - aren't we just incorrigible scamps?' context of the day . . . it's probably understandable that modern audiences too young to recall . . . may find revisiting 'Death Camp' about as uncomfortable as Parker and Stone's generation likely would've found circa-1960s editorial cartoons mocking the Civil Rights Movement." Chipman, "15 *South Park* Episodes That Haven't Aged Well," *Screen Rant,* 16 May 2017, https://screenrant.com/south-park-old-episodes-aged-badly/, accessed 10 March 2021.

15. *Oxford English Dictionary,* https://www.oxfordlearnersdictionaries.com/us/definition/american_english/tolerance, accessed 10 March 2021.

16. Richard Hanley, *South Park and Philosophy: Bigger, Longer, and More Penetrating* (Peru, IL: Open Court, 2007), 65.

17. Griffin, *Satire,* 60.

18. David Remnick, "Larry David on Writing *Curb Your Enthusiasm* and Why He Doesn't Understand 'Squirmish' People," 21 October 2014, https://www.newyorker.com/video/watch/the-new-yorker-festival-larry-david-on-writing-curb-your-enthusiasm-and-why-he-doesn-t-understand-squirmish-people, accessed 14 March 2021.

19. *Curb Your Enthusiasm*, season 4, episode 9 "The Survivor," directed by Larry Charles, aired March 7, 2004 on HBO (HBO Entertainment, 2004), 10:00–12:50.

20. *Curb Your Enthusiasm,* "The Survivor," 24:40–25:06.

21. *Curb Your Enthusiasm,* "The Survivor," 28:56. The Holocaust features prominently in the final episode of the 11th season of the series, when David's character, rendered shoeless before an event at the Los Angeles Museum of the Holocaust after he has stepped in dog excrement, steals a pair of shoes from a display of shoes from Holocaust victims and gets his comeuppance in a way that amplifies the awfulness of his behavior.

22. *Jesus is Magic,* directed by Liam Lynch. Los Angeles: Roadside Attractions, 2005, 41:50–42:28.

23. *Jesus is Magic,* 42:30–42:58.

24. Carrie Batt, "Sarah Silverman's Comedy Is Changing with the Times," *New Yorker,* 1 June 2017, https://www.newyorker.com/culture/culture-desk/

sarah-silvermans-comedy-is-changing-with-the-times?source=search_google_dsa_paid&gclid=Cj0KCQiA0MD_BRCTARIsADXoopZ44_FVCgsLLIbSPkh8HRJJ0s2HxotFNCKN78ajSeAWaG1C-QQU400aAvwAEALw_wcB, accessed 11 March 2021.

25. The Sarah Silverman Program, season 3, episode 10 "Wowschwitz," directed by Rob Schrab, aired April 15, 2010 on Comedy Central (Eleven Eleven O'Clock Productions, 2010).

26. See "The Museum of Boyfriend Wardrobe Atrocities," 19 July 2015, https://www.youtube.com/watch?v=carfJz5vVTc, accessed 17 June 2021.

27. Cited by Kara Manning, "Are We Not Jews?" *American Theatre,* 1 November 2000, https://www.americantheatre.org/2000/11/01/are-we-not-jews/, accessed 14 March 2021.

28. Stephen Vider, "Survivor Challenge: Ten Years after Jerry Seinfeld Got Caught Necking during *Schindler's List*, Reverence for the Holocaust still makes Larry David Squirm," *Tablet*, 26 March 2004, http://www.tabletmag.com/jewish-arts-and-culture/1271/survivor-challenge, accessed 7 August 2014.

29. Rachel Shukert, "Amy Schumer Satirized the Rite of Visiting Holocaust Memorials—and Nailed It," 23 June 2015, https://www.tabletmag.com/sections/news/articles/amy-schumer-satirizes-the-rite-of-visiting-holocaust-memorials-and-nails-it, accessed 14 March 2021.

30. David Remnick, "Larry David."

31. "Kazakhstan Adopts Borat Phrase for Tourism Campaign," 27 October 2020, https://www.bbc.com/news/world-asia-54702974, accessed 14 March 2021.

32. *Borat: Subsequent Moviefilm,* directed by Jason Woliner. Culver City: Amazon Studios Productions 2020, DVD, 00:59:39.

33. Rodney Ho, "Lawsuit by Holocaust Survivor over *Borat 2* Film Portrayal Withdrawn," *Atlanta Journal-Constitution,* 27 October 2020, https://www.ajc.com/life/radiotvtalk-blog/judge-dismisses-lawsuit-by-holocaust-survivor-over-borat-2-film-portrayal/VWTUMRPQ3BGGDC6REUNWB2XBTY/, accessed 19 April 2021.

34. Ho, "Lawsuit."

35. Cate Blouke, "*Borat,* Sacha Baron Cohen, and the Seriousness of the (Mock) Documentary," in *The Routledge Comedy Studies Reader,* 322.

36. "Sacha Baron Cohen's Keynote Address at ADL's 2019 Never Is Now Summit on Anti-Semitism and Hate Remarks by Sacha Baron Cohen, Recipient of ADL's International Leadership Award," 21 November 2019, https://www.adl.org/news/article/sacha-baron-cohens-keynote-address-at-adls-2019-never-is-now-summit-on-anti-semitism, accessed 14 March 2021.

37. Blouke, "*Borat,*" 322.

38. See Brian Logan, "'Once You Can Handle the Insults, You Begin': Inside Philippe Gaulier's Clown School in Étampes," *The Guardian,* 2 August 2016, https://www.theguardian.com/stage/2016/aug/02/philippe-gaulier-clown-school-emma-thompson-sacha-baron-cohen-edinburgh-festival-interview, accessed 14 March 2021, and Lynn Kendrick, "A *Paidic* Aesthetic: An Analysis of Games in the Ludic Pedagogy of Philippe Gaulier," (unpublished paper, n.d.), 2, https://core.ac.uk/download/pdf/11337832.pdf, accessed 14 March 2021.

39. *Historical Roasts*, season 1, episode 3, "Anne Frank," directed by Joel Gallen, aired May 27, 2019, on Netflix (OBB Pictures, 2019), 09:00–10:00.

40. *Historical Roasts,* "Anne Frank," 17:00–18:00.

41. *Nathan for You*, season 3, episode 2 "Horseback Riding/Man Zone," directed by Nathan Fielder, aired October 22, 2015, on Comedy Central (Blow Out Productions, 2015), 21:12–21:25.

42. Talya Zax, "Netflix 'Roasted' Anne Frank: They Could Have Left Hitler's Genitals Out Of It," *The Forward,* 29 May 2019, https://forward.com/culture/425093/jeff-ross-anne-frank-netflix-roast-hitler-fdr-don-rickles-rachel-feinstein/, accessed 15 March 2021, and JTA and Sue Surkes, "Uproar over Netflix Show in which Hitler 'Roasts' Anne Frank," *The Times of Israel,* 30 May 2019, https://www.timesofisrael.com/uproar-over-netflix-show-in-which-hitler-roasts-anne-frank/, accessed 15 March 2021.

43. "Thick Skin With Jeff Ross: Why I Roasted Anne Frank," YouTube webcast, 13 June 2019, https://www.youtube.com/watch?v=MsLiUdc-wNw, accessed 15 March 2021.

44. *Historical Roasts,* "Anne Frank," 25:00–26:00.

45. Niv Hadas, "Demeaning the Memory of the Holocaust? 'The Roast of Anne Frank' Should Be Shown in Schools," *Haaretz,* 3 June 2019, https://www.haaretz.com/life/television/.premium-demeaning-the-holocaust-roast-of-anne-frank-should-be-shown-in-schools-1.7329249, accessed 15 March 2021.

46. Griffin, *Satire,* 128.

47. "Nathan Fielder's New Clothing Line—Conan on TBS," 22 October 2015, https://www.youtube.com/watch?v=D3Im37oRMRE, accessed 15 March 2021.

48. Hyers, *The Spirituality of Comedy,* 177.

49. Diana E. Popa, "*Televised Political Satire: New Theoretical Introspections,*" in *Developments in Linguistic Humour Theory,* ed. Marta Dynel (Amsterdam: John Benjamins Publishing, 2013), 374.

50. Popa, "Televised Political Satire," 369.

51. Baron Cohen, Ross, and Silverman have spoken out against racism and bigotry of any kind, and the latter has repeatedly denounced both Holocaust denial and its misuses.

52. See the work on this by Thomas E. Ford, "Social Consequences of Disparagement Humor," *Personality and Social Psychology Review,* Vol. 8, No. 1 (2004): 79–94.

53. Griffin, *Satire,* 186.

Conclusion

COMEDY, THE SOLEMN, AND THE SERIOUS

This sweep of cinema and television has uncovered a far larger body of comedic work on the Third Reich than one might expect. One may dismiss this reality out of hand as immaterial or detrimental, but that would be incurious and go against the basic premise of scholarship. The phenomenon of comedy about the Nazi era is too vast to ignore, and while many of the productions included in this volume are of middling quality, even they add to a body of work that has something to say about how people confront evil, suffering, tragedy, and death. Scholars Al Gini and Abraham Singer, who have published on satire, cite Mel Brooks in this regard, who said that we need humor because "otherwise our 'collective lamentations' about the trials and tribulations of the world would be unbearable. We all need jokes . . . as a 'defense against the universe.'"[1] How, then, has this manuscript helped to shed any additional light on the subject? What are the takeaways? I believe, for one, that no single genre of comedy is inherently more or less appropriate to address Hitler and Nazism, but that what matters is the comedy's degree of purpose, relevance, and originality. Does the film or television production advance an aim? Does it speak to an issue that is part of a *zeitgeist*? Does it have an element of freshness or surprise in its narrative, delivery, or format? Does it transgress or challenge boundaries and get an audience to think? Does it reveal truth?

It is clear that many productions about Hitler and the Nazis fulfill a basic purpose of comedy: to comfort the afflicted while afflicting the comfortable. In comedy, as Conrad Hyers has said, "Kings become servants, and servants become kings."[2] The many wartime features included in this manuscript demonstrate this purpose in spades. The anti-Nazi comedies of the 1930s and 1940s emerged in an environment where the stakes were life and death, where jokes could be lethal, and where laughing may have been only a brief distraction, a brief act of defiance, against an otherwise deadly reality. Hitler was real. Hitler was powerful. Hitler was evil. Hitler was a danger to human civilization. Humor in this context acknowledged and contested each of these qualities. In this instance, laughing was about taking power away from Hitler and the Nazis and reclaiming it for their victims. Comedies about the Holocaust, which center on the experience of the victims, survivors, and their descendants, also constitute a form of resistance and healing. As Graham McCann maintains in his biography of Woody Allen, "after the death camps, there are at least six million reasons not to laugh anymore, and at least six million reasons to try and laugh again."[3] In many of the productions I have considered, one could also see laughter as symbolic of what Elie Wiesel has described as the limits of spoken language in articulating the experience of genocide. His 1966 book, *The Gates of the Forest,* functions as a commentary on this; the main character of the novel, Gregor, a Jewish teenager whose family leaves him in a cave to hide from the Nazis, encounters another person to whom he gives the name Gavriel, who laughs all the time. This laughter signifies both defiance and loss of language. Gavriel laughs because he cannot describe the indescribable with the signs and codes known to him.[4]

A point about normalization is warranted here. Although deflating Hitler and raising the morale of victims and survivors has continued as an aim of comedic productions in the decades since World War II, the immediacy of the threat has receded, and Hitler and the Nazis have in many ways become harmless foils. Whatever laughter comes from this type of comedy is removed from its original context. Now, for some, Hitler is not only funny but also fun, which is problematic. We diminish his malevolence and the threat of the broader movement he led at our peril. The dangers of normalization are even more acute in comedies with Holocaust referents, and we have seen the difficulties of creating a comedic language that can work in this regard. Bakhtin's notions of carnival and the grotesque, where the surreal becomes the framework for exploring the inscrutable, can be guideposts, but they are not guarantors of effective representation. Many comedies in this book also refer to Hitler and the Holocaust as a way of using the past to critique the present, and there is much to criticize—from continued bigotry and the threat of authoritarianism to collective hypocrisies and performative rituals, but here too, there is a thin line between being fresh and purposeful and being crass and trivializing, and anyone embarking on a comedic project in this regard needs to be ever mindful of where this line is and how to cross it when needed without feeding a minimizing trend.

In my final thought, I offer this quote from John Cleese about comedy and solemnity:

> I think we all know that laughter brings relaxation and humor makes us playful, yet how many times have important discussions been held where really original

and creative ideas were desperately needed to solve important problems but where humor was taboo because the subject being discussed was so serious? This attitude seems to me to stem from a very basic misunderstanding of the difference between serious and solemn. Now I suggest to you that a group of us could be sitting around after dinner, discussing matters that were extremely serious, like the education of our children or our marriages or the meaning of life, and I'm not talking about the film, and we could be laughing and that would not make what we were discussing one bit less serious. Solemnity, on the other hand . . . I mean, I don't know what it's for? I mean, what is the point of it? The two most beautiful memorial services that I've ever attended both had a lot of humor, and it somehow freed us all and made the services inspiring and cathartic. But solemnity? It serves pomposity, and the self-important always know at some level of their consciousness that their egotism is going to be punctured by humor. That's why they see it as a threat and so dishonestly pretend that their deficiency makes their views more substantial when it only makes them feel bigger. Phhhpt. No. Humor is an essential part of spontaneity and an essential part of playfulness. An essential part of the creativity that we need to solve problems. No matter how serious they may be.[5]

Are film and television comedies, purposed to address serious issues, of any less value or inherently more problematic than dramatic productions about Hitler, the Third Reich, or the Holocaust? Perhaps, but both are taking on the unknowable, and both are performance commodities with the same artifice and the same economy. Maybe films and television shows should never go down the path of exploring Nazism or genocide, but this is head-in-the-sand thinking. Hitler and the Holocaust will continue to be a reservoir of ideas, and if this is the case, should there not be some thought, direction, and set of guidelines? Might the product, however tainted and compromised, elicit engagement with these important topics and be the beginning point to deeper inquiry?

NOTES

1. *American Masters,* Season 27, Episode 3, "Mel Brooks: Make a Noise," directed by Robert Trachtenberg, aired May 20, 2013 on PBS (Eagle Rock Entertainment, 2013), in *The Sanity of Satire: Surviving Politics One Joke at a Time,* Al Gini and Abraham Singer (Lanham, MD: Rowman and Littlefield, 2020), 30.

2. Hyers, *The Spirituality of Comedy,* 44.

3. Graham McCann, *Woody Allen* (Cambridge: Polity, 1994), 154.

4. Elie Wiesel, *The Gates of the Forest* (Holt, Rinehart, and Winston, 1966), and Jacqueline Bussie, *The Laughter of the Oppressed: Ethical and Theological Resistance in Wiesel, Morrison, and Endo* (New York: T and T Clark 2007).

5. John Cleese, "Laughing at the Taboo," (20+) Facebook, accessed 20 March 2021.

Bibliography

Atlani, Aviva. "The Ha-Ha Holocaust: Exploring Levity Amidst the Ruins and Beyond in Testimony, Literature and Film." Unpublished Thesis, University of Western Ontario, 2014.
Bakhtin, Mikhail. *Problems in Dostoevsky's Poetics*, trans. Caryl Emerson. Minneapolis: University of Minnesota Press, 1984.
———. *Rabelais and His World,* Trans. Helene Iswolsky. Bloomington, IN: Indiana University Press, 1984.
Barattoni, Luca. *Italian Post-Neorealist Cinema,* Edinburgh: Edinburgh University Press, 2012.
Baron, Lawrence. *Projecting the Holocaust into the Present: The Changing Focus of Contemporary Holocaust Cinema*. Lanham, MD: Rowman & Littlefield Publishers, 2005.
Becker, Jurek. *My Father, The Germans, and I: Essays, Lectures, Interviews*. Ed. Christine Becker. London: Seagull Books, 2010.
Behrman, S.N. *Jakobowsky and the Colonel,* New York: Random House, 1944.
Berger, Asa. *The Genius of the Jewish Joke,* Northvale, NJ: Jason Aronson, 1993.
Bergson, Henri. *Laughter: An Essay on the Meaning of the Comic*. Trans. Cloudesley Brereton and Fred Rothwell. London: Macmillan, 1911.
Bilik, Dorothy. "Singer's Diasporan Novel: *Enemies, A Love Story*." *Studies in American Jewish Literature* No. 1, *Isaac Bashevis Singer: A Reconsideration* (1981).
Birdwell, Michael. *Celluloid Soldiers: Warner Brothers' Campaign Against the Nazis*. New York: New York University Press, 2000.
Biskind, Peter. "Interview with Lina Wertmüller." In *Women and the Cinema,* Ed. Karyn Kay and Gerald Peary. New York: Dutton, 1976.
Borenstein, Miriam. "Heroes, Victims, and Villains: Character Inversion in Holocaust Cinema." Unpublished Thesis, West Chester University, 2009.
Boussac, Paul. *The Semiotics of Clowns and Clowning: Rituals of Transgression and the Theory of Laughter,* London: Bloomsbury, Academic.
Brooks, Mel. *All About Me: My Remarkable Life in Show Business,* New York: Random House, 2021.

Carpenter, Whitney. "Laughter in a Time of Tragedy: Examining Humor during the Holocaust." *Denison Journal of Religion,* Vol. 9, No. 3 (2010).
Caruth, Cathy. *Unclaimed Experience: Trauma, Narrative, and History,* Baltimore, MD: Johns Hopkins University Press, 1996.
Chaplin, Charles. *My Autobiography,* New York: Plume, 1992 edition.
Cohen, Debra Nussbaum. "How Jill Soloway Created *Transparent*—The Jewiest Show Ever." *The Forward,* 21 October 2014.
Cole, Robert. "Anglo-American Anti-fascist Film Propaganda in a Time of Neutrality: *The Great Dictator*, 1940." *Historical Journal of Film, Radio and Television,* Vol. 21, No. 2 (2001).
Collado-Rodriguez, Francisco. "Ethics in the Second Degree: Trauma and Dual Narratives in Jonathan Safran Foer's *Everything Is Illuminated.*" *Journal of Modern Literature,* Vol. 32, No. 1 (Fall 2008).
Crowe, Cameron. *Conversations with Billy Wilder.* New York: Knopf, 1999.
Daub, Adrian. "'Hannah, Can You Hear Me?'" Chaplin's *Great Dictator,* "Schtonk," and The Vicissitudes of Voice." *Criticism,* Vol. 51, No. 3 (Summer 2009).
Dauber, Jeremy. *Jewish Comedy: A Serious History,* New York: Norton, 2017.
Davidson, James. *Hal Ashby and the Making of Harold and Maude.* Jefferson, NC: McFarland, 2016.
Déléas, Josette. "Lina Wertmüller: The Grotesque in *Seven Beauties.*" In *Women Filmmakers: Refocusing,* Ed. Jacqueline Levitin, Judith Plessis, and Valerie Raoul. London: Routledge, 2003.
Des Pres, Terrence. "Holocaust Laughter." In *Writing and the Holocaust,* Ed. Berel Lang. New York: Holmes and Meier, 1988.
Dochartaigh, Pól Ó. "Americanizing the Holocaust: The Case of *Jakob the Liar.*" *The Modern Language Review*, Vol. 101, No. 2 (April 2006).
Doherty, Thomas. *Hollywood and Hitler, 1933–1939.* New York: Columbia University Press, 2013.
Durkheim, Émile. "Preface to the Second Edition." In *The Rules of Sociological Method and Selected Texts on Sociology and its Method.* Ed. S. Lukes, and trans. W. D. Halls. New York: Free Press, 1982 [1901].
Eckardt, Roy. "Divine Incongruity: Comedy and Tragedy in a Post-Holocaust World." *Theology Today,* Vol. 48, No. 4 (January 1992).
Ecker, Jurek. *Jakob der Lügner.* Frankfurt am Main: Suhrkamp Verlag. 1969.
Efron, John. "From Lodz to Tel Aviv: The Yiddish Political Humor of Shimen Dzigan and Yisroel Schumacher." *Jewish Quarterly Review,* Vol. 102, No.1 (2012).
Egerton, Jodi H. "*Kush mir in tokhes!*": Humor and Hollywood in Holocaust Films of the 1990s." Unpublished Thesis, University of Texas at Austin, 2006.
Eyman, Scott. *Ernst Lubitsch: Laughter in Paradise,* New York: Simon & Schuster, 1993.
Fairbairn, Marty. "The Ethics of Representation: A Review of *Jakob the Liar;* An Interview with Peter Kassovitz Report from the Toronto International Film Festival." *Film-Philosophy,* Vol. 3, No. 1 (1999).
Falicov, Tamara Leah. *The Cinematic Tango: Contemporary Argentine Film.* New York: Wallflower, 2007.

Feinberg, Anat. *Embodied Memory: The Theatre of George Tabori,* Iowa City, IA: University of Iowa Press, 1999.
Feinstein, Herbert. "*Me and the Colonel,*" *Film Quarterly,* Vol. 12, No. 2 (Winter 1958).
Fermaglich, Kirsten. "Mel Brooks' *The Producers*: Tracing American Jewish Culture Through Comedy, 1967–2007." *American Studies,* Vol. 48, No. 4 (Winter 2007).
Flanagan, Kevin. "The British War Film, 1939–1980: Culture, History, and Genre." Unpublished Thesis, University of Pittsburgh, 2015.
Ford, Thomas E. "Social Consequences of Disparagement Humor." *Personality and Social Psychology Review,* Vol 8, No. 1 (2004).
Forrest, Tara and Anna Teresa Scheer. *Christoph Schlingensief: Art Without Borders,* Chicago: University of Chicago Press, 2010.
Francis, Lina. "Laughter, the Best Mediation: Humor as Emotion Management in Interaction." *Symbolic Interaction,* Vol. 17, No. 2 (Summer 1994).
Freud, Sigmund. *Jokes and Their Relation to the Unconscious*. Trans. James Strachey. New York: Norton, 1963.
Friedländer, Saul. *Reflections on Nazism: An Essay on Kitsch and Death,* Trans. Thomas Weyr. New York: Harper and Row, 1984.
Friedman, Jonathan, C. "I'm a Survivor! The Holocaust and Larry David's Problematic Humor in *Curb Your Enthusiasm,*" *S:I.M.O.N. Shoah: Intervention. Methods. Documentation.* Vol. 5, No. 1 (August 2018).
Friedrichs, Marie. "Humour as a Way of Dealing with the Trauma of the Holocaust: Discussion of the Use of Humour to Approach the Holocaust by Two Members of the Second Generation—Melvin Jules Bukiet and Roberto Benigni." Unpublished Thesis. University of Gent, 2014.
Frim, Daniel J. "Pseudo-Satire and Evasion of Ideological Meaning in *South Park,*" *Studies in Popular Culture*, Vol. 36, No. 2 (Spring 2014).
Fujiwara, Chris. *The World and Its Double, The Life and Work of Otto Preminger,* New York: Farrar, Straus, and Giroux, 2008.
Gardner, Martin. *The Marx Brothers as Social Critics: Satire and Comic Nihilism in Their Films.* Jefferson, NC: McFarland, 2009.
Gary, Romain. *The Dance of Genghis Cohn,* New York: Signet, 1967.
Gehring, Wes. *Leo McCarey: From Marx to McCarthy,* Lanham, MD: Scarecrow Press, 2005.
Gemünden, Gerd. "Space out of Joint: Ernst Lubitsch's *To Be or Not to Be,*" *New German Critique,* Vol. 89 (Spring-Summer, 2003).
Gilman, Sander. "Is Life Beautiful? Can the Shoah be Funny? Some Thoughts on Recent and Older Films." *Critical Inquiry,* Vol. 26, No. 2 (Winter 2000).
Gini, Al and Abraham Singer. *The Sanity of Satire: Surviving Politics One Joke at a Time.* Lanham, MD: Rowman and Littlefield, 2020.
Gordon, Avery. *Ghostly Matters: Haunting and the Sociological Imagination.* Minneapolis: University of Minnesota Press, 1997.
Gottfried, Martin. *Nobody's Fool—The Lives of Danny Kaye,* New York: Simon & Schuster, 1994.

Griffin, Dustin. *Satire: A Critical Reintroduction*. Lexington, KY: University Press of Kentucky, 1994.

Halbwachs, Maurice. *On Collective Memory*, Ed. Lewis A. Coser. Rev. ed. Chicago: University of Chicago Press, 1992.

Handy, Bruce. "Jerry Goes to Death Camp!" *Spy Magazine*, May 1992.

Hanley, Richard. *South Park and Philosophy: Bigger, Longer, and More Penetrating*, Peru, IL: Open Court, 2007.

Hilsenrath, Edgar. *The Nazi and the Barber*, New York: Doubleday, 1971.

Hirsch, Foster. *Otto Preminger: The Man Who Would Be King*, New York: Knopf, 2007.

Hirsch, Joshua. *Afterimage: Film, Trauma, and the Holocaust*, Philadelphia: Temple University Press, 2003.

Hirsch, Marianne. *Family Frames: Photography, Narrative, and Postmemory*, Cambridge, Massachusetts: Harvard University Press, 1997.

Hughes, David. "Everything in Excess—Christoph Schlingensief and the Crisis of the German Left." *The Germanic Review: Literature, Culture, Theory*, Vol. 81, No. 4 (2006).

Hutcheon, Linda. "The Politics of Postmodernism: Parody and History." *Cultural Critique*, Vol. 5 (Winter 1986–1987).

Hutcheon, Linda. *A Theory of Parody: The Teachings of Twentieth-Century Art Forms.* Champaign-Urbana, IL: University of Illinois Press, 2000.

Hyers, Conrad. *The Spirituality of Comedy: Comic Heroism in a Tragic World*, New Brunswick, NJ: Transaction Press, 1996.

Irwin-Zarecka, Iwona. *Frames of Remembrance: The Dynamics of Collective Memory*, New Brunswick, NJ: Transaction Press, 1994.

Jacobsen, Wolfgang et al. *Lina Wertmüller*. Munich: Carl Hanser Verlag, 1988.

Julin, Grant. "Satire in a Multi-Cultural World: A Bakhtinian Analysis." *The Routledge Comedy Studies Reader*, Ed. Ian Wilkie. London: Routledge, 2020.

Jungk, Peter Stephan. *Franz Werfel: A Life in Prague, Vienna, and Hollywood*, New York: Fromm International, 1991.

Klocke, Astrid. "Subverting Satire: Edgar Hilsenrath's Novel *Der Nazi und der Friseur* and Charlie Chaplin's Film, *The Great Dictator*." *Holocaust and Genocide Studies*, Vol. 22, No. 3 (Winter 2008).

Knepp, Robin Jedlicka. "Laughing Together: Comedic Theatre as a Mechanism of Survival during the Holocaust." Unpublished Thesis. Virginia Commonwealth University, 2013.

Koenig, David. *Danny Kaye: King of Jesters*, Irvine, CA: Bonaventure Press, 2012.

Koestenbaum, Wayne. *The Anatomy of Harpo Marx*, Berkeley, CA: University of California Press, 2012.

La Fave, Lawrence, et al. "Superiority, Enhanced Self-Esteem, and Perceived Incongruity Humour Theory." In *Humour and Laughter: Theory, Research and Applications*. Ed. T. Chapman and H. Foo. London: Wiley, 1976.

Landry, David. "Faint Hope-A Theological Interpretation of Woody Allen's Crimes and Misdemeanors." *Journal of Religion and Popular Culture*, Vol. 22, No. 1 (2010).

Langer, Lawrence. *Holocaust Testimonies: The Ruins of Memory,* New Haven, CT: Yale University Press, 1991.
Langlois, Suzanne. "Images That Matter: The French Resistance in Film, 1944–1946." *French History,* Vol. 11, No. 4 (December 1997).
Langton, Robert Gore. *John Cleese,* London: Essential Books, 1999.
Lax, Eric. *Conversations with Woody Allen: His Films, The Movies, and Moviemaking,* New York: Knopf, 2007.
Levy, Shawn. *King of Comedy: The Life and Art of Jerry Lewis,* New York: St. Martin's, 1991.
Lewis, Jerry and Herb Gluck. *Jerry Lewis in Person,* New York: Athenaeum, 1982.
Lichtner, Giacomo. *Fascism in Italian Cinema Since 1945: The Politics and Aesthetics of Memory,* New York: Palgrave Macmillan, 2013.
Lipman, Steve. *Laughter in Hell: Use of Humor During the Holocaust,* New York: Jason Aronson, 1991.
Louvish, Simon. *Stan and Ollie: The Roots of Comedy: The Double Life of Laurel and Hardy.* New York: Thomas Dunne, 2002.
Low, David. *Autobiography,* London: Simon & Schuster 1957.
Luce, Clare Boothe. *Margin for Error: A Satirical Melodrama,* New York: Random House, 1940.
MacGillivray, Scott. *Laurel and Hardy from the Forties Forward,* Bloomington, IN: iUniverse, 2009.
Manning, Kara. "Are We Not Jews?" *American Theatre,* 1 November 2000.
McCann, Graham. *Woody Allen,* Cambridge: Polity, 1994.
McCormick, Richard. "Transnational Jewish Comedy: Sex and Politics in the Films of Ernst Lubitsch—From Berlin to Hollywood." In *Three Way Street: Jews, Germans, and the Transnational,* Ed. Jay Howard Geller and Leslie Morris. Ann Arbor, MI: University of Michigan Press, 2016.
McGraw, Peter and Warren, Caleb. "Benign Violations." *Psychological Science*, Vol. 21, No. 8 (2010).
Meirich, Hanni. "A Laughing Matter? The Role of Humor in Holocaust Narrative." Unpublished Thesis. Arizona State University, 2013.
Michael, Charlie. *Cultural Politics of a Transnational Cinema,* Edinburgh: Edinburgh University Press, 2009.
Misztal, Barbara. "Durkheim on Collective Memory." *Journal of Classical Sociology,* Vol. 3, No. 2 (2003).
Moeller, Hans-Bernhard. "Bridges between New German Cinema and Today's Generation of Political Filmmakers: An Interview with Michael Verhoeven." *Journal of Film and Video,* Vol. 62 (Spring/Summer 2010).
Mollet, Tracey. *Cartoons in Hard Times: The Animated Shorts of Disney and Warner Brothers in Depression and War 1932–1945.* London: Bloomsbury Academic, 2019.
Monro, David H. "Theories of Humor," in *Writing and Reading Across the Curriculum,* Ed. Laurence Behrens and Leonard J. Rosen. Glenview, IL: Scott, Foresman and Company, 1988.

Montresor, Jaye Berman. "Parodic Laughter and the Holocaust." In *Studies in American Jewish Literature (1981-), Vol. 12, The Changing Mosaic: From Cahan to Malamud, Roth, and Ozick,* University Park, PA: Penn State University Press, 1993.

Morlan, Don. "Slapstick Contributions to WWII Propaganda: The Three Stooges and Abbott and Costello." *Studies in Popular Culture,* Vol. 17, No. 1 (October 1994).

Morreall, John. "A New Theory of Laughter." *Philosophical Studies: An International Journal for Philosophy,* Vol. 42, No. 2 (September 1982).

Morreall, John. "Humor in the Holocaust: Its Critical, Cohesive, and Coping Functions." *Holocaust Teacher Resource Center,* 22 November 2001

Morris, Jon. "Against the Comfort of Catharsis: Teaching Trauma and the Sobering Lesson of *Train De Vie,*" *Transformations: The Journal of Inclusive Scholarship and Pedagogy,* Vol. 16, No. 2, Teaching through Testimony (Fall 2005).

Mulvey, Laura. "Visual Pleasure and Narrative Cinema." In *Film and Theory: An Anthology,* ed. Robert Stam and Toby Miller. Oxford: Blackwell Publishers, 2000.

Niv, Kobi. *Life Is Beautiful, But Not for Jews,* Lanham, MD: Scarecrow Press, 2003.

O'Donoghue, Darragh. *"Laughter in the Dark: The Black Comedy of Lina Wertmüller,"* *Cinéaste,* 22 September 2018.

Olsen, Lance. *Circus of the Mind in Motion: Postmodernism and the Comic Vision.* Detroit: Wayne State University Press, 1990.

Oring, Elliott. "The People of the Joke: On the Conceptualization of a Jewish Humor." *Western Folklore,* Vol. 42, No. 2 (1983).

Ostrower, Chaya. *It Kept Us Alive: Humor During the Holocaust,* Jerusalem: Yad Vashem, 2014.

Pearlstein, Ferne. *The Last Laugh,* Amazon Prime Video. Directed by Ferne Pearlstein, Los Angeles: Tangerine Entertainment, 2017.

Pfaff, Kerry L. et al. "Authorial Intentions in Understanding Satirical Text." *Poetics,* Vol. 25 (1997).

Pfefferkorn, Eli. "The Art of Survival: Romain Gary's *The Dance of Genghis Cohn.*" *Modern Language Studies,* Vol. 10, No. 3 (Autumn 1980).

Popa, Diana E. *"Televised Political Satire: New Theoretical Introspections,"* In *Developments in Linguistic Humour Theory,* Ed. Marta Dynel. Amsterdam: John Benjamins Publishing, 2013.

Pratley, Gerald. *The Cinema of Otto Preminger,* New York: Castle Books, 1971.

Rabinbach, Anson. "From Explosion to Erosion: Holocaust Memorialization in America Since Bitburg." *History and Memory,* Vol. 9, Nos. 1 and 2 (Fall 1997).

Rapaport, Lynn. "The Functions of Humor in Holocaust Tragedy." In *Gray Zones: Ambiguity and Compromise in the Holocaust and its Aftermath.* Ed. Jonathan Petropoulos and John K. Roth. New York: Berghahn, 2012.

Reich, Tova. *My Holocaust,* New York: HarperCollins, 2007.

Richardson, Michael. "Tragedy and Farce: Dani Levy's *Mein Führer,*" In *Hitler: Films from Germany,* Ed. Karolin Machtans and Martin A. Ruehl. London: Palgrave Macmillan, 2012.

Romanska, Magda and Ackerman, Alan, ed. *Reader in Comedy: An Anthology of Theory and Criticism,* New York: Methuen, 2016.

Rosenberg, Joel. "Shylock's Revenge: The Doubly Vanished Jew in Ernst Lubitsch's *To Be or Not to Be*," *Prooftexts,* Vol. 16 (1996): 235.

Rosenfeld, Gavriel. *Hi Hitler: How the Nazi Past is Being Normalized in Contemporary Culture.* Cambridge: Cambridge University Press, 2015.

Rubenstein, Lenny. "Monty Python Strikes Again: An Interview with Michael Palin." *Cinéaste*, Vol. 14, No. 2 (1985).

Safran Foer, Jonathan. *Everything Is Illuminated,* New York: Houghton Mifflin, 2002.

Schneider, Steve. *That's All Folks: The Art of Warner Brothers Animation,* New York: Henry Holt, 1988.

Schoolcraft, Ralph. *Romain Gary: The Man Who Sold His Shadow*. Philadelphia: University of Pennsylvania Press, 2002.

Schorsch, Jonathan. " Jewish Ghosts in Germany." *Jewish Social Studies,* Vol. 9, No. 3 (2003).

Shavelson, Melville. *How to Succeed in Hollywood Without Really Trying. P.S. You Can't,* Los Angeles: MGM Studios, 1974.

Shedlin, Michael. "Review of *Harold and Maude.*" *Film Quarterly*, Vol. 26, No. 1 (Autumn 1972).

Sherman, Dale. *Mel Brooks FAQ,* Montclair, NJ: Applause Theatre and Cinema Books, 2018.

Sherman, Vincent. *Studio Affairs: My Life as a Film Director,* Lexington, KY: University of Kentucky Press, 1996.

Sicher, Efraim. "The Future of the Past: Countermemory and Postmemory in Contemporary American Holocaust Narratives." *History and Memory*, Vol. 12, No. 3 (Fall/Winter 2000).

Sikov, Ed. *On Sunset Boulevard: The Life and Times of Billy Wilder,* New York: Hyperion, 1998.

Slucki, David, et al. eds. *Laughter After: Humor and the Holocaust,* Detroit: Wayne State University Press, 2020.

Sperber, Dan and Deirdre Wilson. *Relevance: Communication and Cognition,* London: Wiley-Blackwell, 1995.

Stier, Oren Baruch. *Committed to Memory: Cultural Mediations of the Holocaust,* Amherst, MA: University of Massachusetts Press, 2003.

Steir-Livny, Liat. *Is it OK to Laugh About it? Holocaust Humour, Satire, and Parody in Israeli Culture,* London: Vallentine Mitchell, 2017.

Tota, Anna Lisa and Trevor Hagen. *The Routledge International Handbook of Memory Studies.* London: Routledge, 2016.

Tutt, Ralph. "*Seven Beauties* and the Beast: Bettelheim, Wertmüller, and the Uses of Enchantment." *Literature/Film Quarterly,* Vol. 17, No. 3 (1989).

Ward, Richard Lewis. *A History of the Hal Roach Studios,* Carbondale, IL: Southern Illinois University Press, 2005.

Weinstein, Valerie. *Antisemitism in Film Comedy in Nazi Germany,* Bloomington, IN: Indiana University Press, 2019.

White, Hayden. "The Modernist Event." In *Figural Realism: Studies in the Mimesis Effect.* Baltimore: Johns Hopkins University Press, 2000.

Wiesel, Elie. *The Gates of the Forest*. New York: Holt, Rinehart, and Winston, 1966.

Wisse, Ruth. *No Joke: Making Jewish Humor*. Princeton: Princeton University Press, 2013.

Young, James. *The Texture of Memory: Holocaust Memorials and Meaning,* New Haven, CT: Yale University Press, 1993.

Zancberg, Eyal. "Critical Laughter: Humor, Popular Culture and Israeli Holocaust Commemoration." *Media, Culture & Society,* Vol. 28, No. 4 (2006).

Ziv, Avner. "Humor as Social Corrective." In *Writing and Reading Across the Curriculum,* Ed. Laurence Behrens and Leonard Rosen. Glenview, IL: Scott, Foresman, and Company, 1988.

———. *Personality and Sense of Humor.* London: Springer, 1984.

———. "Psycho-social Aspects of Jewish Humor in Israel and in the Diaspora." In *Jewish Humor*. Ed. Avner Ziv. New Brunswick, NJ: Transaction, 1997.

Index

100 Years of Adolf Hitler, 11, 77, 92, 196
100 Years of Evil, 82, 87, 90

Adam Resurrected, 149, 164–67, 176, 188n52
Adolf Hitler, 11, 27–28, 61, 75, 77, 79, 87, 92–93, 157, 195–96
Adorno, Theodor, 2, 36, 39
Air Raid Wardens, 105, 108, 110–11
Aleichem, Shalom, 71
All Through the Night, 104–5, 107, 109–11, 137n26, 137n27
Allen, Woody, 87, 149–51, 186nn16–19, 186n22, 216–17, 222–23
Amateau, Rod, 72
The Amy Schumer Show, 9, 12, 194, 200, 203
antisemitism, 8, 62, 64, 71, 75, 82, 117–18, 120, 182, 184, 205–6, 208, 210, 213
Arendt, Hannah, 101–2
Ashby, Hal, 167, 189n64, 189n66, 220
Auschwitz, 1, 8, 30–31, 34, 36, 59, 121–22, 132, 134, 179, 184, 203, 208
Avisar, Ilan, 30, 53n4
Aykroyd, Dan, 114, 177

Bakhtin, Mikhail, 9, 11, 16n34, 52, 60n113, 82, 92, 103, 123, 130–31, 136n6, 141nn102–9, 142nn110–14, 176, 190n87, 216, 219, 222
Baron, Lawrence, 8, 16n31, 34, 36, 53n5, 53n11, 54nn19–25, 219
Baron Cohen, Sacha, 2, 13n5, 194, 205–7, 210, 213nn35–36, 213n38, 214n51
Baruch Stier, Oren, 17n39, 100n98, 145–46, 184, 185n1, 185n6, 226
Becker, Jurek, 7, 16n30, 23–24, 33–34, 48–51, 54n26, 59n102, 60n104, 219
Benigni, Roberto, 15, 23, 35, 36, 47–50, 59nn92–95, 60n104, 60n109, 132, 221
Benny, Jack, 20, 22, 41–42, 53
Berenbaum, Michael, 47
Bergson, Henri, 3, 14n8, 210
Berle, Milton, 107, 109, 137
Berri, Claude, 115, 117, 120, 139n61, 139n73, 156
The Black Bird, 114
The Bloom of Yesterday (Die Blumen von Gestern), 12, 22, 33, 149–50, 161–63, 188n42, 188n45
The Blues Brothers, 114, 138n54
Boothe Luce, Clare, 106, 136–37
Borat (character), 2, 5, 12, 194, 205–7, 213

Borat: Cultural Learnings of America for Make Benefit Glorious Nation of Kazakhstan, 205
Borat: Subsequent Moviefilm, 213
Bosko's Picture Show, 68
British comedies, 104, 122
Brooks, Mel, 4, 8, 21–22, 32–34, 37, 40–41, 43, 45–46, 52–53, 53n12, 54nn14–17, 56nn62–63, 57n73, 219, 225
Bugs Bunny, 11, 61, 65–66
Burnett, Carol, 73–74, 76

"Care Bear Genocide," 194, 197–99, 212n13
carnival, 9, 11, 82, 130–31, 203, 216
cartoons, 11, 61, 63–66, 81, 83
catharsis, 183
The Chamber Quintet *(Ha-Hamishia Hakamerit)*, 149, 163–64
Chaplin, Charlie, 8, 14n14, 19–20, 31, 39, 41–43, 53n9, 55n40, 55n45, 56nn55–57, 65, 67–68, 71, 73, 109, 195, 220
Charles, Larry, 5, 8, 194, 205, 212n19
Cleese, John, 74, 75, 157–58, 160, 187, 216–17, 223
clowns and clowning, 129–34, 141n101, 141n103, 219
collective memory, 12, 17n39, 72, 146, 148–49, 152, 184–85, 185nn3–5, 222
concentration camps, 1, 6–8, 11, 20, 23–25, 43, 46, 101–2, 104, 109, 121–23, 126, 128, 160–61, 164–65
Crimes and Misdemeanors, 149–53, 186n16, 186n22, 222
Cubby's World Flight, 63
Curb Your Enthusiasm, 1, 13n4, 193–94, 200, 208, 212nn18–21, 221

Daffy Duck, 64–66
The Dance of Genghis Cohn, 7, 16–17, 22, 103, 136, 178, 182, 221, 224
Danger, 5, 11, 82, 89, 99

Dauber, Jeremy, 5–7, 15n20, 16nn28–29, 220
David, Larry, 4–6, 9, 13n3, 159, 166–67, 172, 193, 200–4, 206, 210, 212n18, 213n28, 213n30, 222–23, 225
The Day the Clown Cried, 8, 11, 102–3, 121, 123–24, 126–29, 131, 135, 140–41, 157
"The Death Camp of Tolerance," 194, 197–99, 209, 212n12
The Devil with Hitler, 70
Disney, Walt, 64–66, 94, 223
Donald Duck, 48, 64, 66
Downfall (Der Untergang), 75, 78–80, 96n43, 97n54, 97n58, 157
Duck Soup, 67–68, 70, 106
The Ducktators, 64–66
Durkheim, Emile, 146, 185n4, 220, 223
Dzigan, Shimen, 6, 16n28, 163, 220

empowerment, 131, 208
Enemies, A Love Story, 12, 149, 167, 169, 171, 181, 189nn69–72, 189nn75–76.
Everything Is Illuminated, 7, 10, 16n30, 19, 25, 29–30, 36–37, 46, 52, 57n82, 58nn84–85, 145, 220, 225
extermination camps, 24, 48, 51

The Fascist (Il Federale), 149–50, 154–55
Fawlty Towers, 12, 149, 157–60, 187
Fermaglich, Kirsten, 32, 36–37, 53n12, 54nn27–29, 221
Fielder, Nathan, 194, 201, 207–10, 214n41, 214n47
"Final Solution," 79, 86, 98
forgiveness, 174, 194
France, 35, 85, 102, 116–17, 120, 149, 154, 157
Frank, Anne, 7, 30, 194, 207–8, 213nn39–40, 214nn42–45
Frankl, Viktor, 6, 12, 16n26
Freleng, Fritz, 63, 67, 94n19

Freud, Sigmund, 3, 14–15
Friedländer, Saul, 47, 93, 100n98
Der Führer's Face, 64, 66

Gabler, Neal, 64, 94n10
Gary, Romain, 7, 16n30, 17n38, 103, 136n3, 178–79, 182, 191n98, 221, 224–25
Genghis Cohn, 12, 133, 177–79, 182, 184–85
German prisoner of war camps, 117, 122
Getting Away With Murder, 63, 149, 177, 181
ghettos, 20, 24, 33, 39, 41, 46–47, 102, 107, 109, 160, 164
Gilman, Sander, 4, 5, 34, 48–49, 51, 54nn18–19, 55n48, 58n91, 59n92, 59n97, 221
Goebbels und Geduldig, 11, 102, 132–33, 142n119, 196
Gottfried, Gilbert, 61, 207
Grant, Cary, 112, 137
Great Britain, 31, 77, 104, 149, 154, 157, 159, 163
The Great Dictator, 8–10, 14, 19–59, 66–69, 73, 80, 111, 193, 195, 220, 222
Green, Seth, 197, 210
Griffin, Dustin, 10, 12–13, 17n37, 17n41, 43, 46, 56n60, 57n81, 193–194, 197, 199, 209–211, 211nn1–4, 212n17, 214n46, 214n53, 222
grotesque realism, 102, 130

Halbwachs, Maurice, 12, 17, 146, 185n4, 222
Harold and Maude, 12, 72, 149, 167–69, 176, 189nn62–68, 220, 225
Heil Honey I'm Home, 11, 76–77, 96
Herr Meets Hare, 11, 64–66
Higher Than a Kite, 69, 95
Hirsch, Marianne, 163, 188n46, 222
historical memory, 4, 75, 93, 117, 134, 150, 158, 160, 162, 210

Historical Roasts, 1, 12, 194, 207–8, 213nn39–40, 214n44
Hitler, Adolf, 1, 4, 6, 11, 21–22, 26–29, 31–35, 37–46, 51–54, 60–63, 65–102, 106–7, 109–10, 113–14, 157–58, 193–95, 208–10, 214–17
Hitler Goes Kaput (Gitler Kaput), 11, 82, 88
Hitler memes, 61, 78
Hogan's Heroes, 121
Holocaust memory, 12, 34, 145–47, 149, 152, 154, 163–64, 166–67, 179–81
Holoclownsto, 11, 132–33, 148
Hunters, 12, 177, 181–83, 190–91
Hyers, Conrad, 4, 15nn15–16, 204, 209, 214n28, 215, 217n2

I'll Never Heil Again, 69
"I'm Sitting in My Bunker (*Adolf-Ich hock' in meinem Bunker*)," 78, 97n57
Inglourious Basterds, 2, 10, 19, 26, 30, 35–36, 43–44, 46–47, 52, 56–57
"The Interrogator," 74
Irwin-Zarecka, Iwona, 146–47, 160, 163, 185n3, 185nn7–8, 185n10, 188n41, 188n47, 222
Israel, 11, 87, 164, 166
Italy, 62, 67, 70, 102, 149–50, 154–55

Jakob the Liar, 10, 19, 23, 24, 30, 33, 35, 36, 38, 47–49, 50–52, 52n18, 59n101, 59n104, 60n105–108, 111, 220
Jakob der Lügner (East German book and film), 7, 16, 33–34
The Jews Are Coming (Ha-Yehudim Baim), 11, 82, 86–87, 98–99, 163
Jewish comedy, 5, 7, 15–16, 220
Jojo Rabbit, 1–2, 10, 29, 30, 37–38, 41, 43–45, 52, 54n13, 55n32, 57nn67–71, 65
Judaism, 12, 47, 87, 150, 152, 154, 170, 173, 176, 201
Jugnot, Gérard, 139
Juhnke, Harald, 195

Kassovitz, Peter, 24, 35–36, 38, 49–52, 59n101, 60n111
Kaye, Danny, 112, 115–16, 120, 138n49, 138n55, 139n67, 139n74, 221–22
killing centers, 122–23
A Kitten for Hitler, 11, 82, 91–92, 99n92, 100n100
Kraus, Chris, 149, 161–62, 188n49, 188n44

Langer, Lawrence, 12, 17n40, 147, 166–68, 171, 176, 185n11, 189nn56–57, 189nn60–61, 189n65, 189nn73–74, 190n89, 223
Lanzmann, Claude, 30, 53n6, 135, 143n124, 164
The Last Laugh, 8, 15, 224
Laurel (Stan) and Hardy (Oliver), 70, 108–11, 136–37, 223
Levy, Dani, 79, 95, 97, 224
Lewis, Jerry, 8, 11, 49, 102–3, 114, 124–28, 132, 135, 138n52, 140n81, 140nn90–91, 141n95, 141n98, 142n116, 223
Life Is Beautiful, 10, 19, 23–24, 30, 35–36, 38, 47–48, 50, 52, 54, 58n86, 58n90, 59n92, 59nn94–96, 60n104, 101–3, 132, 155, 169, 221
"Lil' Hitler," 82–84
Lipman, Steve, 6, 15
Look Who's Back (Er ist wieder da), 2, 10, 27, 30, 37, 44, 52, 54n31, 57n69, 57n75, 79–80, 193, 196
Lost Embrace, 149–53, 186
Lubitsch, Ernst, 8, 20–21, 34, 40–43, 55n35, 55n44, 55n46, 56n50, 56n52, 56n55, 56n58, 56n61, 65, 220–21, 223, 225

MacFarlane, Seth, 84, 98
Margin for Error, 104, 106, 109–11, 136–37, 223
Marx Brothers, 67–68, 94n20, 95n21, 104, 112–14, 138n43, 138n48, 221

The Matchmaker (Pa-am Ha-eetee—Once I was), 149–50, 164, 166, 176, 188nn51–53, 189nn58–59
Maus, 7, 15n23
Mazursky, Paul, 169, 189n69
McCarey, Leo, 67, 104–6, 109–11, 136n9, 136n18, 137n20, 137n23, 221
Me and the Colonel (Jakobowsky und der Oberst), 115–17, 119–20, 139nn66–69, 155, 219
Mein Führer—The Really Truest Truth about Adolf Hitler (Mein Führer—Die wirklich wahrste Wahrheit über Adolf Hitler), 11, 61, 79–80, 95n33, 97nn59–60, 224
memory and trauma, 10, 31, 136, 145, 148–149, 163–169, 171, 181, 184
Mendel, 12, 167, 172–73, 176, 189n78, 190n81
meta-discourse, 88–89, 91
Mihăileanu, Radu, 35–36, 48–50, 54n23, 59n100
Milligan, Spike, 74–75, 96nn43–44, 157
Misfits, 149, 158–59, 187n34
"Mr. Hilter and The North Minehead Bye-Election," 74, 96n39
Mr. Kaplan, 12, 177, 180–83, 190nn95–97, 191n101
Monsieur Batignole, 11, 115, 117–20, 139n65
Monty Python's Flying Circus, 4, 73–74, 77, 93, 96, 157
My Mother's Courage, 11, 102, 132–35, 142n118, 148
"The Museum of Boyfriend Wardrobe Atrocities," 194, 200, 203, 213n26

The Nasty Girl (Das Schreckliche Mädchen), 12, 73, 134, 149–50, 161–63, 193
Nathan for You, 12, 207–8, 214n41
Nazis and Nazism, 8, 30–32, 38, 64, 72, 74, 88, 101, 104, 106, 108–109, 112, 122, 132, 225
neo-Nazism, 44, 72, 77

Nesher, Avi, 149, 164, 166, 188n51
A Night in Casablanca, 112–14, 138n43, 138n45, 138n47
normalization, 11, 35, 41, 72, 82, 135, 216

Once Upon a Honeymoon, 11, 104–6, 108–11, 137nn20–21, 137n35, 137n39
On the Double, 112–14, 138n44, 138n46
Ostrower, Chaya, 6, 15n25, 224
Oury, Gérard, 117, 156

Pacino, Al, 181, 191n103
Palin, Michael, 74–75, 96nn45–47, 225
The Parrot (Der Papagei), 12, 44, 161, 194–95
Parker, Trey, 81, 209–10, 212n12, 212n14
parody, 3, 6, 65, 69, 76, 78, 81, 83, 85, 89, 222, 225
"The Passion of the Jew," 81, 97n60, 98n65, 98n68
Patt, Avinoam, 9
Pearlstein, Ferne, 8, 15n17, 224
Pfefferkorn, Eli, 11, 17n38, 102–3, 136n3, 179, 190n93, 224
political satires, 30, 44
postmemory, 37, 47, 163, 172–73, 184, 186n21, 188n46, 222, 225
postmodernism, 14n14, 80–81, 90, 100nn94–95, 222, 224
Preminger, Otto, 104–5, 107–8, 110, 121–22, 136n11 136nn13–14, 136n17, 137n30, 140n78, 221–22, 224
The Producers, 8, 10, 19, 22, 30–34, 36, 38, 40, 43, 45, 51, 53n12, 56n64, 114–15
Punch Me in the Stomach, 12, 184, 191n106

reality television, 82, 201, 205
reconciliation, 26, 37, 58, 120, 153, 155, 159

Reiner, Carl, 8, 74–75, 96n42
renewal, 9, 200, 202
Roach, Hal, 70–71, 95n28, 95nn30–31, 225
"The Road to Germany," 83–84, 98n73
Robot Chicken, 82, 84, 98n71, 194, 197–98, 212n13
Rosenfeld, Gavriel, 34, 35, 52, 54n22, 60n112, 95, 97, 225
Røsler, Alexander, 172, 189n78
Ross, Jeff, 1, 207, 210, 214nn42–43
Russell, Ken, 82, 91–92, 100n93
Russia, 6, 39, 88

Safran Foer, Jonathan, 7, 16n30, 25–26, 58nn84–85, 220, 225
The Sarah Silverman Program, 194, 200, 203, 213n25
schadenfreude, 3, 204
Schlingensief, Christoph, 44, 73, 77–78, 89, 92, 96n51, 97nn52–53, 161, 196–97, 210, 211nn10–11, 221
Schrader, Paul, 165–166, 188nn52–53, 189n55
Schreiber, Liev, 25, 46–47, 58n83
Schtonk!, 44, 55, 161, 194–97, 211nn5–6, 220
Schumer, Amy, 200, 203, 204
science fiction, 2, 72
Seinfeld, Jerry, 5, 193, 200
A Self-Made Hero (Un héros très discret), 149–50, 156, 187n30
Seven Beauties (Pasqualino Settebellezze), 8, 11, 102, 121, 123, 125–31, 133, 140–42, 148, 220, 225
Sherman, Vincent, 104, 110, 136n8, 137, 225
Silverman, Sarah, 5, 8–9, 13, 61, 82, 84, 200, 202–4, 206, 214
Singer, Isaac Bashevis, 169, 189n76, 219
slapstick, 3, 30, 48, 70, 115
Slucki, David, 6, 9, 15n25, 225
Snide and Prejudice, 11, 82, 85–86, 98n79.

social commentary, 148, 153–54
Son of Hitler, 11, 72–73, 86
South Park, 81–83, 97n64, 98nn65–69, 194, 197–99, 210, 212n12, 212n14, 212n16, 221
Sperber, Dan, 9, 16n33, 44, 57n72, 114, 138n50, 225
Spiegelman, Art, 7, 15n23
Steir-Livny, Liat, 6, 15n25, 78, 87, 97n56, 99n84, 163, 188n49, 225
Stier, Oren Baruch, 12, 17n39, 93, 100n98, 145–46, 185nn1–2, 185n6, 225
surrealism, 121, 131
survival, 8, 131, 162, 166, 202, 204, 222, 224
"The Survivor," 1, 5, 12, 193–94, 200, 212nn19–21
The Survivors of the Shoah Visual History Foundation, 30, 47, 227

Tabori, George, 134–35, 142, 221
Tarantino, Quentin, 2, 26, 43–50, 52, 56n65, 57nn77–79, 91
Terror 2000—Germany Out of Control (Intensivstation Deutschland), 12, 44, 73, 77, 161, 194, 196–97, 211n11, 212
That Nazty Nuisance, 70
The Three Stooges, 11, 31, 61, 63, 67–69, 71, 93n1, 95nn22–26, 104, 224
The Tollbooth, 149–54, 186n18
They Got Me Covered, 104, 108, 110–11, 137nn35–37
This Must Be the Place, 12, 177, 179, 181–82, 190n94, 190n97, 191n99
Three Little Sew and Sews, 67
To Be or Not to Be, 8–10, 19–20, 22, 30, 32, 38–40, 42, 51–52, 55–56, 65, 111
Train of Life, 10, 19, 24, 35–36, 38, 47–50, 52, 54n23, 59nn98–99, 101, 103, 132, 148,
transgression, 4, 141, 176, 219

Transparent, 1, 12–13, 167, 173–74, 176, 190, 220
trauma, 147–48
trivialization, 76, 101
tropes, 8–10, 46, 52, 61, 123, 130, 147, 152, 154, 159, 166
The Two of Us (Le vieil homme et l'enfant), 11, 115, 117–20, 139nn61–63, 139n72

The United States Holocaust Memorial Museum, 30, 34, 179, 227

Verhoeven, Michael, 73, 132, 134, 142n123, 161–62, 223

Waititi, Taika, 1, 29, 37–38, 44–46, 55n32, 57n71, 61
Werfel, Franz, 115–17, 139nn58–59, 222
Wertmüller, Lina, 8, 11, 102, 123, 126–28, 131–32, 140–42, 222, 224, 225
White, Hayden, 11, 17n38, 102–3, 121, 132, 136n2, 225
Wiesel, Elie, 2, 101, 216–17
Wilder, Billy, 108, 121, 139, 220, 225
Williams, Robin, 49–50, 59n104
Wilson, Deirdre, 9, 16, 225
Wisse, Ruth, 5, 6, 10, 15, 17, 226
Wnendt, David, 27, 37–38, 45–46, 54n31, 57n75
Wondrous Oblivion, 12, 149–50, 159, 187n36
World War II comedies, 8, 11, 26, 33, 37, 45, 53n10, 58n85, 64, 69, 83–84, 87–88, 90–91, 93, 94n3, 96n42, 109, 114, 125, 138n42, 146–47, 151–52, 154, 158, 207, 216
"Wowschwitz," 194, 200, 203, 213n25

You Natzy Spy, 11, 31, 68, 71, 95

Ziv, Avner, 5, 14n14, 15n22, 226
zombies, 72, 90, 95
Zandberg, Eyal, 16n25, 163–64, 188n48

About the Author

Jonathan C. Friedman is currently director of Holocaust and genocide studies and professor of history at West Chester University, in West Chester, Pennsylvania. Author and editor of multiple books, he received his Ph.D. in history in 1996 from the University of Maryland, College Park, and he has worked as a historian at both the United States Holocaust Memorial Museum in Washington, DC, and the Survivors of the Shoah Visual History Foundation.

www.ingramcontent.com/pod-product-compliance
Lightning Source LLC
Chambersburg PA
CBHW020117010526
44115CB00008B/861